PRAISE]

Knowing Her Intimately: 12 Keys for C

M000290660

"We love this book!! We are excited to have someone else promoting concepts regarding women and sex in marriage that correct the common cultural myths and promote what we believe are sound, biblically based approaches to bring about mutual fulfillment for both spouses. Knowing Her Intimately provides practical approaches to self-measure and self-correct that are creative, new and will enhance the process of women knowing themselves and sharing themselves more freely in their marriages."

—**Joyce and Cliff Penner**, Christian sex therapists, authors of *Restoring the Pleasure,*
The Gift of Sex, and *The Way to Love Your Wife*, PassionateCommitment.com

"Our dear friend, Laura Brotherson, has done it once again! In her newest book, Knowing Her Intimately, *she smoothly strips away the awkwardness and reveals exactly what women struggle with when it comes to the bedroom. We all WANT to be more intimate, and this book helps define the* how *and the* why *to get there! Laura dives right in, to identify thoughts and beliefs that keep women from embracing their sexuality in marriage, and the BEST part…?! She shares actionable steps at the end of each chapter to help you obtain that level of intimacy you've always craved. I'm telling you, Laura is a sex-therapist rockstar and this is a must-read! Your husband will thank you!"*

—**Tara Carson**, Founder of TheDatingDivas.com

"Laura Brotherson helps couples focus on changing themselves for the better to create a profoundly meaningful and intimate marriage relationship."

—**Richard Paul Evans**, #1 New York Times Bestselling author of *The Christmas Box,*
and "How I Saved My Marriage" blog post, RichardPaulEvans.com

"We all want the same thing: a truly intimate relationship--to know *and* to be fully known. *Laura Brotherson has written an insightful road map for how to get there. Join the journey!"*

—**Priscilla Hunt**, Executive Director, BetterMarriages.org

"Laura Brotherson is an absolute treasure! Her natural beauty is exceeded only by her wisdom and insights that continue to help so many couples create passion and fulfillment in this crucial aspect of marriage."

—**Mark Gungor**, author of *Laugh Your Way to a Better Marriage*, MarkGungor.com

Knowing *Her* Intimately

12 Keys for Creating a Sextraordinary Marriage

LAURA M. BROTHERSON, LMFT, CST, CFLE
CERTIFIED SEX THERAPIST

INSPIRE
BOOK

Cover design and diagrams by Bryce Andrew, andrewdesign.org
Interior design and composition by Angela Stewart, angelarstewartdesign.com

Published by Inspire Book
Boise, Idaho

ISBN 978-0-9785867-9-9

Library of Congress Control Number: 2016948650

First Printing July 2016

AUTHOR'S NOTE

The examples, anecdotes and characters appearing in case vignettes throughout this book are drawn from my clinical work, and life experience. Names and identifying characteristics have been changed. Because everyone's situation is unique, the ideas and suggestions contained herein should not be considered a substitute for consultation with a trained counselor or therapist.

INSPIRE
BOOK

Another gift, from the heart, to all who seek...

ALSO BY LAURA M. BROTHERSON

And They Were Not Ashamed:

Strengthening Marriage through Sexual Fulfillment

(Softcover, ebook, downloadable audio, CD audio book)

Love 101:

Learning to Love More Meaningfully

(Talk on CD)

Teaching Intimacy 101:

How to Teach Your Children about Sex & Intimacy

(CD audio book)

CONTENTS

ACKNOWLEDGMENTS

Where do I begin to thank the many wonderful people who have had a hand in the creation of this book? I am so grateful to the many fans, clients, friends, colleagues and Think Tank members. They have contributed through anonymous sharing of their stories, providing inspiration, support and encouragement, or taking time to read, review and provide valuable feedback on book covers or manuscript drafts. The following is not an exhaustive list of the many individuals I so appreciate for their time and effort on my behalf:

Carrie Snider	Natalie Greaves	Jory Beal	Stacia Hopkins
Rhonda Cazier	Emil Harker	Jana Griffin	Nathan Coffey
Bryce Andrew	Geoff Steurer	Diane Ehle	Greg Deitchler
Angela Stewart	Jude Black	Kip Griffith	Dr. Mike Systma
Dr. Greg Olson	Michael Boman	Jeremy Boden	The Institute for
Sam Zaragoza	Kim Blackham	Dave Kitabjian	Sexual Wholeness
Vicki Rudd	Ty Mansfield	Caralee Frederic	Debra Greeff

My humblest appreciation goes to my dearest darling children—Tanner, Alyssa and Tyler. I hope my efforts to help strengthen marriages have not been too much of a sacrifice for you, especially now that you are older. Thank you for letting me do what I do to help others have a happy family, too. I love you!

The insights I share within this book would not be possible without Kevin, my awesome husband of 25 years. He has given me the eternal love, support, and inspiration to fulfill my mission to help strengthen marriages intimately. Your steady, loving influence continues to allow me to be all that I am, and to do all that I do. Thank you for your willingness to pick up the slack in our home, especially these last two and a half years as I have written this book. You have been a true partner in sustaining me throughout these endeavors, as I hope I have been to you. I'm so grateful for the secure base you are that allows us to accomplish anything we set our minds to. With this book you have, again, been the source of scriptural inspiration for this fabulous book title *Knowing HER Intimately*. Thank you for your insight and wisdom. Words are wholly inadequate to express my gratitude and deepest feelings. I love you so much...and I really *like* you, too! Hopefully my continual efforts at self-improvement and your work as my "highly compensated research assistant" will reinforce my infinite love and appreciation. ;)

Without God, I would not have the courage or confidence to boldly undertake such a taboo topic in such a toxic world. Because God and I are a team, I can do all things through Christ who strengthens me (*see* Philippians 4:13).

PREFACE

Why I Wrote This Book

Sexual problems in marriage are some of the most perplexing issues couples face. Desire difficulties are the leading sexual complaint among 10–51% of women.[1] This is due in part to the complex nature of female sexuality. Information is sorely needed to help couples understand and satisfy the mental, emotional, physical and even spiritual needs of the wife, plus knowledge of what turns a woman on and how to improve her intimate experience. Women want to love their husbands well. They want to understand how they themselves are wired sexually and how to make their intimate relationship flourish. They often simply do not know what to do. This book will show the way!

My first book, *And They Were Not Ashamed: Strengthening Marriage through Sexual Fulfillment,* was written to share insights from my own study and personal journey towards sexual wholeness. I have been thrilled at the wonderful response I have received from so many readers who have seen improvements in their marriages. As I worked with couples in my counseling practice, it became clear that I needed to dive deeper into this subject. Thus, I have written this book, *Knowing HER Intimately: 12 Keys for Creating a Sextraordinary Marriage.*

Helping couples to strengthen their marriages intimately has been a passion of mine for many years. Completing a master's degree in marriage and family therapy (MS, MFT), becoming a Licensed Marriage and Family Therapist (LMFT), and a Certified Sex Therapist (CST), along with many years of clinical practice, have broadened my understanding of intimate sexual relationships. The insights you will read in this book have been successfully shared with couples who have found great healing and improvement toward a more intimate and passionate marital relationship.

In the sexual dimension of marriage, female sexual wiring is fraught with complexity and confusion for both husbands and wives. This book is *not* focused on specific sexual dysfunctions, but on intimate insights that will help any couple better understand how to have a healthy, sextraordinary marriage. This book attempts to simplify the intricacies of how *women* are wired sexually, with my next book to focus on how *men* are wired. Unfortunately, so many women are lacking important knowledge about their own intimate wiring and what constitutes "sexual wholeness." Husbands don't get it, either.

Both husbands and wives need specific insights to break through intimate barriers and embrace God's gift of sexuality. Women and their husbands are hungry to understand the powerful, yet sensitive and delicate nature of a woman's sexuality, and be able to create the exquisite intimate relationship available in marriage. Taking the marriage relationship further, the greatest gift you can give your children is a mother and father who love each other and are securely and intimately connected.

Seeking professional help for individual or marital issues—much less sexual ones—is difficult. It isn't easy to find those with specialized training in sex therapy and related issues like sex addiction, infidelity, or sexual abuse. In addition, locating someone couples can trust to treat the subject with the respect and reverence God intended is challenging. This book gives couples a chance to resolve many of their own relationship and sexual difficulties, with encouragement to seek additional professional help as needed.

At the end of a recent counseling session, Sarah enthusiastically asked, "So, when am I gonna get to read your new book?!" I told her it would be out soon. She wondered out loud if she already knew most of the material because she'd been doing counseling with me for a while. I said, "That's actually one of the reasons I needed to write this book. Even with counseling, there just isn't enough time to cover all the aspects of intimacy that you'll now be able to learn from the book. And for those who may not be willing or able to see a sex therapist, the book will save them thousands of dollars of counseling if they will read and apply the concepts."

A Self-Help Sex Therapy Resource

In my clinical practice, it's difficult to see as many couples as I would like to help. A book like *Knowing HER Intimately: 12 Keys for Creating a Sextraordinary Marriage* can reach so many more individuals than I can personally. I have created this Christian-based, marriage-friendly, self-help, sex therapy book, so that many more couples will be able to create the kind of intimate and passionate relationship God intended. Being easily accessible, and a more affordable resource for self-help sex therapy, this book will allow couples to take their relationship to the next level intimately—all within the privacy and comfort of their own homes. With 12 key ingredients of healthy and fulfilling female sexuality, this power-packed, how-to handbook will help couples identify what's getting in their way, what areas may need help, and what they can do about it.

According to research, and the tens of thousands of couples who have read my first book, many couples are able to improve their marriages simply by understanding and applying key principles of sexual relating—which are addressed in this book. Some couples will need additional help to delve into the deeper aspects of their relationship. But many will be able to personally apply this information to more closely achieve a wonderfully fulfilling sexual relationship. Gaining intimate insight allows couples to see sex differently in their relationship, and adjust their attitudes and behaviors to make things better. Intimate relationships can go from bad to good, and good to great—even with just a bit of help. Here is what a few happy readers have said about how a good book can help:

I cannot put into words what your book has done for us. It has hit me so poignantly. I'm absorbing the information like a sponge. I do think that if I could have read your book earlier, maybe things could have been better for us sooner. Most importantly, my husband is loving the results of your book. He can sense that I feel so free and lighthearted from what we have learned. I consider myself pretty smart and well educated, but man, I had no idea what I didn't know! I was so missing out!

My wife and I have read your book twice now. We have been working together for many months trying to improve the intimate relationship in our marriage. You and your book have helped us work through several problems that had kept us in an unsatisfying parallel marriage for more than 25 years. We are happier now than we have ever been and feel closer and more unified than I thought would ever be possible. Your work, and your clear and straightforward approach to sexual matters have been invaluable. You have truly changed our lives.

As I started reading your book, I quickly became aware that our sex life was not what it could be. As I read your description of female orgasm, I thought, "that's not what happens to me!" I had been aroused before, but I didn't realize I could have a reaction like my husband does. I engaged in sex for him, not for me. I didn't realize how patient we needed to be with clitoral stimulation until I read your book. Your book taught me so much about the female sexual response, and also about how important sex is to a man. It opened up the subject in our marriage, so that we can talk about it now. It has helped me make my husband more of a priority. It made us more in love. I enjoy sex so much more now, and I have orgasms regularly. I am much happier with our sex life. Thank you so much for the increased happiness and improvement you have made in this special and crucial aspect of our lives. My husband thanks you, too!

Who This Book is For

The primary audience for this book is married women, and then their husbands, or any man who would like to better understand his wife. This book is written primarily for women to better understand their own wiring, and then for men to understand *her* wiring as well. Since sex is a team sport, both spouses need to intimately understand the other's sexual wiring. This book focuses on *her* sexual wiring, while my next book will focus on *his* sexual wiring.

Though this book is written from a Christian, marriage-focused perspective, the actual audience is anyone (married or not) who would like to better understand the intricacies of how women are wired intimately and sexually. The objective is to help couples create what I call a "sextraordinary marriage." A sextraordinary marriage is not just about sex, but about having an intimately connected relationship, which then makes for extraordinary lovemaking.

Since women are also more likely to be relationship book buyers, I speak primarily to them, but I also hope husbands are listening in on how to work more effectively with their wives' intimate wiring. This book takes a respectful approach to this topic, highlighting its wholesomeness in a way that women, especially, can take it in and apply it to their lives. The ideal would be for husbands and wives to read this book together, but it only takes one to change a relationship for the better. If either a wife or a husband is the only one in the relationship willing to read this book, then it can still change lives.

Laura M. Brotherson
July 2016

NOTES

[1] Basson, Rosemary, "Sexual Desire and Arousal Disorders in Women," *The New England Journal of Medicine*, (2006) 354(14): 1497-1506.

INTRODUCTION

To Truly *Know* Her

The Bible uses an interesting term to refer to sex: "Adam *knew* Eve his wife; and she conceived" (*see* Genesis 4:1, 17, 25, emphasis added). Sexual relations between husband and wife are beautifully described with the verb "to know." To truly *know* your spouse and have your spouse truly *know* you—mind, body, and soul—represents the highest form of connection—that of *ONEness.* The "Big O" isn't orgasm. It's oneness!

Knowing our spouse involves so much more than just the act of sex. It's an experience of the heart, mind, body, and soul. The way women are wired sexually provides a perfect opportunity for couples to connect in a much more profound way than just the physical—though that's also an important dimension. To know a woman the way she wants to be known includes the whole relationship, with sex as just one delightful part.

Borrowing the biblical term for sex, this book's title, *Knowing HER Intimately,* is an all-encompassing description of the overarching objective of this book—for both husbands and wives to come to truly *know* each other intimately and sexually. The focus of this book will be "knowing" *her* intimate wiring. To be so known can be a little scary. It requires vulnerability and trust. To be known so fully—warts and all—and still be loved is exhilarating. It's a significant component of what makes for extraordinary lovemaking.

12 T's of Female Sexual Wholeness

In my first book, *And They Were Not Ashamed: Strengthening Marriage through Sexual Fulfillment,* I had three "T's" of female sexual desire—"Talk," "Touch," and "Time."[1] In this book, *Knowing HER Intimately,* that has expanded to include 12 "T's" of female sexual wiring. This how-to handbook puts the essential elements of female sexual wholeness into accessible and understandable aspects, each beginning with one of 12 "T's." The 12 building blocks in this book guide couples through the intricacies, inhibitors, and importance of intimate connection in marriage. Husbands (or the higher-desire spouse) will be given nuggets of information throughout the book of how he can best help her along the journey to sexual wholeness.

Like my first book, this book will be frank and hard-hitting, while also a respectfully reverent resource on sexual intimacy. It again affirms the sanctity of sex in marriage as wholesome, good, and of God. While digging deeper into the underlying aspects of the intimate relationship *outside* the bedroom (especially vital to women), aspects of the sexual relationship *inside* the bedroom will be tackled as well.

12 Essential Ingredients for an Extraordinary Sexual Relationship

The table of contents for this book reads like a condensed recipe of key ingredients for fulfilling female sexuality—necessary for a sextraordinary marriage. This list of 12 "T's" is an overview, providing a quick peek of what will be discussed in more depth throughout this book. We'll address what it takes to have an intimately connected sexual relationship—especially from the perspective and needs of a woman:

1. *Transformed.* A woman must transform her identity by embracing the idea that she is a sexual being. It needs to be seen as a good and important part not only of her marriage, but also of her wholeness and aliveness. She must commit to awakening and nurturing her sexuality, taking responsibility for her sexual desire and fulfillment.

2. *Thoughts.* Women need to program their minds with positive, affirming thoughts and core beliefs about sex, their sexuality, and their bodies. Not only that, but they need to program their minds about their husband, his body, and their marital and sexual relationship. Developing the mental discipline to be able to focus one's thoughts, and keep out inhibiting mental distractions during lovemaking, is needed.

3. *Tenderness.* This ingredient, along with thoughtfulness, trust, respect, etc., represents the foundation of a secure emotional connection upon which a sextraordinary marital relationship is built.

4. *Time.* With so many things on a woman's plate, it's vital that she provide enough time and energy for sexual learning, and fulfilling lovemaking, so that these things receive priority time and attention.

5. *Transition.* Because women are generally a few steps away from a state of sexual desire most of the time, they must develop a transition process to get them from 0 (or wherever they are starting from) to 60 sexually.

6. *Talk.* Talk is the primary means by which emotional connection is created and personal sexual preferences are discussed. Conversation is necessary for couples to be able to tune into each other well. Talk is a powerful part of the arousal process through sensual communication within the context of lovemaking.

7. *Touch.* Non-sexual touch or affection (with no strings attached) is needed, particularly outside of bedroom activities. Within lovemaking, a significant degree of sexual and especially clitoral stimulation is needed in order for mutual sexual fulfillment to occur.

8. *Technique.* Couples must be educated on sexual wiring differences between husband and wife, and know the specific intricacies of the female sexual response,

in order to work well within those realities. Each spouse must identify and share their specific sexual preferences and desires, which can't be learned from a book.

9. ***Tuned In.*** Couples need to tune in well to themselves and to their spouses. The ability to read and respond effectively to each other's nonverbal cues and body language is critical. This is true both within the emotional relationship, and for creating a passionate sexual experience within the bedroom.

10. ***Teasing.*** Flirty playfulness adds the spark that's often missing from long-term relationships. Understanding the benefits of fun and playfulness, as well as some how-to's, can take the relationship to a whole new level of intimate enjoyment.

11. ***Treats.*** While the element of teasing and playfulness improves the tone of the overall relationship, adding "Treats" into the mix increases the novelty, creativity and adventure in the marriage. This is necessary for long-term marriages to thrive by keeping things fresh, new, and exciting.

12. ***Transcendence.*** The sexual climax is an involuntary response requiring a state of transcendence. It isn't something a husband can fully do *for* his wife without her willing participation. Sexual surrender is something she must be willing and able to relax into, and let herself experience, in order to fully enjoy the ecstasy of sexual intimacy and oneness.

Each of these keys builds upon each other. It will be especially difficult to engage in intimate "Teasing" (Chapter 10) or "Treats" (Chapter 11) if a woman hasn't yet "Transformed" her identity as a sexual being (Chapter 1). It will be difficult to be truly "Tuned In" to each other (Chapter 9) if both husband and wife haven't mastered the individualized art of emotional connection and "Tenderness" (Chapter 3). Women will find it nearly impossible to achieve "Transcendence" and sexual surrender (Chapter 12) if they have not yet developed the mental discipline (Chapter 2 - "Thoughts") or the "Touch" (Chapter 7) and "Technique" (Chapter 8) needed for full arousal.

Women's brains are wired like the World Wide Web in an interconnected way; so too are each of the 12 T's interwoven, and they even overlap some. Keep in mind that while the 12 T's will help you focus on a particular aspect of female sexual wiring, they don't have clear-cut separating lines between them. Sexual relationships are as different as the individuals in them. With so many variables at play, such as personality, age, mental health, etc., this book attempts to provide a blueprint for couples to tweak in order to fit their unique situation and circumstances. One wife commented on this list of intimate ingredients, "There's a lot of power here and permission, too. It's like you are saying 'Go...with this information, find your own way! Learn. Trust. Grow. Share. You can do it!'"

What This Book Will Do for You

As you begin your journey to the intimate relationship of your dreams, you may want to start by taking the "Sexual Self-Evaluation" in the Appendix to see where you currently are in the 12 dimensions of sexual wholeness. It would be great for your spouse to take it as well. As you take it again after reading and applying the concepts in this book, you will be able to see your progress. Readers of this book can hope to achieve the following objectives:

- Identify what's getting in the way of a more fulfilling and passionate intimate relationship, what areas need help, and what you can do about it.
- Become an expert at your own intimate wiring.
- Help your husband become an expert at your intimate wiring.
- Create a happier and more intimately and securely connected relationship.
- Create a sextraordinary marriage, which includes an extraordinary sexual relationship.

Often minimized, a woman's sexual potential is incredible. This book celebrates that concept while helping husband and wife make the most of the intimate experience. For the benefit of her wholeness, and for the strength of her marriage, an awakening and development of sexuality within marriage is vital. Sexual wholeness may seem unimportant to the wife who has not yet made sexuality a priority. Nevertheless, sexual development in marriage goes to the heart of her personal development and completeness. This ultimately allows for the ecstasy of mutual intimate enjoyment in marriage. This is God's intended gift for husband and wife.

NOTES

[1] Brotherson, Laura M., *And They Were Not Ashamed: Strengthening Marriage through Sexual Fulfillment.* Boise, ID: Inspire Book, 2004, 67.

CHAPTER VIEW

❧

Transforming Your Sexual Identity
    Embracing Sexuality
    Accepting and Embracing Your Sexual Self
    Positive Sexual Messages
Why a Healthy Sexual Identity is Foundational
Satan Seeks to Destroy Marriages
    Pornography: Designed to Destroy Marriages
Restoring God's Wholesome Luster to Sex
    Put in a Good Word for Sex
    Good Girls Do
Unleashing Your Sexual Potential in Marriage
    Levels of Sexual Development
    Characteristics of a Healthy Sexual Identity
    Healthy Sexual Identity Assessment
    A Sexy State of Mind
Developing Your Physicality and Sensuality
    Awakening Sensuality with Massage Therapy
    Nurturing Touch
How To's for Embracing Your Sexual Identity
    1. *Take the Healthy Sexual Identity Assessment*
    2. *Reprogram your mind*
    3. *Merge your identity and welcome sexual thoughts*
    4. *Start a Sexual Self-Discovery Journal*
    5. *Get educated*
    6. *Do the Action Items and some counseling*
    7. *Do it for you*
    8. *Dance and use music*
    9. *Awaken sensuality with massage therapy*
There is Hope
Self-Evaluation - "Transformed"
ACTION ITEMS — Chapter 1 - "Transformed"

Chapter 1

TRANSFORMED — EMBRACING YOUR IDENTITY AS A SEXUAL BEING

"I just don't know how to want to. It's just not me. I want to want to, but I just can't seem to really want to. It just seems so not something worthy of my time and attention." Janet shared her frustration that she couldn't figure out how to really "get" being a sexual person.

I said, "Janet, you know how you spend a lot of time and effort to develop your spirituality? You go to church regularly. You pray every day. You read your scriptures…It seems that doing those things helps you to see yourself as a spiritual person. Likewise, developing and nourishing your sexuality, so that it becomes a well-developed part of your wholeness—part of your divine identity—might be likened to developing your spirituality. Since we're trying to change from having a mindset that rarely thinks about your sexuality to one that embraces your sexuality, it may help to see yourself as a sexual being. What if we can transform your identity, if you will, at a core level?

"Where you do not currently see sex as a valid or welcome part of your being, we want to get to a place of thinking, 'I am a sexual being, and it's good and of God.' We want to have a mindset of welcoming sexual thoughts and feelings. We want to develop a default of thinking of your spouse from a place of, 'I do want you sexually!' 'I need you.' 'I'd be happy to have sex with you right now.'" Janet couldn't imagine herself in that state of mind or how to get there.

We decided to nurture her sexuality in a similar way to how she nurtures her spirituality:

1. *We identified things she could read or listen to on her cell phone to positively affirm and reprogram her mind about sex. This was similar to how she had been reading and listening to spiritual materials regularly to nurture her spirituality.*

2. *She started listening to romantic songs on the radio, like she had often listened to hymns. She compiled a playlist of songs that made her desire intimate connection with her husband. This created more balance in her life between music that nourished her spiritually and music that nourished her intimately.*

3. *She started praying about and changing her self-talk about sex. This was akin to the prayerful thoughts she often had in her heart and mind regarding other things. She focused her attention on developing her sexual self with thoughts like: "I want you, physically and emotionally," and "I like sex. It makes me feel connected to my husband. It makes me feel whole. It makes me feel alive."*

Transforming Your Sexual Identity

Janet is a good example of the many women who have not embraced their sexuality as a good and godly part of their being. While men's challenge is to control or bridle their sexual energy, women struggle to awaken and develop both their sexuality and sexual identity. What is a sexual identity? It's seeing yourself as a sexual being and embracing that as a good thing. Part of a healthy sexual identity is understanding and embracing that your sexuality is of God. We need to have a deep regard and respect for ourselves as divinely created sexual beings. This is vital to creating sextraordinary marriages that are at least partially comprised of extraordinary sex—the way God intended. Transforming your sexual identity is an extension of overcoming the Good Girl Syndrome addressed in my first book.[1]

Women are endowed with great sexual potential and magnificent sexual power. We are divinely designed to develop a spiritually based, authentic, complete self, which can then help us create a strong and solid marriage. Female sexuality is often minimized or ignored rather than encouraged and empowered because many will not appropriately discuss the topic. Few are focused on helping women develop this vital aspect of their being. Other women misdirect their sexuality to the world, instead of focusing it on their spouse. This can happen when women surgically enhance themselves or dress revealingly to those other than their spouse. With such incredible power and potential, it's unfortunate when Satan is able to undermine our God-given sexuality.

"Female sexuality is often minimized or ignored rather than encouraged and empowered."

Embracing Sexuality

God is very pro sex. He created it. One of the adversary's subtle tactics to subdue godly women has been to entice them to disregard and disavow their sexuality. He makes sex an unwholesome, awkward, uncomfortable, and unwelcome part of what could be a great gift in marriage. In our society, there are few positive, affirming messages about the godly nature of sexuality, or sex in marriage. We rarely hear messages that it's good and healthy to develop one's sexuality as a vital dimension of marriage. Consequently, few make it into marriage with a good, healthy, and divinely ordained sexual identity. It's not of God to be anti-sex. I invite women everywhere to awaken and transform their identities into a godly understanding of the vital role sexuality plays in our individual wholeness and marital oneness.

Sex is of God. He created it for procreation and for pleasure. A woman has a small bit of sexual anatomy—the clitoris—that has no other purpose than sexual pleasure. This sends a clear message that God designed women for pleasure and enjoyment. This awareness can be a helpful element of embracing one's sexuality as good and of God. Maybe you already have a healthy identity as a sexual being. Maybe you have happily and fully embraced that fact. If so, that's a wonderful thing and will make the rest of this book much easier. You may not have the mental barriers that the lack of a healthy sexual identity imposes. For the rest of us, this chapter provides the foundation upon which to build a sextraordinary marriage.

Accepting and Embracing Your Sexual Self

God created each of us as sexual beings. It's part of our wholeness—our completeness. Living your sexual truth in marriage allows you to be more fully alive and functioning as the multi-dimensional person you were divinely designed to be. It's important to recognize that fact. Your sexual identity goes to the heart of your "completeness" and personal development. From a place of sexual wholeness, living your sexual truth in marriage allows you to be more fully alive, more passionate in all areas, and more fully functioning as the multi-dimensional person you were divinely designed to be.

We are all comprised of various parts of the self—mental, emotional, social, physical, sexual, and spiritual. Women who struggle with sexuality tend to have an "asexual" view of self.[2] They do not see or accept themselves as sexual beings. This is akin to not fully accepting the unique and differentiated parts of who you are. Without a sexual component to one's identity, it's no wonder that women struggle with sexuality in marriage.

A healthy sexual self might be considered as having sexual self-esteem or confidence. This is where your sexuality is viewed in a positive light. There is a comfort and willingness to assert your sexual thoughts and needs towards your spouse.[3] Religious institutions don't often talk about

Parts of Self

healthy sexuality, or they tend to focus primarily on what *not* to do. At the other end of society's spectrum is a sexual free-for-all, seen prominently promoted in popular culture. It's difficult to find that space where there is reverence for the sacredness of sexuality, as well as some affirmation of its positive and wholesome purposes within marriage.

✤

"God is very pro sex. He created it."

✤

Positive Sexual Messages

When does a young woman receive the message that her sexuality is a good and godly thing? When are young women encouraged to honor, respect and embrace their sexuality for its full expression within marriage? In our efforts to teach our youth that sexual activity is reserved for marriage, we often forget to mention that after marriage, good girls do!

That mental transition from "not good" before marriage to "good" after marriage never fully occurs for many couples (wives and husbands included). Because young adults hear fear and shame-based messages, many distance themselves, and even disown their sexuality completely. This paves the way for disconnection, frustration and heartache within marriage.

Due to their different sexual wiring, young women especially take in negative messages about sex. What they need instead is encouragement and affirmation of their sexuality as a wonderful gift within marriage. It is certainly wise counsel for both young men and women to learn to master their sexual feelings. But, there is a shortage of positive and affirming messages about the goodness of embracing your sexuality for its proper expression within marriage.

As a sex therapist, I'm saddened to see the dislike women have for sex, and the pain and rejection husbands feel in their marriages. Many factors contribute to the lack of intimate expression and enjoyment in marriage, as evidenced by the 12 "T" ingredients outlined in this book. But I have often found that women have simply not yet accepted and embraced their sexuality. This puts husbands in a particularly helpless and hopeless predicament. One husband shared his situation. It's similar to many others who are without hope of a mutually fulfilling, intimate sexual relationship with their wives.

I have decided that I need to "give up on the dream" of having a sexual relationship that is truly fulfilling. I need to turn it over to the Lord, and just try to be the best husband that I can be. It has taken me years to get to this point. I do feel calmer, most of the time, than I have in the past where I was often on the edge of even being able to function.

It is better now than when I would try so hard to do everything possible, and then emotionally crash when my hope was shattered. I do still try hard to be a good husband, but I don't expect anything from it anymore. I do it because I am deeply in love with my dear wife, in spite of everything.

A thought that buoys me up is knowing that Satan is trying his best to use our sexual disconnect to drive a wedge into our marriage. I need to do everything I can to keep that from happening, but it's not easy.

We can and must do better at instilling the goodness of our sexual selves as an honorable aspect of our identity. God designed each of us as sexual beings. We can embrace that sex is something God created as a wonderful gift for a husband and wife to enjoy in marriage. It's not only our marital relationship, but also our personal wholeness that is at stake.

Why a Healthy Sexual Identity is Foundational

When a woman has not yet fully embraced her sexuality, or accepted that part of herself, it will undermine any other efforts to create a strong and healthy marital relationship. When there is a void of positive and affirming sex-related thoughts going into marriage, it's a challenge for a woman to change that thought pattern once she's married. It's like going from "No, no, no" to "go, go, go" in one night. It can be done, if needed. But, it would just be so much more effective to be better prepared to enjoy the exquisite gift of sexual expression in marriage.

Especially for women, enthusiastic sexual expression is a by-product of a healthy sexual identity. Once a woman has fully embraced her sexuality as part of her identity, a flow of positive sex-related thoughts and feelings within marriage is still a necessary component of nurturing sexual desire. This may be a foreign concept to some men who have plenty of sexual thoughts. Women generally must consciously cultivate sexual thoughts and feelings, since they do not tend to occur spontaneously. As you continue through this book, you will learn about the 12 key ingredients of "knowing her intimately," and what it takes to create a "sextraordinary marriage":

1. **Transformed** — Embracing your sexual self.
2. **Thoughts** — How powerful they can be.
3. **Tenderness** — Why we need a lot more of this for true intimacy.
4. **Time** — Giving our spouse more of our time.
5. **Transition** — From our regular day into lovemaking.
6. **Talk** — Its role inside and outside the bedroom.
7. **Touch** — In all its forms.
8. **Techniques** — To get things right and enhance the experience.
9. **Tuned In** — Really "getting" each other.
10. **Teasing** — Being playful and fun with each other.

11. Treats — These add novelty, and adventure.

12. Transcendence — Letting go into sexual surrender.

There is no point in addressing your thoughts and beliefs about sex if you're unsure if sex is good or of God, or that God approves of you really enjoying your sexuality. Why would you strive to increase the tenderness and thoughtfulness in your marriage if it just leads to something like sex—that really isn't a good thing anyway?

Why talk about sex or learn better sexual techniques, if you're just going through the motions for your husband's sake? And how in the world could you possibly let go and transcend sexually—surrender to the sexual experience—if the whole thing is suspect anyway? It's necessary to believe that sex is good and of God, and worthy of your time and attention, in order to master it. Ellen had been listening, in between counseling sessions, to some of my "Marital Intimacy Show" podcasts where I talk about awakening and embracing your sexuality. In a recent session she said:

> You tell us that taking responsibility for our sexuality is a decision we must make. I realized that long ago, probably before I was even married, I made a decision NOT to be a sexual being given the negative experiences I'd had during my dating years. I got married still unconsciously refusing to be a sexual person.
>
> Now I've been married all these years without being an active sexual participant in my marriage. You talk about women being all flirty and playful with their spouses. I can't even fathom doing that. I know where it would lead, and I just can't go there. I don't want to. I know I've got to change, but it scares me.

Ellen has come a long way, but she still has work to do. The suggestions throughout this book are necessary ingredients for her and many women like her. In order to make way for a wholesome sexual identity, women need to overcome their inhibiting thoughts and feelings. Embrace your sexual identity. Happily see yourself as a sexual being. It is the foundation for mastering the art of lovemaking as God intended.

Satan Seeks to Destroy Marriages

Satan has made sex his territory, practically high-jacking the whole thing. It's as if we've relinquished any attempt to maintain any godly ground on the subject. We seem to have relegated to taboo territory or low priority the message that God created sex, and that it's a good and wholesome thing in marriage. The secular message is one of sex anytime, anywhere, with anyone, or alone with an image on a screen. Sex has become so distorted and such forbidden subject matter that few are willing to speak up to restore its divine light. Satan, the author of deception, uses people's desire to "be good" against them—keeping them away from the subject altogether. This leaves them poorly prepared to enjoy the God-given sexual relationship in marriage. Avoiding discussion of even appropriate and positive aspects of the subject leaves Satan with no competition for his counterfeit message about sexuality.

Of course, we want to keep kids from inappropriate sexual information and media. But, when good, intelligent adults won't address the subject of healthy sexual relationships, even within marriage, then something seems out of balance. When good people *are* willing to address the subject of sex in a public forum, the only messages that get some air time are the negatives—like pornography addiction. What about help for how to have healthy intimacy in marriage? This is one of the ways Satan uses good folks against the divinity of marital sexuality. It's no surprise that Satan has many tactics to get marriages off course. He's mastered using the sexual dimension in otherwise good marriages in a way to weaken and destroy relationships.

Some like to believe that sexual difficulties only occur when there are other major problems in the marriage. I have found that many couples with pretty good relationships still have a real disconnect in the sexual dimension. They often have a dangerous void in their intimate relationship that can take a terrible toll on the marriage. Satan is thrilled that although he is unable to get otherwise good people to succumb to his more obvious snares, he is able to wreak havoc in the sexual dimension of many marriages. He creates an incredible reservoir of contention and disconnect for many couples.

God wants strong and happy couples who are intimately connected—emotionally, spiritually and sexually. Satan is overjoyed when they are not. I encourage all those who might be ignoring, discounting, or neglecting the sexual relationship in their marriages to consider this an Achilles heel that gives the adversary access to their lives. Satan will do anything he can to get good couples to disengage. I don't imagine God is too happy with Satan destroying something so sacred and precious as sex in marriage. I suspect God is unhappy about Satan having all the airtime on the subject too. Even though it seems Satan has been pretty successful in his efforts to mess up sexuality and destroy marriages, we can increase our efforts to stand up for the sanctity of sex, and not allow anyone else to take over God's creation of sexuality.

Pornography: Designed to Destroy Marriages

Pornography—video or print material that includes explicit sex acts or organs, intended to illicit arousal can ruin even the seemingly best marriages. Pornography is a counterfeit of true, intimate love. Sex and/or pornography abuse is common in too many marriages. In the age of easy Internet access where pornography is so prevalent, it is a powerful tool to devalue sex and marriage. It wreaks great havoc on the couple's emotional bond by destroying trust and exacerbating insecurities. The negative effects of pornography could be a book by itself.

I'd like to share a real-life example of the effects a husband's pornography addiction had on the intimate marriage relationship. After reading some of her husband's very raw process writings about his many dissatisfactions with her, Sherry wrote the following to me. I share this anonymously, but with their permission, in hopes it may help other couples who too may be dealing with the poisonous affects of pornography addiction. (Names and details have been changed.)

Cam has come a long way in his recovery, and I am proud of him. However, he is still blaming me for many of his issues, seemingly incapable of taking full responsibility for his actions. He is also sending strong messages that I am simply not good enough. He continues to be controlling in our relationship. I still struggle to let myself get too close to him. I am protective of our kids as well. He tends to shame them. He sends a message that they aren't good enough. Last night I came across the email that he sent you to vent some of his frustrations. It was awful! It came from the "addicted" Cam—not the Cam that I love. It did validate so many of the feelings I've felt from him throughout this addiction recovery journey.

We have had access to each other's email accounts for some time now in the name of transparency. I don't usually read his email, but for some reason I felt the need to check it. As I read it, two things became very clear to me. First, my husband wrote that email from a selfish, addicted, lustful place. I was clearly the source of all of his problems in his mind. It was apparent that his problems were extremely carnal and selfish. I realized that he is simply unaware that he has been seeking a fantasy wife. I believed I could actually be the wife he wants, if he could only love and cherish me.

Second, his email confirmed to me that I am not crazy, despite how he has made me feel. I have my issues, but I now know I'm not the problem, despite his success at convincing me I was! He genuinely does not think I am good enough. To him I am not in good enough shape. My breasts aren't big enough. I am not good enough in bed, or affectionate enough. I am not a good enough mother, or a good enough steward of my time.

Despite the shock and pain of reading his email, it actually felt really good to finally be validated. I now realize I am not the cause of all the problems in his life, or in our marriage. I am good enough. I am a good person. I am caring. I am wise. I have God with me throughout my day. I am always working to improve. I know God knows my heart and soul. That is all that really matters. I may never be good enough for Cam in his mind, and that's okay. Wherever our relationship leads, I will be at peace. I want a wholesome, happy, loving marriage. I might not ever get it with Cam. But, I have always been good enough—good enough to God and to our dear children.

After reading Cam's email, I was determined to be kind, but felt a newfound strength to be straightforward with my husband. I walked upstairs and told him how I have been feeling this week with the trauma we had been working through. I told him how I realized I was holding onto some of the trauma, as if it was a cushion to protect me and my heart from further pain.

Cam has not proven that he will protect me and love me unconditionally. He continues to betray our relationship with his slips, and with his angry and selfish behavior towards me and our children. I told him that even when he is "sober," he still shames me, and is harsh (telling me I am boring in the bedroom, and a bad kisser, etc.). I don't yet feel right about leaving him, but now realize that may be necessary for me at some point.

I told him that his actions continue to destroy my feelings of safety and trust. A woman cannot blossom, or be vulnerable, or be sexually intimate in a relationship if there is no trust. I told him I want desperately to heal and flourish. I want him to be whole, too. He deserves the healing power of Christ as much as I do.

I then revealed that I had read his email to you. He began to throw it back at me that I should not be reading his email. I reminded him that we had committed to be open with things like our email. He will sometimes get curious and read mine as well. That seemed to calm him down. I then told him everything that I just shared with you.

In the long run, we both determined that we are not giving up on this marriage. I asked him for a hug, and we hugged for a while. I felt like God was telling me to hug him. But that was hard for me. I needed it too, though. Hugs seem to at least start to break down our barriers and begin to heal our hearts.

Cam still has a long way to go in his recovery. I think my job now is to continue to own my stuff, but require him to own his stuff more fully. I recognize much better the demon he is battling with his addiction, and know now that I am more than good enough for him.

When we think about transforming our sexual identities, one particular issue that can make it hard to move forward is pornography addiction. Here are some of the damaging effects research has found on the emotional connection in intimate relationships[4]:

1. Rating partners as less attractive.
2. Being less satisfied with their partners' sexual performance.
3. Greater desire for sex without emotional involvement.
4. More sexual callousness.
5. Trying to get partners to act out scenes from pornographic films.
6. More likely to have an affair.
7. Using more sexual terms to describe women.
8. Less child-centeredness during marriage.
9. Engaging in more behavioral aggression.
10. Engaging in marital rape.

Additionally, Dr. Sue Johnson, founder of Emotionally Focused Couples Therapy, highlights the fact that pornography removes the relational aspects of lovemaking. It reduces sex to just the physical—the sensations and the intercourse—with no respect for the user's partner. Contrary to the myth that pornography provides good sex education, she perfectly points out that any attempt to imitate pornography in the marital bedroom is a surefire recipe for being a lousy lover.[5] So you can see why pornography needs to leave a marriage before a transformation can begin. If this is an issue in your marriage, I encourage you to look into the Recommended Resources listed in the Appendix for help. It may be necessary to get help from a therapist to work through it.

Restoring God's Wholesome Luster to Sex

In order to help couples truly embrace their God-given sexuality as God designed it to be, there needs to be a restoration of goodness and wholesomeness to sex itself. Sexual intimacy is one of God's great gifts to a husband and wife. But this concept needs more than just empty lip service. We need to take sex out of the darkness—out of Satan's territory—and restore it to God's light to do our part in overcoming those negative beliefs we personally hold. We need to do what we can to promote sex as a positive and wholesome expression of love, and a pleasurable, even passionate means of intimate connection in marriage.

I especially like the notion of sex as a "wholesome recreational activity" in a marriage. To truly embrace sexuality, transform one's identity as a sexual being, and unlock one's sexual potential, we must work to restore God's luster to sex, and reclaim sex as a divinely ordained endeavor.

Put in a Good Word for Sex

At a conference where I was presenting, I invited the attendees to be a positive advocate for marital sexuality in some way when they returned home. Not long after, I began to receive emails from people telling me about the opportunities they had taken to stand up for the goodness of sexual intimacy. I have been thrilled to see that many good people have begun to speak out in defense of sex in marriage as a good thing—whether with their friends, their children, or in their churches or communities. Just setting an example of confidently, openly, and appropriately addressing the topic can go a long way towards changing the energy surrounding the subject.

I encourage us all to watch for opportunities to put in a good word for sex. Sex needs a new public relations team to restore its divine light and luster. We all need to help remind each other that in marriage, good girls (and guys) enthusiastically do!

"Sex needs a new public relations team
to restore its divine light and luster."

Good Girls Do

One of the trends I continue to see in my work with couples is that there is still an ingrained belief and something of a cultural norm that says, "Good girls don't." Instead, I wish we were better at communicating that in marriage, "Good girls do!"[6] The suggestion is that good girls shouldn't think about sex, talk about sex, or engage with it in any way. Good girls are certainly not supposed to enjoy sex, either. The problem occurs when that mindset gets carried over into marriage. The lie is that good girls aren't supposed to think about it, learn about it, or enjoy it; nor should they fully embrace or develop their sexuality even within marriage. Many men struggle with similar beliefs wreaking havoc in their lives as well.

Unleashing Your Sexual Potential in Marriage

In order to unleash your sexual potential, you must commit to awakening and nourishing your intimate hunger for emotional and sexual closeness. Women need to nurture their sexuality, as if awakening and developing any of the other parts of themselves—mental, physical or social. Women have an untapped power that can be awakened when they embrace and cultivate their sexuality for its full expression within marriage. Women often do not fully understand what a profound power and potential they possess. They have the power to connect in a transcendent way with their spouse and exude passion in all areas of their lives.

A man once titled a comment he made on my website, "How Women Could Rule the World." He concurred with the idea that if women would learn to embrace their God-given sexuality, they could rule the world. I imagine there are forces at play to keep women from awakening and embracing the godly powers they possess. As women take responsibility for their sexuality,[7] and believe it is God ordained, they will experience greater enjoyment, fulfillment, and profound intimate connection with their husbands. Sexual nourishment that feeds both husband and wife is the dessert of married life. Sexual intimacy is as important for the health and vitality of your marriage as is emotional closeness and spiritual connection. Cultivating your sexual potential in marriage leads to greater overall mental, emotional, and physical health, as well as greater happiness and wholeness.

Levels of Sexual Development

In working with couples, I have noticed a continuum of three differing levels of what motivates a woman's sexuality to be expressed, and how fully she has embraced her sexual self. It may be helpful to understand these levels of sexuality. See if you can identify which one best describes you, and which one you might want to be working toward.

3 Levels of Sexuality

Level 1	Level 1 sexuality is having sex mostly to meet your husband's needs. You don't really want to have sex for your own sake. We might call this "duty sex" or "charity sex" where your body is involved, but your heart and mind aren't. This level represents a fairly negative motivation to be sexual. Level 1 sexuality is motivated either by a reluctant desire to be a "good wife," or because your husband is getting grumpy and irritable, so you feel it's time to give in and give him sex again. You mostly just want him to leave you alone. Even if you are able to muster a fairly civil attitude, you mostly have a negative mindset about sex. This level is more focused on a minimum quantity of sex needed for the husband to basically get by, versus the quality of the sexual encounters. The focus is one-sided toward the husband's needs rather than mutually attending to the wife's emotional and sexual needs as well. A woman at this level is often unaware that she even has any sexual needs and does little to communicate them. This level is a beginning step for wives who haven't regularly been sexual with their spouse. It's not generally the end goal for women.
Level 2	Level 2 sexuality is having sex still mostly to meet your husband's needs, but you do try to be more emotionally engaged and mentally present. You only "sort of" want to be intimate for your own sake. We might even call this "lovemaking" where your body is certainly involved, but so is your heart and mind to some degree. Level 2 sexuality is mostly motivated by a desire to be a "good wife," and/or as a genuine expression of love toward one's spouse. There may also be some mutual enjoyment or pleasure involved in the sexual experience. This level is not as much focused solely on the quantity of sex, but includes some focus on the quality of the connection as well. The focus on meeting needs may be more mutual, but this wife is often still unaware of her own needs for sexual intimacy and expression. It's more something she does for the benefit of her husband and marriage, though she participates much more willingly and happily. This level is certainly a significant improvement over Level 1, but is still hopefully not the end goal for women.

Level 3	Level 3 sexuality is true, enthusiastic, shared lovemaking not just for your spouse, but for you, too—to feel more whole, alive and complete. You actually want to be intimate for your own sake, as well as your husband's. Your hunger for sex comes from a place of fully embracing your God-given sexuality and your sexual self. You see yourself as a sexual being. You see sexuality as a powerful gift from God to both husband and wife. You proactively take responsibility for your desire and enjoyment. At this highest level of connection, not only are you mentally, emotionally, physically, and spiritually engaged and present, but you work to continually nurture and develop this dimension.

Level 3 sexuality is motivated by a genuine desire to connect completely with your spouse—mentally, emotionally, physically, and spiritually. It comes from a place of safety and secure attachment to your spouse. It's organic and self-perpetuating, because you both have a reservoir of trust and goodwill sustaining you. Not only is there great enjoyment and pleasure in the experience, but there is also an active, passionate, fully surrendered giving of yourselves to each other within the encounter. Instead of focusing on one spouse's need for sex, there is a deeper desire for mutual connection and true oneness. This level of sexuality provides a mutually intimate experience where both partners' sexual connecting needs are realized and fulfilled.

This level is definitely focused on the quality of the connection and intimate communication, with little thought needed regarding the quantity. Built-in is a focus on assuring that each other's healthy needs are attended to. This is truly "tuned-in" sex. There is a conscious recognition that both husband and wife have sexual needs, even though the wiring behind those needs may differ (i.e., hers being more emotionally based, and his generally being more physically based).

Like a beautiful sunset, Level 3 sexuality is something you both desire to experience together in order to make it its most meaningful. It's a shared intimate encounter that comes from a place of wholeness, as a true oneness of body and soul. It's a place of giving, receiving, sharing and fully experiencing.

While I have some concern about creating a categorized standard against which women may compare themselves, I hope those who truly want to reach the level of sexuality God intended will find these descriptions helpful in their strivings for sexual oneness.

Characteristics of a Healthy Sexual Identity

As women embark on this identity transformation to fully embrace and internalize their sexuality, it can be helpful to have specifics of what it looks and feels like to work toward. The following are some of the characteristics of a sexually confident wife. Identifying with these characteristics inevitably creates sexual self-confidence—the internalization of a healthy sexual identity. Take the following healthy sexual identity assessment by rating yourself on how true each statement is for you on a scale of -5 to +5. This can help you see where there might be negativity, neutral feelings, or positive acceptance of sexuality.

Healthy Sexual Identity Assessment

(Definitely Not True) -5 -4 -3 -2 -1 0 +1 +2 +3 +4 +5 (Definitely True)

1. I have a healthy sexual self-concept. I see myself as a sexual being with a sexual body.
2. I embrace my sexuality as good and as of God.
3. God created me as a sexual being and approves of my sexuality.
4. I work to overcome any inhibiting thoughts and beliefs I have about myself, my spouse, and sex itself that may hinder the intimate connection in my marriage.
5. I have positive thoughts, feelings, and underlying beliefs about sex and my sexuality.
6. I recognize that I have my own divine need to connect intimately and sexually with my spouse.
7. I understand the power of lovemaking to bond husband and wife.
8. I sense the divinity instilled within the sexual act.
9. I nurture sexual thoughts and feelings for my spouse, so that they are more accessible to me in lovemaking.
10. Embracing my sexuality makes me feel more whole, alive and complete.
11. I feel confident about myself sexually. I feel self-assured sexually.
12. I enjoy my sexuality as a vital part of my being and my marriage.
13. I can move into a "sexy state of mind" as needed.
14. I initiate sexual encounters fairly regularly, and take an active role in connecting with my spouse sexually. I make sex a priority by setting aside priority time and energy for connecting and lovemaking.
15. I have developed a welcoming attitude of being open to lovemaking opportunities.
16. I have made peace with my body, despite its imperfections.
17. I understand my own sexual wiring. I have learned and will continue to learn what I need to do to not only prepare for lovemaking, but also what I need throughout the arousal and orgasmic process.

18. I realize I am ultimately responsible for my sexual needs, and I am active in taking responsibility to see that those needs are met.

A Sexy State of Mind

Feeling sexy comes from within. It's how you feel about yourself as a person, as a wife, and as a sexual being. One's sexual identity is a creation of the mind, not the size or shape of the body. Nothing is more exciting and sexually fulfilling to a man than a "turned on" wife. But for women, they are most likely to feel sexy and get turned on when they feel good about themselves. When she is tuned into her own sexuality and shares that with her spouse, it has a powerfully positive effect on their sexual relationship.

Women need to believe they are worthy of sexual pleasure and have the right to be intensely sexual with their spouse. A woman needs to be able to enjoy her sexuality, her husband's sexuality, and her husband's enjoyment of her sexuality. To have real passion, a woman must be willing and able to receive and be "taken" within the sexual experience.[8] To develop a sexy state of mind, I often encourage women to practice looking at themselves in the mirror and saying, "Hi ya sexy!" You might ask yourself, in a written conversation, what it means to you to be sexy. It's difficult to develop a healthy sexual identity if "sexy" is something you fear or feel is not good.

Developing Your Physicality and Sensuality

When talking about sexual identity, one thing many women struggle with is being able to connect with their physicality and the sensuality of sexual relations. You often hear of women deriding the physicality or carnality of sex as if it were a bad thing. But, it is not. The physical body is a gift from God. Sensuality is a gift from God. The expression of sexual desires within marriage is also a gift from God. Sensuality is the essence or experience of feeling one's physical sensations, including pleasurable sensations, such as with a touch, a kiss or a caress.

I was the poster-girl for not really having a healthy sexual identity. I was not in tune with my physical and sensual self in the beginning of marriage. In time, by applying the principles I teach in this book, I not only learned to embrace my sexuality, but also my physicality and sensuality. Where I used to have a hard time with affectionate touch, I now touch my husband almost as much or more than he does me. There is definitely hope for those who may think they can't change their orientation to physical touch.

Awaken Sensuality with Massage Therapy

Transforming our sexual identities takes practice. But besides sex itself, how else can we practice awakening our sensuality? One great way is through massage therapy. Massage therapy is "no strings attached," meaning there are no psychological pressures to return the favor or have it lead to something more. You are likely to feel more free to fully experience the sensations.

Many women have a hard time relaxing, or they may even find themselves "checking out" during lovemaking. Their mind is on what they have to do tomorrow, or what they did yesterday, rather than on the sensuality of what they are experiencing at that moment. Thankfully, learning to relax and focus on pleasurable sensations can be developed, through something like massage therapy.

As women proactively practice calming their mind and body, they can tune into their physical sensations, which helps to awaken sensuality. The learned sensuality can then flow over into lovemaking more easily. Surrendering to sensuality is a necessary component of fully engaging ourselves in the intimate experience of lovemaking. Learning to breathe deeply and focus on the pleasurable touch during a massage provides a great opportunity to practice the sensual skills that can be beneficial during lovemaking. It helps us practice relaxing, being present, surrendering, and developing our physicality.

Getting a massage provides an added benefit of helping women work through any body image issues and feelings of vulnerability. Though you are appropriately covered during a massage, there is still some connection to the feeling of being exposed and vulnerable that often occurs within lovemaking. Women might consider taking advantage of getting a professional massage as a therapeutic activity. Here are just some of the benefits women may gain:

1. Learning to relax, let go, and surrender to tactile pleasure.
2. Awakening, tuning into, and savoring physical sensations.
3. Being mentally present during sensual touch.
4. Training yourself to slow your mind and shut out mental distractions.
5. Practicing deep, relaxing breathing.
6. Working through body image issues and feelings of vulnerability.
7. Disassociating pleasurable touch with having "strings attached."

Nurturing Touch

If massage therapy is too big of a first step for some women, I also encourage the use of "Nurturing Touch" that can also help women develop their physicality and sensuality.[9] Women can take a few minutes to simply caress their hand, arm or neck to learn to pay better attention to pleasurable tactile sensations. This helps them get more familiar with loving touch.

Nurturing touch is naturally done for you in a massage therapy session. It can also be done if you can talk your husband into a no-strings-attached massage with the intent for you to practice breathing, relaxing, and learning to let go, as you bask in the sensual touch. You can then move to massage therapy as a next step.

How To's for Embracing Your Sexual Identity

How do we go about developing a healthy sexual self-concept? The following nine suggestions can help you embrace your sexuality and nourish your mind with healthy and positive sexual messages.[10]

1. ***Take the Healthy Sexual Identity Assessment.*** Do the "Healthy Sexual Identity Assessment" shared earlier in this chapter to identify where you may need some shoring up. This will help you identify your limiting beliefs and other barriers to help you fully embrace your sexuality. Record your thoughts in your Sexual Self-Discovery Journal (see 4 below).

2. ***Reprogram your mind.*** Reprogram your brain with healthy, positive sexual messages. You might read and re-read this chapter, or listen to this book over and over until it roots out the negative beliefs you have about sex. Listening to positive sexual information, like my books or "The Marital Intimacy Show" podcasts, helps keep sex on your radar as a priority among the other things competing for your attention. One client shared, "When I can, I listen to your book and podcasts as the 'background music' of my day. It helps me change my negative sexual beliefs and notice otherwise fleeting sexual thoughts and feelings."

3. ***Merge your identity and welcome sexual thoughts.*** Begin to merge your identity as a mom, school teacher, executive, or whatever else you are, with the fact that you're also a sexual being. Welcome positive thoughts and feelings about sex and your sexuality. Nourish positive feelings toward your spouse to help fuel a healthy sexual identity.

4. ***Start a Sexual Self-Discovery Journal.*** A Sexual Self-Discovery Journal is something you will be encouraged to write in throughout this book. As you write your thoughts and feelings, you will better discover who you are sexually, and what you want to change. You won't believe what a huge impact journaling can have. Throughout this book, you will hear me refer to journaling as "process writing," "journal therapy," and even "notebook therapy." They all refer to the process of reflecting upon and writing about your thoughts and feelings specifically about sex. A simple notebook will suffice where you can be completely honest with yourself. This is not for others to read unless you want to share parts of it with your spouse. Some even find it helpful to shred or destroy their process writings immediately, so they can feel safe about being fully honest. The objective is for you to be able to process emotions and gain clarity by sorting through your thoughts and feelings about sexuality. Like reading your own mind, this exercise helps you develop greater self-awareness by tuning into your internal experiences, reactions and perceptions.[11] It can even help you realize how much you've grown. Journaling has so many physical, mental and emotional benefits.[12] Start by writing about any aspect of sex or your sexual development with which you are struggling or feel uncomfortable. This may include negative experiences

or regrets you may have from your past. Putting emotions into words helps to process them and change their negative impact.[13] Reflect on and write out your thoughts regarding the Sexual Beliefs Assessment questions found in Chapter 2 – "Thoughts." Here are a few of the questions to get you started:

   a.   What do I think about sex? What does sex mean to me?
   b.   How did I learn about sex? What was I taught?
   c.   What would I have to change or give up if I fully embraced my sexuality?
   d.   What would it mean to my husband if I fully embraced my sexuality?
   e.   How might it benefit my children?
   f.   What would it mean for me to be "sexy"?

5.   ***Get educated.*** Read or listen to good books to get more familiar with healthy sexuality. This entire book is designed to help you develop a healthy sexual identity. (See the Recommended Resources in the Appendix for more suggestions.)

6.   ***Do the Action Items and some counseling.*** With the help of a good counselor or sex therapist, address any sexual history or negative beliefs that are interfering with your sexual relationship. The homework and Action Items throughout this book, and in my first book, *And They Were Not Ashamed: Strengthening Marriage through Sexual Fulfillment,* can help with this process.

7.   ***Do it for you.*** Make sure your motivation for developing your sexuality is not just for your spouse, but also for you and your own wholeness. Work together with your spouse to identify how to make lovemaking an enjoyable experience for both of you, so that it will be more motivating to "want to!"

8.   ***Dance and use music.*** Some additional tools that can be helpful are music and dancing. Dancers may already intuitively connect better with the physicality of their bodies. For those of us non-dancers, just having some fun dance music to listen to and dance to can help you connect with your body. It can help you get more comfortable with physical and even sensual movement. Dancing just for fun can also help you get out of your head and into your body. Like Janet in the opening story, listen to mood-inducing music to give yourself the opportunity to be tuned in to your romantic and more sensual self. Whether you just listen to the music or also move your body to it, music can help you connect with and nurture physical and sexual feelings.

9.   ***Awaken sensuality with massage therapy.*** To practice tuning into your sensuality, consider practicing by getting a massage or two. Massage therapy is a great way to engage in and practice many of the skills needed to awaken sexually, but in a non-sexual environment.

There is Hope

In the beginning of this chapter, we talked about Janet and how she had struggled to embrace her sexuality. She worked hard to get to where she really wanted to be intimate with her husband. So, it was exciting to hear what her husband had to say after a few months of them working together on their intimate relationship:

Since she's been listening to your book and podcasts regularly, she's now speaking my love language so well. She is so much more comfortable with herself sexually. She's a lot more flirty, too! I used to feel starved sexually, but not anymore! The best part is that I know she's not just doing this for me. Our sexual relationship is so much more of an enjoyable shared experience now.

Creating a foundation of healthy sexual thoughts, feelings and beliefs is vital to accepting one's sexual identity and embracing one's sexuality. If this is an area that needs some work in your sexual development, don't delay in getting the mental inhibitors rooted out and working to nourish a healthy and confident sexual identity.

Self-Evaluation - "Transformed"

To give yourself a guide as to how you are doing in this dimension, how would you currently rate yourself and your spouse overall in the area of a "Transformed Sexual Identity"? Write your thoughts in your Sexual Self-Discovery Journal. — *I embrace the idea that I am a sexual being. It is a good and important part of my marriage and my wholeness and aliveness. I commit to awakening and nurturing my sexuality and take responsibility for my sexual desire and fulfillment.*

RATING (0 - disagree to 10 - agree):   You _____   Your Spouse _____

ACTION ITEMS — Chapter 1 - "Transformed"

- Overcome your negative sexual beliefs. Do what you can to promote sex as a positive and wholesome expression of love, and a pleasurable—even passionate—means of intimate connection in marriage.
- Stand up and speak up for the sanctity of sex. Watch for opportunities to put in a good word for sex.
- Identify where you currently fit in the three levels of sexual development.
- Do the Healthy Sexual Identity Assessment in this chapter to identify your limiting beliefs and other barriers to fully embracing your sexuality.
- To develop a sexy state of mind, practice looking yourself in a mirror and saying, "Hi ya sexy!" Ask yourself in writing what it means to you to be sexy.
- Get a professional massage to practice being present, relaxing your mind and body, awakening, tuning into, and basking in physical sensations to develop your physicality and sensuality.

- Start a Sexual Self-Discovery Journal to record your feelings as you go on this journey.
- Reprogram your mind with healthy, positive sexual messages by reading and re-reading this chapter or listening to this book over and over until it roots out the negative beliefs you may have about sex.
- Merge your identity as a mom, or an executive, or whatever else you are, with the fact that you're also a sexual being. Welcome and nourish sexual thoughts and feelings about your sexuality and toward your spouse to help fuel your healthy sexual identity.
- Reflect upon and do some writing about any aspect of sex or your sexual development with which you may be struggling or feel uncomfortable. This may include negative experiences or regrets you have from your past. Reflect on and write out your thoughts regarding the Sexual Beliefs Questionnaire questions in Chapter 2.
- Read or listen to good books to get more familiar with healthy sexuality.
- With the help of a good counselor or sex therapist, address any sexual history or negative beliefs that are interfering with your sexual relationship. Do the homework and Action Items throughout this book and in my first book, *And They Were Not Ashamed: Strengthening Marriage through Sexual Fulfillment,* to help with this process.
- Make sure your motivation for developing your sexuality is not just for your spouse, but also for yourself and your own wholeness. Work to make lovemaking an enjoyable and mutually fulfilling experience, so that it will be more motivating to "want to!"
- Have some fun dance music to listen to and dance to as a way to help you connect with your body. It can help you get more comfortable with physical and even sensual movement.
- Listen to mood-inducing music to give yourself the opportunity to be tuned in to your romantic and more sensual self.

NOTES

1 Brotherson, Laura M., *And They Were Not Ashamed: Strengthening Marriage through Sexual Fulfillment.* Boise, ID: Inspire Book, 2004, Chapter 1.
2 Foley, S., "Women in Sex Therapy: Developing a Sexual Identity," *Contemporary Sexuality* 37(9) (2003): 7-13.
3 Ménard, A. Dana, and Offman, Alia, "The Interrelationships Between Sexual Self-esteem, Sexual Assertiveness and Sexual Satisfaction," *The Canadian Journal of Human Sexuality* 18.1/2 (2009): 35-45.
4 Layden, Mary Anne, Testimony for U.S. Senate Committee on Commerce, Science and Transportation, Center for Cognitive Therapy, Department of Psychiatry, University of Pennsylvania, November 18, 2004, 2.
5 Johnson, Dr. Sue, *Love Sense: The Revolutionary New Science of Romantic Relationships.* New York: Little, Brown and Company, 2013.
6 Brotherson, Laura M., *And They Were Not Ashamed: Strengthening Marriage through Sexual Fulfillment.* Boise, ID: Inspire Book, 2004, Chapter 1.
7 McCarthy, Barry, "Marital Sex as it Ought to Be," *Journal of Family Psychotherapy* 14(2) (2003): 1-12.

8   Penner, Dr. Clifford, and Penner, Joyce, "Counseling for Sexual Disorders," Richmont Graduate University, Atlanta, GA. November 6-8, 2015. Advanced Sex Therapy Training.

9   Brotherson, Laura M., *And They Were Not Ashamed: Strengthening Marriage through Sexual Fulfillment.* Boise, ID: Inspire Book, 2004, 52.

10 Foley, S., "Women in Sex Therapy: Developing a Sexual Identity," *Contemporary Sexuality* 37(9) (2003): 7-13.

11 Adams, Kathleen, "The Development of Journal Writing for Well-Being." Center for Journal Therapy, accessed May 26, 2016. http://journaltherapy.com/get-training/short-program-journal-to-the-self/journal-to-the-self/journal-writing-history.

12 Baikie, Karen A., and Wilhelm, Kay, "Emotional and Physical Health Benefits of Expressive Writing," *Advances in Psychiatric Treatment* Aug 2005, 11(5): 338-346; DOI: 10.1192/apt.11.5.338.

13 Johnson, Dr. Sue, *Love Sense: The Revolutionary New Science of Romantic Relationships.* New York: Little, Brown and Company, 2013.

CHAPTER VIEW

How Thoughts Affect Sex

How to Have a Sexy State of Mind

    Develop healthy sexual thoughts and beliefs

    Develop healthy self-acceptance

    Take responsibility for your sexuality

Developing Positive Mental and Sexual Blueprints

    Identifying Inhibiting Thoughts and Beliefs

    Tools for Overcoming Inhibitors

Exercises for Developing a Healthier Sexual Blueprint

    Good Girl Syndrome Self-Awareness Assessment

    Sexual Beliefs Questionnaire

    Identifying Mental Weeds and Flowers

    Positive Sexual Affirmations

    Sexual Effects Inventory

What's Okay and What Isn't Sexually?

    Feel Free to Express and Explore

    Principles Over Practices

    The Spirit of the Law

    Spiritual Self-Confidence

    Inappropriate Versus Inhibited

Characteristics of Healthy Sex

Resolving Sexual Differences

Body Image and Lovemaking

    Women and Body Image

    Body Image and Feeling Sexy

    Body Image Issues and the Impact on Husbands

    Believing Our Husbands

    What Is Real

    Making Peace with Your Body

Good Sex is a Mental Discipline

There is Hope

Self-Evaluation - "Thoughts"

ACTION ITEMS — Chapter 2 - "Thoughts"

Chapter 2

THOUGHTS — SEXY IS A STATE OF MIND

Karla came in for counseling because she wanted to enjoy sex with her husband. She just couldn't figure out how. There were quite a few factors getting in her way. Some of the biggest issues were her thoughts and beliefs about sex. Anxiety and depression needed to be addressed, and she needed more information about how women are wired sexually.

Some of the impeding issues she had were a lack of trust in others, even her husband; fear of getting pregnant again; feeling that she didn't deserve sexual enjoyment; discomfort with having needs and not wanting to voice them; feeling unattractive with her post-baby body; general fear that men could be unfaithful at any time; fear of feeling out of control during sex; belief that if she liked sex her husband would just want more and kinkier activities; and disbelief that her husband's enjoyment was connected to her enjoyment...

How Thoughts Affect Sex

Karla's beliefs were getting in the way in their relationship outside the bedroom, and also inside the bedroom—within lovemaking itself. Thoughts and beliefs play a huge role in a woman's sexual accessibility and her sexual enjoyment, because sex starts in the brain. A woman's ability to develop a positive mental blueprint, and have mental discipline during sex, is essential in sextraordinary lovemaking. Having a healthy mental blueprint directly affects having a healthy sexual blueprint, or view of sex.

At one level, a negative mental blueprint allows one's deeply held beliefs to sour the whole concept of sex. At another level, negative thoughts and feelings can interrupt the relaxation and surrender process. It keeps the mind distracted and disengaged from arousing lovemaking activities.

The purpose of this chapter is threefold: 1) to help women have positive thoughts and feelings about sex, outside the bedroom (a positive mental blueprint), 2) to help women have positive thoughts and feelings about sex within lovemaking (a positive sexual blueprint), and 3) to develop mental discipline. Mental discipline helps her overcome the mental distractions that often occur during sex, and to stay focused on enjoying the intimate experience.

Sex starts in the mind. The mind is the most powerful sex organ. It's the most important body part when it comes to sex.[1] While medical advances such as Viagra may help increase blood flow to the genitals, they do little to help increase the flow of positive thoughts to the mind. Even physical arousal can be stunted by inhibiting thoughts of anger, fear, disgust, etc., during the lovemaking process. Banishing negative thinking about sex is paramount. Like Karla, having negative thoughts like, "I don't want to enjoy this, or my husband will want even more sex," or a fear of pregnancy are both significant impediments in the lovemaking process. More helpful thoughts might be, "I sure love my husband," or "I can't wait to feel close and connected with him."

A woman's attitude about various aspects of sex has a powerful impact on the sexual relationship. For example, the negative effect of thoughts comes into play when a woman struggles with body image issues where she feels insecure and unattractive in her own mind, especially when naked. A man can tell her how beautiful and enticing she is until he's blue in the face. She still won't feel desirable, because she doesn't believe him. This is the power of thoughts and beliefs! She needs to believe she is at least acceptably attractive, plus have the ability to maintain positive thoughts and feelings within the sexual experience. This mental focus is needed to bypass mental barriers and concentrate on emotional and physical stimulators.

Because of the power of thoughts on the sexual experience, sex therapy is really mental therapy. Cognitive work to address negative and unproductive thoughts and beliefs is needed for mastery of our thoughts and fears.[2] You may be able to change your thinking on your own, but if your sexual identity is deeply rooted in negative thinking, then therapy may be necessary. A woman's general state of mind regarding sex comprises her sexual blueprint from which sexual feelings either flow or are stunted. A "sexy state of mind" is a healthy positive-about-sex mental environment from which the desire to be sexually intimate can flourish. This leads to a mutually fulfilling and passionate intimate relationship.

How to Have a Sexy State of Mind

Feeling sexy comes from within. It's a state of mind. Because a woman's sexuality is primarily a product of her thoughts and beliefs about herself, her spouse, and sex in general, what goes on in a woman's mind is of utmost importance. Having healthy, positive, and productive thoughts, core beliefs, feelings, and attitudes form the foundation for true sexiness. Developing a sexy state of mind requires you to do three key things:

Develop healthy sexual thoughts and beliefs. Healthy sexual thoughts and feelings include positive thoughts about sex and positive thoughts about one's body—having a healthy body image. It isn't necessary to have a perfect body, but you have to love and accept your body as it is, even as you continue to work to improve it. We'll discuss body image issues more in a bit. On the flip side, it's almost impossible to have healthy sexual thoughts and beliefs if you think negatively about yourself. The mind is very powerful. Negative thoughts in the form of fears can dangerously become self-fulfilling prophecies in our relationships. Whether the recurring thought is, "I'm never in the mood," or "I'm probably not going to have an orgasm anyway," both thoughts can become unfortunate realities.

When we allow room in our minds for fears to flourish, it's more likely for them to become self-fulfilling prophecies. Trent and Vanessa both had fears of being rejected and abandoned in their marriage. By allowing those fears to have a home in their hearts and minds, those very fears then showed up in their behavior—ultimately destroying their marriage. You can either choose to believe the positive or the negative, but you can't do both. Choosing to have faith over fear greatly increases the chances of having your hopes and dreams fulfilled both in the bedroom and in your relationship. Healthy sexual thoughts and feelings also include having an accurate understanding of the divinity of sex—that sex is good and of God—not something to be ashamed of or embarrassed about. It also requires that you have sufficient sexual knowledge and an understanding of how you and your spouse are wired sexually.

Develop healthy self-acceptance. Healthy self-acceptance means liking yourself in general—mentally, emotionally, physically, etc. It has more to do with your relationship with your "self" than even your relationship with your spouse, though that is certainly an important element. How important is this sexual self-confidence for a wife? Let's just say it's the difference between a mediocre marriage and a passionate intimate relationship. Truly liking one's self—as is—is a vital aphrodisiac for a healthy and fulfilling sexual relationship. Feeling sexy or sexually self-confident is the feeling that says, "I like who I am, and I'm happy to share that with you!"

This is an area where accepting imperfection and "good enough" is part of healthy sexuality.[3] Feeling sexy comes from how you feel about yourself as a person, as a wife, and as a sexual being; so if you don't have a good self-image, it will certainly show up in your sexuality. If a woman does not like herself inside and out, it is very difficult for her to share herself freely and fully with her husband. Think of the self-confidence it takes to get naked. Think of the confidence it takes to be naked with lights on in front of your spouse. Liking yourself, regardless of your imperfections, is a crucial dimension of fully engaging yourself in the sexual experience.

One tool I often suggest to those struggling with feelings of self-worth is to keep a daily list of five things they like, love or appreciate about themselves. They're basically compiling a list of anything positive they can think of about themselves. This helps their mind to focus more on their positives. It can begin to reprogram feelings of worth by fueling the mind with positive thoughts. One client had such a hard time coming up with positives about herself that she instead wrote out every night the same list of positives we had identified together in counseling. She kept at it until she felt like she actually believed the positives.

Healthy self-acceptance is not only liking yourself in general, but also feeling secure about yourself and your body. It's about being at least somewhat immune to your spouse's and other people's negative opinions or moods. This helps create a solid, secure self. This self-acceptance makes it much easier to engage mind, body and soul in the vulnerable marital and sexual relationship.[4] One client wondered about the practical application of this "secure self." What if your spouse doesn't like something about your body? How can you be immune to their negative thoughts about you? How do you share your body with them, if they aren't fully accepting? And if you just ignore your spouse's negative assessments of you, will your spouse feel disregarded?

There will always be things that others may not like about you. That doesn't mean you have to agree or be defined by that, especially if it's not a positive or productive opinion. When you are solid in your own being, then you also recognize that you are doing the best you can and will continue to do so. If your spouse thinks you need to lose weight, and you agree, then you can be working on it while acknowledging and accepting your imperfection in that area. You can still share your imperfect body with your spouse if *you* have accepted your imperfection, and continue to do what you can about it (even if sometimes that isn't a lot).

If your spouse is so bothered by your body that it affects sex, then that becomes your spouse's issue that you don't have a lot of control over anyway. When you don't have control over something (or someone), it's not really worth you giving it a lot of energy. It's likely to pull you down. You can be respectful of your spouse's wish that you lose weight by acknowledging and working on it (in your own way, not your spouse's), without letting go of your secure acceptance and sense of self. We make positive changes a lot better from a state of acceptance than criticism anyway—whether the criticism is from ourselves or others.

Take responsibility for your sexuality. To take responsibility for one's sexuality, and the sexual relationship in one's marriage, involves a willingness to go through the pain of personal growth. Women need to be willing to engage in some serious mental calisthenics to develop the mental habits and discipline necessary for sex to flourish.

Husbands do have a role, however. There are many things husbands can do to help the sexual relationship in the 12 key areas addressed throughout this book, especially in the areas of Tenderness, Thoughtfulness, Trust, Touch and Technique. However, the area of "Thoughts" is a bit of a trump card. Women hold particular power to make or break the sexual relationship in a marriage with their thoughts. A man can't do much directly to change a woman's thoughts and beliefs, though he can certainly help her on her path. Husbands can help her want to work on changing her thoughts and beliefs about sex by saying and doing things that build trust and security in their current relationship. For example, he can compliment her about her appearance, giving her the chance to believe the positive things he says. A wise husband pays careful attention to the psychological foreplay he engenders in his wife whether through his thoughts, words, or actions.

When it comes down to it, however, changing her thoughts and beliefs about sex is primarily a work she must tackle herself. It's important for women to realize that their husbands can't do a lot to directly undo any psychological damage from a negative childhood experience or from her negative core beliefs. He can help, but he can't do it for her.

An impediment to progress is when husbands develop the attitude that all the couple's sexual troubles are due to a wife's negative thoughts (that he can't directly change), and that he is absolved of any responsibility to help her heal. For women, creating a sextraordinary relationship begins with her wanting to do so. It's hard to want to if she feels like she's married to a thoughtless jerk, or if she is the only person putting any effort into positive change in the relationship.

As women work to overcome their psychological inhibitors, and program in positive, affirming thoughts and beliefs, they're on their way to cultivating a sexy state of mind that is available for intimate and passionate lovemaking. This concept may help you understand how to change your thoughts—but being able to change can be difficult. There is a lot that can hold us back. This will take some time and effort that at some times will be hard. Many times there are mental weeds crowding out the mental flowers.

Let's talk now about developing a positive mental blueprint, and how to identify what's on it. Identifying the mentally inhibiting aspects of your sexuality is important, so that you can replace the mental weeds with mental flowers that support healthy sexuality. Once you reprogram your mental blueprint, the day-to-day thoughts about sex can be healthier and more productive. That leads to developing the mental discipline needed to stay present and more fully engaged in the sexual experience itself.

Developing Positive Mental and Sexual Blueprints

A blueprint is basically a map of what is going on, in this case in the brain. Throughout this book, I will talk about two main blueprints:

Mental: Having a positive mental blueprint means that you have healthy thoughts, beliefs, attitudes, feelings, perceptions, teachings, expectations, experiences, etc., about things, including sex and its related aspects.

Sexual: Having a healthy sexual blueprint manifests itself in appropriate automatic reactions to touch and sex. A positive sexual blueprint includes thoughts and beliefs that allow for healthy sexual engagement and activities, as well as having an emotionally healthy intimate relationship.

The two are very interrelated. Just as your sexual self-concept is an aspect of

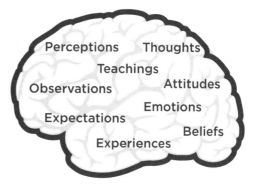

Mental Blueprint

Perceptions Thoughts
Teachings
Observations Attitudes
Emotions
Expectations
Beliefs
Experiences

your mental blueprint, there are other areas of your sexual blueprint that need positive, healthy, and productive thoughts as well. Having a positive sexual blueprint means that you have positive thoughts and beliefs about the following items:

- The act of sex itself
- Your sexuality
- Your body
- Your spouse's body
- Your relationship with your spouse

To develop a positive sexual blueprint usually requires identifying the inhibiting factors and overcoming those negative thoughts and beliefs. The information and exercises below can help you begin to identify what's on your mental blueprint, and where things may need to be changed to help your sexual blueprint.

Identifying Inhibiting Thoughts and Beliefs

Inhibiting thoughts and beliefs are those that create resistance to intimacy. Although there is some overlap, inhibiting thoughts and beliefs may be categorized into mental, emotional, and relational inhibitors. Mental inhibitors include negative or unproductive thoughts, beliefs, and attitudes about sex—Good Girl Syndrome issues.[5] This also includes a lack of education about sex and intimacy. Inaccurate or unrealistic expectations are other culprits in inhibiting a great sexual relationship. Some examples of mental inhibitors include negative thoughts and beliefs such as: "Sex is messy;" "I'm too tired;" "Good girls don't;" "All he ever thinks about is sex," and so forth.

Emotional inhibitors include negative feelings or negative automatic responses. Some examples of emotional inhibitors include: stress, grief, feelings of guilt, shame, fear, embarrassment, or awkwardness associated with lovemaking, etc. Relationship inhibitors still tend to stem from thoughts and beliefs that have developed over time about one's spouse and relationship. Overcoming these inhibitors not only requires changes to one's attitude and expectations of one's spouse, but often requires changes in behavior as well. Some examples of relational inhibitors include: lack of emotional connection, lack of kindness, trust issues, anger, resentment, etc.

For Sharon, she had some inhibiting thoughts and beliefs that flowed into all three categories. She wanted to overcome her sexual inhibitors. Her husband liked to be able to suck on her fingers during sex, but that felt dirty, inappropriate, and unwholesome to her. She went on to share that technically *everything* about sex felt dirty to her. She said, "I feel dirty just engaging in sex at all, even though I know I shouldn't." She explained that sex had never been presented to her in a positive light, so the whole subject was fraught with negative thoughts and feelings. Thankfully, Sharon was willing and able to use some of the tools and exercises below and throughout this book to work through her inhibiting thoughts and feelings towards her husband, and toward sex as well.

Tools for Overcoming Inhibitors

As we dive into some exercises that can help you identify specific thoughts and beliefs that may be inhibiting you sexually, it may be helpful to be aware of some valuable tools to use for overcoming inhibiting thoughts and beliefs. In turn, these are helpful in developing a positive sexual blueprint. Many of these processes were used by Karla, in the opening story, to work through her difficulties:

1. ***Talk therapy.*** Talk about your thoughts and feelings regarding sexual matters with both your spouse and a therapist, if possible. It can help to read and discuss this book, the assessments, and the writing exercises below with your spouse and/or a therapist.

2. ***Journal therapy/process writing.*** This exercise entails completing written questionnaires, like the ones below, or free writing any thoughts and feelings you have about sex. This can be done in your Sexual Self-Discovery Journal. It can be helpful to have written conversations with yourself, your spouse, your therapist, or God about your sexual difficulties. Functional magnetic resonance imaging (fMRI) studies show that suppressing emotion is detrimental to well being. Instead, putting your thoughts and feelings into words helps you reflect upon and better regulate them. Process writing is therapeutic because it calms the brain and helps you better tolerate and change the negative impact the thoughts and feelings may be having on you.

3. ***Bibliotherapy/reading books.*** Getting educated about sex, intimacy, marriage, relationships, etc. (like you are already doing by reading this book), is a powerfully therapeutic way to change your thought processes by adding new information into the mix. Some helpful books are listed below in the "Program in positives" section and the Recommended Resources section in the Appendix.

4. ***Emotional Freedom Technique (EFT).*** This tapping technique based on energy meridians in the body is one of the best self-help tools for removing deeply embedded inhibiting thoughts and beliefs. See EmoFree.com, EFT.mercola.com, or 123EFT.com for more information or to find a practitioner.

5. ***Program in positives.*** It's not enough to identify the mental weeds on your mental blueprint. It's also important to replace the negatives with positives. This can be done by affirmations, tapping in positives with EFT, and listening to affirming audio books, podcasts, etc., to replace the negatives. A few of my favorite audios for positive programming are: my book *And They Were Not Ashamed: Strengthening Marriage through Sexual Fulfillment*, my "Marital Intimacy Show" podcasts on iTunes or at TheMaritalIntimacyShow.com (see the full list of episodes in the Appendix), *The Good Girl's Guide to Great Sex* by Shelia Wray Gregoire, *The Sexually Confident Wife* by Shannon Ethridge, and *Sheet Music* by Kevin Leman.

6. ***Meditation.*** Meditation is a simple and elegant way to develop mental discipline. Mental discipline is needed to relax tightly held negative beliefs and make room for more positive replacements. It can help with the relaxation process needed within lovemaking.

7. ***Surrender process.*** Working through the surrender process I've developed is often necessary in order to let go of things you can't control, while maintaining faith that things will be okay. We'll go into more detail on this in Chapter 12 as we discuss "Transcendence" and surrender.

Exercises for Developing a Healthier Sexual Blueprint

The following exercises are just a few examples to help you get started on the process of identifying inhibiting thoughts and beliefs, and then reprogramming them to be more positive and productive:

- Characteristics of a Healthy Sexual Identity Assessment
- Good Girl Syndrome Self-Awareness Assessment
- Sexual Beliefs Questionnaire
- Identifying Mental Weeds and Flowers
- Positive Sexual Affirmations
- Sexual Effects Inventory

If you haven't already completed the exercise in Chapter 1 - "Transformed," then the "Characteristics of a Healthy Sexual Identity" assessment in that chapter is a good place to start. It's important to see if your identity includes affirming beliefs about being a sexual person. Another exercise to help identify the weeds on your mental blueprint is my "Self-Awareness Assessment" for the Good Girl Syndrome adapted from my first book, *And They Were Not Ashamed.*[6] As you work through each of these exercises, record your results, responses and thoughts in your Sexual Self-Discovery Journal.

Good Girl Syndrome Self-Awareness Assessment

Listed below are some of the symptoms of the negative sexual conditioning many people have acquired regarding sex and the body from their families, religious training and society. This negative conditioning and lack of affirming sexual knowledge may be a significant underlying and oft-ignored source of sexual dissatisfaction in marriage.

Directions: *Rate on a scale of 0 (none) to 10 (a lot) the effect of each issue in your life. An honest, in-depth assessment can help you become more aware of the negative conditioning you may have internalized, and help you to see areas that need to be addressed. You might also have your spouse rate you on these items if you'd like to have their perspective.*

<u>0 (none)   10 (a lot)</u>

0 1 2 3 4 5 6 7 8 9 10   Discomfort, embarrassment or inability to appropriately discuss sexual matters.

0 1 2 3 4 5 6 7 8 9 10   Underlying belief that sex is bad, wrong, dirty or sinful.

0 1 2 3 4 5 6 7 8 9 10   Lack of belief in the divine purposes of sex—particularly that God intended it for pleasure and connection—as well as for procreation.

0 1 2 3 4 5 6 7 8 9 10   Inability to relax and let go fully within the sexual experience.

0 1 2 3 4 5 6 7 8 9 10   Lack of enjoyment of sexual relations, and/or participation out of duty.

0 1 2 3 4 5 6 7 8 9 10   Lack of sexual understanding and "know how"—a simplistic perception that if I can just "be a good person" I will have blissful, intimate relations.

0 1 2 3 4 5 6 7 8 9 10   Unnecessary or inappropriate inhibitions, guilt, shame or awkwardness associated with sexual relations within marriage.

0 1 2 3 4 5 6 7 8 9 10   Discomfort or distaste with sexual parts of the body and body functioning.

Sexual Beliefs Questionnaire

Another tool I use with clients is my "Sexual Beliefs Questionnaire" to help them not only identify negative or unproductive thoughts, attitudes, and beliefs, but also to begin to process through those inhibiting factors by writing about them. In your Sexual Self-Discovery Journal, write your thoughts regarding the following questions:

1. What do I think about sex? How do I feel about it? "I think sex is…" (List all your honest thoughts about sex.)
2. What do I think about my body…all parts of it? Are there any parts I am uncomfortable with?
3. What do I think about my spouse's body…all parts of it? Are there any parts I am uncomfortable with?
4. What or who played a role in my sexual learning and development (i.e. parents, peers, church, media, etc.), and in what ways?
5. What did I learn about sex? What was I taught?
6. What do I think God thinks about sex?
7. What negative experiences with sex have I had in my past?
8. What positive experiences with sex have I had in my past?
9. What inhibitions or psychological barriers do I think I may have regarding sex?
10. How important is the sexual relationship in my marriage? How important is sexuality to me?
11. Write down everything you can think of to finish the following phrase: "I remember …" (List sex-related memories, personal experiences, and feelings, e.g. your first kiss (positive or negative); your first sexual experiences, or honeymoon experiences (positive or negative); memories from movies or conversations with

friends; the first time you saw someone naked (e.g. accidentally seeing someone just out of the shower, or when viewing porn), etc.)

12. Write down everything you can think of to finish the following phrase: "I don't like …" "I hate …" (List all your dislikes or inhibitions about sex.)

13. Write down everything you can think of to finish the following phrase: "Sex …" (List anything else that comes to mind regarding sex.)

14. List as many genuine, positive thoughts and feelings as you can about sex.

15. Write out any additional information or observations related to your thoughts, beliefs, attitudes, etc., about sex.

It's likely that you may need some help from a good therapist to help you work through these issues. Doing this writing will at least get you started on the road to better understanding your sexuality, and creating a healthier, more positive sexual blueprint.

Identifying Mental Weeds and Flowers

It might be useful to create a two-column table as shown below to list out all the negative thoughts, feelings, beliefs, attitudes, etc., you've been able to identify about sex. Then choose a more positive thought or feeling that you could use to replace and reprogram the negatives. Once you identify the mental flower, or positive thought or belief, read them out loud regularly, tap on them with EFT, or write them out frequently. The concept is to identify the weed, or inhibiting thought or belief. Then pull it out like you would a weed, plant a flower in its place, and nourish the flower until it becomes your new norm.

Mental Weed	Mental Flower
List any negative, unproductive thoughts, feelings, beliefs, etc., you can identify about sex and related issues.	*Identify healthier, more positive messages to replace each mental weed. Make them positive, specific, and present tense.*
i.e. I don't like sex.	i.e. I enjoy being intimate with my spouse and look forward to our intimate time together.
i.e. I hate my body.	i.e. I am grateful for my body and all that it can do. I'm especially grateful that I can be intimate with my spouse.
i.e. I have little interest in being sexual.	i.e. I want to develop my sexuality so that I can feel whole and be able to love my spouse well.

*Feeling sexy comes from within. It's the feeling that says,
"I like who I am, I like my body, and I'm happy to share it with you!"*

Positive Sexual Affirmations

Below are some positive affirmations about sex to use to reprogram your mental blueprint. The list can also help you come up with your own statements to replace the mental weeds you've identified in the exercise above. I've had clients who have either used my list below, or compiled their own and recorded them via voice recording. They are then able to listen to them over and over until they become embedded new beliefs. It's a great way to change your "self-talk." You could also write them in your Sexual Self-Discovery Journal and read them daily.

- I am grateful for this body that God has given me.
- Our sexual relationship is a high priority to me.
- I want to experience the joy of sex.
- I know God wants me to experience the joy of lovemaking.
- I deserve to enjoy this God-given gift.
- I give myself permission to enjoy and explore this divine gift.
- I like sex.
- I'm grateful my body works as God intended it by responding to mental, emotional and sexual stimuli.
- I am grateful for my body—all parts of it.
- I love my spouse's body—all parts of it.
- It's okay to enjoy sexual touch.
- It's okay to let my body express its God-given sexuality.
- I trust my spouse to be tender and attentive to me in lovemaking.
- I can relax and let go sexually.
- I can let go of negative past experiences and enjoy sexually connecting.
- I am safe and allow myself to be vulnerable during sex.
- Even though letting go sexually feels scary sometimes, I know it will be all right.
- I am proud of myself for learning to relax, let go, and surrender to the sexual experience.
- I know sexual love is or can be a sacred, spiritual experience.
- It's okay to be physical and sensual.
- It's okay to bask in the sensual pleasure of sexuality designed for husband and wife.
- It's okay for me to learn and grow into my God-given sexuality.
- Sex is healthy and wholesome with my spouse.
- I thoroughly enjoy the whole experience of lovemaking.

- I feel whole and more alive when I am sexually intimate with my spouse.
- Sexually interacting is one of my favorite ways to express my love to my mate.
- Fully engaging myself sexually is an empowering experience for me.
- I thoroughly embrace my sexuality and enjoy its full expression with my spouse.
- Lovemaking is a natural and healthy part of a strong and intimate relationship.
- Our intimate relationship is mutually enjoyable and sexually satisfying.
- I can feel my desire increase in between our lovemaking encounters.
- Sex is a wonderful means of nurturing and healing each other.
- I bask in the ecstasy of the pleasurable sensations and orgasm during lovemaking.

Sexual Effects Inventory

Another tool for changing negative thoughts and beliefs is the "Sexual Effects Inventory." It helps you begin to identify the effects that negative experiences have had on your sexual attitudes, reactions, behaviors, and relationships. This is used especially when there has been any sexual abuse in one's past (adapted from *The Sexual Healing Journey* by Wendy Maltz[7]). The Sexual Effects Inventory helps to identify what concepts resonate with you. You might also write about your thoughts or any insights you are having in your Sexual Self-Discovery Journal. Here are a few sample items to write your thoughts about, particularly if sexual abuse, of any degree, has impacted your life:

Attitudes about Sex

- I feel sex is a duty I must perform.
- Sex feels dirty to me.
- I think sex benefits men more than women.
- Sex means danger to me.

Sexual Self-Concept

- I hate my body.
- There is something wrong with me sexually.
- I feel I will lose control if I let myself go sexually.
- I'd be happiest in a world where sex didn't exist.

Automatic Reactions to Touch and Sex

- I have little interest in being sexual.
- I believe that when a person touches me, he or she wants to have sex.
- I get panicky feelings when touched.
- I feel emotionally distant during sex.

Sexual Behavior and Boundaries

- I am unable to initiate sex.
- I avoid situations that could lead to sex.

- I am unable to say no to sex.
- I feel I have no physical boundaries when it comes to sex.

Intimate Relationships

- I am afraid of being emotionally vulnerable in relationships.
- I have difficulty being intimate and sexual at the same time.
- I have difficulty communicating my sexual wants and needs.
- I am afraid to be emotionally close with my partner.

What's Okay and What Isn't Sexually?

Right up at the top of the list of things I get asked about the most are the "what's okay and what isn't" type questions. These questions and concerns often act as distracters and inhibitors to intimacy. Because women tend to be particularly sensitive to things they consider spiritually based, these issues often create mental conflicts. Resolution is needed in order to allow a woman's mind to be at peace so lovemaking can flow freely.

Some common "what's okay/what isn't" topics include things like oral sex, vibrators/sex toys, wearing lingerie, etc. Think through them as I discuss the following principles to help resolve such conflicts. "What's okay/what's isn't" issues have also been addressed in my book *And They Were Not Ashamed*,[8] and on my website StrengtheningMarriage.com in Q&A's and other articles. Here are some of the overriding concepts to consider as you work through your own "what's okay and what isn't" type issues.

Feel Free to Express and Explore

Couples should feel free to express and develop their lovemaking within the intimate sanctuary of marriage. Sexual intimacy is approved and ordained of God as a divine gift for husband and wife to enjoy. The sexual learning of a husband and wife is meant to occur within an atmosphere of love, respect, and trust, not in an atmosphere of fear, anxiousness, guilt, or shame. Some people experience overactive feelings of guilt, shame, and discomfort about sex, already inhibiting their sexual desire and response. It can make it difficult to grasp the idea of the intimate relationship being a sacred sanctuary free of anxiety, embarrassment, or guilt.

The husband and wife relationship must be seen as a haven of God-given privacy. This allows couples to freely and openly express, learn about, communicate regarding, and understand the unique and powerful blessings of sexual expression. Both husband and wife should feel free to share their thoughts, feelings, and bodies. Couples should become comfortable with their bodies and learn how they respond sexually. Within the divine context of a private marital sanctuary, and following the guidance of the Spirit, couples can work through their personal beliefs, preferences, and boundaries. They can create a wonderfully close and mutually satisfying relationship.

Principles Over Practices

Some couples look for a laundry list of do's and don'ts to guide the intimate relationship in marriage. Because of the variety of individuals, experiences, history, personalities, etc., it may be more effective to operate on the principles of love, mutual respect, trust, fidelity, etc., rather than seek a list of specific practices in determining what's okay and what isn't. God doesn't need to command in all things, especially when we can go to Him directly for specific personal counsel and guidance. This requires that we understand God's principles governing sexual intimacy. We must then work to develop our spiritual senses, so that we can trust in the inspiration we receive.

Many people have wanted me to give them a "yes" or "no" answer to specific questions, but my response is always the same. It doesn't really matter what I think. It only matters what you and your spouse think, and what you both feel comfortable with and willingly agree upon. What's the point of someone even saying that a particular behavior is okay, if your spouse feels that it isn't? The counsel would only be useful for one spouse to, in essence, beat the other spouse over the head about it. That's not the best way to create a close and intimate loving relationship. This is why couples must take responsibility for working through their intimate differences between themselves and God, if needed, based on divine principles. A professional may be helpful when the relationship is being negatively affected by their differences of opinion.

The Spirit of the Law

Jesus Christ replaced the strict and specific written commandments (the do's and don'ts) of the Old Testament's Law of Moses with the New Testament's higher law. Blind obedience to specific behaviors—the letter of the law—was replaced with following the spirit of the law. It almost makes lists of moral do's and don'ts unnecessary given that the underlying law is presupposed. What's added is the intent of our hearts in determining what's right or wrong for one's relationship based on divine principles of love, respect, trust, etc. Graduating to the spirit of the law regarding intimacy in marriage not only includes maintaining appropriate behavior, but also relies on following the intent of God's counsel for sex in marriage.

The Savior used symbols and parables to teach divine truths. Parables and symbols allow for people to learn what they are ready to understand at that moment in time. Parables rely upon the Spirit to teach what is right according to when one is ready, willing, and able to receive. This might mean that husband and wife may have different impressions based on their uniqueness as an individual. Depending on the knowledge, experience, and degree of spiritual understanding an individual has, parables can potentially allow for each person to understand the same principle a little differently. If the Savior chose to use parables to teach, then maybe we too can give each other greater latitude in our learning. We can let it be okay for others to see things differently.

Following the spirit of the law requires refinement of the heart, greater spiritual insight, and a greater ability to hear and heed spiritual direction. We must, therefore, examine the intent of our hearts regarding our desires within the sexual relationship in order to determine what's appropriate. The spirit of the law allows for flexibility in making decisions for our particular situation. It means making a decision, then checking with the Lord for confirmation. One caution here is to beware of using the spirit of the law as simply a way to rationalize the law away.

An example of applying the spirit of the law might be when a husband is overly fixated on a particular sex act, even though the behavior isn't expressly forbidden. His insistence makes his wife upset and resistant to sex altogether. The spirit of the law might then be that while something isn't technically "not okay," it is affecting the relationship in a way that is harmful to the warmth and connection.

Spiritual Self-Confidence

I applaud couples who are trying to create a healthy and godly sexual relationship. God wants couples to enjoy His divine gift of sex. By personally tackling the difficult issues of what's appropriate regarding intimacy in marriage, couples will be able to develop greater confidence in their ability to identify and receive spiritual direction, and rely more directly on God for guidance.

I see couples wanting approval for or against certain behaviors. My concern comes when couples are not sufficiently versed in the language of the Spirit of God, and/or are not confident in their ability to receive divine guidance on this delicate subject. Some may not want to put in the effort required to study and gain insight directly from the Lord on this. But on matters especially as sacred and personal as sexuality, God may be the only true source of sound guidance versus relying on human opinion and validation.

No one outside the couple has enough information about the circumstances in the relationship to make accurate judgments about what's okay and what isn't. Only God perfectly knows each one of us. He knows our strengths, our weaknesses, and the dynamics of our marriage relationship. He is the only one who can answer our "what's okay" questions correctly.

We must be careful not to condemn or judge our spouse, or others, based upon our personal interpretation or perceptions of right and wrong. We must work together as husband and wife, with the help of the Lord, to determine what will enhance and strengthen our intimate relationship. Each couple has a responsibility to develop their own spiritual self-confidence—especially within the delicate and intimate relationship of marriage. Couples need to work together using wisdom to govern themselves. Spiritual self-reliance is as vital today as ever, if not more so.

Inappropriate Versus Inhibited

Negative thoughts, beliefs, and experiences we accumulate about sex create distorted perceptions about sexual intimacy that we may incorrectly see as reality. We internalize this conditioning, which manifests itself in varying degrees among both men and women, though women seem to absorb it more easily. These negative core beliefs can affect one's perceptions of right and wrong. Men (and women), too, can pick up negative conditioning about sex through pornography and its influence.

Being able to receive definitive divine guidance is a complex, delicate matter. Personal revelation involves preparation, study, righteousness, and a sufficiently developed sense of or familiarity with God's voice in order to be able to accurately hear and heed the whisperings of the Spirit.

Distinguishing between sexual inhibitions caused by negative conditioning, and reticence prompted by divine direction, is no easy task. Couples must consider the possibility of negative sexual conditioning, as well as the strength of their spiritual connection when determining what's okay and what isn't in their intimate relationship. Let's say a husband wants his wife to participate in a particular behavior, but she feels uncomfortable with it. She considers her feelings to be a spiritual indication that the behavior is wrong. It is possible that the husband is out of tune with his spiritual guidance system, or it could be that things like pornography are unfavorably influencing his appetites and desires. He may not see anything wrong with the behavior, even though it may actually *not* be in keeping with God's designs for sexual relations in marriage.

On the other hand, it is possible that the wife is unaware of her underlying negative conditioning (Good Girl Syndrome)[9] that causes her to believe or feel something is sinful when it is not.

As the husband develops spiritually, or roots out the effects of pornography, for instance, he may come to see that the particular behavior he previously desired isn't appropriate. As the wife overcomes her unnecessary inhibitions, the sexual activities she previously felt were sinful can now be seen as perfectly acceptable, and even enjoyable within the loving and intimate relationship of marriage.

Though there is no clearly defined list of do's and don'ts, the Lord has not left couples alone with the important issues of intimacy in marriage. Couples can counsel with the Lord in all their doings—even in the area of sexual relations—and He will direct them to that which is good. The Lord knows every individual, and is intimately aware of their lives and circumstances. He can lead each couple to the right counsel for them. He can direct them to certain books or information, or put people in their path in the form of friends, family, or professionals to guide them to light and truth regarding the matter.

Characteristics of Healthy Sex

Wendy Maltz, in her book *The Porn Trap*[10] and on her website HealthySex.com, outlines the differences between healthy sex and porn-related sex. It's a list of comparisons between sex based on love and sex based on lust. It's especially helpful to those who may not be clear about the differences. Her list identifies the characteristics of healthy sex as couples work together to resolve sexual differences in their own relationships:

- Healthy sex is caring for someone, not using someone for selfish gratification.
- Healthy sex is sharing with a partner.
- Healthy sex is a natural drive, not compulsive.
- Healthy sex is about genuine connection.
- Healthy sex is an expression of love.
- Healthy sex is nurturing.
- Healthy sex is emotionally close.
- Healthy sex is safe.
- Healthy sex is always respectful and never degrading.
- Healthy sex requires morals and values.
- Healthy sex requires healthy communication.
- Healthy sex requires honesty.
- Healthy sex has ethical boundaries.
- Healthy sex enhances who you really are.
- Healthy sex enhances self-esteem.
- Healthy sex is lasting satisfaction, not impulse gratification.[11]

Resolving Sexual Differences

As noted in Sharon's personal situation above, she really struggled with a particular sexual activity her husband wanted. "He wants to suck on my fingers during sex," she shared, "but it just feels dirty, inappropriate and unwholesome to me." In reality she had other issues with sex itself, not just that particular act. Couples could look at conflicting desires and see the sexual activity as simply a personal preference or a personal boundary, rather than a psychological inhibitor. It was helpful for her husband Ron to think of her reticence to his request as simply a differing sexual preference. This helped him not put so much weight on her as being "the problem to be fixed" or "the broken one."

Husbands can be mindful of putting undue pressure on their wives for certain behaviors whether they are "appropriate" or not. The principle over the practice is that if he puts pressure on her, or guilts her into doing something she considers uncomfortable or demeaning, it will have a negative effect on the overall relationship. That is sure to be an intimate inhibitor itself. It becomes a vicious downward spiral.

Certainly is would be good if women would put in the efforts suggested here to work through any potential inhibitors they may have. But, if the husband can't stay in a space of love, respect, trust, patience, etc., then the foundation for healthy sexuality is already lost. It often doesn't seem fair to men, given that their desires may be benign, but pressure, guilt, and shame are not good motivators for wives if you want a healthy intimate relationship. In Sharon's case, we were able to resolve the underlying issues she had by using the tools for overcoming inhibitors addressed throughout this chapter.

Steps to Resolving Sexual Differences

The process for resolving differences of opinion, or conflicts in preferences for various sexual behaviors, is similar to that which has been addressed above:

1) Read together. Couples might first spend time reading together, out loud if possible, the entire section "What's Okay and What Isn't." This can help them have some of the overriding principles in mind before addressing their specific disagreement.

2) Talk about it. Couples need to fully discuss each other's needs, desires, and perspectives on any issues of concern. With many couples, one spouse tends to be less likely to speak up and be honest about their true feelings. If the issue has become heated, it can make it even more difficult for both spouses to be truly heard.

It may be necessary to have this conversation in writing. This minimizes defensiveness and reactivity. It allows each spouse to feel more fully heard. Couples might use the "Questions to Consider" below in their verbal or written discussion. The goal regarding such discussions over disputed sexual activities is to maintain an open, soft, and receptive heart. One couple also reminded me of the need to attend to who is doing most of the asking, and who is doing most of the changing:

> As Heather and John discussed some activities they had recently added to their lovemaking repertoire, I wondered how Heather was really feeling. John was the more dominant personality and would often ask her direct questions that I knew she'd have a hard time answering forthrightly. He turned to his wife, and almost with an assumption that she was, asked, "Are you okay with such and such?"
>
> Before she could answer I said to him, "You know, I think there's a chance she won't answer that question as truthfully as she might want to, given that she may not want to hurt your feelings." She carefully nodded in agreement.
>
> Coming from a neutral stance, I asked them who was generally the one who had to adjust their perspective or opinion most often sexually. Thankfully they could honestly say that they had both moved towards each other as they worked together to discuss their sexual issues. He had learned to lessen his intensity and quantity of requests, and she had worked to be more willing to try new things.

Asking who does the most changing in the sexual arena is another good way to determine what's best for the overall relationship. If one person is doing most of the changing or sacrificing of their opinion or position, it may mean that the intimate relationship has a unilateral method for resolving difficulties, rather than it being an equally united journey. For an intimate relationship built on trust and respect, there should be a balance in the give and take of resolving any what's okay, what isn't type questions.

3) Pray together. Make the issue a matter of prayer both individually and as a couple. It's harder to get off-track in your intimate relationship when you invite God into the mix. Prayerful communication with God may help clarify what the inhibiting issue is really about, and who seems most likely to be able to change something to improve the situation. The concept of "the only one you can directly change is yourself" especially comes into play here.

The Lord can guide us to know when an activity is genuinely wrong, and bless us with a lessening desire for it. He can also help us know when resistance to a behavior is due to an unnecessary inhibition, and guide us to overcome that as well. God is the best resources to change hearts and guide couples in distinguishing between genuinely sinful behavior, and inappropriate inhibitions caused by negative conditioning or past traumatic experiences. Husbands who are prompting the addition of a particular sexual activity would do well to examine their heart and their motives. If the disputed activity seems to be an unnecessary psychological inhibition on the wife's part, it will require even more patience and compassion on his part. Continuing on with the steps for resolving sexual differences of opinion, a wife may decide that she does have some inhibitions that she'd like to overcome.

4) Work through inhibitions. She may need to work through the exercises in the beginning of this chapter to identify any inhibiting, or unhelpful thoughts and beliefs, etc., and replace them with more positive and productive ones. This would include being sure that a good mental mindset or blueprint is in place of the sanctity of sexuality itself.

5) Align yourself with God. Either husband or wife may need to spend more time in prayer or written conversation with the Lord to be sure they are accurately aligned with His spirit and His divine designs for marital sexuality.

Questions to Consider in Resolving Sexual Differences

Here are a few questions to ask yourselves to help you sort out the many what's okay and what isn't questions. What might be okay for one couple might not be okay for another. These questions can help you identify your uniquely individual/couple answers:

1. What is the purpose or intent of the desired sexual behavior?
2. Does either spouse feel demeaned, degraded, or objectified by the behavior in question? Does the behavior maintain the dignity of both spouses?
3. Is either spouse demanding a particular behavior, or seem overly preoccupied with it?
4. What is motivating the desire for the behavior? What is motivating the other spouse's resistance to the behavior?
5. Do you think God would approve of the behavior? Why or why not?
6. What are the short-term and long-term outcomes or consequences of adding this activity to your intimate relationship?

7. Is the marriage relationship more likely to be strengthened or weakened in the long-run?

8. Who generally has to do the most changing sexually? Is there compromise, or a balanced mutuality in resolving differing sexual interests and desires?

9. Do both of you feel fully heard about the issue at hand? Are you both confident that the other has honestly and openly expressed their true feelings? Have either of you shut down to avoid confrontation or negative reactions?

Once a resolution is reached, be sure that both husband and wife willingly agree to the action—neither feeling coerced, nor talked into it. I've always appreciated this quote by Susannah Wesley. It's an excellent yardstick by which we can measure anything we are wondering about regarding sex in marriage:

> *Whatever weakens your reason, impairs the tenderness of your conscience, obscures your sense of God, or takes off your relish for spiritual things, whatever increases the authority of the body over the mind, that thing is sin to you, however innocent it may seem in itself.*

Cleaning out any unnecessary negative conditioning, and resolving what's-okay-type questions, is an important first step toward developing a healthy sexual blueprint. It then helps you develop a sexier state of mind that can support and sustain a sextraordinary marriage. This step gets at the level of more global outside-the-bedroom thinking, which paves the way for developing mental discipline within lovemaking itself.

Body Image and Lovemaking

Another of the top contenders for thoughts and beliefs that inhibit sexual relations is that of body image issues. It often feels like an uphill battle for women to love and accept their own bodies, but it is a necessary ingredient of a sextraordinary marriage. Many, if not most, women struggle with their body image, no matter how they look. Body image is a big part of a woman's self-esteem, which is a big part of her sexuality.

> *Candace had been struggling with body image issues for some time. We had worked on it quite a bit in both individual and couples' therapy sessions. She didn't look like someone who would feel insecure about how she looked, but she did. Her husband felt he wasn't "seeing enough" of her in their sexual interactions.*
>
> *One day Candace walked into my office and said, "Guess what I did this week? I vacuumed naked!" I said, "You did what?!" She continued, "I actually vacuumed naked…while my husband was watching even!" Wow! I was stunned and thrilled all at the same time. I asked what made her decide to do that. She said she thought it would help her get more comfortable with her body. I asked if it worked, and she said, "Yes!"*

No matter how attractive a woman is, most tend to have some kind of body image issues that often get in the way of really letting go and engaging fully in lovemaking.

Learning to love and accept ourselves, and our bodies, is a necessary ingredient of passionate and truly transcendent lovemaking. It's difficult to really "go there" intimately and give ourselves—body and soul—to the experience when we're consumed with the cellulite on our thighs or our sagging body parts. Vacuuming naked may not be a bad idea for anyone who wants to overcome their insecurities and learn to be more okay with their body. And if you need a way to start out a little easier, you could even just vacuum naked in your locked bedroom.

Another fun way to make friends with your body might be to turn on some party tunes and dance naked in the shower. Either way, it will help you to relax and get more comfortable with your nakedness as you confront and let go of any body image issues.

Women and Body Image

Most women wish they could change a few things about their appearance. Given the unrealistic media comparisons that constantly bombard women (and men), it's difficult to maintain healthy acceptance of one's natural body. This can significantly affect one's intimate relationship. What's going on inside a woman's mind about herself and her body, prior to and during lovemaking, is of utmost importance. While the thing on men's minds many times a day is sex, by comparison, women think about their appearance (mostly negatively) many times a day.

Neuroscientists did a study of healthy, fit females with healthy body images to then compare to women who have eating disorders. They chose women without overt body image issues, according to standardized assessments, then showed them images of overweight women to record their brain activity through an MRI.[12]

Unfortunately, they found that even healthy women exhibit brain activity that shows anxiety and negative self-reflection, similar to women with eating disorders. In the study, men did not show similar signs of anxiety or comparison in their MRIs. It appears that women may be hard-wired, or at least well conditioned, for unhealthy body image comparisons. As women, we need to acknowledge how easy it is to compare ourselves unfavorably, then work at disputing the comparisons.

While discussing how women think about themselves, and their lack of body image acceptance, Kyle was pooh-poohing the idea of even trying to be complimentary to his wife anymore. He felt like she responded so dismissively anytime he tried to say something nice about her, it felt like a waste of time. I agreed that women aren't always good at accepting compliments, especially when they don't believe that they look good. But, I also endeavored to explain that if husbands simply stop even trying to compliment their wives, then women are left alone with only the negative assessments and comparisons they make about themselves.

Husbands can do much to help their wives feel better about themselves by continuing to express positive feelings about her and her appearance, regardless of her response. This helps her feel safe and more willing to risk herself sexually. A husband's compliments can help counteract her negative body image issues, especially when his comments have no sexual overtones.

Body Image and Feeling Sexy

Just like the questions and mental conflicts about "what's okay and what isn't" issues discussed above, what a woman thinks about herself and her body is key in how relaxed, open, and engaged she will be with her husband during sex. Sexy is not a certain size or a certain age. Marilyn Monroe was a size 14 and was considered a sexy and an ideal beauty in her time. It's not about your size, but what you think about yourself, and what you do with what you have that matters.

Sexy is technically self-confidence, or body-confidence. Sexy is accepting who you are, and how you look, focusing on your positive features, and thinking less about your perceived negatives. Sexy is allowing your body to be imperfect, yet good enough. There are many women who don't look anything like the media images of what's considered sexy. Yet, they have found a way to accept themselves and embrace their sexuality in spite of, or regardless of, their appearance. You don't have to wait until you lose 15 pounds in order to start feeling sexy. You can feel sexy now, but it may take some effort.

Body Image Issues and the Impact on Husbands

The visual aspect of lovemaking is particularly important to husbands. Men are visually wired. I remember one couple I had counseled where the wife had not allowed her husband to see her naked throughout their 10+ years of marriage. For husbands, being able to see their wives' bodies, especially during lovemaking, is an important element of the sexual experience. When wives are so concerned with how they look, and how they couldn't possibly be attractive to their husbands because of this or that, it's pretty difficult for them to be able to relax into their husbands' arms and fully surrender to the sexual experience.

Husbands are hungry for wives who get and respect a husband's visual nature. Men long for their wives to understand the importance of visual sexuality, and to embrace their albeit imperfect bodies, so that they can still feel sexually confident for both of their sexual sakes. One husband shared the following:

> *I know my wife has body image issues. One night I mentioned as lightly as possible that I missed seeing her wear something sexy. She said, "I don't like my body right now." I told her I thought she looked great. My wife is beautiful and amazing. She is a mother of four children, and takes very good care of her body. I find her very attractive. I tell her this, but it just seems to just bounce off her.*
>
> *I've always felt this way about her throughout our whole marriage, especially when she was pregnant. I wish wives would understand that we do love them, and find them attractive. They are sexy to us especially when they feel sexy themselves. I*

wish my wife knew how beautiful I think she is. I wish she wasn't so hard on her-
self. I love her just the way she is.

The world's view—the media, tabloids, etc.—are so unfair to women. It is so
sad and wreaks havoc in so many marriages, like mine. I wish women knew that
when they feel sexy and show it, even just sometimes, we are putty in their hands.
They have real power over us!

Most men are turned on by their wives and their bodies, regardless of whether they are in perfect shape or not. Men are certainly susceptible to the media's conditioning about what is sexy, but thankfully most men are more interested in the woman they are married to, and can actually have sex with, than that she look like a super model. Your husband doesn't need you to have a perfect body for him to be thoroughly attracted to you and to want you. Nor does he need you to have a perfect body to thoroughly enjoy having sex with you. The good news is that most husbands are generously able to overlook our inevitable imperfections, especially if they think they might get lucky!

Certainly women want to be healthy, and so do their husbands, but most women are genuinely doing the best they can with their bodies. A husband who is loving and accepting of his wife's physical idiosyncrasies, and is complimentary and encouraging, is more likely to bring about actual improvement in his wife's appearance anyway.

Believing Our Husbands

It is a real struggle in a lot of marriages where the husband thinks his wife is beautiful and attractive, regardless of how she feels about her carrying some extra pounds. Where a husband sees beauty, a woman sees wrinkles or rolls. His words are often powerless in penetrating his wife's heart, if she does not believe in her own attractiveness. A husband cannot always convince his wife of something that she simply cannot or will not believe. In order to receive his compliments well, and surrender to him sexually, she needs to believe she is attractive and acceptable to herself. Women must overcome negative self-perceptions and embrace more positive observations of themselves.

Many women have the dilemma of a distorted body image as their default way of thinking about themselves. They need to be attentive to that shortcoming and work to overcome it. I was delighted to receive the following comments from a woman who had what she considered a "sexual awakening" about herself and her husband. She was able to finally believe the positive things her husband had been trying to tell her for years:

After having somewhat of a revelation that God did indeed want to bless our
marriage bed, I had a revelation of how my husband sees me, and how beautiful
I am to him. I suddenly realized how much he desired me. I now believed it when
he told me how beautiful I was to him. I didn't resent it like I used to, where I felt
like he only wanted my body. I knew that my soul was part of the package. I knew
he wanted all of me…and I finally felt the goodness of it.

I have also worked with couples where pornography has conditioned a man's sexual circuitry to no longer feel attracted to his wife's realistic, un-altered, and un-Photoshopped body. Men may need to not only stop feeding the media-sensationalized body images to their brains, but they also need to work to reprogram what they see as sexy and attractive. Without this internal change in their thinking, it will be difficult for them to communicate genuine attraction to their wives.

Another way men can do this is to focus on the many other important characteristics that they like, love, and appreciate about their wives. This helps to diminish the physical and sexual characteristics on which they have been conditioned to focus. Men might also constantly remind themselves that the images in their minds are often those that have been surgically altered, or Photoshopped, rather than being real bodies given to real women by God. It may be true that your wife has a few pounds to lose. She may not look like she did prior to having children. (Darn that gravity!) If men will work to discipline their minds to focus only on positive and productive thoughts about their wives and their bodies, both will benefit within the bedroom.

What Is Real

Sometimes it's difficult in our society to know what is real and what isn't, especially when it comes to one's appearance. A woman told me about an acquaintance who had a flat stomach, and looked really good after having three kids. She said she would beat herself up because her exercise and weight loss efforts weren't getting near the same positive results. This friend's breasts didn't seem to have been affected by gravity at all. She hadn't even suspected it, but found out later that this friend had had some surgical work done, including liposuction. She said she was actually relieved because she didn't feel like she had to compare herself to her anymore. Now when she sees women who have slim figures, wrinkle-free skin, or perky breasts, she just reminds herself that they might have had some extra help. She says, "It's actually really cut down on my stress level and feelings of inadequacy knowing that it might not be real."

It's tough not to compare. But in our day and age where there are many options for enhanced appearance, it's helpful to remember what is real, and what may not be. This can cut down on body misperceptions or comparing ourselves to unrealistic images or expectations. Feeling good about ourselves and our bodies does not have to be contingent on how we look, especially when we may be competing against unrealistic images.

As a therapist, I definitely lean toward working to change one's self-image before trying to change things surgically. Changing how we think about ourselves and our bodies to be more positive and accepting can be a great way to manifest a change in ourselves physically. Feeling good about ourselves is a more empowering way to work on losing weight, for instance, than condemning and criticizing ourselves.

Making Peace with Your Body

In order to make peace with our bodies given all the complicating factors in today's media-heavy society, we need to empower ourselves to counter the comparison monster and shore up our own sense of self. The following are some suggestions for what women can do to make peace with their bodies, and improve their body image. This can lead to being more personally and sexually confident in their own skin.

Emotional Eating. Most women will tell you they'd really like to lose some weight. That alone is a significant cause for a lot of women to feel "less than" about their bodies. Probably the biggest cause of weight issues among women (and men, too) is something we might call "emotional eating," or compulsive overeating.

Food can be an addictive, self-medicating drug. It's an easy "go-to" for mood altering. It's the drug of choice for many people. If men tend toward pornography as a common drug of choice, then food could easily be considered a woman's drug of choice. Any kind of compulsive behavior you can't seem to stop on your own may need some professional help. Addressing the underlying anxiety-inducing issues and working an active addiction recovery program may be needed. The first step in most programs is to acknowledge your powerlessness over the compulsion and turn to God for divine power and healing.

God's Help. What we know from successful addiction recovery programs is that God may be the only true source of help and healing for compulsive or self-destructive behaviors. Developing your connection with God can assist in drawing on the powers of heaven in overcoming body image issues, and developing a stronger feeling of self-worth.

One of the ways to bring God into the mix is to ask Him to help you see yourself and your body the way He does. You might even make this one of your affirmations addressed below—"God helps me to see my body, and myself the way He does." Having a glimpse of divine insight can be very helpful and healing with body image issues. Ultimately, our greatest sense of self-worth and wholeness comes from God. Instead of turning to food, or any other mood-altering counterfeit like porn, drugs, alcohol, etc., we need to turn to God to fill us instead. It may be helpful to talk to a therapist and check out organizations like Overeater's Anonymous (OA.org) to help walk you through the 12 steps of addiction recovery with a focus on emotional or compulsive overeating.

Grateful List. One of the ways to begin to make peace with your body is to make a list of everything you can think of that you appreciate about your body, and what it does for you. This might include some of the following:

- I'm grateful that I can walk.
- I'm grateful that I can see.
- I'm grateful that my body digests food properly.
- I'm grateful that I can hug my husband and children.
- I'm grateful that my body responds sexually, etc.

As you think more about your body being a tool, or a creation of God that can do so many wonderful things, you shift the focus from how it looks, to the many ways it blesses your life by what it can do.

Positive Characteristics List. You might also create a long list of all your positive characteristics. When you spend time focusing on your positive personality traits, and other attributes as a multi-dimensional being, it reminds you that you are more than just your size or weight. You might include things like: I am a positive person. I help others. I am a good mom. I love to learn, etc. I encourage you to come up with a list of 100 positive statements about yourself that don't include anything about your appearance. Write them in your Sexual Self-Discovery Journal.

Heart Circles. Another path to making peace with your body is to program affirming thoughts and beliefs into your psyche. It can help change the negative and often unconscious self-talk that tends to run non-stop in our minds. One tool I especially like is what I call "Heart Circles." It combines positive self-talk, or affirmations, with a tactile element. This is a great little habit to use every time you look in a mirror. What you do is take your hand and make a fist, putting it in the center-left of your upper chest (over your heart). Then do circular clockwise motions while repeating any or all of the following affirmations:

- "I deeply and completely love and accept myself just the way I am."
- "I deeply and completely love and accept my body just the way it is."
- "I deeply and completely love and accept my whole body just the way it is."
- "I'm grateful for my body and all that it does for me."
- "I'm doing the best I can, and my best is good enough."
- "God helps me to see my body and myself the way He does."
- "I turn to God rather than to food."

These are just a few sample affirmations. You may be able to think of others that work even more powerfully for you. These positive statements also work well using the Emotional Freedom Technique (EFT) tapping tool discussed earlier in this chapter to help you program in these positive beliefs.

I had shared this concept of stopping negative self-talk about our bodies with my teenage daughter. A while back when we were shopping and trying on clothes, I started to complain about how I looked. I remembered our recent conversation and started doing the heart circles with this affirmation: "I deeply and completely love and accept my body just the way it is." We both laughed. Changing your self-talk, whether it's internal or external is a powerful way to counter your negative core beliefs about yourself or your body. To beat those body image blues, I recommend doing heart circles and repeating one of the affirmations at the following times: 1) anytime you are getting dressed or undressed, 2) anytime you look in a mirror, and 3) anytime you are tempted to say something negative about yourself or your body.

Body Acceptance. This exercise can help you change your mental programming about your body by affirming each part of your body, while acknowledging the areas you struggle with and affirming those parts anyway. Doing this exercise naked in front of a full-length mirror is ideal, but if that's too much, you could start clothed in front of your mirror instead.

Using the heart circles discussed above, make a fist over your heart then move it in a circular clockwise motion while repeating, "I deeply and completely love and accept my _____ (body part) just the way it is," listing every body part (including sexual ones). You can also use the affirmation: "I'm grateful for my _____ (body part)."

After affirming each body part, move on to the ones you struggle with, and do the heart circles while repeating the following: "Even though I struggle with my _____ (body part), I deeply and completely love and accept myself and my body anyway." You could also say, "Even though I wish my _____ (body part) was _____ (how you wish it was instead, i.e. "Even though I wish my hips were smaller..."), I deeply and completely love and accept myself and my body anyway."

You could also get in the habit of focusing on just a few body parts at a time when you hop out of the shower. For some that's easier, because it's built into your regular routine. The EFT tapping technique also works well for this body acceptance exercise. There are many benefits to this exercise. It can: 1) help you connect with your physical body, or the physicality of your body. Many of us spend so much time in our thoughts or mind that we are somewhat disconnected from our physical bodies. This exercise also helps 2) to develop greater comfort with your naked body. Many women are uncomfortable with or embarrassed by their naked bodies. And 3) it helps to stop and reprogram out the negative things we say to ourselves about our bodies.

Your Body — A Gift from God. Your body is one of God's greatest gifts. In life we are to obtain a body, take good care of it, and learn to become the master of it—rather than letting it control us. As we treasure our bodies, we become a friend and advocate for our bodies instead of beating ourselves up about our imperfections. Imagine how you would treat a highly valued gift. It makes me think of my good husband, who recently had one of our cars detailed. I was stunned when he told me how much he spent on the detailing. He is very attentive to keeping the cars clean and in great condition. This is what we need to strive to be doing with our bodies.

We've talked about how to talk to or think about our bodies. But, how do we actually treat our bodies? How are you doing with getting the sleep you need? How are you doing with feeding your body healthy, energizing foods, or do you mostly feed it junk food? Do you wear nice, attractive clothing to look your best—no matter your size? How often do you exercise your body and work to keep it fit? When you cherish something, you tend to take better care of it. Remember that your body is one of your greatest and most valuable possessions. Treat it accordingly.

As you come to accept and appreciate your body as the gift from God that it is, your self-worth will grow, and the motivation to make your body healthier will increase. It's the higher energy of love and acceptance that allows things to get better. This not only affects us personally (and physically), but also has a positive effect on the intimate relationship in marriage. We want to be able to love and accept our bodies and our whole selves. This allows us to more fully appreciate the gift we are to our husbands, and be able to freely and enthusiastically share that gift with them.

Good Sex is a Mental Discipline

We know that a mind with positive sexual beliefs and easy access to helpful thoughts and feelings is probably the most vital aspect of lovemaking. But once you have a positive sexual belief system in place (your mental/sexual blueprint), it still takes mental discipline to stay focused and engaged within the sensual experience itself. Earlier we addressed the "outside-the-bedroom" efforts to improve your mental blueprint. We're now moving into the "inside-the-bedroom" mental discipline that's also needed.

Sex often begins with a conscious decision to go there. It then requires an influx of positive, connecting thoughts and feelings, in order for the lovemaking process to flow. A woman best stays in the flow of lovemaking with the additional skill of keeping out the easy flood of mental distractions and other inhibiting thoughts and feelings. Especially for women, good sex is really a mental discipline.

As a simple self-check, how would you rate yourself on the following statement regarding your ability to stay present and focused—avoiding mental distractions—during sex (0 = completely untrue - 10 = completely true)? Write your answer and thoughts in your Sexual Self-Discovery Journal: *"I keep my thoughts focused on the present moment, and the pleasurable sensuality of the sexual experience. I don't get distracted by other thoughts, feelings, fears, etc."*

For most of us, this mental discipline is a learned behavior that takes lots of conscious effort. A man's challenge is to keep his mind from being overrun with sexual thoughts, and getting too far ahead in the arousal process. A woman's challenge is to keep her mind from being overrun with all the other thoughts that constantly fill her mind—distracting her from the arousal process. For different reasons, both men and women have to work on their mental discipline for good sex to occur. You might think of it as if men have one window they are trying to close 15 times a day, while women have 15 different windows open they are trying to close, in order to focus on one window—sex.

What's on Your Mind?

Because good sex requires the full engagement of the heart and mind, it's important to know what's on your mental screen during lovemaking. Is your mind "deliciously engaged" in the lovemaking process? Trina told me that she usually just focuses on the plant in her bedroom when they have sex. I found that very sad for her and her husband. Thankfully the "Arousal Helpers" discussed in Chapter 5 - "Transition" helped her to turn things around. Do any of these distracting thoughts sound familiar?

- "I wonder if my husband is turned off by my body?"
- "I wonder if I'm doing this right?"
- "My husband seems bored."
- "Is it going to happen this time?"
- "Gee, this is taking too long."
- "Boy, I don't know about this orgasm thing. I don't know what it's going to feel like. What if I don't like it? What if I do or say something embarrassing?"
- "I wish my husband would do such and such instead."
- "I wonder if the kids can hear us?"
- "I should water that plant."
- "I hope I won't disappoint my husband again."

With such thoughts, it is very difficult for your mind to fully engage in the sexual experience. What's needed instead is to instill thoughts more along the lines of: "This feels awesome!" or "I could eat you right up!" It may help if you first write out some thoughts you'd like to be thinking during sex to help you get in the habit.

Nurture Loving Thoughts and Feelings

What you focus on, you tend to get more of. If you focus on the positive aspects of lovemaking and your husband, you are more likely to get more positives back. It is a mental discipline to be conscious of your thoughts and focus more on what you want, rather than on what you don't want. Ultimately, it's a choice.

Men tend to more easily embrace their sexuality. They don't usually need to nurture sexual thoughts and feelings to feel amorous. In fact, they usually need to be working to bridle their sexual thoughts and feelings. Because women are wired differently, they actually need some encouragement in that area. I suggest women spend time pondering upon positive aspects of: 1) themselves, 2) their own body, 3) their spouse, 4) their spouse's body, and 5) lovemaking itself, in order to learn to savor and nurture sexual thoughts and feelings.

A common homework assignment I give clients is to keep a daily list of at least five positives about themselves, their spouse and/or about sex itself to feed more positives into their mind. Similar to some of the exercises above for developing a healthy sexual blueprint, this daily list helps you to identify and focus on the good instead of the bad. Your list might include things like:

- I like how I'm learning to enjoy sex more.
- I like how I'm feeling more connected during lovemaking.
- I appreciate how patient my husband is with me during lovemaking.
- I love how my husband keeps things slow and gentle while I'm trying to get warmed up.

- I love how my husband is such a great daddy!
- I can see better now how good sex is supposed to be in a marriage.

Rather than entertaining such thoughts as, "I'm just not in the mood," and "I don't know how to get there," you can instead feed yourself thoughts that will fuel your desire for connection with your spouse. As a simple self-check, rate yourself on the following statement using a scale of 0 (no) to 10 (yes): *"I nurture positive thoughts and feelings about myself, my spouse, and sex itself."*

Pay Attention to Your Intimate Thoughts

Another aspect of nurturing romantic thoughts and feelings is to simply pay more attention to them when they show up. For women, sexual thoughts tend to be pretty fleeting. When they do show up, as you are watching a movie, or listening to a song on the radio, or when you see your honey being patient and cute with your kids, notice and hold onto those thoughts.

Elizabeth shared that she was beginning to have more "glimmers" of romantic feelings for her husband. At first she was surprised by them. Because we had talked about welcoming such feelings, she was able to relax into them and utilize them to benefit their relationship. As you pay attention to loving, intimate thoughts and feelings, you can save them for later retrieval within the bedroom. It's as if you are saving and cataloging a reservoir of intimacy-inducing fuel for the mind.

One client shared how just working on some of our homework assignments, knowing she'd be coming to see me again in a few days, seemed to pique her interest in being intimate. She admitted that if she hadn't been watching for it, she may not have even noticed the amorous feeling. She happily took that feeling and used it to initiate sex when she had an opportunity the next night. I encourage you to nourish sexual thoughts and feelings on a daily basis, as if looking for intimate fuel. It can help you warm your mind for use within the bedroom when the time comes to put it into action.

Gentle Eyes

Having mental discipline means you are attentive to your thoughts and are able to focus them in positive ways. I love the concept of "gentle eyes" that Shari and I discussed as she worked on having more loving thoughts toward her husband. She said, "My husband has mentioned that he can see in my eyes if I am upset with him, so I have worked on having 'gentle eyes.' Gentle eyes are a way to remind myself to look at my husband with positive, loving thoughts." Spouses truly can feel what you are thinking about them. The way you look at them says a lot. Work on looking at your spouse with loving eyes, which is simply disciplining your thoughts to be positive. This helps you be able to send them positive vibes. (This works with children, too!)

Your Spouse Can Feel Your Thoughts

I first realized the power of our thoughts towards our spouses during a couples' massage class my husband and I took at a marriage conference. I was intrigued by the suggestion that our spouses could feel what we are thinking. The presenter instructed all of us to be sure we were having loving thoughts about our spouses as we touched them during the massage. As the giver and receiver, I could feel the difference in the massage by paying attention to my thoughts.

It's true that spouses can feel what we are thinking and feeling—especially through our touch. Try giving your spouse a massage when you don't want to. You'll see that the feel of it is very different than if you are touching your spouse from a place of love. They will sense that you don't really want to. We all want our loved ones to want to love us. Keep in mind that what we are thinking and feeling will come through in our eyes and our touch. If you are wanting to improve the Thoughts dimension of lovemaking, get in the habit of asking yourself if a particular thought you are having helps or hinders. Is it useful or useless, productive or unproductive, positive or negative? With the mind as the most important sexual organ, you'll want to become master over your thoughts.

Faith as a Mental Discipline

To further the concept of mental discipline, consider how the discipline required for good sex is similar to the mental discipline required to have real faith. Having faith requires you to believe in something that you may not have any other evidence to support (*see* Hebrews 11:1). You may even have a lot of counter-evidence working against you. Believing anyway requires a practiced and prepared mind, able to withstand the temptations of thought that will likely occur especially within the act of lovemaking. Maintaining a faith-filled mindset is good practice for the similar mental discipline needed to keep out distractions and stay focused sexually during lovemaking.

Faith—on steroids—adds the element of surrender. It's the addition of emotional detachment from needing a specific outcome. For example, you absolutely believe that you will have an orgasm, but you are totally okay if it doesn't happen. You have turned it over to God, and you are willing to let His will be done. You have faith in your desired outcome, but also steadfastly believe that God's will is even better than yours. You are okay with the outcome being different than what you thought you wanted.

The mental discipline of faith, and surrender, is one of the hardest things for women to do in their approach to having an orgasm. But, it's a necessary mindset. The more we get worried or obsessively worked up about having an orgasm, for example, and the more we "want" or "need" it to happen, the less likely it will. It's a challenging paradox to believe in something, but also let go of needing it.

The words that best describe this necessary state of mind is a confident, trusting, believing, yet relaxed "letting go." All of this begins in the mind with our automatic thoughts and core beliefs. This is why any Good Girl Syndrome issues,[13] or even just any negative or unproductive thoughts, beliefs and attitudes about sex can so easily get in the way of thoroughly enjoying sex and/or experiencing an orgasm. Women need to develop the mental discipline to be able to focus their thoughts and keep out inhibiting distractions during sex. Hopefully it's clear why developing this mental skill is necessary for women to fully experience sex, as it was intended by God.

Meditation for Mental Discipline

One of the habits I encourage clients to develop is daily meditation. Meditation is powerful spiritual medicine for the mind. Even five minutes a day can help you get better at reducing stress and mastering your thoughts. Meditation provides an opportunity to develop self-discipline by channeling your thoughts. This helps to channel your energy and emotion as well. It can help you quiet your mind and relax your soul.

Meditation is an accelerator for rewiring the brain—especially for changing negative core beliefs. Meditation is self-directed rewiring of the brain through focused attention and repetition. Through meditation, you get to practice "being" instead of "doing." You bring both your heart (intuition) and your mind (intellect) together for greater synergistic power.[14] I find that it allows me to be still and better tuned into my own thoughts. It provides even just a few moments of quiet time in this otherwise fast-paced world. Meditation is excellent practice for the mind to develop greater control over one's thoughts. This can be very useful in the bedroom or anywhere else.

If you're not sure how to start a simple daily practice of meditation, follow these beginning suggestions. Find a quiet place where you won't be interrupted. I find that a locked bedroom or office is best. Sit comfortably on a sofa, chair, bed, or floor. I prefer sitting cross-legged on the floor, on a small decorative pillow, sitting upright against the bed. You might start with a couple of cleansing breaths. Breathe in through your nose. Exhale through your mouth like you are blowing out a candle. Close your eyes and simply observe your breath as you inhale and exhale. As you inhale, slowly say to yourself, "in." As you exhale, simply count each breath by repeating the number "one" in your mind. This helps your mind stay better focused on your breathing.

You might even repeat some other calming word, such as "Relax," "Calm," "Still," "Sunshine," or "Peace,"—whatever feels good for you. Each time you notice your thoughts wandering, just turn your attention back to focusing on your breath. As you move into a relaxed, meditative state, you'll notice your breathing slowing down and your mind being more at ease and calm. Consciously relax the muscles in your face as well. (It might even help with the wrinkles!) Just keep practicing each day until this becomes a natural and welcome part of your daily routine.

I also suggest adding an element of mental imagery to your meditation. This often helps to engage one's attention even better than just focusing on one's breath. Here is a sample imagery you might use, in addition to the above steps:

Close your eyes and observe your breathing...Notice your inhale and exhale...Notice your breathing slowing down as you let it flow in and out. See yourself standing in a beautiful place surrounded by trees, mountains, and a clear blue lake...Notice the leaves gently rustling in the trees...Notice the beautiful blue sky above and the majestic mountains in the distance...See the sunlight sparkling across the lake as you hear a small river flowing nearby...Feel the warmth and aliveness all around you. Breathe in the fresh spring scent in the air. You can feel the warmth of the sun shining down, as if creating a pathway of light reaching from you into heaven. See yourself ascending this pathway of light into God's presence.

With this imagery, you might bask silently in the heavenly presence, or you might pour out your heart to God mentally in a private and very personal conversation. I like to just "be" there in God's presence, repeating the words in my mind, "I'm listening..." as if realigning myself with God each day. Whenever you feel ready, return to the present moment by opening your eyes. You might also let a slight smile cross your lips just before opening your eyes.

Developing mental discipline through meditation allows you to feel more centered, focused, and better able to overpower mental distractions during sex—whether they be thoughts of an errand you need to run, or any other negative thoughts, fears or doubts.

There is Hope

Let's continue with the rest of the opening story about Karla and Sean:

Karla struggled to keep herself engaged and her thoughts in line during lovemaking. She struggled with reaching orgasm. She had put in significant effort to identify and overcome her inhibiting thoughts and beliefs. She had worked to develop more mental discipline. Karla used the mental discipline tools shared here and others discussed throughout this book. She found them to be very helpful in her quest to create an enjoyable and mutually fulfilling sexual relationship. She stopped thinking about how long sex seemed to take, and how bored her husband might be. She stopped worrying that she was being selfish if she actually relaxed and enjoyed sex. She simply stopped thinking so much, and started just feeling.

She had so many diverting thoughts during sex that she started using the Arousal Helpers (B-F-A-V-E) to help her push out all her negative and distracting thoughts that would inundate her mind. The tools helped her keep from getting fixated and frustrated with herself and the process of lovemaking. Without them, she would inadvertently shut down sexually. Many times she felt like she'd reached a seven or eight on the arousal scale, when some thought would get stuck in her mind and shut her down. She found that of all the tools she'd tried, focusing on her breathing, plus actively touching her husband, made all the difference for her.

She was okay with her husband's verbalizations during sex, but was totally embarrassed about doing it herself. She agreed to try to practice it a little on her own to get more comfortable expressing herself that way. A big piece of the puzzle was when she began listening to sexually affirming audios throughout the day, like "The Marital Intimacy Show" podcasts, and my audio book And They Were Not Ashamed. *Sometimes she even did the EFT tapping along with the audio to help it sink in. She felt like these activities made her think about sex a lot more than she usually did. This helped her get from 0 to 60 sexually a lot more easily. She was surprised to find that thinking about sex more often actually made her more interested in it as well.*

Sex had also not been an easily accessible topic of conversation for Karla and Sean. This created emotional distance between them. Thankfully, they had both gotten better at talking about their thoughts and feelings, including her likes and dislikes about sex. As a result of their conversations, Karla began to feel more connected and safe emotionally in the relationship. She felt more love for her husband, and even felt more relaxed about her body issues. She began to believe that her husband was genuinely attracted to her despite what she perceived as her physical flaws.

Because Sean had also begun to tune into her better (see Chapter 9), the emotional environment in the relationship was stronger. This motivated her to say "yes" to sex, and to feel more connected with him within sex itself, even though she still hadn't had her first orgasm after many years of marriage. Karla had been planning to let me know that she was okay now with not having an orgasm, given that she had learned to surrender it to God. She was okay with Him bringing it about in His perfect timing. We had talked about that being the ideal mindset for orgasm to naturally occur anyway.

But, happily, a few nights before our next session, she and her husband figured out some additional helps for her during foreplay that pushed her over the edge into orgasm. This included the sensory experience of dimly lit scented candles, and a soothing soak in a bath to help her relax. She needed more breast play, and just the right kind of clitoral stimulation at the right moment. Also, it was more effective for her to be on top to direct things a little better. With sustained effort over time, all these different ingredients—like pieces of a puzzle—finally came together for them to better create the sextraordinary relationship they desired.

There are many valuable insights and tools women can use to develop a positive mental blueprint about sex. They also help women have positive thoughts and feelings within the sexual experience itself. This is accomplished by developing the mental discipline needed to overcome mental distractions, and stay focused on the ecstasy of the sexual experience with one's spouse.

Self-Evaluation - "Thoughts"

To give yourself a guide as to how you are doing in this dimension, how would you currently rate yourself and your spouse overall in the area of "Thoughts"? Write your thoughts in your Sexual Self-Discovery Journal. — *I have positive and affirming thoughts and core beliefs, not only about sex, my sexuality, and my body, but also about my husband, his body, and our marital/sexual relationship. I have the mental discipline needed to be able to focus my thoughts and keep out inhibiting mental distractions during sex.*

RATING (0 - disagree to 10 - agree):   You _____   Your Spouse _____

ACTION ITEMS — Chapter 2 - "Thoughts"

- Utilize your Sexual Self-Discovery Journal as you go through these items.
- Keep a daily list of five things you like, love or appreciate about yourself. You're compiling a list of anything positive you can think of about yourself.
- Take the "Characteristics of a Healthy Sexual Identity" assessment in Chapter 1.
- Take the "Good Girl Syndrome Self-Awareness Assessment."
- Complete the "Sexual Beliefs Questionnaire" to help identify negative or unproductive thoughts, attitudes, and beliefs. Also do some writing about each of your inhibiting factors to help process them.
- To work through sexual differences, do the following:
  1. Read and discuss the "What's Okay and What Isn't" section, including the overriding principles.
  2. Fully discuss each other's needs, desires, and perspectives on any sexual issues of concern either verbally or in writing, if needed. Also discuss the "Questions to Consider."
  3. Make such issues a matter of personal and couple prayer.
  4. Work through the exercises in this chapter to identify and overcome any unnecessary inhibitions and develop more positive sexual beliefs.
  5. Spend more time with the Lord to be accurately aligned with His divine designs for marital sexuality.
- Vacuum naked, even just in your locked bedroom, to overcome your insecurities and learn to be more comfortable with your body. You might also turn on some party tunes and dance naked in the shower.
- Write a list of positive thoughts you'd like to get in the habit of thinking during sex.
- Work on looking at your spouse with loving "Gentle Eyes," which means disciplining yourself to have more positive thoughts about him.

NOTES

[1] Granvold, D. K., "Promoting Long-term Sexual Passion," *Constructivism in the Human Sciences* 6(1) (2001): 73-83.

[2] Hertlein, K. M., Weeks, G. R., and Sendak, S. K., *A Clinician's Guide to Systemic Sex Therapy*. New York: Routledge, 2009.

[3] Metz, Michael E., and McCarthy, Barry W., "The 'Good-Enough Sex' Model for Couple Sexual Satisfaction," *Sexual and Relationship Therapy* 22(3) (2007): 351–362.

[4] Meltzer, A., and McNulty, J., "Body Image and Marital Satisfaction: Evidence for the Mediating Role of Sexual Frequency and Sexual Satisfaction," *Journal of Family Psychology* 24(2) (2010): 156-164. doi:10.1037/a0019063.

[5] Brotherson, Laura M., *And They Were Not Ashamed: Strengthening Marriage through Sexual Fulfillment*. Boise, ID: Inspire Book, 2004, Chapter 1.

[6] Ibid, 135-142.

[7] Maltz, Wendy, *The Sexual Healing Journey: A Guide for Survivors of Sexual Abuse*. William Morrow Paperbacks, third edition, 2012.

[8] Brotherson, Laura M., *And They Were Not Ashamed: Strengthening Marriage through Sexual Fulfillment*. Boise, ID: Inspire Book, 2004.

[9] Ibid.

[10] Maltz, Wendy and Larry, *The Porn Trap: The Essential Guide to Overcoming Problems Caused By Pornography*. Collins Living, 2008, 182.

[11] Maltz, Wendy, "Do You Know the Difference? (Porn-related Sex vs Healthy Sex)," *Healthy Sex*. www.HealthySex.com, accessed March 18, 2016.

[12] Owen, T. E., Allen, M. D., and Spangler, D. L., "An fMRI Study of Self-reflection about Body Image: Sex Differences," *Personality and Individual Differences* (2010): 849-854.

[13] Brotherson, Laura M., *And They Were Not Ashamed: Strengthening Marriage through Sexual Fulfillment*. Boise, ID: Inspire Book, 2004, Chapter 1.

[14] Fralich, Terry, *The Five Core Skills of Mindfulness*. Eau Claire, WI: PESI Publishing & Media, 2013.

CHAPTER VIEW

The Crucial Emotional Climate in Marriage
Emotional Connection is Our Foreplay
What Do You Understand about the Emotional Climate?
The 0 to 60 Scale Sexually
   Emotional Desire
20 Characteristics of Living at a "40" on a 0 to 60 Scale
   Emotional Connection Self-Assessment
      Respect
      Trust
      Love
      Like
      Appreciation
      Selflessness
      Priority
      Responsiveness
      Positivity
      Acceptance
      Tenderness
      Affection
      Honesty
      Openness
      Vulnerability
      Safety
      Compassion
      Friendship
      Admiration
      Attention
Emotional Foreplay — How to Live at 40 on a 0-60 Scale
   Courtesies and Kindnesses
   Couple Time
   Date Night
   Meeting Your Spouse's Needs for Love
   "Daddywork"—A Great Aphrodisiac
Self-Evaluation - "Tenderness"
ACTION ITEMS — Chapter 3 - "Tenderness"

Chapter 3

TENDERNESS — CREATING A SECURE FOUNDATION

My husband is so much more tender and sweet with me than he's ever been before, since we found your book. He's been more loving and considerate of my feelings on a regular basis. I feel so much closer to him that our intimate relationship has also greatly improved.

This morning he was running late for work and was being critical of me not doing things the way he wanted them done. I gently said, "I am not sure why you are talking to me that way." He stopped, came over, and asked for my forgiveness. He said he should not have talked to me that way. It used to be that he would deny he was even being inconsiderate, then continue being unkind to me.

The other night we were praying together. Afterwards he told me that he could not find the words to let me know how much he loved me. He had tears in his eyes when he said it. I have noticed both of us sharing more of these tender feelings over the last couple of years since reading your book. We are both becoming more selfless and thoughtful of each other. We are much more focused on meeting each other's needs.

The Crucial Emotional Climate in Marriage

Men and women are both wired for connection. But, it is especially true for women when it comes to sex. Emotional intimacy is a wife's primary fuel for connecting sexually with her husband. It's the quality of the emotional relationship that matters more than physical aspects like sexual technique. Think of it as 80 percent emotional connection, and just 20 percent physical or physiological. I like to call it the 80/20 rule. This analogy highlights the crucial emotional context of female sexuality, and ultimately her marital and sexual satisfaction.[1] This important dimension of emotional foreplay tends to occur primarily in outside-the-bedroom interactions before sex even begins.

Especially for women, tenderness, thoughtfulness, and trust in the marriage describe some of the key ingredients of a sexually intimate and fulfilling relationship. Creating a safe haven in marriage lays the foundation for women to be able to open up and connect sexually. Being your spouse's safe haven is vital. It's what allows women to turn off their fears and relax into sexual arousal.

When we feel emotionally bonded, we experience the greatest sense of security and well being. It creates the conditions for sexual abandon—a total giving of body and soul to each other. In contrast, our greatest fear underlying all unhealthy relationship patterns is a core fear of emotional abandonment.[2]

The very best sex is built on emotionally bonded, securely attached relationships. Husband and wife are tuned into each other and responsive. They can talk, tease, and be playful with each other. A connected couple has the most enjoyable, adventurous, and mutually rewarding sexual relationship, because of the mutual trust and respect they have for each other. They are a team. They know they are safe in each other's arms.

The sexual repertoire of couples that are securely connected includes both "dopamine sex," which is enthusiastically passionate sex, and "oxytocin sex," where there is tender, loving sexual intimacy. Truly, married sex—where spouses are well-connected—is the best sex!

As you'll learn in Chapter 8 – "Technique," being sexually intimate is first and foremost a decision for women. It's a conscious choice to go there. A lack of libido may have more to do with a lack of emotional connection in the marriage than anything else—especially for women.[3] Couples often need therapeutic help addressing both the marital relationship and the sexual relationship as well.[4]

Consider what would entice a woman to want to flip her mental switch to a "Yes!" It's generally the feeling of safety and emotional connection she feels with her husband that increases her sexual responsiveness. Feeling connected makes it easier for her to decide to say yes when an opportunity for sex presents itself. This chapter will help husbands and wives improve their relationships in ways that make it naturally easier for her to want to say yes to sex.

"A woman's most important foreplay happens outside the bedroom."

Emotional Connection is Our Foreplay

Dr. John Gottman has a fabulous slogan: "Every positive thing you do in your relationship is foreplay."[5] He's right on the money. I call these various experiences "emotional foreplay." This is a vital concept for husbands to get. If they miss this, then not much else in this book will matter.

Women are not generally walking around with constant feelings of desire to have sex at the drop of a hat. If there is not a good amount of connection, warmth, tenderness, thoughtfulness, trust, etc., outside the bedroom (where her decision to "go there" is generally made), then she will not be very willing to decide to say yes. She will likely be hesitant to put herself in such a position of vulnerability by "getting naked" in front of

her husband, giving herself to him. For her, having sex when feeling emotionally disconnected might be compared to having sex with a stranger.

For women, the desire to be intimate is more of an "emotional desire," whereas for
men it's more of a physical desire. Husbands often struggle to understand the concept of
women needing to feel emotionally close and safe before they can "decide" to have sex.
This is especially true given that husbands are not wired to *have* to feel emotionally close
before they want to have sex. They also don't have to mentally "decide" to go there sexually. Their minds and bodies practically do that for them.

Men usually have enough sexual desire floating around to easily say yes to sex,
whether their spouse has been kind or considerate of them that day or not. For a
woman, it isn't so easy to overlook it if her husband has been a jerk that day. It isn't easy
to say yes if, in general, her husband simply refuses to acknowledge, respect, and meet
her emotional needs in the marriage. Let me share an example from some of my clients
that may help husbands understand this concept a little better.

> *In a recent counseling session with Bill, we were discussing his and his wife's dif-
> fering ways of feeling loved. He kept almost brushing off the fact that his wife felt
> emotionally connected through words. He just couldn't imagine how anyone could
> feel loved by words, instead of actions or touch. "Talk is cheap," he said. It made
> no sense to him.*
>
> *I firmly and repeatedly explained, "If you want your wife to feel loved by you,
> and create that warm, environment where she feels close and connected to you (her
> 'emotional foreplay'), then it doesn't matter if you don't understand or agree with
> it. You just have to accept it. You need to learn how to do it, and then do it faith-
> fully. If not, she'll have a hard time feeling loved or opening up to you sexually."*
>
> *He tried to tell me how good he was at doing the dishes and other acts of ser-
> vice. He told me she SHOULD feel loved by his efforts. I asked him how loved he
> would feel if she always told him how much she loved him, but refused to ever be
> sexual with him (his "Love Language"). He got the picture.*
>
> *I asked him what he thought the message was she was receiving all these years
> of him not recognizing her need for conversation and intimate, verbal expressions
> of love. He realized that she probably didn't feel very loved. He finally recognized
> why she had decided to withdraw from him and try to find connection and emo-
> tional fulfillment elsewhere.*
>
> *The kicker for him, which is often the case with couples, is that the thing she
> needed most from him was the thing that was most difficult for him to give. He
> said, "If I had to pick one of those 'love languages' that would be the most difficult
> for me, it would be words of affirmation." He didn't want to open up emotionally.
> He didn't like sharing his own vulnerabilities—his worries, fears or other tender
> emotions. He was struggling to grasp how any of that could be foreplay for her.*

If it's just a matter of husbands not understanding this concept of women needing emotional connection in order to pave the way for lovemaking, then great. But if there are significant difficulties with couples being genuinely thoughtful, tender, and emotionally open and safe with each other, then they will likely need to elicit the help of a good counselor.

This may be necessary in order to get the marriage working well enough for the sexual relationship to be able to flourish. Some of the deeper issues that keep couples disconnected and away from bedroom festivities are anger, selfishness, resentment, defensiveness, trauma, abuse, betrayal, addiction (especially sex/pornography addiction), mental health issues, or medical issues, etc.

What Do You Understand about the Emotional Climate?

We've talked about the crucial emotional climate as a foundation for sex. We've discussed how things like not feeling connected, not meeting each other's needs, or dealing with deeper issues can affect the relationship—especially the sexual relationship in a marriage. If you were sitting in my counseling office at this point, I would probably ask you to tell me what you understand here about the emotional climate of your marriage and its connection to sex. I'd want to see if you understand or really get it. There's not much point in moving on to more "sexual" aspects of improving the intimate relationship if a husband doesn't understand or refuses to accept his wife's emotional wiring and intimate differences.

A husband needs to do everything he can to meet his wife's needs for trust and emotional connection in her specific ways. If he does, he will be able to help create the conditions that are more likely to produce the exquisite intimate connection he desires. If husbands want greater connection—intimately and sexually—what will help much more than asking for more sex, or more variety, is to instead develop a stronger, secure connection with his wife first.

I also get that women can do a lot to make it easier for their husbands to be more thoughtful and considerate of them by making sex (the husband's needs) a higher priority. It just depends on which part of the relationship dynamics we are focusing on. In this book, the focus is about understanding the female wiring and what helps her sexually. My next book will focus more on better understanding the husband's wiring. Here is one client's story about how he finally "got it." He finally understood his wife's needs, as well as his own:

Jody had done a lot of incredible work to develop her sexuality and improve the intimate relationship in their marriage. During a recent counseling session, her husband, Kendall, had an "ah ha" moment about the significance of the emotional connection to his wife.

He said, "I had always been wanting Jody to find her sexuality and share it with me. I didn't realize that all this time, she has been asking me to share myself with her emotionally. We've both been asking each other to be naked in a very scary way. For her, it was being naked physically. For me, it is being naked emotionally. These are the keys for us. I finally get it. I get what she wants from me."

He explained how he had never really been open with anyone in his life. He said, "I never even shared with my mom things like who I liked as a kid. I just kept all that stuff in. To share more of my inner feelings is pretty foreign to me. But, now I get the gravity of what Jody has wanted and needed from me. I'm not very good at this yet, but now that I get it, I think I can actually do that for her—especially given all that she has done to change for me sexually."

The 0 to 60 Scale Sexually

Truly, tenderness and thoughtfulness are needed for her to be ready for intimacy. In Chapter 8 - "Technique," I discuss my "Fuel for Female Sexual Desire" handout where I more fully address the concept of women having at least a four-step process of getting to where they can begin to feel "sexual desire." Men generally feel sexual desire at Step #1, whereas for women it shows up at their Step #4. In contrast to how men are wired, women require a warm up process that takes them through those four steps. It's like getting from 0 to 60 sexually.

Let me provide a quick overview. Because we're first talking about more of a contextual factor than an actual step, Step #0 in my Fuel for Female Sexual Desire is a climate of warmth, safety and emotional closeness being present between husband and wife. Step #1 is where she must mentally "Decide" to go there. Step #2 is where "Connecting Emotionally" (or Talking) is needed. Step #3 is "Foreplay" (or physical Touch—leading to the beginnings of sexual arousal). It is at this point, Step #4, that a woman arrives at "Desire."

Referring to the 0 to 60 concept, when there is little warmth, kindness, consideration, and connection in the marriage, the couple is living closer to a 0 emotionally. When a couple generally feels securely connected through a mutual sharing of self in tender and vulnerable ways, and they seek to put the other's needs above their own, then that couple is living closer to 60.

It's quite the feat for a woman to be living at 0 in the emotional environment of her marriage, and to then have to "choose" whether to have sex or not. She would then have to get from 0 up to 60 emotionally and sexually (often mostly on her own). This is needed for sex to be even somewhat sexually fulfilling. For couples living near 0, sex generally feels more like a chore—an almost impossible one—for her. It's simply going through the motions, rather than it being an emotionally fulfilling expression of love.

Emotional Desire

If, instead of living at 0, a couple can learn to live at a "40" on that 0 to 60 scale, then transitioning into lovemaking is much easier and quicker for the woman. The "emotional desire" is already present in her heart and mind. Men have "physical desire" floating around available much of the time. Women need to have a relationship that supports them having emotional desire floating around more often. This allows them to more easily flip the mental switch to decide to connect sexually.

A client asked me what it looks like to live at a "40" on that 0 to 60 scale, and how to get there. This is exactly the purpose of this chapter—to help couples build an emotionally connected foundation. This creates a genuinely sweet and emotionally fulfilling relationship in and of itself. It also makes it so much easier to choose to say, "Yes" to begin the transition into lovemaking.

Preliminary Steps for Those Living in the 0 to 20 Range

For those living down in the lower 0-20 range in their relationship, there may need to be preliminary measures taken in order to make the best use of the rest of this chapter. Where there is often a lot of anger, resentment, and accumulated bitterness, you may need to do the following steps first to get you on the road to Tenderness, Thoughtfulness and Trust:

1. Work through my "Clearing Out Your Emotional Closet" process writing worksheet.
2. Work through my "Letting Go of Resentment" worksheet. (Both worksheets can be found on my website StrengtheningMarriage.com. Check the Appendix for access information).
3. List at least 100 things you feel frustrated, angry or resentful about. This list is just for you to process the toxic emotions, to begin to let them dissolve.
4. Elicit the help of a counselor to work through personal and couple issues, if you find yourself stuck in unhealthy patterns of interacting.

It's important to remember that any time you want to change, it requires: 1) Insight (into self and others), 2) New Information (know how), 3) Deliberate Effort, and 4) Time (and patience). The four suggestions addressed above can help both husband and wife with these steps of change by providing greater *insight* into themselves, and why they do what they do in their patterns of interacting.

This book can also provide the needed *new information* to learn how to do things differently and hopefully better. You will then have to put in *deliberate effort* to change your behaviors. Remember that any change takes *time* and patience, in order to make the changes genuine and permanent.

What Emotional Intimacy and Connection is All About

The sexual union in marriage requires an emotionally intimate relationship where spouses are able to share their deepest, most personal, and most vulnerable parts of themselves. They are able to do this by trusting that the other person will receive them safely and kindly, and return the open, full sharing of self in like manner.[6] This is why intimacy is often referred to as "in-to-me-see."

A warm, emotional connection in marriage is what provides the psychological safety to be so deeply open and vulnerable, both emotionally and sexually, precisely because of the security, permanence, and exclusivity it provides.[7] When psychological intimacy is present in the relationship, the brain (and body) can relax.[8] Psychological intimacy lets you lower your defenses, knowing you can trust your spouse. You have the assurance that your spouse is honest, loyal and committed to you.

Dr. Sue Johnson reminds us that it is from a securely attached relationship base that we feel safe enough to be able to branch out into more vulnerable, anxiety-inducing endeavors like sex. How emotionally and physically accessible, responsive, and engaged our spouse is makes all the difference sexually.[9] She would also say, "Hot sex doesn't lead to secure love; rather, secure attachment leads to hot sex—and also to love that lasts...It's not good sex that leads to satisfying secure relationships, but rather secure love that leads to good, in fact, the best sex."[10] Hot monogamy is not a myth in long-term relationships, though our culture would have us think it is.

Recognizing how vital the emotional dimension of marriage is to the sexual dimension, this chapter outlines a blueprint of what constitutes emotionally close and connected relationships. It also provides specific suggestions on how to create such a marriage.

20 Characteristics of Living at a "40" on a 0 to 60 Scale

Living at a "40" emotionally on that 0 to 60 scale embodies many of the characteristics one might think of regarding couples with really good, happy marriages. Here are 20 key ingredients that make up such a relationship: respect, trust, love, like, appreciation, selflessness, making your spouse a priority, responsiveness, positivity, acceptance, tenderness, affection, honesty, openness, vulnerability, safety, compassion, friendship, admiration, and attention.

It's helpful to know what these characteristics might look like in a relationship. Descriptions and examples of these qualities, in action, follow. I'd suggest rating yourself, and then your spouse, in each area for an honest self-assessment of how you're currently doing. Record your responses in your Sexual Self-Discovery Journal. This will give you an idea of what areas to work on in your relationship. Many of these characteristics overlap, but each are listed here because of the unique elements of that characteristic.

Emotional Connection Self-Assessment

On a scale of 0 (poor) to 10 (excellent), rate how you think you and your spouse are doing in each of the following areas. Have your spouse do the same, from his perspective.

Respect. Relationships based on mutual respect are those where couples work as partners and love and honor each other. As much as possible, by consulting with and taking counsel from each other, they work as a team. When couples respect each other, they listen to and value each other. They allow each other to think, feel, and be different and can even disagree without it affecting the emotional connection. Respect requires that you consciously listen to understand your spouse. Balancing self-respect with spouse-respect is necessary in mutually respectful marriages. Spouses are not only attentive and respectful to the other, but also to themselves and their own boundaries. *How well do you show respect to your spouse? How well does your spouse show respect to you?*

RATING:　　You _____　Your Spouse _____

Trust. Trust in the relationship lets you know that the other is there for you and has your back. You know you can depend on them to follow through and do what they say they will do. Trust is the authentic sense that you are safe with your spouse—emotionally, spiritually, and physically. Husbands often overlook how little things like being home from work on time, or taking care of the kids without the home getting trashed, affect a wife's ability to rely on and trust her spouse. Trust means she knows you will stand up for her when needed. She knows you would never intentionally say or do anything to hurt her.

One wife explained how much it hurt that her husband did nothing when her in-laws were disrespectful and treated her poorly. He explained he didn't want to offend his family. Another woman felt completely alone in standing up for one of their children. She had to take action all on her own. She couldn't help but make others upset and uncomfortable by confronting the situation. She wanted her husband to stand with her and help share the emotional weight. He was a nice guy and didn't like confrontation or to cause any problems. Instead, he caused problems with his wife by losing her trust. This affected not only things in the bedroom, but also the very foundation of their marriage.

Trust is strengthened when spouses are there for each other, especially in times of anxiety and need. Added emotional bonding occurs when you feel your spouse is there to support you—particularly when you are under duress or are feeling vulnerable. Imagine how these women felt about trusting their husbands sexually when they didn't feel like they could depend on them emotionally or socially. For a woman to be able to let go within lovemaking, she needs to have a deep and abiding trust in her husband—inside the bedroom and out.

John Van Epp has created a Relationship Attachment Model (RAM)[11] identifying the ideal process for how healthy relationships develop. First there's "Talk" over a period of "Time," so "Trust" can develop before "Touch" should be added. Trust must come before Touch, or the relationship can easily get out of balance and weaken. If things have happened in the relationship that have affected the level of trust, then those things will need to be addressed and resolved in order to create a trusting foundation so necessary in marriage. *How well do you trust your spouse? How well does your spouse trust you?*

RATING: You _____ Your Spouse _____

Love. Love is an action. Love is a choice. Love is a decision to think, speak, and act in loving ways even if you may not "feel" like it at times. Love—the feeling—may come and go, but deciding to act in loving ways must be a constant, if you are truly committed to the covenant of marriage. It reminds me of a favorite quote by Diane Sollee, founder of Smart Marriages: "To get divorced because love has died is like selling your car because it has run out of gas." And you don't have to wait around for loving feelings to show up if they've faded. It's much more empowering to choose to love, rather than being dependent on what you may be feeling or how the other is behaving. Love is doing things for each other. It's putting your spouse and their wants, needs, and opinions ahead of your own at times. Love doesn't mean you let others walk on you, or take advantage of your kindness or goodness, though. Ultimately we're looking for unconditional love. It's the sense of being loved despite our weaknesses. It's being allowed to be imperfect. Unconditional love is the epitome of being "fully known"—warts and all—and still being loved and accepted. *How well do you "love" your spouse? How well does your spouse "love" you?*

RATING: You _____ Your Spouse _____

Like. I often tell my husband I really "like" him! To me, liking him is almost more important than loving him. In some ways, we may feel that we *have to* love our spouse, but we don't always like them. Liking your spouse is almost a step up from love. To like your spouse means that they do a bunch of the things you like or appreciate. Someone can love their spouse, because they are their spouse, but really dislike how their spouse treats them, for instance. This "like" factor is a huge, almost intangible characteristic of the emotional climate in marriage, which fuels the desire to be intimate. I have often told clients that I, like most women, may not really feel like having sex at times, but because I like my husband so much, it is much easier for me to make that mental decision to go there anyway. *How well do you "like" your spouse? How well does your spouse "like" you?*

RATING: You _____ Your Spouse _____

Appreciation. One of the assignments I most often give couples is to start express-ing their appreciation for each other more frequently. Sometimes the words don't get heard or are overlooked. Invariably, a husband or wife may feel unappreciated by their spouse. You can change that. With the help of technology, it is quick and easy to send a simple text expressing gratitude for the many positive things you could focus on about your spouse. You may not be able to change how your spouse shows appreciation, but you can focus on yourself, and how you could be more expres-sive of grateful feelings towards your spouse. An overall attitude of gratitude will do wonders for the loving emotional climate in the marriage. *How appreciative are you? How appreciative is your spouse?*

RATING: You _____   Your Spouse _____

Selflessness. This one is a biggie! It is through the maturing process of personal growth and development that we turn from self-centeredness into a more other-ori-ented state of selflessness. This is necessary for oneness in marriage. Selflessness is the ability to exercise self-discipline and restraint and put your spouse's wants and needs ahead of your own. Randall lamented that his wife never makes him a prior-ity. "She's always busy with other things, and won't even read your book with me. When we talk on the phone, we always talk about her. She hardly ever asks about me, or what I'm thinking or doing."

I loved the article by *New York Times* bestselling author, Richard Paul Evans, when he shared in a very personal blog post how selfishness nearly destroyed his marriage. In the post, "How I Saved My Marriage,"[12] he shared how after one of many difficult fights with his wife, he cried out in anger to God. He came to realize he couldn't change her, and was instead inspired to focus on changing himself. He turned to her needs and began asking her every day, "How can I make your day better today?" That simple yet profound question followed by selfless action saved his marriage. We all would do well to set aside our own concerns and focus on the needs of our spouse a little more.

Selflessness can only be done well from a healthy, solid "self"—from a full cup, not an empty bucket. Otherwise the more naturally selfless person often gets taken advantage of. Selflessness only works well in a healthy, balanced relationship. I have quite a few clients who are dealing with things like manipulation, addiction, and narcissism in their relationships. In circumstances like that, the focus needs to be on maintaining healthy boundaries and requiring respect, rather than selflessly giv-ing in to endless, unhealthy, and inappropriate demands. In healthy relationships, there's a balance of selflessness. Externally imposed boundaries are not needed in healthy relationships, because both individuals have healthy internal boundaries and natural respect for each other. Self-focus is in equal proportion with spouse-focus. If not, resentment grows, weakening the relationship. Both spouses need to make sacrifices for the other in a mutual give and take. *How selfless are you? How selfless is your spouse? How often do you do something for your spouse that you know they would like even if it's a little inconvenient for you?*

RATING: You _____ Your Spouse _____

Priority. A divorce lawyer shared that divorces she sees are not so much about the standard "sex" or "financial issues." She observed that the spouses simply weren't making each other a priority anymore. One or the other didn't feel important. Their needs weren't being met. They felt disregarded, misunderstood, and discounted by their spouse. Over and over she'd hear one of them say that a spouse's needs and requests were ridiculous. One spouse was often simply unwilling to stretch to meet the other's needs. Making your spouse a priority may mean getting off work in time to have dinner together as a family. Making your spouse a priority may mean making sex a priority over household duties. Making your spouse a priority, in whatever way that means to them, cannot be understated. When your spouse is your highest priority (next to God), your marriage can flourish. *How well do you make your spouse your priority? How well does your spouse make you their priority?*

RATING: You _____ Your Spouse _____

Responsiveness. According to decades of research on couples, Dr. John Gottman tells us that one of the main factors in happy, long-term marriages is that couples respond positively to each other's requests or "bids for connection."[13] These could be large or small, verbal or nonverbal. They might be things like: Will you do the dishes tonight? Or it could be: Put your phone away while we talk. It could be a simple request to come look at something they want to share on their phone or computer. It can also be nonverbal requests in the form of playful teasing, tickling or wrestling. It can even be a heavy sigh that invites an inquiry into your spouse's thoughts or well-being. Responding positively means you "turn toward" your spouse rather than "turn away." Like loving our spouse in their own love language, these positive responses to a spouse's "bids for connection" are deposits into our spouse's emotional bank account.

I was reminded of the value of responsiveness one morning while trying to get myself to wake up. I'm not a morning person, so I called out to my husband, who works from home. He came to me in the bedroom. I told him I was having a hard time waking up and needed him to talk to me. So, he laid down beside me, put his arms around me, and starting teasing me and talking to me. He was being responsive. That kind of responsiveness definitely fills one's emotional bucket and makes it so much easier to say "Yes" to sex, or any other need one's spouse might have.

For deep, emotional connection, couples in happy marriages make identifying and responding to "bids for connection" a high priority in their lives. Dr. Sue Johnson, in her groundbreaking work with Emotionally Focused Couples Therapy, concurs with the need for couples to respond positively to requests for connection.[14] She reminds us that emotional responsiveness is comprised of three things: Accessibility, Responsiveness, and Engagement (A-R-E). Encompassing other characteristics like trust, selflessness, and making our spouse a priority, we all want a positive response to the questions: Do I matter to you? Are you there for me? Can I count on you to be there for me? *How responsive are you in your relationship? How responsive is your spouse in your relationship?*

RATING: You _____ Your Spouse _____

Positivity. Couples might have a lot of good things going on in their marriage, but if one or both of them focuses on the negative, it makes it difficult for marriages to thrive or partners to feel close. Positivity in your marriage means you assume the best and look for the good in your spouse by focusing on things to appreciate in each other. Positivity is a form of faith. It's believing that you are each doing your best, have good intentions, and are both looking for things that prove your positive beliefs. What we focus on, we tend to get more of. When we focus on and reflect the good, we get more of it. *How positive are you in your relationship? How positive is your spouse in your relationship?*

RATING: You _____ Your Spouse _____

Acceptance. It can be pretty scary for a spouse to risk opening themselves up to the other emotionally, spiritually, or sexually, then find that they are then rejected. Acceptance in marriage sends an overall message that says, "I know you. I love you—warts and all. I realize you aren't perfect, but I love and accept you anyway." Like the couple in the opening story, acceptance means you don't need things to always go your way. Your spouse's way is good and okay, too. A state of acceptance, or unconditional love, is the path that most often leads to spouses making needed changes in themselves to create an even better marriage relationship. *How well do you accept your spouse unconditionally? How well does your spouse accept you unconditionally?*

RATING: You _____ Your Spouse _____

Tenderness. Tenderness is being soft, kind, warm, and approachable in your interactions with each other. It's the little kindnesses in a relationship that really count. Like the couple in the opening story, when we are unkind with our spouse, we can stop, apologize, and instead express tender feelings of love. Tenderness flows best from a softened and humble heart. If pride is an issue in your marriage, it will need to be rooted out. *How much tenderness do you show your spouse? How much tenderness does your spouse show you?*

RATING: You _____ Your Spouse _____

Affection. Without loving touch, the emotional environment in marriage gets pretty empty and cold. So many couples get into the sexual dimension of marriage, and leave the affectionate aspects far behind. Women are especially hungry for affectionate touch, for its own sake. This lays a foundation for more intimately affectionate touching. Affection in marriage means that spouses make a point to touch each other in fun, soft, and loving ways as a regular part of their relationship. I'm always saddened when I see couples walking together not holding hands. It's a missed opportunity for affection when couples are sitting together on a couch, but not close enough to touch. Wives will often tell me that their husbands rarely touch them affectionately, unless they are wanting to have sex. These husbands are ignoring an important part of the mental, emotional, and physical environment necessary for a wife to want to connect sexually. *How affectionate are you with your spouse? How affectionate is your spouse with you?*

RATING: You _____ Your Spouse _____

Honesty. Honesty and transparency are crucial to the foundation of trust in marriage. Transparency prevents distrust. Keeping secrets of any kind—big or small—is generally a weakening agent in marriage. Not doing anything you'd be ashamed of certainly makes honesty easier. To affair-proof their marriage, one couple came up with the concept of a "Threat Scale." This helped them share when either of them felt attractions to or concerns about other individuals. They developed the kind of open and honest relationship where they could share attractions and be able to ask where the individual was on the threat scale for them. This transparency helped them continually build trust.

Steering clear of secrecy, and the shame that follows, takes the buzz out of the forbidden and instead builds trust and transparency. Couples dealing with pornography, or other sexual addictions, for instance, usually find that it's especially important to be honest and speak up about a slip, even more so sometimes than the fact that he *had* a slip. Honesty means that you can count on your spouse to compassionately tell you the truth, even if the truth might be painful, or create negative consequences for either person. Honesty, with kindness, is key. *How honest are you with your spouse? How honest is your spouse with you?*

RATING: You _____ Your Spouse _____

Openness. Openness is a willingness to be honest about who you really are and a willingness to express or show all parts of the self. Confiding in each other, as husband and wife, is what openness looks like. When was the last time you confided something even a little anxiety-inducing to your spouse? Openness necessitates keeping your emotional walls down and your heart softened. Openness is a willingness to see things another way, like trying to see things from your spouse's perspective, and being open to the possibility of their way being as right or as valuable as yours. *How open are you with your spouse? How open is your spouse with you?*

RATING: You _____ Your Spouse _____

Vulnerability. Openness and vulnerability refer to that "in-to-me-see" concept. Vulnerability is a willingness to share your tender, sensitive, or even upsetting thoughts and feelings. Self-disclosure, where you are so deeply and fully *known,* is a big part of what builds emotional bonding and connection. Couples must be willing to allow themselves to be fully seen and fully accessible—even the vulnerable parts of the self. Instead of responding with easier emotions like anger or frustration, couples are willing to expose their softer side where pain, sadness, and fears reside. Unfortunately, many couples have a history where accumulated hurts often build a strong emotional wall to protect themselves. *How willing are you to be vulnerable with your spouse? How willing is your spouse to be vulnerable with you?*

RATING: You _____ Your Spouse _____

Safety. Mental, emotional, and physical safety are pre-requisites for women to be open and willing to make themselves vulnerable—especially sexually. If a spouse doesn't feel safe emotionally or physically, they will be in fight, flight, or freeze mode much of the time. This will not only affect their ability to relax and respond sexually, but will also make it difficult for them to even communicate effectively. Brain studies show that in women, physical and emotional safety is inseparably connected with sex. Women's brains naturally pair sexual cues with questions of safety and security. Sex is a riskier, more vulnerable endeavor for women. They are smaller, weaker, naked, and often on their backs in a vulnerable position. Women unconsciously ask themselves how sure they are about you. They wonder if they can trust you with their heart and their body.[15]

Being emotionally safe for your spouse means being open and accepting of what they have to say, even if you don't agree with or like it. Many couples unwittingly train their spouses to NOT open up or connect with them because of the way they respond so negatively to genuine thoughts and feelings. A wife recently said to me, "Why in the world would I tell him what I am thinking, when every time I do he gets defensive or bites my head off?" Sometimes a spouse brings the feeling or belief of being unsafe into marriage because of abuse or other negative experiences in their past. Sometimes a spouse has not developed the skills to manage their own emotions or to freely share their inner emotional self with another. These are some things that may need to be addressed with the help of a good counselor. *How safe does your spouse feel with you? How safe do you feel with your spouse?*

RATING: You _____ Your Spouse _____

Compassion. Compassion is the ability to respond with understanding and love, instead of criticism or judgment. Compassion is charity instead of contempt. A close relative of compassion is empathy. Empathy is the ability to feel what your spouse is feeling, and to see from their point of view. Empathy and compassion allow you to read, or tune into your spouse, and respond with kindness. This allows you to understand where your spouse is at emotionally, and what they may be feeling or experiencing. This requires a healthy degree of self-awareness and selflessness to be able to set aside your own needs and step outside yourself, and see how something may be impacting your spouse instead. *How well do you show compassion towards your spouse? How well does your spouse show compassion towards you?*

RATING: You _____ Your Spouse _____

Friendship. The richness of having your spouse as your best friend and cheerleader cannot be overstated in building a strong foundation for fantastic lovemaking. The warm companionship of friendship includes a genuine interest in the life and well-being of the other. It includes doing and saying thoughtful things. I've seen many couples where they show little interest in what's important to the other. I often tell clients, "You might need to practice caring about things that are important to your spouse, even if they aren't important to you, simply because you care about your spouse." It's an exercise in selflessness. Friendship requires letting go of selfishness so everything isn't about you. In addition to being genuinely interested in your spouse, and being their devoted cheerleader, friendship includes a mutual sharing of each other's thoughts and feelings. *How often do you do something nice for your spouse, just because? How good of a friend are you to your spouse? How good of a friend is your spouse to you?*

RATING: You _____ Your Spouse _____

Admiration. For admiration, I always think of "that look" in a person's eyes that says, "I like who you are. I think you're pretty great!" Remember the concept of "gentle eyes" discussed in Chapter 2 - "Thoughts." Admiration requires that you not only love, but actually "like" your spouse. Admiration involves a willingness to focus on the strengths of our spouse and to think only thoughts that are encouraging and affirming. Admiration is the outward manifestation of loving, positive thoughts about your spouse. *How well do you admire your spouse? How well does your spouse admire you?*

RATING: You _____ Your Spouse _____

Attention. Couples that neglect each other and spend much of their time, energy and attention elsewhere will find the emotional bank account in their marriage lacking. Giving each other attention can be little things like phone calls or texts throughout the day. It might be a kiss and a hug when coming together after being apart. Paying attention is how you get good at reading and understanding your spouse, and tuning into them, so you can get better at connecting with them. It also means listening and showing the respect of giving your undivided attention when your spouse is talking to you. That means putting aside your phone, TV remote, video game controller, or the laundry. It is hard not to be distracted these days. All couples (and families) can benefit from an hour or two of planned "technology-free" time every day.

Many a cell phone, tablet, laptop, and TV screen have caused a lot of emotional disconnection between husband and wife. This phenomenon is aptly called "Relationship Technoference"—the interference of technology on relationships.[16] Janie simply calls it "death by cell phone," because of how she felt about her husband's phone use. She found herself increasingly angry any time he was on the phone in the evenings. Especially when there were children, or her, he could attend to instead. To her it was as if he was saying, "There's nothing of interest, or importance going on around me, so I'll just play a game or check my email."

Ken had a few choice words for his wife's preoccupation with social media. "She's always on that stupid 'F-book!'" Paying attention to your spouse may mean you need to set aside scheduled time where neither has to compete with texts, email, apps, or video games. The message you are sending by spending time on your phone may be inhibiting the very intimate relationship you desire. *How well do you pay attention to your spouse? How well does your spouse pay attention to you?*

RATING: You _____ Your Spouse _____

By rating yourself and your spouse in each of these areas, you can hopefully see where to focus your attention on making your marriage better. We're talking primarily to or about women here. Yet, this dimension of tenderness/thoughtfulness/trust is one where a husband can do the most to help change the sexual dynamics in the marriage. I especially hope husbands will read and diligently apply this chapter to their relationships. It's important to remember that the only one you can change is yourself. Don't waste your time and energy trying to get your spouse to change. You are most likely to change your spouse by changing *you* first. Focus on what you can think, say and do differently to make things better. It's the best way to bring about change in your spouse anyway.

Emotional Foreplay — How to Live at "40" on a 0-60 Scale

Now that we've talked about the importance of the emotional climate in the marriage, and the characteristics of a securely attached relationship, let's talk about some specific things couples can do to stoke their intimate fires. Consider this a prescription for developing the emotional climate in your marriage.

Courtesies and Kindnesses

The following suggestions are ingredients of courtesy and kindness that lay the foundation for emotional closeness: opening her car door; saying please and thank you; touching her more often in affectionate, no-strings-attached ways (i.e., holding hands, hugging, sitting close enough to touch, etc.); giving her your undivided attention when she is talking to you; or doing little things for her that you know she likes. Sometimes after couples have been married a while, basic courtesies diminish.

Brenda explained it well when she said, "I just need my husband to be kind and thoughtful throughout the day. I don't really feel valued, loved, or accepted except within the bedroom. That makes it really hard for me to respond to him sexually. It seems like he is only willing to do what I ask or be nice to me if he wants sex. I don't know if he really cares about me—my hopes and dreams, my needs, or what's important to me. He just doesn't seem to realize that the best foreplay happens outside the bedroom for me."

It's the little things. Husbands, you might consider asking her to make a list of small and specific kindnesses you could do for her. They may seem small or unimportant to you, but would help to show your wife you care. Little things can go a long way in warming her heart and making her feel loving towards you.

This list may be particularly important for husbands to be able to identify little tweaks they could make in things they may already be doing, but that they could do more effectively. One wife spoke with resigned frustration about the fact that she always had to ask her husband to take out the trash, and that he would also forget to put the new garbage bag back in. It's sometimes difficult for spouses to accept that what they may do for their spouse (i.e., take out the trash) may not have the intended desirable effect. That's especially true if what their wife really wanted was for them to be thorough and do the whole job by putting in a new bag as well.

Some may argue that their wives should be grateful for what he did do instead of what he didn't do, and I agree. But if husbands want to have a sexually responsive wife, they will want to meet their wife's requests as closely as possible. The more attentive and responsive he is, the more she will feel loved.

Begging me to make things better in the bedroom. Since husbands are often begging me to tell them how they can make things better in the bedroom, I explain how important those little "dumb" things are. Doing the little things sends a powerful message to their wives: "I know you. I know what you like, and how you like things. What's important to you is important to me" (even if it really isn't that important to him).

Sam, whose marriage was hanging by a thread due to past indiscretions, finally "got it" when he recognized how "done" his wife was with him over something he thought was pretty minor. So, it was heartening to hear him say:

Husbands really need to listen and pay attention to their wives more. They need to not be so insensitive. I have been guilty of disregarding what's important to my wife. I really wasn't trying to be insensitive. It's just that the thing she was so upset about didn't seem like a big deal. So, of course I just got defensive. Thankfully, I was able to recognize what was going on, since we had talked about it in session with you. I let her know I was sorry, and would try to fix the situation. I let her know I would be more attentive in the future.

I reminded him that if things are a big deal to her, and he wants to send a message that he loves her, then he might want to make it a big deal to him, too. Ignoring the little things tells her she's not important to him. That's a great way for her to not want to make sex a priority.

Self-reflecting questions for husbands. I really like the following questions from a blog post entitled, "Sex Starts in the Morning."[17] I've also added a few questions of my own that husbands can ask themselves to better show their love and attentiveness to their wives. These questions, and the self-awareness it can give husbands, can ease the weight that women often carry in their day-to-day lives. Such burdens keep wives from responding as favorably to sexual overtures.

- Have I put my wife's needs above my own today?
- Am I really listening to her when she's sharing something with me? Or, am I distracted by my phone, the football game, or something else?
- When I get home from work, am I really there? Am I present and engaged with the people I love the most?
- What's it like to interact with me? What's it like for her to be married to me?
- What are my motives when I do listen and interact positively with my wife? Is my focus on sex? If so, then I may act in ways that turn her off, because I feel entitled to sex. If my goal is connection, then she is more likely to feel loved and have a greater interest in being intimate.

Couple Time

"We never seem to have time to talk—I mean really talk. We're always just running here and there, transporting kids and taking care of household responsibilities. When we do finally crash, we both seem to slip into the habit of hiding behind our cell phones, televisions and tablets. That's just what we do. I guess we assume the other person doesn't want to talk." This is a common dilemma for many couples. When they don't plan for and set aside time together, it may not happen.

Ken and Jada were finding it difficult to make time to connect during an especially busy few months. They were both feeling it. Some of their bigger connectors, like date night and sex, were slipping. Sometimes we have to just accept and work with our realities, so I asked them how they could connect more in little ways during a regular crazy day. Jada suggested that if Ken would listen better, and not argue with her opinions, that would help. We came up with a simple mnemonic device to make it easy to remember three easy ways to connect—V-E-T. V was to Validate what Jada had to say. E was for Ken to stop what he was doing and make Eye Contact. It helped him give her his undivided attention. T was to encourage them both to Touch more often throughout the day. This meant simple, non-sexual affection like a kiss, or a hug, or a hand on a shoulder.

I discuss the concept of making time in Chapter 4 - "Time," but suffice it to say that couples need at least a decent amount of time together to be able to talk and connect. Talking does need to be about more than just the logistics of their lives.

Couple time won't happen by chance. To develop the emotional relationship—emotional foreplay—couples must make it a priority, and give it priority time and attention. That often means it needs to be scheduled. Couple time can take many forms. Some couples make sure they have pillow talk time at night to either just talk, or to read something together. Some couples go out for lunch together regularly. Some couples make sure they have a set-aside date night.

Date night is a great way to have plenty of time and attention, to really reconnect as husband and wife—instead of always just connecting as mom and dad. Some couples are good at regularly connecting when communicating about daily logistics. Some have couple time just by expressing random thoughts and feelings throughout the day just to keep in touch—whether by text, phone, or email.

Some couples have set aside Sunday night for a "Marriage Meeting," where each contributes to an ongoing list or agenda of things to discuss. It might include things like how to motivate a child with their homework or chores, where to go for an anniversary getaway, what to do with a child being bullied at school, or concerns either may have about work, with other responsibilities, or in their personal lives. It's an important way to remember that you're a team.

This Marriage Meeting works well in connection with maybe a Monday night "Family Meeting" to coordinate everyone's schedules. You might discuss any concerns or issues family members may be having. You'll see as we talk about "Daddywork" later in this chapter, that family functioning is right up there on the list of ingredients for good, emotional connection for women. Again, this is a component of the marriage climate that makes her more likely to want to be intimate with her husband.

A vital form of couple time is couple prayer, where husband and wife can kneel together to express gratitude, and plead together for that which they are in need. This might also be thought of as "spiritual foreplay." Emotional connection is very closely aligned with spiritual connection. Husbands especially need to be sure they help to make spiritual connection a priority as well. Don't wait for your spouse—initiate prayer or other forms of spirituality or worship as a couple.

Couple time, in all of its forms, is a necessary vehicle for emotionally connecting through Talk, Touch, Tenderness, Tuning in to each other, and even some playful Teasing. You need to spend time together to do these things. Your homework is to individually, or as a couple, come up with specific ways you might be able to fit more couple time into your lives.

Couple time ideas. It may help to jumpstart your own couple time habits by sharing a few things, other than sex, you might do during your time together as a couple:

- Discuss your day—the joys and frustrations.
- Read about or discuss a book, an article, or something from the news.
- Pray together.
- Study the scriptures or other religious materials together.
- Discuss a question or two from a list of "couple questions" found on the internet or from books (i.e., *365 Questions for Couples* by Michael Beck).
- Watch a favorite TV show together (while touching in some way).
- Cuddle. Be affectionate.
- Have a planning session to plan your day, week, life.
- Go out on a date.
- Have lunch together.
- Talk on the phone during the day.
- Text each other throughout the day.
- Play a game or do a crossword puzzle together at night.
- Share five things you like, love, or appreciate about each other.

Date Night

Date night is technically a form of couple time, which we've already discussed. But, because it's so important, it's worth its own section. Couples need to be sure they are fully utilizing this connecting activity. I had a client tell me that their relationship was in such a mess that date night was not even an option. They had serious work to do to first get the relationship back to a basic level of civility. There were few basic courtesies or kindnesses shown, and many underlying issues kept them in a constant negative cycle. When couples are in such a state, they usually need some help from a counselor to break their negative patterns. If date night is an option, but you just aren't making it a regular part of your marriage, then I hope this section will encourage you to move date night to the top of your to-do list.

Don't forget date night. The need for date night can't be overstated. Many couples find themselves falling out of love, and falling into dangerous disconnected territory mentally, emotionally, and physically. It's significantly more difficult to fall out of love when you are spending regular amounts of fun, enjoyable time together.

Date night keeps the good times in marriage in better balance with the inevitable difficult times. It's a proactive way to continually create positive associations and memories of fun and enjoyment with your spouse. To keep a marriage out of vulnerable territory, it's important that couples keep the scales tipping in the direction of positive interactions with each other. Date night helps to add fun and playfulness to the relationship. When the fun goes out of the marriage, then the motivation to deal with the inevitable challenges goes, too. Date night gives you a chance to get away from it all and slip into "couple mode" for a few delightful hours.

There was a time in my life when Friday night date night was a real light at the end of the tunnel each week. Being a full-time, stay-at-home mom of young kids was a real challenge for me. But, I knew I could make it through the week, because Friday was on its way. Date night allowed me to remember that I was an individual and a wife—not just a mother.

Date night gave me a chance to interact with my husband on a more personal, individual basis, rather than being only a mom or housekeeper. It helped me to remember those wonderful feelings from our courtship days. It put a sparkle back into my eyes and into my soul. It continues to be something I look forward to every week. I might even say that date night is one of my very favorite things!

Husbands, don't just date your spouse, but court her. Woo her in a way to make her feel like you would choose her all over again. It's a wonderful way to make her feel wanted and cherished.

Marriages need nourishment. Sometimes we forget that a marriage needs to be nourished. We can't just stop doing all the things we used to do when we were courting and expect our marriage to stay exciting, alive, and vibrant. Our marriages need constant nourishment emotionally, spiritually, and sexually. Wives, especially, need the emotional nourishment that's hard to provide better than with ongoing date nights. The emotional intimacy and connection that develops through regular date nights is the fuel that makes both husband and wife feel loved, cherished and desirable. Date night is *not* optional for couples who want to create a close and connected intimate relationship.

The power of date night. David and Cindy provided an excellent example of the power to change your relationship, simply by adding date night to the mix.

> *David and Cindy came into my office with a lot of frustration and resentment on both sides. She felt unloved, unimportant, and found herself being constantly angry with him about every little thing. He couldn't understand why his wife was so upset. It didn't make sense why she was acting so crazy and over the top about dumb little things. He thought he was a pretty good guy and doing a pretty well at being a good husband and father.*
>
> *We identified that Cindy felt loved best through quality time, especially date night. They hadn't really had date night to speak of for years. David felt loved not only through physical touch, but also by having a calm home environment where kind words of affirmation were spoken. We talked about these differences, and how*

both of their needs weren't really being met. That influenced how they interacted with each other.

David shared how all he wanted to do was come home from a long day at work and stay home. The last thing he wanted to do was go out for a date night. Cindy, on the other hand, was at home or running kids around all day. She just wanted to get away for some time alone with her husband once in a while. They decided to make date night a higher priority. She was going to try harder to keep her frustrations with her husband in check. He was going to make the effort to go out for a date night on the weekends. When they came back after just a few sessions, they had been doing date night faithfully each week for some time. The whole tone of their relationship had changed.

When I asked what made things so different, she explained that now that they were going out together regularly she felt closer to him—like he was a friend, instead of the enemy. She acknowledged that she genuinely felt loved now. She knew it was a sacrifice for him to go out when he'd prefer to stay home at the end of a busy week. David explained that Cindy was so much nicer and calmer now. They hadn't even had any arguments since our first visit.

It's not every day that I get to send couples home half-way through a counseling session. They had genuinely made the one profound change they needed after just two and a half counseling sessions. They were simply better at meeting each other's needs. Their experience was a testament that when couples understand each other's need for a specific kind of love, and will do those things sincerely and consistently, the whole emotional environment of their relationship can change. They had truly shifted from living in the 0-10 range emotionally into living at least at a 40 on the 0-60 scale. Connecting with him sexually was even easier for Cindy, now that she genuinely liked him again.

David was happy to report that the date nights had actually become quite enjoyable for him. He liked how they talked more about things other than just the logistics of running their home and family. He appreciated having a calmer, kinder wife, and noticed how they both simply liked each other better. They were able to remember how much they loved each other after all. They were a good example of choosing to act in loving ways by meeting each other's needs better, even when they didn't have much in the way of loving feelings toward each other.

When I asked on a scale of 0-10 how each of them now felt toward the other, she answered a "9," and he answered similarly. Had he not been willing to do something he didn't want to do (go out on regular date nights), he'd still have an angry, critical wife, and be spending a bunch of money on counseling.

My hope is that many of you will be able to make the changes you need simply from reading this book. If you do, you can save yourself a lot of time, money, and heartache!

"Date night is not optional for couples who want to create a close and connected intimate relationship."

Date night and emotional foreplay. The whole experience of date night builds emotional connection between a husband and wife—the key ingredient in emotional foreplay for wives. Date night itself is great foreplay. It just makes it so much easier for women to move from feeling emotionally connected (emotional desire), to wanting to be physically intimate (sexual desire). Since sexual touch is the dessert of married life, date night may be a great time for you both to look forward to a little bit of lovemaking. Especially after all that emotional foreplay during your date.

It's important to get home early enough to not be too tired for some "nooky." Amanda complained that they went out on date night so late that by the time they got home, she was spent. She couldn't keep herself awake, much less actively involved in lovemaking. They decided to do date night on a different night when they could get away sooner.

Men, keep in mind that doing this date night thing just for the possible bedroom benefits is not usually the best approach. When men have an expectation about sex, it can be a real turn off for women, especially if they don't yet share his passion for love-making. Couples that are on the same page about sex being dessert on date night won't have that difficulty.

Wives are experts at identifying when loving behavior has strings attached. It can be a turn off if there is not enough emotional connection outside of his sexual interests. It can even undo the positives of a great date, depending on where your wife is emotionally and sexually. Nobody wants to feel as if she is being "wined and dined" because of something that is expected in return. Since we're focusing here on improving the emotional connection, especially for wives, date night works best if couples can just relax and enjoy each other. The focus needs to be on emotional connection—whatever that means for them—not on sex, unless that is a shared desire.

If the focus of this book was the husband's intimate wiring, then connecting sexually first may be more effective for women to improve the emotional connection in the marriage. If husband and wife have addressed and improved the 12 keys of marriage discussed throughout this book, then you can more likely trust that the rest of the night will take care of itself beautifully.

Just enjoy each other. Whether your date nights are actually an evening out, or a lunch date, or even just time spent together after the kids are in bed—this time is sacred time. Some of my favorite dates were when we would put our little ones to bed a bit early, then read and discuss a book or article together.

Other times, we'd take the book *365 Questions for Couples* by Michael J. Beck,[18] with us on our dates to help us have interesting things to talk about—other than the things we always talked about. We'd ask each other questions like, "What is your greatest fear?" or "What is your greatest hope?" or "What are your best characteristics?" etc. It helped us to keep learning about each other. Conversations like that help to keep things fresh, new, and interesting as ever-changing individuals.

Date night is a perfect mix of how women and men generally connect best. Women tend to connect best through communication, and men tend to connect best through doing things together. Date night provides both! Whatever you decide to do on your dates, just enjoy each other. Pay attention to feelings you may have forgotten about like why you ever started dating and fell in love with each other in the first place. If you need some help coming up with fun ideas for your date nights, be sure to check in with our friends at TheDatingDivas.com. You can also visit our website StrengtheningMarriage.com for more date night information and resources.

Raising the bar on date night. I am always thrilled with whatever couples can do to create a habit of date night. But, I do have a few suggestions for those who are ready to raise the bar on their date nights:

- *No Cell Phones or Other Electronic Devices.* Even if your phone is a major part of your job, or you are in the habit of checking your social media or sports scores, plan to put your phone away for date night. Surely it can wait, so that you and your spouse can have a few hours of uninterrupted couple time. Remember it sends a great message that says, "You are most important to me."
- *Minimize Babysitting Distractions.* Train and prepare your children, and their babysitters, to handle all but life-threatening emergencies on their own. This is also good practice for moms to learn to let go a little and shift their focus to their spouse.
- *Show Uncommon Courtesy.* Date night is the perfect time to practice gentlemanly skills of courtesy and kindness. Treat each other in ways that you would want to teach your own children to act on their dates. Imagine showing your sons how to treat their future wives. This might include opening her door, lending your jacket if it's cold, and escorting her through the maze of tables, as if she is under your tender care.
- *Touch More.* Date night is a perfect opportunity to engage in affectionate touch, even if it's not yet a regular habit for you. Holding hands, extending your arm to hold, and sitting close enough to touch ought to be a natural part of your dating (and married) life.

Remember that the main purpose of date night is to have some uninterrupted time alone together so you can have fun and reconnect mentally, emotionally and even physically. If you'll apply these four suggestions, you will be able to maximize the benefits of date night in helping to create the relationship of your dreams.

Meeting Your Spouse's Needs for Love

No discussion of connecting emotionally as husband and wife would be complete without addressing the need for both to know and "speak" each other's language of love effectively and frequently. Over the years, I've seen couples trying to express their love in many ways, yet not fully reaching the heart and soul of their loved one. They may be trying their best to love their spouse. But, like two ships passing in the night, they often express that love in the way *they* want to give it, or the way they would like to receive it themselves. Instead, they need to express their love in the way *their spouse* wants it, and can actually feel it. In marriage it's not so much the "Golden Rule" we need to remember, but the "Platinum Rule"—do unto others as *they* would have you do unto them.

Fulfilling each other's needs is at the root of marriage itself. There's almost an unwritten assumption that when two people love each other and marry, they will do everything they can to meet each other's needs. When husband and/or wife don't feel like their needs are being met on a fairly consistent basis, it creates a huge vulnerability in their marriage. Couples need to be tireless in understanding each other's needs and striving to meet those needs regularly.

Just like Bill and his wife in the story at the beginning of this chapter, the challenge to love each other effectively is usually two-fold: 1) couples lack the knowledge of what their spouse wants and needs in order to feel cherished, and 2) what the spouse needs to feel loved is often the hardest thing for the other to do. Like Bill, our spouse's love language is often that which we least want to do.

A common dynamic for couples is when she loves conversation with words of appreciation and affirmation in order to feel loved. Yet, those are the hardest things for her spouse to do. He, on the other hand, wants sexual connection in order to really feel loved. And, you guessed it, that's the hardest thing for her to do as well.

Two principles for loving your spouse more effectively. The overriding principles in making sure your spouse feels loved are: 1) make sure you know what specific behaviors make your spouse feel cherished. Just knowing their primary "love language" isn't quite enough; and 2) be prepared to have to stretch some in order to be able to meet your spouse's needs.

According to Gary Chapman in his fabulous book *The Five Love Languages*,[19] there are five general ways that people feel loved:
1. Quality Time
2. Words of Affirmation
3. Receiving Gifts
4. Acts of Service
5. Physical Touch

I'll never forget how moved I was by a story in *The Five Love Languages* that solidified my desire to help couples learn each other's love language. The story involves Norm and

Jean, a couple married for 35 years. They go to see their marriage counselor, and Jean says she doesn't feel loved. Norm and Jean don't have money problems, and they don't argue. They go to church together regularly, and seemingly have all the basics for a good marriage.

Norm lists all the things he does for his wife—makes dinner, does the dishes, laundry, vacuuming, etc., but she emphatically states how those things just don't really make her feel loved. She tells the counselor that she just wants her husband to sit and talk with her, but he's always too busy doing stuff. Norm doesn't feel loved either, but has never really said anything. The counselor asks him about the ideal wife, and he lists practically all the things he's been doing for his wife. The counselor is able to help them understand that she needs 15 minutes of his undivided time and attention in order to feel loved by him. (She's a quality time gal.) For Norm, he needs her to do things for him in order for him to feel loved. (He's an acts of service guy.)

The heartrending part for me was when the husband said, "Why didn't somebody tell me this thirty years ago? I could have been sitting on the couch talking to my wife for 15 minutes every night instead of doing all these other things." Thankfully, they went home and started loving each other in the right way, even though it took them 35 years to figure it out. Their love and connection was reborn. Better late than never.

In this story, the challenge for Norm and Jean in meeting each other's needs was principle #1—they simply did not know what the other needed. Happily, they were able to actually provide the kind of loving behavior each other needed. But as we can see in the story of Bill and his wife, just knowing your spouse's "love language" isn't enough. You also have to be willing to change your behavior, and maybe even stretch a bit in order to meet the specific needs for love that your honey may have.

Principle #2 is that you might have to stretch in order to love your spouse effectively. I find it interesting how many couples attract someone whose needs for love are not their strong suit. Rhonda was a "receiving gifts" kind of gal. Her husband, Steve, struggles to spend money, being raised in a family that didn't have much. It was like pulling teeth for him to buy gifts for his wife, even though he knew that was how she best felt loved. When the loving behaviors are particularly difficult, they are often felt as an even greater gift from the heart.

Inconvenient acts of thoughtfulness. Making difficult sacrifices to love our spouse well reminds me of the many couples I've worked with where the wife's primary language of love was best described as "inconvenient acts (or words) of thoughtfulness." It became pretty humorous to me when I'd had multiple couples in succession where the wife expressed a similar need for her husband to do thoughtful things that were inconvenient to him. It was the only way for these women to feel real love from their spouse. It was something about the sacrifice they needed him to willingly make. In most of these instances, the husbands tended to be more focused on attending to their own needs instead of their wives'. These women felt neglected and unimportant. Their husbands just didn't want to do things they didn't want to do. Sometimes a husband will take issue with his wife's desire for inconvenient acts of love. A self-focused spouse will take issue with any of their spouse's needs that aren't easy or convenient. With most couples, one tends to be more other-oriented, and the other spouse tends to be more self-oriented. These wives (often the other-oriented ones) did not regularly experience thoughtful acts of love from their husbands. This made those behaviors all the more rare and needed.

Meeting these wives' needs provides an excellent opportunity for the husbands to stretch and grow, if they want their wives to feel loved. Husbands are able to become more thoughtful and other-oriented if they will work to meet her needs. Cameron had an "Aha" moment when he realized how much it meant to his wife that he text and talk with her throughout the day. He was not a texter. He told me how he'd just get busy with work and not even think about it. He thought texting was kind of dumb, anyway.

He finally got that texting was important to her. He knew if he wanted her to feel loved, he'd have to change his tune about texting and make the extra effort to do so. He realized he needed to start seeing things as important, simply because they were import- ant to her. He thought it wouldn't be a bad idea to get over the fact that he didn't like to text and learn to enjoy it because of how it made her feel. It was painful for him to realize that this shift in behavior was very different than what he would have done in his previous marriage. He acknowledged that he probably wouldn't have texted his first wife, because he wouldn't have known of its importance. She wasn't a big communicator about her needs, and he hadn't previously been very willing to put himself out.

Husbands who are willing to do those inconvenient and selfless acts of love will be richly rewarded in their relationship with their spouse. They will find great joy in the personal development gained by stretching to meet their spouse's individualized needs for love. They will also more likely find greater connection in the bedroom as well.

Identifying her needs and his needs. In addition to Gary Chapman's *Five Love Languages,*[20] Willard F. Harley, in his book *His Needs, Her Needs,*[21] says there are ten common emotional needs. Five are more prevalent in women, and five are more preva- lent in men:

Wives' Emotional Needs	Husbands' Emotional Needs
1. _____ Affection	1. _____ Sexual Fulfillment
2. _____ Intimate Conversation	2. _____ Recreational Companionship
3. _____ Honesty and Openness	3. _____ Attractiveness of Spouse
4. _____ Financial Support	4. _____ Domestic Support
5. _____ Family Commitment ("Daddywork")	5. _____ Admiration
_____ Other _____	_____ Other _____

The five love languages and the ten emotional needs listed here provide valuable insight to help husband and wife discover each other's primary needs for love. While these categories are very helpful, I think it is even more important to identify the specific behaviors that are meaningful to you and your spouse.

Your homework for this section is to do the Love Language Worksheet on my website StrengtheningMarriage.com (see the Appendix for access information) to identify 10 specific behaviors that most make you feel loved and cherished. This list will be like gold to your marriage, because it provides the very keys to each other's heart. It makes it so much easier to know what to do to love your spouse more effectively.

In addition to creating your love language list of what specific actions make you feel loved, I also recommend both of you rate each of the ten emotional needs above on a scale from 0 (none) to 10 (a lot) to identify which are your highest priority needs. You might even want to add your own. After you have done both of these things, then focus your time and effort solely in those areas. I recommend you choose one to two things to *stop* doing for your spouse, so that you have more time and energy to do the things that mean the most for them. These may be things that you tend to like to do for them, but that do not rank high on their priority for feeling loved. Especially in today's busy, fast-paced society, we just can't do it all. I'm a big believer in doing that which gives you the biggest bang for your buck!

The refining process of meeting each other's needs. If either of you struggle with meeting your spouse's specific needs for love, I encourage you to seek out a good marriage counselor to help you work through your obstacles. We tend to attract a spouse whose needs for love are perfect for us to finish our own development and help us grow in areas where we may be less developed. Marriage is a refining process meant to polish and perfect each spouse. It reminds me of one of my favorite quotes by sex therapist Dr. David Schnarch: "Marriage's 'polishing process' uses each spouse as the abrasive to finish the other's development."[22] Learning to speak our spouse's love language is an opportunity for personal development.

If sexual love hadn't been such an important way for my husband to feel loved, I'm not sure I would have gone to the lengths I have to develop that part of my being. As I watch my clients also struggle with their challenges, I can see God's wisdom in designing marriage to help couples complete each other's development, as they strive to love each other better. I chuckled, and sighed, as I again heard a wife say that she finally figured out what her love language was after we talked through the options. She said, "I think Words of Affirmation might be my primary love language, and of course, that's the hardest one for my husband to do!"

Again, while the focus of this book is the wives' sexual wiring, it's important to note that most men have either a primary or close secondary love language of physical/sexual touch. Women may need to accept that they have work to do to develop themselves sexually, in order for their husbands to feel loved. Meeting those needs provides you a perfect opportunity to develop your wholeness at the same time.

"Daddywork"—A Great Aphrodisiac

It's hard to find much that's sexier than a daddy who loves his kids. They say men doing housework is a great aphrodisiac for women, but I think "Daddywork" is way up there on the list as well. Not much beats the feeling that comes from seeing your husband play with your children, help them with homework, teach them how to ride a bike, read to them, or tuck them in at night. Now that's a turn on!

> *Jake couldn't figure out what happened to his wife one Saturday when he sur-prisingly "got lucky!" He'd been working with the girls all day on various projects around the house. He even patiently helped one of them practice driving. Mindy filled in the blanks during a counseling session. She said, "I couldn't help myself, given how cute you were being with the girls that day. I thought about waiting until later that night. But I've also been trying to work on initiating more often, so I took the chance when the girls wanted to go run some errands for a bit."*
>
> *I added, "Jake, that's the power of Daddywork. It can be a huge turn on for women, given that we are intimately connected to the well-being of our children. It's kinda like how God says when we take care of His children, we are in essence taking care of Him (see Matthew 25:40). You being patient and nurturing of your children makes Mindy feel close to you. This makes it easier for her to want to express her feelings in the way you most want—sexually."*

Men might find it strange that their wives would experience any erotic effect from them being actively and lovingly engaged with their children. Daddywork may be a great unrecognized reservoir of fuel to stoke their wives' intimate fires. On one hand, it relieves some of her stress when you focus on the kids, and on the other hand, she is seeing how loving and caring you are, which makes her have those feelings for you. This is also why when husbands make a point to put away their cell phones, so that they can be fully present and engaged with their family, they are likely to have a very happy wife.

My prince is a daddy. One day I was walking through a quaint arts and crafts fair in a small town when I saw this beautifully framed quote that to me captured the essence of Daddywork. It said, "My prince has come…His name is Daddy!" I loved it because it perfectly captured one of the best things I love about my husband—that he's a great dad! My prince is a daddy. He's my kids' daddy. I realize that the meaning I gave to the state-ment was probably not what was originally intended. It works perfectly for many wives who so appreciate the tenderness and love their husbands show their children.

Within the same week, I had two couples with significant issues about how the hus-bands were treating the children. It was negatively affecting the wives' feelings toward their husbands. In both situations, the wife perceived the husband as being unduly mean, intense, impatient, and unkind to their children. This directly affected her desire to be intimate with him. Both husbands couldn't understand how their interactions with their children had anything to do with the marital relationship, or bedroom activities for that matter. They were upset that their wives wouldn't keep the issues separate. The wives could have easily argued the opposite, not understanding how, to men, the interactions weren't related to the marital relationship.

Remember that women are like the World Wide Web, where everything is connected to everything. Men, on the other hand, can more easily separate different components of their lives as they naturally tend to compartmentalize things. It's important for husbands to know that even seemingly unrelated things—like how they parent—are still part of the emotional environment of the relationship. These other issues can act as intimate accelerators or brakes for a wife.

The power of Daddywork. Brad's experience shows how well Daddywork can work on a wife's libido.

> *Brad had felt pretty distant from his wife lately, so he was shocked to get a text at work from her. She asked if he wanted to come home "for lunch." He happily obliged, and told me that he didn't even break any speeding laws getting there! She was surprisingly warm to him and seemed quickly "ready to go" intimately.*
>
> *Having recently discussed my Fuel for Female Sexual Desire diagram (Chapter 8 – "Technique"), I asked Brad what he thought had made the difference in her being so amorous with him, and so quickly. He thought that maybe it was that he had recently decided to develop a better relationship with his kids. He had lately been more fun and playful with them. I suspected that was probably a pretty good guess.*
>
> *I explained this concept of Daddywork as a great aphrodisiac for women when dads are genuinely cute and caring with their children. What likely made it even more powerful to his wife was that he wasn't trying to do it to get a "bedroom benefit," but that it was a genuine desire on his part to connect with their children.*

Daddywork might include things like attending a child's school or sporting event, patiently helping the kids with their homework, or reading them a story and tucking them into bed at night. Daddywork efforts can certainly help to fuel those intimate fires in a wife's heart and mind, making it easier for her to decide to "go there," and express her love in ways that husbands tend to really like.

As you improve the emotional connection, and increase the tenderness, thoughtfulness, and trust in your marriage, your intimate connection will skyrocket. The following are the highlights of this chapter as "Action Items" to help you be able to live higher up on the 0 to 60 scale. This is what makes it easier for wives to be able to respond more favorably to lovemaking.

Self-Evaluation - "Tenderness"

To give yourself a guide as to how you are doing in this dimension, how would you currently rate yourself and your spouse overall in the area of "Tenderness"? This ingredient is the primary foundation of emotional connection upon which a sextraordinary relationship is built. Write your thoughts in your Sexual Self-Discovery Journal. — *I am doing well with the 20 characteristics of emotional connection. I make couple time and date night a priority. I know and speak my spouse's love language well.*

RATING (0 - disagree to 10 - agree): You _____   Your Spouse _____

ACTION ITEMS — Chapter 3 - "Tenderness"

- Take the "Emotional Connection Self-Assessment" and work on the areas where you are lacking.
- Get in the habit of asking your spouse, "How can I make your day better today?"
- Husbands, ask your wife to make a list of small and specific courtesies and kindnesses you might do for her. They may seem small or unimportant to you, but would really show your wife that you care and that she is important to you.
- Get in the habit of giving or sending regular expressions of appreciation to your spouse. When you focus on the good about them, you'll get more good from them.
- Individually, and/or as a couple, come up with a few ways you might be able to fit more couple time into your daily/weekly schedule.
- Develop a regular date night, so that you can have that opportunity for connection in your marriage.
- Do the "Love Language Worksheet" on my website StrengtheningMarriage.com to identify 10 specific behaviors each of you most prefer that make you feel loved and cherished. (See the Appendix for access information.)
- Conscientiously work to meet your spouse's specific needs for love, so that they will unquestionably feel your love.
- Rate each of the 10 Emotional Needs on a scale from 0 (none) to 10 (a lot) to identify which are your highest priority needs.
- After you have done both the "love language" list and rated the 10 emotional needs, choose one or two things you used to do that you can stop doing, so that you have more time and energy to do the things that mean the most to your spouse.
- Remember Daddywork. How you treat your children has a big effect on how your wife may feel about you, and how easily (or not) she'll be able to respond to you sexually.

NOTES

1 Pascoal, P. M., Narciso, I., and Pereira, N. M., "Emotional Intimacy is the Best Predictor of Sexual Satisfaction of Men and Women with Sexual Arousal Problems," *International Journal of Impotence Research* 25(2) (2013): 51-5. doi:http://dx.doi.org/10.1038/ijir.2012.38

2 Johnson, Dr. Sue, *Love Sense: The Revolutionary New Science of Romantic Relationships*. New York: Little, Brown and Company, 2013.

3 Ibid.

4 Bulow, S., "Integrating Sex and Couples Therapy: a Multifaceted Case History," *Family Process* 48(3) (2009) Sep: 379-89. doi: 10.1111/j.1545-5300.2009.01289.x.

5 Gottman, John, and Silver, Nan, *The Seven Principles for Making Marriage Work*. New York: Harmony Books, 2015.

6 Weir, Kyle, *Intimacy, Identity, and Ice Cream*. Cedar Fort, Inc., 2016.

7 Ibid.

8 Skinner, Dr. Kevin, "Addiction & Intimacy - How & Why Addictions Prevent Intimacy," YouTube Video, 44:36. Posted March 2014. https://www.youtube.com/watch?v=7ITIpGq1ZNA

9 Johnson, Dr. Sue, *Love Sense: The Revolutionary New Science of Romantic Relationships*. New York: Little, Brown and Company, 2013.

10 Ibid, 21.

11 Van Epp, John, *How to Avoid Falling in Love with a Jerk*. McGraw-Hill Education, 2008.

12 Evans, Richard Paul, "How I Saved My Marriage." Richard Paul Evans Blog, accessed July 18, 2016. http://www.richardpaulevans.com/index.php/2015/02/09/saved-marriage.

13 Gottman, John, *The Relationship Cure: A 5 Step Guide to Strengthening Your Marriage, Family, and Friendships*. New York: Three Rivers Press, 2001.

14 Johnson, Dr. Sue, *Hold Me Tight: Seven Conversations for a Lifetime of Love*. New York: Little, Brown and Company, 2008.

15 Johnson, Dr. Sue, *Love Sense: The Revolutionary New Science of Romantic Relationships*. New York: Little, Brown and Company, 2013.

16 BYU News Release, "Daily 'Technoference' Hurting Relationships, Study Finds." Brigham Young University. December 2, 2014, accessed March 30, 2015. http://news.byu.edu/archive14-dec-technoference.aspx.

17 Berry, Mike and Kristin, "Sex Starts in the Morning." Confessions of a Parent. October 20, 2014, accessed March 30, 2015. http://www.confessionsofaparent.com/sex-starts-in-the-morning.

18 Beck, Michael J., *365 Question for Couples*. Holbrook, MA: Adams Media Corporation, 1999.

19 Chapman, Gary, *The Five Love Languages: The Secret to Love that Lasts*. Northfield: Later Printing edition, 2004.

20 Ibid.

21 Harley, Willard F., *His Needs, Her Needs*. Grand Rapids, MI: Revell, 1986.

22 Schnarch, David, *Passionate Marriage: Keeping Love and Intimacy Alive in Committed Relationships*. Beaufort Books, 2011.

CHAPTER VIEW

❧

Making Time and Prioritizing
Cutting Back
How Husbands Can Help
Scheduling Your Priorities
Making Sex a Personal Priority
Making Your Husband a Priority
Improving the Emotional Climate
Benefits of Making Sex a Priority
How to Spend the Time
    Making Time for the Relationship
    Making Time for Sexual Learning
    Making Time for Enough Sexual Stimulation
Don't Forget the Clitoris
Quickies and Gourmet Sex
Self-Evaluation - "Time"
ACTION ITEMS — Chapter 4 - "Time"

Chapter 4

TIME — MAKING SEX A PRIORITY

I don't think my wife really understands what sex means to me. I think if she did, she would make it a much higher priority than she does. Sexual intimacy is probably a little different for everyone, but for me I never feel more alive in ALL my senses than through true sexual intimacy with my wife.

I have tried to communicate to her that for me, sexual intimacy is tied closely with emotional and spiritual intimacy. When we make love, I feel I am giving all that I am and ever want to be to her. It's like I am giving all of me into her. It is sacred, and symbolic, yet very real.

When my wife genuinely wants to make love to me, and for me to make love to her, I never feel more needed, accepted, appreciated, wanted, and alive. I exist for this love. To me, this love is the purpose and meaning of life, and all creation. I believe every man and woman is designed to desire and need this love—this total acceptance, this total giving and receiving with one's spouse. The object of our existence is to become ONE with our spouse and Deity. There is no greater happiness, joy, and peace.

My wife has basically given up on having a healthy intimate relationship with me. She seems to think it takes too much effort. She goes out of her way to perform all of her other wifely duties, though. She keeps a meticulously clean house, is a fantastic cook, and in every other way is amazing. What frustrates me is that although those things are important, I would ten times rather have an affectionate, loving relationship with my wife than any of those other things.

When enough time goes by and she senses my frustration building, she'll throw me the "obligatory bone" sexually. It has about as much romantic feel as taking out the garbage. My wife says that in order for her to get physically worked up for a satisfying sexual experience, it will take her three or four days of just mentally focusing on it. That is only if nothing like a cross word or problem with one of the kids occurs . . . What are the chances?

It's very difficult to not let a cross comment slip when there is so much built-up frustration. And then to make it even more frustrating, when she does respond I know that it is purely out of duty, and not because she desires it. She says she loves me, which I believe. It's just a physical/mental desire thing, she says. It's not that she's not attracted to me, it's just the physical desire for sex isn't there. She has mentally given up, and moved on to other things.

In these experiences, husbands share some of the meaning that sex has to them, and how painful it can be when sex is a low priority to their wives. It helps to understand what sex means to your spouse, and how important it is to them. But, as discussed in the previous chapters, women have work to do to awaken and develop their unique sexual wiring. Couples have work to do to develop the emotional environment, for the fuel it provides female desire. On top of that is simply the busyness of our lives. It's hard to find the time to be together. It's difficult to have enough time and energy to make sex or our sexual development a priority. To husbands, it just feels like they are not a high priority.

In this chapter, we'll discuss how the element of "Time" plays a role in the challenges of sexual intimacy. We'll also suggest solutions regarding the time troubles that occur outside the bedroom, and the issues at play within the bedroom. We're not only looking to help you make time for lovemaking (and to spend enough time at it to be mutually satisfying), but also to make time for personal sexual development, and sexual learning as well.

Making Time and Prioritizing

When it comes to priorities, it seems that women have about 59 things on their plate at all times. But, if something is important, we tend to find time for it. Women seldom have lingering sexual desire on the stage of their minds, to the surprise and chagrin of their husbands. It may be helpful to understand the time and priority issues that women face, and how to help entice women to make sex and the intimate relationship a higher priority.

Cutting Back

Many husbands have lamented that they don't feel like they are a priority to their wives. With so many things on a woman's plate, they might need to consider where they could cut back. A good general guide for prioritizing our lives is to put God first, self-care second, marriage third, children fourth, then other things fifth. Following this guide can help women be sure they are taking care of themselves, so that they can more effectively take care of everything else…and not feel guilty about it. It's hard to do anything well, if we aren't first making sure we are personally functioning well.

How do you spend your time? I encourage you to make a list that will likely include personal, household, family, employment, church/community responsibilities, etc. After listing everything that takes your time, choose one or two things that you could delegate, hire out, cut back on, or stop doing all together. I know this isn't an easy thing to do. It may involve a lot of soul searching and prayer.

Utilize God as your guide. He can help you know where to cut back in order to make time for the most important things. Sometimes you just need to de-clutter your life to find a few things that can be removed from your daily schedule in order to make more room for your relationship.

Over the years, some things that have helped me make more time for my marriage are: cutting back on school/church/community service, using paper plates more often, doing all the laundry in one day and delegating the folding and putting away responsibilities to our children, hiring help for some of the household cleaning, not letting children's activities take over date night, minimizing TV watching, cutting out all technology on Sunday to make it a down day to rejuvenate and connect, and saying "no" more often to requests for my time. For a few years I had to say "no" to all speaking engagements, which I love, in order to make time for other higher priorities. It's not always easy saying "no," especially for women, who tend toward people pleasing, but it is worth it when you realize you are trading your time from something *good* to something *even better.*

How Husbands Can Help

Husbands always ask me how they can help their wives make sex a higher priority. One of the best things men can do is help their wives find some "down time" to rejuvenate. Specifically, they need to be completely off-duty from their cares and responsibilities. While it may seem counterintuitive to a good sexual relationship, helping wives have some personal down time is probably one of the most cherished acts of love given the hectic lives of today's women. One of my clients even suggested that "downtime" for women may be akin to "foreplay" for men. Feeling fatigued and overwhelmed are common contributors of low sexual desire. With women being wired like the World Wide Web, having many plates spinning at all times, it often feels that they never have time to themselves to breathe.

One wife shared how her husband would take over all the childcare and household responsibilities from 6 to 10 p.m. every Thursday night. She said it was like heaven to be able to hide herself away in her room or office, go to a movie alone, or have a fun girl's night out. This may be another great aphrodisiac where husbands can be proactive in helping to create the climate that can light her fire.

Husbands need to be sure their wives don't come home to a bigger mess, or the goodwill gained by the night away will be quickly lost. If men can refrain from expecting that sex will happen that night, things will likely turn out better for them in the long run. Overwhelmed and fatigued wives will just bristle at the feeling that there were strings attached to the act of service. It is important for men to note that being helpful around the house does not immediately translate into erotic thoughts and feelings in the wife. In fact, she may appreciate the help and feel loved, then simply add other things onto her plate. This can certainly be frustrating for men. When the husband makes helping his wife a priority, he lovingly removes some of the obstacles that prevent her from being able to make sex a higher priority. But, it still takes a conscious decision on the wife's part to use that time to help her sexual feelings grow.

Scheduling Your Priorities

I'm a fan of the concepts taught in the book *Automatic Millionaire*.[1] The gist is that if you pre-schedule your money to go into savings before you even see it, or have the chance to impulsively spend it, anyone can become rich. The same concept applies to how we spend our time. It's like budgeting our time to make time for our spouse and our relationship. One husband pleaded with his wife, "Why can't you make some time for me?! I just need to know I matter. Please don't make me beg for scraps of your time. I don't even need a lot of time or attention, but I do need some. It doesn't even have to be just sex. I'm happy to see you even thinking about our sexual relationship or reading something to try to learn how to make things better."

By scheduling into our lives anything that's important to us, we make it happen. It's easy to complain about the lack of spontaneity in scheduling sex. It may not sound very sexy. But then, neither is a lack of intimacy. If you have a hectic life, common in today's society, it may be necessary. By setting aside this time for connecting with your spouse, you are better able to physically, mentally, and sexually prepare, in addition to assuring that it will more likely happen. We can't mentally prepare if we are unaware of what is coming.

Husbands will often tell me that sex never seems to make it to the top of their wives' to-do list. Scheduling sex may be preferable to no sex at all. Since women are juggling a lot, unless there is a set-aside time for lovemaking, then sleep or some *other* vitally important endeavor may take precedence. Men have the luxury of being able to compartmentalize, which means it's easier for them to shut out the dirty dishes, or the children playing downstairs, to want to make love.

Some couples may need to make a "Sex Plan" to clear out the logistical barriers, in order for them to be able to connect sexually. Curt and Katherine had been married for 38 years but just couldn't seem to get in the flow of a good intimate relationship. We decided to sit down and figure out what they needed to do to make couple time and lovemaking a priority. Here are the specifics of their plan to do things differently:

- Plan for couple time and lovemaking every Saturday and Sunday night, plus one other weeknight to be decided together on Sunday nights.
- Stop working these nights by 6 p.m. and have dinner ready early enough to have time for a nice evening together.
- Don't use garlic in the dinner those nights, so sex isn't unpleasant.
- Turn off all electronics by 6 p.m.
- Play a game together after dinner.

- Shower together. (His job was in construction, so showering was already a regular part of his evening routine.)
- Light candles and turn on music for her enjoyment.
- For homework they were to also add anything else that they needed.

Try scheduling at least one planned occasion of lovemaking per week, or more, if you're up for it. This needs to be priority time with priority energy, not just whatever is left over. If that doesn't sound attractive to you, you may need to spend that time on the Action Items in previous chapters. We don't really want anyone to schedule sex just to have sex. We want them to want to, and be enthusiastically engaged.

Some couples find it best to not schedule specific nights, but to know that each of them will initiate sex at least once that week. Date night with its built-in foreplay is especially ideal as a great opportunity to plan to make love. I'd love for couples to make once-a-week sex a minimum recommended requirement for their marriage. If wives will make lovemaking an automatically scheduled event, then their never-ending to-do list won't rule over the romance in the marriage.

The challenge is to discuss and then schedule time for sexual learning and/or love-making. Some clients have scheduled sex on date night, and one other night during the week. Sunday nights can be set aside to read an article or chapter from a book. Other couples have made reading something about sex a part of their bedroom routine. For some, it's even part of their foreplay. You decide what works best for your situation and calendar, then schedule it.

Making Sex a Personal Priority

When wives see sex as an important part of their personal wholeness and aliveness, the whole issue of making time for sex is easier. In Chapter 1 – "Transformed," I lay out the how to's for developing your sexual identity and identifying your own sexual needs. This chapter is about doing internal work that can help you to overcome the obstacles of time and energy and make your sexual relationship a higher priority. When you see sexual fulfillment as a way to feel whole and alive, or as a needed form of intimate expression, then you can see how much easier it will be to make sure some of your priority time and energy is available for lovemaking.

The wife in the second client story went out of her way to do other loving things for her husband. It was a way to compensate for her feelings regarding sex. Whether the underlying issue for her was not embracing her own sexuality, feelings of failure sexually, negative past experiences, etc., the work involved in transforming one's sexual identity tends to address underlying issues in a woman's heart and mind.

Making Your Husband a Priority

Spouses need to know that they are a priority in each other's lives. How you show someone that they are a priority has to do with how much time and energy you devote to them. The quality of the time they are given matters as well. Do they get left over time, or do they get priority time and attention?

Adam felt like his wife was constantly adding "projects" to her to-do list. He was never one of them. He wanted her to work on their intimate relationship, but she just always had too much else to do. He said, "I just wish she would put me at the top of her to do list sometimes instead of always at the bottom." Making your spouse a priority is a necessary ingredient in making your spouse feel loved. Sex is a team sport. It's not a solitary activity. In a loving, mutually respectful relationship, when sex is a high priority for one spouse, then it needs to be a high priority for the other.

As illustrated in the opening client scenarios, most men consider sex to be of utmost importance. Whether wives like it or agree with it or not, husbands generally consider sex to be the highest expression of love. Sometimes just knowing how men define sex in such a profound way can help wives to want to make more time for such expressions of their love.

Over time, when the newness and novelty of sex wears off, women tend to see sex as simply a means of physical release for their husbands. Or they see it as an inappropriately important need. Such thinking does little to inspire the necessary effort to make lovemaking an important part of your marital life. Most women want to be good wives. They want to love their husbands well. But the clamors of life and the lack of understanding about our differing meanings of sex can easily build barriers to frequent lovemaking in today's marriages.

"In a loving, mutually respectful relationship when sex is a high priority for one spouse, then it needs to be a high priority for the other."

Improving the Emotional Climate

Physical attraction tends to flow from emotional connection. For women, the quality of the marital relationship has a lot to do with the priority women give to sexual intimacy. This is such a huge issue, especially for women, that Chapter 3 - "Tenderness" is dedicated to helping couples improve the emotional climate in their marriage. While it takes both spouses to create a good emotional climate, this is certainly one area where the husband probably has the greatest ability to make a difference in his wife's receptiveness to his sexual advances.

An emotionally connected relationship between husband and wife is one of the best motivators for making sex a higher priority. When both feel close and connected, and there is genuine warmth between them on a regular basis, it sets the stage for women to more easily flip their mental switch and decide to "go there." As illustrated in the diagram of "Fuel for Female Sexual Desire" in Chapter 8 - "Technique," the psychological environment of the relationship is in essence "Step #0" of the multi-step process for women to get to a state of desire. That emotional connection between husband and wife provides the fuel for her to decide to open the door and be receptive to sexual advances.

Benefits of Making Sex a Priority

Making intimate passion a priority is not just for husbands—it's also for wives. Benefits of making time for your mate sexually include: awakened senses, a deepened relationship, and feeling more whole and complete as a sexual human being. Don't forget that physical touch alone has healing powers. Research shows that orgasm, as well as skin-on-skin contact, releases the powerful hormone oxytocin, which is considered the "bonding" or connecting hormone.[2]

Making your marriage and sexual relationship a priority not only makes your life better in many ways, it also reduces your stress and frees up your psychological energy. Jon and Maria had worked hard at improving their relationship and the sexual dimension of their marriage. Jon recently reflected, "You know, I used to feel almost consumed by the lack of intimate connection in our marriage. But now that it's better, I don't think about it so much. The anxiety in our relationship has significantly diminished."

It reminds me of the t-shirt a client saw that says, "Sex is like air. It's not a big deal until you're not getting any." The quality of the sexual relationship represents another 80/20 rule. When the relationship is struggling, it feels like it consumes 80 percent of our thoughts and energy. But when it's good, it takes a more balanced place among the other important dimensions. We have more time and energy to focus elsewhere. This helps us live a more productive and balanced life—mentally, emotionally, spiritually, socially, physically and sexually.

Making sex a priority is not just for your spouse's sake, or even for your sake. It's also for the sake of your children. Not much would benefit your children more than providing them with the strong foundation of securely and intimately bonded parents. Making your spouse and your marriage a priority also shows your children what it looks like to have a good, strong, happy marriage. Setting that example makes it easier for them to create a strong marriage for themselves in the future.

How to Spend the Time

Now that we've discussed the obstacles to setting aside time for sex, let's talk about what we might need to do with that time. Time is a necessary ingredient, not only for building the emotional relationship (outside-the-bedroom stuff), but also for many inside-the-bedroom activities. Couples need Time to do the following:

- Work on negative core beliefs.
- Embrace your sexual identity (as discussed Chapter 1 - "Transformed").
- Learn about each other sexually.
- Learn about the intricacies of the sexual response.
- Foreplay—including clitoral and other sexual stimulation.
- Lovemaking itself.

While knowing to spend more time on these things may make logical sense to you, incorporating them into your life may still be a challenge. Let's discuss how you can make the needed changes in order to give more time to sex.

Making Time for the Relationship

Keep in mind that "Step #0" in fueling female sexual desire is having a connected emotional climate the relationship. This is a woman's ongoing foreplay. In Chapter 3 - "Tenderness," we went into this in much more depth. As you may be beginning to see, when it comes to women, all things are interrelated and can affect other aspects of their sexuality for good or for ill. The emotional connection in marriage is fed by things like date night (my personal favorite), regular pillow talk, daily texts and phone calls, as well as many other tender and thoughtful acts of love and kindness. These all require time. It is especially effective when those activities are based upon the specific love language of one's spouse.

What can you do to make time for being together to strengthen the intimate relationship? Can you schedule a regular date night? Can you commit to put things away by a certain time each night, so that you can spend time together? Can you plan to go to bed at the same time, so that you have a little pillow talk time at night?

For good lovemaking, it's not optional to spend time on the emotional dimension of the relationship. While a focus on emotional connection is needed as a fuel for female desire, this is not just for her benefit. The greater the emotional connection in the relationship, the greater the sexual satisfaction for men. There's a definite return on the investment for men to spend time on the relationship as well. It improves their sexual experience, too.

Making Time for Sexual Learning

Couples will benefit from making time to learn about what builds a healthy sexual relationship. Contrary to popular opinion, good sex is a learned behavior. Sexual skill building takes time.[3] It takes time to read good books or articles, or listen to audio resources on the subject. It takes time to learn from each other as well. Couples need to set aside a specific time in the evening, at least a couple times a week, to do any of the Action Items at the end of each chapter, or for reviewing the Recommended Resources in the Appendix. It's difficult to find the time unless you schedule it.

In addition to obtaining good general sexual learning, it's especially important to take time to "practice" and get "to know" each other sexually. Good sex is ultimately an adventure of trial and error to figure out just the right ingredients, in the right amounts, for a mutually fulfilling sexual relationship. Just think of how much fun it can be to figure it all out!

In Chapter 1 – "Transformed," I suggested starting a Sexual Self-Discovery Journal. This is where you can begin to identify specific things that are a turn on, and specific things that aren't. This helps women get to know their sexual accelerators, brakes and preferences (see Chapter 9 - "Tuned In"). She can then share those insights with her husband—best done outside of lovemaking. Throughout this book, I ask you to do process writing and various self-assessments. Write about these exercises in your Sexual Self-Discovery Journal. It will help you gain insight about yourself and show your progress over time.

Making Time for Enough Sexual Stimulation

Truly meaningful and fulfilling lovemaking requires time. Men function more like a microwave, whereas women tend to be more like a slow cooker. Women need time for their minds to focus. They need time for their desires to simmer and begin percolating through their sexual senses for full expression.

Within the context of lovemaking itself, many couples don't spend enough unrushed time on foreplay before diving into the "main event" of intercourse. I love seeing the look on husbands' faces when I give them "foreplay homework." This is when they must spend at least 15-20 minutes talking, touching, kissing and caressing anything other than the obvious erotic body parts before they can touch any of the "good" stuff! They often have a look of, "What am I going to do for 20 minutes?!"

When couples spend enough time on the whole body—before diving into the breasts and genitals—it enhances the entire experience. This is the slower and softer focus of foreplay. It helps her warm up and "get up to speed" quicker. She can then join her husband at higher levels of arousal where he is usually waiting.

I was discussing this concept of a slow boil for female foreplay with my husband. He talked about how opposite that is for men. Men tend to be more interested in a direct, fast, and furious approach. If the husband will slow things down for her to warm up her way, it makes it so much easier for his wife to return the favor, and take on his preferred fast and furious approach. Unfortunately, the reverse is not as true. If a woman were to dive in with a fast and furious approach, let's say specifically to please her husband, it isn't as likely that he would in turn slow down, and take a slower, more sensual approach in lovemaking.

Men, your assignment is to take it slow. Spend enough time in foreplay before moving to her hot spots and the main event of intercourse. Watch her and read her well, to know when she's warmed up and ready for you. You want her to be on the same page with you sexually, instead of her dragging along behind you. Foreplay is like the appetizer to the main culinary experience. Although foreplay isn't technically the main course, it too is a delicious, even vital part of the overall experience. Foreplay is particularly needed for wives who are working their way from the first step of flipping their mental switch to "on," through getting talked and touched into a state of arousal. This is where they can then find and express their own sexual desire.

Don't Forget the Clitoris

In addition to making sure there is enough time for wives to get the emotional, verbal, and tactile foreplay they need to really get in the game, they also need a special kind of sexual stimulation that often gets overlooked or underplayed. Just like a man would have a difficult time being fully fulfilled from a sexual interaction without stimulation of his penis, so too do women need clitoral stimulation. The clitoris and the penis originally come from the same embryonic tissue. Both have the highest concentration of nerve endings, so don't forget the clitoris.

Sufficient stimulation of the clitoris is necessary for her to have a satisfying sexual encounter. Husbands, be sure you spend enough time and attention there. It could take even an hour of direct and indirect clitoral stimulation the first few times. (See Chapter 8 - "Technique" for more specifics.) Her mind and body work together to attain the heightened arousal she needs. Both must be ready to relax and let go, to involuntarily release the built up pleasurable tension accumulated for an orgasm.

Couples need to set aside sufficient, unrushed, pleasuring time, especially for the wife's clitoral needs to be satisfied. The focus must be leisurely enjoying every sensation, NOT on the outcome of an orgasm itself. Much like "trying" to go to sleep just makes sleep all the more elusive, chasing an orgasm makes the orgasm all the more elusive as well. Make time to enjoy the experience, and the orgasm will come.

This is all easier said than done. How do you maintain a state of firm faith that orgasm will occur, but not over focus on it to the point of inhibiting it by "spectatoring" (mentally observing, instead of physically experiencing)? It's very important to be patient not only within the lovemaking experience, but also throughout the course of "practicing" together until you get there. Homework for couples is to spend time exploring and communicating about what kind of touch, in what amounts, and at what point in the lovemaking process clitoral stimulation best provides the desired orgasmic response.

Quickies and Gourmet Sex

You can't talk about time, and sex, without mentioning quickies. Quickies can be great little treats in and of themselves. They can be a gift, especially to fulfill a husband's needs without a ton of time and effort. Women may want quickies, too. Female sexuality can include an interest in a "fast and furious" approach not just to meet a husband's needs, but also for her own sake. If sex is always a quickie, then women may not have enough time to be able to experience their full arousal, and orgasmic potential.

Making sure you spend enough time for luxurious lovemaking on a fairly regular basis is vitally important for mutual fulfillment. I often encourage couples to schedule at least one quickie and one gourmet lovemaking session per week to make sure that both husbands and wives are getting enough sexual time and attention for their needs to be met.

This chapter was designed to inspire you to make your sexuality and your intimate relationship a higher priority. That means finding ways to make time for these endeavors and to be together more. Priority time is needed for strengthening your marital relationship, learning sexually, and having enough time for fulfilling sexual intimacy. These things contribute to creating the sextraordinary marriage you desire.

Self-Evaluation - "Time"

To give yourself a guide as to how you are doing in this dimension, how would you currently rate yourself and your spouse overall in the area of "Time"? Write your thoughts in your Sexual Self-Discovery Journal. — *I make my sexuality and intimate relationship with my spouse a high priority. I make time to be together with my spouse. I find ways to cut back on other less important things in order to make time for developing my sexual self, strengthening my marriage relationship, learning sexually, and having enough time for fulfilling sexual intimacy.*

RATING (0 - disagree to 10 - agree):   You _____ Your Spouse _____

ACTION ITEMS — Chapter 4 - "Time"

- Schedule sex at least once a week, if possible.
- Make a list of everything you spend your time on, and choose one thing to take off your to-do list.
- Do the work in Chapter 1 - "Transformed," so that making time for sex is an easier endeavor.
- Discuss, and then schedule time for sexual learning, and/or lovemaking. You decide what works best for your situation and calendar, then schedule it. Set aside at least one evening a week for sexual learning, and/or lovemaking.
- Write in your Sexual Self-Discovery Journal to get to know your sexual accelerators, brakes, and preferences.
- To do "foreplay homework," spend at least 15-20 minutes talking, touching, kissing and caressing before moving on to touching any of the "good stuff!"

- Spend time exploring and communicating about what kind of touch, in what amounts, and at what point in the lovemaking process clitoral stimulation best provides the desired orgasmic response.
- If you can, schedule at least one quickie and one gourmet lovemaking session per week to make sure that women are getting enough sexual time and attention for their intimate needs to be met.

NOTES

[1] Back, David, *The Automatic Millionaire: A Powerful One-Step Plan to Live and Finish Rich.* New York: Crown Business, 2015.

[2] Johnson, Dr. Sue, *Love Sense: The Revolutionary New Science of Romantic Relationships.* New York: Little, Brown and Company, 2013.

[3] Granvold, D. K., "Promoting Long Term Sexual Passion," *Constructivism in the Human Sciences* 6(1) (2001): 73-83.

CHAPTER VIEW

✤

Chapter 5

TRANSITION — GETTING THERE

Cade and Mandy were having a busy summer. Kids were running around all day, and teenagers were up until all hours. Cade headed to bed early, in order to get up for work. Mandy waited up for the teenagers to get home. They became ships passing in the night. She started to feel a little disconnected. One night they had a rare chance to be intimate. It felt like climbing a mountain for her, because of the emotional distance she'd been feeling. She explained that she wanted to, but didn't really want to, either. She wanted to connect, but felt miles away from being interested in anything sexual.

As they got into bed she said, "Cade, if I'm gonna get there, you're gonna have to talk and touch me into it tonight." I had previously given them homework where Cade couldn't touch any erogenous zones for at least 15-20 minutes. This gave them a chance at a healthy dose of non-sexual foreplay, before they could move on to more intimate touch.

They talked about a variety of things. She was able to share and discuss some of the things on her mind while he stroked her shoulder. She began to feel that her husband wasn't so much of a stranger anymore. She moved into a spooning position. He asked if he could rub her back for a bit. They continued to talk.

Their talking moved from innocuous topics to more connected verbal intimacy. A bit later he asked if she wanted to take her top off while he continued to massage her back. She said yes. The transition from "no interest" to "willing interest" was nearly complete. The time they took together helped her transition from feeling like strangers, to gently and genuinely leading her into desire and arousal. She now truly wanted to connect sexually. The rest was history.

In a counseling session, we discussed what happened that made things flow so smoothly and turn out so successfully. She was willing to go there, even though she didn't "feel like it" at first. He was willing to take her "where she was" without being offended that she wasn't interested. He didn't take it personally that she wasn't as anxious to have sex as he was, even though it had been awhile. He was willing to be patient and trusted the transition process would allow her to warm up to him. Believing it would work itself out, he understood the value of verbal intimacy and affectionate touch, to move her from a "not-really-interested" position to a more receptive state.

He scored bonus points in his wife's and my eyes when he turned down the quickie she initially offered. Because of our discussions, he knew gourmet sex was a possibility if he would just patiently work with her and her sexual wiring. He knew it could lead them both to a shared state of mental, emotional, and physical connection. When husbands practically beg me to help their wives be more interested in sex, I can't help but think of Cade and Mandy, and wonder how much the husband is doing to help his wife along. Mandy too played a key role in being open to the possibilities, even though the sexual feelings hadn't shown up yet.

The Transition Challenge

Because women are generally slower to warm-up—like slow cookers—to the idea of sex, and also to get fully aroused, they have more difficulty getting in the mood for lovemaking. It's on top of everything else they have going on in their lives. They often have to go from "mommy mode" to wife and lover mode. It isn't quick or easy for them most of the time. I like the analogy of women having 15 windows open on their mental computer screen. They need to learn to close down each of those windows, to get their mind off of things like dishes or some stressor, and focus on being intimate instead.

While sexual desire is pretty readily available for most men, many women find that they rarely get around to thinking about sex, and don't often do so automatically. Even getting from the "thought" of it to a "desire" for it can feel like an impossibly wide gap. Many women have shared this thought, "I enjoy sex once we're 10 to 15 minutes into foreplay, and I think, 'Wow! We should do this more often! This is great!' But during the week I hardly ever think about it at all." Those many open windows in their mind prevent them from focusing on lovemaking.

Need Transition Time

Let's take a quick look at a woman's sexual wiring again, so that we can see why there is even a need for help to get from 0 to 60. The higher-desire, or more spontaneous-desire spouse (often the husband), may see getting from 0 to 60 as a simple, automatic process—a no-brainer almost. But for the lower-desire, or "cultivated-desire" spouse, there's a conscious transition from what they are currently doing (i.e., tending to kids or paying bills) to the thoughts and feelings of making love.

For women, the first step in the process is making a conscious decision to clear their mind of all other competing thoughts to enable their body to respond. Once there, she generally needs some emotional connection (usually some form of conversation), and then some degree of affectionate touch. This leads toward physical arousal. Sexual desire will then begin to show up for her.

Because women tend to be a few steps away from the feeling of sexual desire, they need a transition process. They need some warm-up time to fuel their fire. This gets them from 0 (or wherever they are starting from) to 60 sexually. The transition stage bridges the gap between the "thought of sex" and the "desire for sex." The transition process involves a number of essential ingredients addressed throughout this book:

- Embracing her identity as a sexual person.
- Her thoughts need to be positive about sex going into the process.
- A good emotional connection with tenderness and thoughtfulness on the part of the husband is needed.
- Time and patience on both of their parts to "get there."
- Some talk to help fuel the emotional connection during lovemaking itself.
- Definitely some touch…beginning with non-sexual touch, before moving into more intimate touch.
- The husband being tuned in to her and her state of mind—reading her state of arousal so he knows what to do, and when.
- Some teasing and playfulness to keep the process light and enjoyable.

Female sexual wiring specifics and the entire process of getting from 0 to 60 sexually is addressed in more depth in Chapter 8 - "Technique." In this chapter, we will focus on the earliest steps in the transition, or warm-up process. For women, getting from 0 to 60 may include going from:

1. No thought about sex.
2. To considering thinking about sex.
3. To thinking about sex.
4. To wanting sex.
5. To being taken away into desire, arousal, and orgasm.

While not an automatic process for women, thankfully there are things women can do to transition into sexually connecting with their husbands. There are also things husbands can do to help their wives. There are things couples can do together to assist in the transition into lovemaking. You might consider these things "during-the-day foreplay."

Closing Your Mental Windows

One of the most important parts of transitioning into lovemaking is developing the mental discipline to get good at closing down the many mental windows open in a woman's mind. A woman must be able to turn off, in order to be able to turn on!

My friend, Mark Gungor, comedian and popular speaker on marriage, talks about how men's brains are more like individual boxes that don't like to touch, whereas women's brains are more like an interconnected web of wires with a constant flow of energy—where everything touches everything.[1]

I also think of a woman's brain as similar to what you might see at a circus, where a juggler is trying to keep 15 different plates spinning at one time. With PET scans, and other brain imaging techniques, research has shown that the resting female brain is as active as the activated male brain. In other words, the female brain is never really at rest.

Both husbands and wives need to understand the difficulty and importance of women being able to channel her thoughts in a direction that supports engaged—even passionate—lovemaking. One husband helped his wife close her mental windows, and be more present sexually, by having her walk through a verbal "Stress List." As she listed all the things that were worrying her, the thoughts began to melt away. She could now pay attention to her husband.

Though it's probably most accurate to think of women as the World Wide Web with many different interwoven thoughts and feelings flowing continually, I tend to most often use the analogy of a woman having multiple windows open on the screen of her mind. This just makes it a little more manageable. It's easier to conceptualize how a woman might develop the ability to minimize or close those screens. This allows her to focus her energy and attention on just the "lovemaking screen."

Bridges to Desire

Given the extra steps women generally need in order to get to a state of genuine interest in connecting sexually, "Bridges to Desire"[2] may be helpful. The idea of Bridges to Desire, coined by sex therapist Barry McCarthy,[3] is a helpful one for many women. Here's what one client had to say about how valuable Bridges to Desire had been for her:

I'm glad you talked about the concept Bridges to Desire. It has been visually helpful to me. Where I live, we have a lot of rivers and bridges that we drive over often. I can easily picture a river with a bridge to get to the other side. When I put this idea in a sexual context, it helps. It perfectly fits my experience. Often my husband wants sex, because it has been a while. I, on the other hand, haven't been thinking about sex at all. I've just been busy and overwhelmed with life. It feels like I'm on one side of the river while the idea of having loving, meaningful sex is on the other side. To me it feels like there's no bridge. It seems impossible to get to the other side.

I could swim (or try to force desire), but that thought makes me feel even more exhausted and overwhelmed. The situation seems all the more impossible. When I feel this way, the pressure to engage anyway, and say "yes" to the whole nine yards, is very difficult for me. Sex becomes just a yes or no question of whether I'm going to take care of my husband's sexual needs or not. It pretty much kills any chance of me having any desire myself. This makes me get into an avoidance mode. My husband is trying to be patient, but often feels neglected and hurt.

If we could build a bridge or two, or ten, or twelve, we would have a variety of things to choose from to help me. These would be things that don't put pressure on me. We could find ways to help me relax, while bringing us closer together. This way, my own desire, followed by orgasm and intercourse, are more likely to happen. Even if things don't happen perfectly each time, at least we feel closer and

more loving towards each other. We can rest assured that a more mutually fulfill-
ing sexual experience is right around the corner.

Some of the bridges my husband and I have come up with thus far that we
do together include: taking a bath or shower together, giving each other massages,
watching a romantic movie together, or going away for the weekend. There are
also bridges I can do by myself like: simply thinking about sex more often in a
positive way during the day, or wearing perfume or lingerie. Even doing Kegel
exercises helps me out.

My husband also has bridges he can do like touching me inconspicuously in
teasing ways throughout the day when we are out and about. It's especially fun
because we can't "do anything about it." There's no pressure attached. That really
gets me simmering! Being helpful around the house and attentive with the kids is
always welcomed and helpful to me as well.

Sometimes we may also have a "10 minute free-for-all." This is just 10 min-
utes of anything goes—touching, fondling, etc., but it ends at 10 minutes with
no strings attached to sex. I like this one when we go to bed late because I know
it can't turn into anything else. It's been helpful for me to have a wide variety of
bridges I can now use to help get me to desire.

How Bridges to Desire Help

Bridges to Desire have many helpful advantages. Tanya liked to say that their Bridges to Desire helped her go from "I should want to," to "I do want to!" The following are just a few ways bridges to desire can help women with the transition into lovemaking:

- Increase her thoughts about sex.
- Help her decide to "go there."
- Warm-up and prepare her mind for intimacy.
- Help her relax and let go of other thoughts and concerns.
- Increase anticipation.
- Get her mental, emotional, and physical arousal simmering.

With women's wiring like a slow cooker, these Bridges to Desire provide an invaluable means of helping her warm up to sex. They help level the playing field sexually between husbands and wives.

Identifying Bridges to Desire

For this exercise, I'd like you to think about your own list of three specific types of bridges: 1) bridges for you, 2) bridges for your spouse (how they could help), and 3) shared bridges of things you can do together to help in the transition process. You might think of them as "Hers" (self-made bridges), "His" (spouse-made bridges) and "Ours" (shared bridges). The following is a list of some examples in each of those categories. This can help get you thinking of your own ideas to bridge the distance to desire:

Examples of "Hers" / Self-Made Bridges to Desire

- Keep an ongoing list of "What I like/love about sex/my spouse…"
- Make time, and be willing to put in some effort to mentally prepare yourself for lovemaking. Think about sex in a positive way. Keep out negative thoughts and distractions. Ask yourself, what kind of mental foreplay you need throughout the day to prepare your heart and mind for lovemaking?
- Focus on and cultivate romantic emotions towards your spouse.
- Listen to mood music throughout the day (i.e., love songs, romantic music).
- As a form of nurturing touch, gently touch or stroke your hand or arm to reconnect to your physical self. Train yourself to connect with the sensual pleasure of touch.
- Schedule lovemaking, so the decision is already made.
- Decide to initiate sex.
- Download and listen throughout the day to audio books or my "Marital Intimacy Show" podcasts to help get sex on the mind. (See the full list of episodes in the Appendix.)
- Send playful/teasing text messages to your spouse during the day.
- Wear something sexy during the day to put you in the mood.
- Do Kegel/P.C. muscle exercises during the day, and/or during lovemaking.
- Go for a walk to unwind from the day.
- Touch lovingly or playfully during the day (maybe even sexually).
- Kiss or hug when you come together after being apart.
- Take a bath and relax.
- Wear perfume during the day or right before lovemaking.
- Consciously close your mental windows. Do some process writing. Make a to-do list. Write your stressors to free your mind to be able to focus on lovemaking.
- Daily, or even just prior to lovemaking, meditate or sit quietly with eyes closed, breathing deeply and relaxing your mind and body.
- Use candles in your bedroom.
- Wear lingerie to help you feel sexy and/or to get into a romantic mindset.
- Read a book or articles about lovemaking.
- Read naked in bed to unwind and transition mentally.
- Think of something new or different to try during lovemaking for added fun and variety.
- Keep track of how often you make love, and who initiates, or what type (quickie, gourmet), etc. That which you keep track of you tend to have on your mind more.

Examples of "His" / Spouse-Made Bridges to Desire

These can be tricky in making sure she doesn't feel pressured, or that there are strings attached.

- Hold hands.
- Give her a massage (i.e., hand, foot, back, etc.).
- Touch lovingly or playfully throughout the day.
- Kiss or hug when you come together after being apart.
- Call or text your wife during the day just to let her know you love and appreciate her.
- Help with kids and household responsibilities.
- Help her have down time to relax. Help her go off duty for an hour before lovemaking, or for an evening, but with no strings attached.
- Do and say things that you know your spouse likes or loves.
- Learn her love language and "speak it" regularly.
- Let go of trying to "fix" her, so that she can own her own sexuality.
- Develop the ability to be okay—even happy—whether your wife responds well to your sexual needs or not.

Examples of "Ours" / Shared Bridges to Desire

- Prepare the environment to be more romantic and enticing by adding music, candles, soft lighting, etc.
- Kiss or hug when you come together after being apart.
- Shower together.
- Give each other a massage (i.e., hand, foot, back, etc.).
- Watch a romantic movie together (i.e., chick flicks).
- Spend time together as a couple.
- Have set-aside times of affectionate touch with no strings attached to relearn the pleasure of touch for its own sake.
- Have pillow talk time. Ask each other couple questions to continue to get to know each other better.
- Have date night regularly.
- Schedule a getaway for a night or weekend as often as you can.

Your homework is to list out all the "Hers" (self-made), "His" (spouse-made) and "Ours" (shared) Bridges to Desire that you can think of to help in the transition process. You can do your lists together or separately (perhaps in your Sexual Self-Discovery Journal). Come together to discuss which ones you think would work best in your situation. You might even want to talk through some of the logistics of incorporating some of these new activities.

As you move on into Chapter 8 - "Technique," you'll be identifying more specific activities that you consider sexual accelerators and sexual brakes. Beyond the mental transition from "no thought of sex" to having "some desire for sex," you and your spouse need to know the specific things that turn you on, and also things that turn you off.

Date Night and Chick Flicks

I'm a fan of date night and "chick flicks" (otherwise known as romantic comedies). How can I not at least mention them here as a wonderful resource for helping couples in the transition process into lovemaking? Date night is an all-around great night for love-making, since so much of the needed emotional foreplay is built into the event.

Date night is vitally important for healthy intimate relationships. It was addressed quite extensively in Chapter 3 - "Tenderness." Suffice it to say, without regularly sched-uled date nights, couples are missing out on fabulous ingredients necessary for healthy marriages—not to mention the mental, emotional and physical foreplay it provides.

Many couples rarely touch each other in affectionate ways throughout the week. Thankfully, they will at least hold hands or touch a little more often if they are out on a date. That affectionate touch can be a great aphrodisiac for women. It's especially good for those who have addressed the issues that were keeping them from anticipating date night, and the intimate desserts that may accompany it.

From diapers, dishes, and discipline, to dealing with coworkers and bosses, it's easy for women (and their husbands) to get caught up in day-to-day living. Date night pro-vides an escape into the wonderful world of courtship. You get to be that special, chosen someone, with set-aside time and undivided attention focused on each other. As the wife steps into the role of "girlfriend," it can greatly benefit her (and her husband as well)! As Dr. Laura Schlessinger often says, "Never stop being your husband's girlfriend!" Don't overlook the power of date night. It's a great way to nourish the relationship in ways that help a woman want to connect with her husband more intimately.

"Date night is an all-round great night for lovemaking, since so much of the needed emotional foreplay is built into the event."

Chick Flicks and Foreplay

To give husbands a little help with understanding the value of chick flicks, I start with a funny experience my husband and I had with TV and radio personality Glenn Beck. We attended one of his live shows when he was in town some time ago. His show was a mix of comedy, hilarity, and politics. His marriage-related tirades were side-splitting. Until he moved into the topic of what he called "bonnet movies." As he began one of his marital rants involving "bonnet movies," I knew exactly where he was going to go with this. I've heard it many times before.

As a marriage counselor and sex therapist, I'm saddened when I see that men have not tuned into the value of chick flicks. They apparently don't get their connection to them "getting lucky!" I could also say something similar about women not understanding men, but that's a topic better suited for my next book about male sexual wiring.

I knew full well Glenn Beck was getting ready to go on a tirade about chick flicks… and not just any chick flicks, but my absolute favorite "bonnet movies" based on Jane Austen's books, such as *Pride and Prejudice, Sense and Sensibility* and *Emma*. While I understand the inevitably unrealistic nature of romantic comedies, I still felt sorry for him and others who have little understanding of the female psyche and its attraction to chick flicks. Unfortunately, many men still misunderstand how women are wired, and why the slowly simmering romance portrayed in these movies can be helpful emotional foreplay for their wives. Chick flicks help awaken those romantic feelings that women don't often have automatically. Chick flicks ignite a desire to be cherished and romanced. This fuels her desire to connect, which leads to more easily transitioning from the many varied happenings in her life to connecting sexually with her husband.

Chick Flicks and Anticipation

A key ingredient in female foreplay is anticipation. It's a build-up of tender, yet passionate, and intimately enticing emotions. My husband recently sat and dutifully watched a "bonnet movie" with me. I pondered why these movies were such an emotional turn on for women. Throughout the movie, I noticed that it was like a two-hour build-up of anticipation of that first longed-for kiss or passionate embrace.

I can imagine men thinking, "Just get on with it! Just kiss her already!" One of the key differences between male and female sexual wiring is that for women, it's more about the slow stirrings. For men, it's more about the big release. I get that men might think these kinds of movies are ridiculous. But, if they will accept their wife's differing wiring, they'll gladly work with it to bring out the desired outcome.

Husbands can help if they will embrace these differences, exercise restraint in their own escalating desire, and take things slow. If they will do so, they can often bring their wife to a state of breathless longing and anticipation for the rest of the sensual experience. That slow boil is a perfect analogy for female foreplay. Since "bonnet movies" are often filmed within the context of English Victorian culture, the gradual pace of relationship formation is an excellent ideal for the simmering feelings of attraction and desire to slowly build.

I'm convinced that if more men understood the emotional nature of women's sexual wiring, they would adjust their attitudes about chick flicks, and maybe even learn to enjoy them. They just might be amazed at how helpful such romantic movies can be in helping their wives fuel their intimate fires. It just might make it much easier for them to get from 0 to 60 sexually…and for men to "get lucky!"

Chick Flicks and a Caution

One argument against chick flicks is that they are not realistic. That's true. There is a danger in thinking that real life and real relationships will be like what they see in the movies. Women need to consciously remind themselves that these movies are fanciful, and not true to life. Even so, they can utilize the romantic feelings for good, by embracing and directing them towards their spouse.

Because women are wired with a slower transition rate, and need emotional foreplay, it can be helpful for women to awaken their romantic feelings. These feelings are easily directed toward one's spouse. A woman's libido is more emotionally focused on their spouse than on the physicality of the sexual act. This makes the argument of women and chick flicks very different than the issue of men and pornography. Chick flicks are just one of the many ways for women to stir up those wonderful feelings of love that are necessary precursors to helping her want to be intimate with her husband.

The Transition Process and Mental Discipline

As evident from Chapter 2 - "Thoughts," the transition process into lovemaking requires mental discipline. This is a learned behavior for women. It's not something we tend to do easily, especially since our minds tend to function like the World Wide Web where there is a lot of different information ever present on the screen of our minds.

> *Jenny and George were really struggling with the transition process because she said she felt like a million miles away when he would approach her about sex. She asked me how she could either make the transition more easily or not be so far away from it all the time. We talked about some Bridges to Desire they could incorporate for her, for him and for them together.*
>
> *We reviewed the 12 key ingredients addressed in this book, and she realized that a big part of the issue for her was that she really hadn't embraced her sexuality. She didn't really consider herself a sexual person and didn't have many positive feelings about it. We also talked about how much of a mental discipline it is to get one's self into sex or even a sexual mindset. She heartily agreed about there being a chasm between "mommy mode" where she was most of the time, and "wife and lover mode," which felt foreign and even dreaded. She needed help to transition.*

"Arousal Helpers" for the Mind

Women need to learn to stop thinking, and start sensing. The many sensual suggestions in Chapter 11 - "Treats" can also help. These include having music playing or candles lit. Both help take you out of your thinking mode to be more present in your sensual mode.

Jenny and George agreed that many of the bridges we identified would be helpful. But she felt like she still struggled with her thoughts, especially in the beginning stages of lovemaking. So, I shared with her the following five suggestions for developing mental discipline where she could focus on the pleasurable process and make an easier transition into lovemaking. These are great ways to help couples get and stay more actively engaged in the sexual experience. They can help women be more mentally, emotionally, and physically present during the arousal phase of lovemaking. I call them "Arousal Helpers" because when the mind is engaged sexually, arousal more easily and naturally occurs.

Shantel found herself getting distracted during sex by thoughts about what her husband might be thinking. As a "spectator" rather than a participator, she'd drift into thoughts about what was happening sexually rather than feeling what was happening. These Arousal Helpers got her out of her head and refocused on her sexual senses. I love mnemonic devices to help remember important information. The letters B - F - A - V - E will hopefully help you recall the following suggestions in the heat of the moment. Each suggestion will increasingly demand your attention. They will help you get out of your thoughts and into your body, keeping you more focused during sex and allowing you to more easily ascend the arousal scale to reach the pinnacle of climax.

B — BREATHE. Breathe slowly and deeply to ground yourself and get out of your thinking mind. Pay attention to the inhale and exhale of your breathing to distract yourself from your thoughts. It will help you stay more present during lovemaking. With each breath, say the word, "one" as if counting each breath. You might even breathe in sync with your spouse. It demands your attention and increases connection.

F — FOCUS ON TOUCH (Receptive Touch). Soak in all the pleasurable sensations you are receiving. Notice every touch, kiss, and caress you are feeling. This step is more of a "receptive" tool than an active one, but helps you better focus. It can lead you more easily to the next suggestion.

A — GET ACTIVE (Proactive Touch). Be an active participant in the process by proactively touching, kissing, caressing, and feeling your spouse's body instead of just passively receiving your spouse's touch. No "dead-fish" sex allowed! Feel the softness of his neck with your lips. Feel the hardness of his shoulders with your finger tips, basking in the strength and security he provides. Giving and receiving touch are great ways to help you get out of your mind and into your body, where you can feel and sense... instead of think.

V — VERBALIZE. Verbalize your pleasure with sounds and/or words that communicate what you are feeling or what you are wanting, etc. You decide if it's more helpful for *you* to do the verbalizing or for *your spouse* to help, too. Even just verbalizing "Mmmm," and "Ahhhh," or "Oooh, I love that!" can help you move into a surrendered state. This allows your body to take over and lead you into the exquisite involuntary response of orgasm. If this is difficult for you, you might consider practicing such expressions in a mirror. Many women aren't terribly comfortable verbalizing sexual feelings. Being verbal sexually can be a huge turn on for women to help them get more fully absorbed in the arousal process. Husbands will love it, too! (For more specifics, see the "Auditory Arousal" section in Chapter 6 - "Talk.")

E — EYES OPEN. Try keeping your eyes open during sex to visually share the sexual experience with your spouse. Eye contact demands your attention and increases intimate connection by releasing the love and bonding hormone oxytocin. For some, it may be more helpful to keep your eyes closed in order to maintain focus. Play with both options to see which works best.

> *Jenny gratefully agreed to incorporate these actions into her lovemaking and found them to be very helpful. She realized that once she had learned more about female sexual wiring and how she was naturally a few steps away from where her husband started, then she was able to accept and work with her wiring to make her way into a more passionate state.*
>
> *Her husband explained that it sometimes seemed like the whole transition process was comparable to a bullet-proof vest that you have to find a way through in order to get to her heart and mind to unlock the passion. I reminded them both that as couples come to understand her sexual wiring better, there wouldn't be a bullet-proof vest to remove, or at least they'd have a better understanding of how to more easily remove it when the time came to go from mommy-mode to lover-mode!*

When couples do not understand the need for a transition process, then the outcome of lovemaking will not usually be a marriage-strengthening experience for either spouse. The warm-up or transition process including specific bridges to desire are necessary components of successfully transitioning into fully engaged, enjoyable and passionate lovemaking.

Self-Evaluation - "Transition"

To give yourself a guide as to how you are doing in this dimension, how would you currently rate yourself and your spouse overall in the area of "Transition"? Write your thoughts in your Sexual Self-Discovery Journal. — *I understand the need for a transition process to warm up into lovemaking. I have some "bridges" that help me transition into desire and arousal. I am developing the mental discipline to help me stay focused.*

RATING (0 - disagree to 10 - agree):   You _____   Your   Spouse _____

ACTION ITEMS — Chapter 5 - "Transition"

- Women need to find ways to close all of their "mental windows" in order to transition to sex.

- List all the "Hers" (self-made), "His" (spouse-made) and "Ours" (shared) Bridges to Desire that you can think of that can help in the transition process. You can either do your lists together or separately (in your Sexual Self-Discovery Journal), then come together to discuss which ones you think would work best in your situation. You might even want to talk through some of the logistics of incorporating some of these new activities. Don't forget to include date nights and possibly a chick flick now and then.

- For women to develop greater mental discipline, and to stay more mentally, emotionally and physically present, they can use the B-F-A-V-E "Arousal Helpers" during sex.

- Husbands can help with the transition process by building breathless anticipation in their wives. They must embrace the sexual wiring differences, exercise restraint in their own escalating desire, and take it slow.

NOTES

[1] Gungor, Mark, "Tale of Two Brains: Unlocking the secrets of life, love and marriage." 2009. YouTube video. 13:34 minutes. Posted February 2011. https://www.youtube.com/watch?v=3XjUFYxSxDk.

[2] McCarthy, Barry W., and McCarthy, Emily, *Rekindling Desire*. New York: Routledge, 2013.

[3] McCarthy, Barry W., Ginsberg, Rebecca L., and Fucito, Lisa M., "Resilient Sexual Desire in Heterosexual Couples," *The Family Journal* 14: 59, 2006. doi: 10.1177/1066480705282056.

CHAPTER VIEW

Chapter 6

TALK — TALK ME INTO IT

In my marriage, I have been very guarded about sex—even talking about it. I just didn't want to…at all! I especially didn't want my husband to get any ideas that I was interested in doing anything, if we did talk about it. I found that I couldn't even talk about anything that made him feel close to me, or he'd want to have sex.

Something's been different lately, though. My husband seems to have taken to heart the counsel to pull back trying to "fix me" sexually. He has willingly agreed to not push for sex, while I work through some of my issues. It now feels safe for me to talk to him again, because I know it won't lead to sex.

It's quite strange, actually, to be able to talk with him now. He feels like a friend again. I feel like I have choices, instead of just shutting down and waiting for the storm to pass. We've been doing the emotions exercise you gave us where we share some of our thoughts and feelings with each other. It's actually been nice. He listens. It's strange. He's seems interested, with no sexual expectations. Every time we talk now, it builds my trust in him. I feel safer with him now. There might be hope for us after all.

Needed Forms of Talk

Communication has many important purposes in marriage. It is a vital component of both marital and sexual satisfaction.[1] [2] Conversation is not only necessary for couples to be able to resolve problems well, but it's also the primary fuel for emotional intimacy. Emotional intimacy is the primary fuel for a woman to want to be sexually intimate with her spouse. As we get into the specific steps that fuel female desire in Chapter 8 – "Technique," you'll see that a huge part of lighting her fire is being "talked" into it.

In the client story above, sometimes past abuse or other negative sexual experiences can make a woman avoid intimate communication, or anything that might lead to sex. If communication is that restricted, it is probably a good time to get professional help.

One client, Shaun, shared a good analogy for ongoing communication. He said, "Communication in marriage is like a dam. If you keep it all in, at some point it will break and flood the relationship." Keeping a stream of communication flowing will help prevent damage to the relationship. Anger and resentment are common causes of inhibited communication. This can occur when couples are trying so hard to be nice that they can't be honest.

Ben and Karen hadn't been married very long when they came in for counseling. In one of our sessions, they both expressed complaints about various marital issues that they couldn't seem to bring up with each other outside of the counseling office. They each would get defensive and put up an emotional wall that sometimes lasted for days. They felt like they were in a vicious downward spiral.

When Karen brought up some issues with finances, Ben just bristled and wouldn't talk. She'd get the message and shut down as well. She was accumulating quite a list of topics she felt unable to address with him. Their growing resentment was fueling their emotional distance. When I asked what was behind the defensiveness, I could see Ben was hesitant to say for fear of hurting her feelings. "She'll probably just be upset."

Looking at her to read her, I said, "She's a big girl. I think she can handle it." Having an idea of what he was feeling, given some of our previous individual sessions, I also said, "You can either tell her, and trust that we will be able to work through whatever it is, or you can continue to say nothing, and increase the resentment and distance you're both feeling."

He finally explained what was making him so mad about their financial situation. She was a little taken aback by his true feelings. She had taken pride in being financially intelligent, while he felt she often made poor financial decisions. I suggested that being open and honest with each other was probably better in the long run. They might need to practice being okay with the possibility of saying something potentially hurtful, but that their love and the genuineness were worth the risk.

I continued, "I'm sure you've noticed that when you are both so concerned about not hurting each other's feelings that it gets in the way of even talking about important or sensitive issues. It drives a wedge that affects all aspects of the relationship. Of course, you want to be as kind as you can be while being honest with each other. You still have to be willing to put your real self out there, in order for genuine connection to occur. It may feel emotionally risky sometimes, but you both know you love each other. We can work through your true feelings."

In this chapter, we'll discuss five important reasons why talk is one of the essential ingredients of a sextraordinary marriage. The forms of talk needed for nurturing intimacy are: 1) talking to connect, 2) talking to teach, 3) talking to learn, 4) talking to help close mental windows, and 5) talking to arouse. Before we dive into these topics, let's talk briefly about some of what gets in the way of couples talking together about sex.

Why We Don't Talk about Sex

Sex is one of the most taboo subjects around. Many husbands and wives go throughout their lives having sex, yet rarely—if ever—do they have good, instructive conversations about their sexual relationship. If you can't talk about sex, it becomes even more taboo, more emotionally charged, and more difficult to adequately discuss. Plenty of comedy routines use jokes about how much men despise "talking," especially about feelings. Fear of being vulnerable is one of the main reasons people hesitate to share important information about themselves. It can be scary. Intimacy can make you feel exposed and vulnerable by allowing another into your heart, mind and soul in an open, honest and transparent relationship.

Good communication is an act of faith. You are trusting that the other person won't purposefully hurt you or use your words against you. Good communication works best in an atmosphere of honesty, mixed with emotional safety and trust. Communicating about daily logistics in our marriages or emotions is difficult enough. If we move to a whole new level of talking about sex, things can get more difficult, for the following reasons:

- **Embarrassment.** Sex is very personal and private. Even in marriage, it can feel pretty taboo to talk about openly. It's not a commonly discussed subject, so it can feel awkward and embarrassing.

- **Too personal.** Some feel that sex is so personal or sacred that it shouldn't be talked about...even with one's spouse. One woman shared with me, "Your book has taught me to be open and communicate with my husband about things I felt were so sacred they should not be talked about very much. Somewhere I developed the idea that once you know the mechanics of sex, you no longer needed to discuss it. My eyes have now been opened to the necessity of communicating our thoughts and needs about sex."

- **Negative conditioning.** If the topic of sex has been shame-filled, or mostly fear-based in your past or even current relationship, then it's going to feel like an inappropriate or dangerous subject. If there's also been abuse or other negatively impacting sexual experiences in your past, then it will also feel scary and off-limits to talk about sex.

- **Lacking intimate education.** Feeling unsure about your sexual knowledge, or not knowing your personal preferences, can make sex even more difficult to talk about openly. Because of women's different wiring and sexual conditioning, women may not be as tuned in to their sexuality. Many a husband has asked his wife what she likes, or what he could do differently, only to have her say, "I don't know." There's not much to talk about when that's the answer to most of the questions.

- **No example to follow.** How often have you heard anyone discuss sex openly, appropriately and confidently? At a conference, I asked the audience when the last time was that they had heard anything positive said about sex in an open and confident way. Only one man in the audience of at least 200 people raised his hand. He had recently attended another conference where the presenter had said some positive things about sex in marriage. I also asked them how many had received a sex talk from their parents before marriage that was more than just, "Do you have any questions for me?" Only a few hands went up. That's not good. We must do better than that if we want to have good, healthy, intimate marriages. We have also got to do better if we want our kids to be able to have sextraordinary marriages.

- **Don't know what's okay and what isn't.** Another dilemma for many concerned couples is a lack of understanding about what's "okay" sexually. Many lack confidence about finding answers and making peace with their particular resolutions to those difficult questions. (Review Chapter 2 - "Thoughts" for help in determining answers to such questions.)

- **Think talking about it indicates a problem.** Sex is supposed to just be easy and natural for everyone, right?! So, if we have to talk about it, then something must be wrong. Sexual compatibility is a learned behavior in marriage. Regardless of how knowledgeable one might be, it will still take a fair bit of communication to share and learn each other's intricacies and preferences.

- **Expect spouse to be a mind reader.** We secretly hope that we won't have to talk about sex, because our spouse will just miraculously read our mind, magically knowing what we like and want (even if we don't know ourselves)—not to mention *how* and *when* to do what we might like or want. This is an unrealistic expectation, and a sure recipe for disaster. Carmen felt that her husband should just know what to do, like all the guys on TV and in the movies. This is one of the dangers of getting our sex education from the media. It's rarely based in reality of what is real for a husband and wife.

It can be daunting to dive into the deep end of talking about sex with your spouse. It might help if you first go through this list above together, and discuss which items may be inhibiting factors for you. Discuss what keeps you from talking more openly about your intimate sexual relationship.

1. Talking to Connect

Our first purpose for talk is "Talking to Connect." Connecting conversation is the kind of talk that happens throughout the day and at the dinner table. It's what happens during pillow talk at night, or on date night. Both husband and wife need to be able to express their thoughts, feelings, and opinions with each other openly and honestly. Each must truly feel heard.

This "verbal intimacy" includes self-disclosure and honesty. It requires letting yourself be vulnerable. It requires accepting your spouse's vulnerability and tending it carefully. Trusting and being trusted by your spouse with your inner-most thoughts and feelings can be incredibly bonding and intimate. It's letting yourself be truly known—inside and out. To know your spouse means to know their heart, mind, and soul. Communication is a profound way to truly know and be known—to see and be seen. It's that emotional nakedness that bonds us so completely that it makes physical nakedness so much richer and more rewarding.

Sometimes husbands and wives see communication differently. Men tend to view communication primarily as a way to resolve a problem. Women may simply be interested in talking as a way to share and connect emotionally or explain their thoughts. For husbands to connect well with their wives, they need to listen to *understand* rather than to *fix*. You'll find a fabulous video online created by Jason Headley entitled, "It's Not about the Nail." This video humorously and exquisitely illustrates this gender difference regarding how and why men and women communicate. I often encourage couples to watch this video to help them better understand each other's communication needs.[3]

Steve and Tonia provided an excellent example of the need to work through their communication differences and learn to interact more effectively:

> *Steve and Tonia hadn't been married long before their conflicting understandings, and differing needs for communication, began to cause problems. Tonia longed for them to share their thoughts and feelings with each other. This helped her feel close and connected. Steve viewed her attempts to communicate as either interruptions, or as a means of bringing up problems that often couldn't be fixed. He felt a bit panicked and wanted to avoid the confrontations. Tonia felt he was simply ignoring her needs. She interpreted his actions as a message that he didn't care about her. This caused her to panic. She began to pursue him more intently to get him to talk to her. This created a downward spiral in their relationship. Both began to experience communication as a dreaded—even dangerous—endeavor.*
>
> *We discussed the idea that her escalating desire to talk to him was really her moving into a state of emotional emergency. She was starving for verbal intimacy through conversation—much like a man might starve for sexual intimacy. She felt perilously insecure to have to ask for this form of intimate connection. No husband or wife wants to have to ask (or beg) for their desired form of intimacy, any more than a man wants to have to ask for sex. Both people want the other to willingly want to, simply because of their love for each other.*
>
> *We addressed the anxiousness and intensity she exhibited in wanting him to listen to her. He felt flooded emotionally to where he felt he could only fight back or flee. Such an unproductive cycle of communication needed to be broken. This required them to understand each other better and work on their approaches. They needed to learn to address and respond to each other in healthier, more effective ways. Ultimately, this allowed them to both feel safe, loved, and connected.*

Openly expressing one's self is easier for some than it is for others. Listening is also easier for some than it is for others. My husband and I initially were a perfect complement to each other because I was great at talking, and he was great at listening. Over time, marriage tends to require both partners to be good at both sides of the communication equation—speaking and listening.

I remember a poignant moment in our marriage when my husband told me he wasn't really feeling heard. I didn't really get it until he said, "You ask me questions so quickly, that I'm still working out my response to your first question when you're on your fourth question. I need a little more time to think through things than you do. That's probably why I don't say much."

In that moment, I got it. I had an opportunity to develop greater understanding and patience, so that I could love and communicate with my husband better. I had to practice being okay with people processing things differently than me. I have needed to use those same skills with our kids and my clients. Husband and wife both need to be good at talking, as well as listening. While I worked on listening more effectively, my husband worked on speaking up a little more. After all these years, we've gotten pretty good at communicating to connect!

Many couples have an imbalance in their communication styles and abilities. To level the playing field, I often suggest that clients communicate with each other in writing on important or sensitive subjects. The spouse who is quicker to communicate verbally or get defensive no longer has the verbal advantage. The spouse who is less likely to say what they think for fear of a negative reaction is now able to communicate and be heard more fully. Neither can interrupt or shut down the conversation with anger or defensiveness or silence. Written communication can create a safe space for both to fully process their thoughts and the other's responses allowing for better connecting communication.

Talking as Emotional Connection

Throughout this book, I refer to the fact that for most women, it's emotional connection that fuels our feelings of desire. Emotional connection can happen in a variety of ways, since there are a variety of love languages. Connection is most often accomplished through verbal and nonverbal communication. There's just something about thinking out loud, and sharing our feelings, that helps us feel connected.

Janie and her husband had been so busy lately. He'd been out of town for work a lot, so they hadn't had much time to talk at all. Janie said, "When we don't talk enough, it's like the Wi-Fi connection is weak. We have to talk more until we can get the strength of the connection back up. I start feeling lonely and a little insecure when we go too long without talking and connecting. I literally just want to know what he's thinking and feeling. It doesn't even really matter what he says."

If finding things to talk about is sometimes hard in your marriage, there are many resources available. One of my favorite books is *365 Questions for Couples* by Dr. Michael J. Beck. It's filled with questions that couples can ask each other. It's a great way not only to emotionally connect, but also to get to know each other better. It gives couples something else to talk about besides the basics of kids, work, finances, etc. You can also search for couples questions online, which make for great date nights or pillow talk material. You'll find some Couples Questions in Chapter 8 - "Technique" or in the Appendix.

There was a time in our difficult, busy lives with young children that our date night consisted primarily of finding a quiet place to park and talk. I did most of the talking to unload my frustrations and fears. We practiced a form of active listening called the Couples Dialogue.[4] It gave me an opportunity to talk through my thoughts and feelings, allowing me to feel heard, validated, and empathized with. It lifted my heavy load at the time. It was a true gift of love for my husband to provide this form of emotional connection. It paid great dividends in helping me to feel closer and more connected to him. It ultimately paved the way for me to work diligently on the forms of connecting that were important to my husband.

Such communication as a form of emotional connection is what couples can nurture "outside the bedroom," making it easier for wives to decide to "go there" when "inside the bedroom." Talking in connecting ways allows couples to live at a "40," on a 0 to 60 scale. It makes it so much easier for women to get to a state of "wanting to connect sexually" than if she has to start at 0.

Talking to Connect Activities

Some activities couples can do to talk to connect are:
* Ask each other fun couples questions. This help you get to know each other better—beyond the basics.
* Communicate by actively listening. Repeat back what the other has said, until they feel understood, before you respond with your own thoughts. You can find the Couples Dialogue process to follow along in my book, *And They Were Not Ashamed: Strengthening Marriage through Sexual Fulfillment.*[5]
* Share your thoughts and feelings by doing the "9 Core Emotions" exercise (Chapter 8 - "Technique"). This is an opportunity to reveal more of your day-to-day experiences and related emotions. It provides deeper insight into each other's inner world.
* Read articles or books together about relationships, and discuss how the principles might apply to your marriage.
* Read anything to each other. One woman loved to have her husband read to her just to hear the soothing sound of his voice. She described how it felt like that familiar comfort of a mother reading to her child.

How Your Thoughts Affect Talk and Tone

It's not just the words being spoken that couples need in order to feel connected. Talking and listening may seem fairly straightforward. If you add in the element of what you're thinking while you're speaking, then that's where couples invariably get into trouble.

Think of nonverbal and verbal communication as having the 80/20 rule. Eighty percent of the weight in a conversation goes to the nonverbal message. It far outweighs the 20% that goes to the words that are actually said. As you say words to each other, what you are thinking and your other facial and bodily expressions are what come through the loudest. The nonverbal message is felt much more profoundly. This is what we refer to as your "tone" or the "attitude" that was sent along with the words.

In my husband's and my "talk dates," if my husband was thinking how boring it was to listen to my concerns, or if he was taking offense about something I said, then I would have sensed that message from him much stronger than anything he could have said. Thankfully, my husband's loving thoughts matched his kind and caring words—creating connection instead of conflict.

Kyle and Julie struggled with their communication, especially because of the thoughts and feelings behind what they were saying. If their words were technically neutral, but the thoughts and feelings behind them were that of impatience or frustration, then the communication would feel incongruent. The weight of the communication would go to the nonverbal message where negative thoughts were being sent.

We often say things that seem reasonable, but the message is perceived negatively because of the thoughts of the sender. Saying the word "Fine" can mean "Sure, that's okay with me," or it can mean "Fine, go ahead, but I'm gonna be ticked if you do!" The sender can either radiate a feeling of love, or a negative emotion depending on the thoughts behind their words.

I explained to Kyle and Julie a common concept I come across in counseling with couples. Couples need to just assume that whatever they are *thinking* when talking is what their spouse is going to "hear" the most. This was definitely affecting their communication. In our sessions, I'd ask things like, "Now, what does 'tone' mean again?" I wanted to see how they were doing at understanding and really getting it. Kyle would quickly add, "Tone is actually what I am thinking and feeling when I am speaking. That's the message that is coming through louder than my words." He was right on.

Kyle was a confident and capable man, but the tone he was inadvertently sending his wife with his words said, "I know better than you do. You should think this way, or do things my way because I've thought it through better." Not being aware of his nonverbal message, he was creating a lot of defensiveness and disconnect in Julie. He reluctantly acknowledged that he may have been thinking those kinds of things.

No wonder she wasn't terribly excited to be sexually intimate with him. They were missing some mutual sharing through Talk as a form of closeness and connection. She was trying to be a "good wife" and meet his needs, but that translated into her mostly giving him "duty sex" rather than "making love." Husbands generally don't want "duty sex" or "charity sex" as the main fare. They want to connect at a deeper level than just the physical, even when they may not fully realize it at times.

It took some time for Kyle to get better at recognizing his thoughts and feelings, and then go about changing them. He needed to work on refraining from constantly sending a nonverbal message that was disparaging to Julie. Instead of negative thoughts about her lack of sexual efforts, he had to practice a more surrendered state of faith about her and their sexual relationship. He needed to develop the habit of having thoughts like, "It's okay if she doesn't change this or that. I'm going to love and cherish her anyway." This feeling from Kyle was needed to reduce Julie's resentment and make him safer for her emotionally. He got there in time. She was happily able to respond to him sexually so much more genuinely and deeply.

"Couples need to just assume that whatever they are thinking while they are talking is what their spouse is going to 'hear' the most."

2. Talking to Teach

Talking to teach requires a willingness to share intimate insights about yourself. It requires an emotionally safe environment where neither spouse will be dismissed or denigrated. Talking to teach is primarily the sender's responsibility. Spouses can't read minds without you first informing them of your intimate intricacies. Sexual communication certainly helps partners educate each other about their sexual wants, needs, and preferences. A couple's sexual satisfaction is enhanced by the frequency and quality of sex talk between husband and wife.[6]

If couples don't or can't talk to teach each other about their intimate thoughts, feelings, likes, dislikes, etc., then couples will have a hard time creating a mutually enjoyable and passionate intimate relationship. This husband agreed that he had no clue about his wife sexually, and needed more information…especially from his wife.

After reading your book, I was amazed how much I misunderstood about intimacy. My thinking has flipped 180 degrees. My wife laughs at me now that finally, after 10 years of marriage, I have a clue about women sexually. I thought I knew all there was to know, but I actually didn't. I can now love my wife so much better than ever before. I know now that we do need to understand our wives better. We need to know how they think, and how they experience intimacy… especially as a guy.

It was especially surprising how our communication improved just from talking about intimacy. At first it was very uncomfortable. It was even somewhat painful to hear some of the things my wife had to say about sex. But in the end, I felt more emotionally close to my wife. I felt so much more love for her than I ever had. It's been amazing! I'm so glad we've learned to talk about this subject. I'm so glad she was willing to share such personal and private insights with me.

As we are discussing "Talking to Teach," it may be fun here to take a pop quiz. In your Sexual Self-Discovery Journal, write down five specific things you think your spouse likes most during lovemaking. Share your list with your spouse to find out how well you each did at knowing each other sexually.

20 Questions–Your Conversation Starter about Sex

One way to help you identify and talk about your sexual turn-ons and turn-offs is to start with my 20 conversation-starter questions about sex found in Chapter 9 - "Tuned In." This exercise makes it easier for you and your spouse to learn important insights about each other, from each other. It's an opportunity to discuss specifics of your sexual relationship.

One or both of you might feel a little gun-shy about sharing such intimate information. It's important to remember that no one and no book can teach your spouse about your specific sexual accelerators (or brakes) better than you can. Both husband and wife need to be willing and able to identify their turn-ons and share them with each other. This is how couples learn each other's preferences and personal arousal process.

Discussing these intimate questions can make a fun date night activity. It could be something to discuss on a walk together. You might also make this part of pillow talk, maybe once a week, with no expectation that it will lead to anything else. It might also be something you do as a part of foreplay.

Another idea some couples have found helpful is for both of them to write out their answers to each of the questions, then give them to the other. This allows each of them to read the answers in their own time and space before discussing them. This can make it easier to think through your own answers, and process the answers to your spouse's questions about sex, without feeling on the spot. Here are a couple of the questions, but you'll find the full list of 20 questions in Chapter 9 - "Tuned In."

1. What do you think are three of *my* favorite parts of lovemaking?
2. What are three (or more) of *your* favorite things about lovemaking?
3. What are three things you think I like least about sex?

As a bonus question, it may be interesting to ask each other this question: On a scale of 0 - 10 (0 = not at all to 10 = a lot) how comfortable was it to answer these questions and have this conversation? This question can create an interesting conversation.

Talking to Teach — Inside the Bedroom and Out

It's one thing to talk about sex outside the bedroom, in order to be more knowledge-able inside the bedroom, but there needs to be a form of communication inside the bed-room as well. This is especially needed as couples are first learning each other's intimacy intricacies. I'm not a fan of direct communication about what to do, what not to do and when, while in the midst of lovemaking. It's counterproductive to letting go and surren-dering into the lovemaking process.

There is a way to communicate, and even direct things by using positive reinforce-ment with "Mmmms" and "Ahhhhs," for instance, when he's moving in the right direc-tion. Wives must take some responsibility for seeing that their husbands understand their sexual needs and desires by communicating to teach inside the bedroom and out.

Talking to Share Expectations

Shauna had been disappointed and was accumulating resentment because of her hus-band's lack of effort. Instead of hoping her husband would just know what to do to make her birthday a special and romantic evening, she decided to share specifically what she was hoping for. He was more than happy to oblige. Shauna could see that her hus-band was usually trying to make her happy, but that he often failed—he didn't really understand why. Her willingness to speak up and share her expectations averted a ruined evening. It blocked her having additional resentment. Husbands are wired to please their wives. Wives, you just need to make sure your spouse knows what you want. Husbands are generally quite grateful when wives don't expect them to read minds. Her birthday was the best it had ever been, because she decided to help him out. Her communication to teach him about her wants and needs outside the bedroom also helped a lot when it came time for inside-the-bedroom activities.

3. Talking to Learn

Closely related to talking to teach is talking to learn. Talking to learn requires a willingness to ask questions, to listen, and to gather intimate information. It's a more receptive process than "talking to teach." Talking to learn is particularly important for understanding your partner. It helps you be able to know their intimate wants and needs. It helps you tune into and read your spouse, especially when in the midst of love-making. Talking to learn can be enhanced as couples read good books together and dis-cuss how to apply the material.[7]

It's pretty counterproductive to have to be directing traffic in the midst of sex, when the focus should be on relaxing into and enjoying the sensual experience. The need to communicate about sexual turn-offs and turn-ons outside the bedroom becomes para-mount. This communication makes it easier for your spouse to learn how to read you well inside the bedroom. Talking to teach and talking to learn can both be tough at times. They call for self-awareness and empathy. Self-awareness requires that you know yourself enough to understand your strengths and weaknesses. You need to know your likes and dislikes. Empathy requires the ability to think from another person's perspective. You then must suspend your own opinions in order to truly see and understand through another's eyes.

Talking to Understand Expectations

Part of learning each other's intimate needs and desires is asking about underlying assumptions we may make about each other. Laney was feeling a lot of anxiety and pressure over an anniversary getaway she and her husband were planning. She was sure her husband was expecting fabulous sex, all day, every day. She knew she couldn't meet those expectations, and didn't really want to, either. Rather than letting her mind run wild, she simply asked her husband what he was thinking their weekend would be like.

She was pleasantly surprised to learn that he wasn't expecting what she had been anticipating. He was also a lot more easy going about the whole getaway experience than she thought he'd be. He asked her what she was expecting out of the weekend as well. They were able to discuss their hopes and plans, and make a few tweaks to accommodate both of their desires. Her anxiety and wife guilt greatly diminished by willingly discussing their previously unspoken expectations.

> *John and Lynette also needed to learn to communicate about their lovemaking. They weren't great at checking out their silent assumptions. In a counseling session, Lynette was frustrated with their previous sexual encounter. She wanted to please John sexually, and found it enjoyable to touch him. She began fondling and caressing him, as she felt her own arousal rise. She was surprised, and frustrated, that he wasn't touching her as well. All she could assume was that he didn't really care about her needs. She thought he was just caught up in all the pleasure for himself.*
>
> *I had Lynette ask John what was going on for him during that time. He was visibly discouraged by her assessment of him. He explained that so many times he would try touching her only to receive a negative reaction that stopped everything. He admitted that he generally thought it was better to do nothing. After some discussion of their underlying assumptions, and their updated sexual desires, they were both able to see the other's thought process, and stop assigning negative meanings to their actions or lack thereof. John also decided he'd pay closer attention to her arousal cues. That helped him move ahead with caressing and pleasuring her body as well.*

Checking Out Assumptions

In Chapter 9 - "Tuned In," some of these similar issues of communicating to better understand each other are addressed in more depth with additional exercises. To help you start developing the ability to better understand your spouse's underlying thoughts and feelings, the following is a great exercise for checking out assumptions. Not only will this help you "talk to learn," but more especially it helps you "talk to better tune in."

Be thinking about your assumptions regarding your spouse in the following five areas. When you have a few minutes together to talk (i.e., date night, pillow talk, or instead of watching your favorite TV show), take turns sharing your assumptions about a particular topic or situation. Record your answers in your Sexual Self-Discovery Journal. Next, ask how correct your assumptions were on a scale of 0 (not at all) to 10 (right on). If you aren't right on, ask your spouse to tell you where you were off. Repeat back what they share until they genuinely feel that you understand their perspective.

This exercise helps you get better at identifying and discussing what you think your spouse thinks. It also gives them a chance to correct any misconceptions. These are just a few sample ideas to get you started, but you're welcome to use other more pertinent topics, if you prefer:

- **Sex.** I think your feelings regarding sex are _____.
- **Finances.** I assume your perception of how I handle money is_____.
- **Parenting.** If I had to say what your thoughts are regarding my strengths and weaknesses in parenting our children, I'd say they are_____.
- **Household Responsibilities.** When I don't do _____ I think you tend to feel _____. Is that correct?
- **In-laws.** I think you tend to feel _____ when we visit my family. Is that correct?

4. Talking to Close Mental Windows

Working to close one's mental windows, and redirect one's focus, is a real struggle for women. It may even be one of their biggest difficulties, particularly in the initial stages of lovemaking. Closing mental windows in order to focus on lovemaking is one of the primary purposes of Chapter 2 - "Thoughts," and Chapter 5 - "Transition."

Talking to minimize one's mental windows requires an understanding by both husband and wife; both must know that such a step is even needed to help prepare her for more engaged and enthusiastic lovemaking. It requires a willingness to attend to where her mind is first, before diving right into the physical dimension. She often needs help if her heart and mind aren't there yet. Women can learn to do this on their own, as a developed mental discipline, but it sure can't hurt if husbands will help.

One of the best tools for helping women clear their mental plates, and channel their many, varied thought processes, is for them to be able to talk things out, i.e. Pillow Talk. Sometimes they simply need to vent. This helps women be able to shift their focus from their immediate/pressing concerns over to the sexual dimension. Talking together in this way helps to fuel female sexual desire. As long as her mind is spinning with a wide variety of distracting thoughts, it will be hard for her to tune into her sensual side.

Husbands can help their wives by talking with them in a way that helps slow down their minds and clear off their mental plates. The following exercises are a few ways of communicating when a wife needs help getting focused on her spouse and on sexual intentions.

Stress List. Whether "outside the bedroom" still, or after lovemaking has been agreed upon, it can be helpful for a woman to be able to verbally walk through a list of things that are currently stressing her. You might also think of this as a way for her to verbalize all the items on her mental to-do list.

The simple act of verbalizing these things helps to dissolve them. This allows her to shift her focus elsewhere, specifically to more intimate activities. The sentence stem for these statements might be: "I feel stressed/frustrated/angry/annoyed/worried about…" or "I am stressing over…" etc.

> When Sandy got into bed one night, she felt the concerns from the day weighing her down. Wisely reading her, her husband said, "Tell me everything that's on your plate, honey." As she began to list each item, she was surprised that there weren't a lot more items on her list. Once she got to the end of everything she could think of that was bothering her, or weighing her down, she found it was easier to re-direct her attention to her husband and connect with him. She said, "If we hadn't done the verbal list I wouldn't have realized my stresses weren't as many as I thought."

Happy List. A variation of the verbal Stress List is a verbal "Happy List." Kari said the Stress List didn't work as well for her, because she didn't like to focus on the negative when she was trying to get in the mindset for being intimate. She preferred to do a list of ten things that she was happy about. That worked wonders for her to focus in on the positives in her life. She could then set it all aside to focus on making love.

Grateful List. Another variation of the Stress List and the Happy List is the "Grateful List." This is one of the more common homework assignments I give individuals and couples, because it is so beneficial to one's well-being.[8] The Grateful List can work both ways—husband to wife, wife to husband or some of both.

Some couples have found it particularly useful for the husband to verbalize 10 things he likes, loves or appreciates about his wife. This process not only commands her attention, but also does a great job of filling her emotional love bucket. It's hard not to feel closer to someone who has so many nice things to say about you. Some wives prefer the extra demand on their attention to do the verbal list themselves. The content is then focused on what they like, love and appreciate about their husbands.

Whatcha Thinking? One of my favorite and most frequently used ways to connect with my husband is to ask the simple question, "So, what do you think?" or I'll say, "Tell me something." My husband is usually a bit caught off guard by this, and then he valiantly tries to come up with something to say. He realizes that I just like to hear him share his thoughts and feelings in order to connect with him. It's an effective connector, because it helps me feel like I know my husband again. Even just a few minutes of sharing some of his thoughts, or whatever is on his mind, can help me feel reunited with him. Even one work day apart can leave couples feeling a little disconnected. Sharing in this way makes it easier to choose to be intimate, since he is no longer a stranger.

5. Talking to Arouse

One of the most profound forms of "talk" that is vital to passionately connected lovemaking is talking to arouse. This auditory stimulation could be a key missing ingredient in many couples' lovemaking repertoire. It may be just the thing to take her over the edge into ecstasy. This form of talk takes us right into the bedroom—into the heart of foreplay and arousal, stoking the fires of lovemaking. Continuing with the concept of "talking to connect," women may especially enjoy the simple act of being read to, as a form of talking to arouse. Being read to can help women connect and close her mental windows. It can also help her focus on getting intimate with her husband.

Earlier, I noted the woman who loved to have her husband read to her, simply to hear the soothing sound of his voice. She told me she had also found some romantic poetry that really lit her fire. It was a great means of foreplay for her. Like a child who loves a bedtime story, women may especially enjoy a relaxing, verbal massage as an intimate turn on.

In the midst of lovemaking itself, talking to arouse can be difficult for couples. It requires a husband to really know and read his wife well (see Chapter 9 - "Tuned In"). He needs to know what to say, how to say it, and when. It also requires a wife to be willing and able to express her pleasure and delight verbally within the lovemaking process. This is something she may have to work on if she tends to be more on the reserved side.

It may be helpful, particularly in the beginning, to simply practice making some of the sounds suggested below. She might practice in front of a mirror or in the shower. She might practice when she is alone in bed sometime. Though it may feel awkward at first, this can help women get a little more familiar with, and comfortable expressing themselves sensually.

Auditory Arousal

While it's obvious that people can be aroused visually, and by touch, we must not overlook the dimension of verbal stimulation. This use of "talk" within lovemaking is a concept I refer to as "Auditory Arousal." Auditory Arousal is defined as the utilization of some form of verbal expression or auditory stimulation, such as "Mmmms" and "Ahhhs" and "I love the way you…." This is erotic fuel for escalating arousal and desire. It may be provided by the husband, the wife, and/or both within the sexual interplay of lovemaking. There are multiple levels of Auditory Arousal defined below. As women (or their husbands) increase their verbalizations during lovemaking, it can significantly increase sexual arousal. This is due to the added mental focus and foreplay it provides. Verbal stimulation is a way for a woman to focus her attention and be more fully engaged in the lovemaking experience.

Music would also fit into the category of auditory stimulation. It too has a profound effect on lovemaking given the added ambience it generates. Auditory stimulation can help with shutting out distracting thoughts that might otherwise dominate one's mind. When one's focus is on fully experiencing and savoring every touch, kiss, and caress, while verbalizing the associated pleasure, it keeps the mental clutter from derailing the pleasure train.

Words as Touch

Words can have a profound effect on another, as if they were "touch" itself.[9] Sexual verbalizations can have an added effect, much like a sexual touch. Intimate verbal communication may be considered part of a couple's seduction process. It can help coordinate their couple sexual style. It may also help with the sexual flow of that particular sexual encounter. It's an added component of caressing each other with words and sounds—particularly to unlock the gateway to her ecstasy. Men will certainly enjoy this added active component, but it's especially beneficial for women who tend to be more auditorily stimulated than visually stimulated. It's simply a helpful addition for either spouse who has a hard time staying focused enough on the sensuality of sex to allow arousal to build. Rita shared a positive experience she had with words as a source of arousing stimulation:

> One evening my husband gave me a long, full-body massage with tropical scented lotion. He slowly talked me through a romantic imaginary island escapade. He had Hawaiian music playing in the background. I couldn't believe how aroused I was. The added verbal stimulation and the music was awesome! Normally a massage alone doesn't have quite that effect on me. He hadn't even touched any of my "hot zones," yet I was ready for him to TAKE ME!
>
> I think it also helped that there were no expectations how things were going to go that night. I felt completely relaxed. His proactive efforts to creatively steer my thoughts worked very well to keep me in the moment. His narrative kept my mind from wandering! We've learned that smooth verbal caresses can be a powerful tool in our intimacy toolbox!

Benefits of Auditory Arousal

The following are some of the passion-inducing benefits of utilizing Auditory Arousal:

- Increased focus on the sensuality of lovemaking, instead of getting stuck in one's mind.

- Increased power over mental distractions.
- Decreased self-consciousness and spectatoring (mentally observing yourself during lovemaking instead of being fully immersed in the experience).
- More open, active engagement in lovemaking instead of feeling inhibited or passive sexually.
- Increased sexual arousal and orgasmic responsiveness due to the physical and sensual focus.
- Enhanced ambience and heightened romance.
- More harmonious connection between husband and wife by staying closer to each other's state of arousal.
- Better understanding and negotiation of sexual rhythm, needs, and desires.
- Increased sexual self-confidence through immediate and affirming feedback.
- Increased surrender to the sexual experience, leading to greater sexual satisfaction and increased incidence of orgasm.
- Added variety by incorporating the sense of sound.
- Increased novelty, variety and adventure.

Levels of Auditory Arousal

This talking-to-arouse technique thankfully comes in many different shapes and sizes. The multiple levels help to clarify the concept and assist with identifying an application that fits within your comfort zone. It's specially fitted to match the individuals utilizing this form of verbal intimacy. A few beginning examples are suggested to help couples ease into using this talk-to-arouse technique.

It's important to realize that comfort with a particular level of Auditory Arousal will be dependent on a variety of factors. It's not only dependent on the person, but will also depend on the degree of their arousal within the lovemaking experience. The beginning stages of lovemaking may necessitate staying at lower levels. As arousal increases, with its unique ability to change one's entire state of being, comfort with higher levels of auditory arousal may be feasible.

AUDITORY AROUSAL	
Level	**Description**
1	**Sensual Sounds** Level 1 is a starting place for utilizing Auditory Arousal in lovemaking. This level describes the addition of the softer, yet still erotically stimulating verbal expressions of pleasure, such as "Mmmms," "Ahhhhs," "Uhhuhs," and moans. It's a great way to provide verbal reassurance of enjoyment. ***Examples:*** *"Mmmmm," "Ahhhhhh," "Uhhuh!"and "Oh Yeah!"*

2	**Sensual Communication** Level 2 Auditory Arousal steps it up from sensual sounds to include "sweet nothings." This communication may consist of erotically enhancing "sex talk," or other sensual communications. The content may be about how one is feeling, what one is experiencing, or what is happening in that moment. It might also include what one likes about what is happening, what one is doing to the other, or wants to do to the other, or what one wants to have done to them. *Examples: "I love you so much!" or "Your body is so beautiful!" or "I love it when you touch me like that!" or "I love how you kiss my neck like that!" or "I love how you look at me like that!" or "I love it when you run your fingers down my spine!" or "I love how you slowly unbutton my shirt!" or "I love it when you tease me with your tongue!" or "It turns me on when you…!"*
3	**Sharing Sensual Scenarios** Level 3 lets you escape into any sexy scenario you can create in your mind without ever having to leave your bedroom. Couples can either decide ahead of time what they want to do in this regard, or they can just let the moment take them to a moonlit beach on a deserted island, for instance. They might make love in the soft, warm sand. Couples can play verbally with many different tantalizing scenarios. This significantly enhances the ambience of the sexual experience. Couples can determine what scenarios or role playing seems appropriate to them. Every couple will feel a little different. The relationship, and your spouse, is still the sexual focus. This isn't about imagining having sex with someone else. Creating and sharing sexual scenarios and fantasies is a great way to pretend you're NOT just in your bedroom. It's a romantic opportunity to escape the realities and distractions that await after your escape into arousal. Many couples have found that sometimes, if one spouse has a particular fantasy, it may be easier, safer, and more fun even for them to mentally and verbally role play the scenario than to do it in real life. With the power of the mind, lovemaking can be an incredibly exciting experience, even when it's just make believe. *Examples: Act out making love on a secluded beach on a warm moonlit night. Act out making love in a semi-public place. Act out making love in an elevator. Act out having sex in a backseat of a car, etc.*

4	**Naughty Talk**

Level 4 is an extension of level 2, but because it tends to be further outside one's comfort zone, I define it as level 4. This level of Auditory Arousal basically ratchets things up a few notches for a sizzling, more intimate encounter. This is often what people think I mean when I talk about "Auditory Arousal." It's important to understand the differing levels. Especially as arousal increases, some women find it particularly arousing to move beyond soft and flowery expressions of love to more suggestive, rough, raw, naughty, steamy, passionate and erotic communication. Women sometimes want to be "taken" and "seduced," or want to do the seducing themselves from a more "fast and furious" state. Again, this will be dependent on the couples' sexual conditioning, their comfort levels, and their individual arousal levels.

This level 4 verbal stimulation may need to be something discussed together ahead of time. Couples may have sexual terms that, while they may be profane to use in public, can be erotic, endearing and even sacred in the context of their intimate, private experience. It's a form of communication specifically reserved for each other, and approved by both within the safety of their shared experience. It's important to remember that the state of arousal affects how we might experience or perceive things. What may seem inappropriate outside of lovemaking may be just what's needed within. For some, it might be worth it to stretch themselves to give it a try.

Husband and wife will need to be exquisitely tuned in and attentive to each other emotionally. Prior to lovemaking, they may need to discuss what feels okay. They will also need to effectively read each other's arousal level and responses to any such "sexy talk" within lovemaking. This is needed to not overdo the Auditory Arousal. Accurately executed auditory stimulation won't squelch the burgeoning passion and erotic excitement, but will enhance it. It may be a missing erotic key for some couples.

Examples: "Do me!" or "Take me!" or "I want you bad!" or "You're so hot!" or "You turn me on!" or "I want to rock you all night!" or "Talk sexy to me!" or "Do what you want with me!" or "I'm gonna do what I want with you!" or "You make me so crazy for you!"

Talk is right up there as one of the essential ingredients for a sextraordinary marriage. Talk is an element that spills over as an integral part of many of the other 12 T's throughout this book. As you consider how you're doing as a couple in the area of "Talk," think through the five forms of talk needed for nurturing intimacy: 1) talking to connect, 2) talking to teach, 3) talking to learn, 4) talking to help close mental windows, and 5) talking to arouse. See where you can shore things up in your relationship and make it even better!

Self-Evaluation - "Talk"

To give yourself a guide as to how you are doing in this dimension, how would you currently rate yourself and your spouse overall in the area of "Talk"? Write your thoughts in your Sexual Self-Discovery Journal. — *I talk with my spouse in ways that help us connect. I can share my inner self. I am comfortable talking with my spouse about sex to better understand each other intimately. I utilize sensual communication as an arousing part of lovemaking.*

RATING (0 - disagree to 10 - agree):   You _____   Your Spouse _____

ACTION ITEMS — Chapter 6 - "Talk"

- Before talking about sex with your spouse, go through the list of "Why We Don't Talk about Sex" items, and discuss which ones are inhibiting factors in your intimate sexual relationship.
- As connecting activities:
  - Ask each other fun couples questions to get to know each other beyond the basics.
  - Communicate by actively listening, where you repeat back what the other has said, until they feel understood, before you respond with your own thoughts.
  - Share your thoughts and emotions by doing the "9 Core Emotions" exercise (discussed in Chapter 8). This is an opportunity to reveal more of your emotion-based experiences and see deeper into each other's inner world.
  - Read articles or books and discuss how the principles might apply to your relationship.
  - Read to each other.
- Take the pop quiz to highlight "Talking to Teach." Write down five specific things you think your spouse likes most during lovemaking. Share your list with your spouse to find out how well you each did at knowing each other sexually.
- Use the "20 Questions — Conversation Starter about Sex" (listed in full in Chapter 8 – "Technique") to talk in ways that help you teach each other about your specific wants, needs, and preferences sexually.
- Be thinking about your assumptions regarding your spouse in the following five areas. When you have a few minutes together to talk (i.e., date night, pillow talk or instead of watching your favorite TV show), take turns sharing your assumptions about a particular topic or situation, then inquire as to how correct

your assumptions are on a scale of 0 (not at all) to 10 (right on). If you are less than right on, ask them to let you know where you are off. Repeat back what they share until they genuinely feel that you understand their perspective. This exercise can help you get better at voicing and discussing what you think your spouse thinks.

- *Sex* — My assumptions about your feelings regarding sex are…
- *Finances* — My assumptions about your perspective regarding how I handle our money are…
- *Parenting* — If I had to say what your thoughts are regarding my strengths and weaknesses in parenting our children, I'd say they are…
- *Household Responsibilities* — When I don't do _____ I think you tend to feel _____. Is that correct?
- *In-laws* — I think you tend to feel _____ when we visit my family. Is that correct?

- Utilize the following exercises to help communicate in a way that can help close your mental windows: Stress List, Happy List, Grateful List, Whatcha Thinking?
- Practice making some of the auditory arousal sounds suggested in the chapter. You might practice in front of a mirror, in the shower, or when you are alone in bed sometime. Though it may feel awkward at first, this can help you get a little more familiar with and comfortable expressing yourself sensually.
- As you consider how you're doing as a couple in the area of "Talk," think through the five forms of talk needed for nurturing intimacy: 1) talking to connect, 2) talking to teach, 3) talking to learn, 4) talking to help close mental windows, and 5) talking to arouse, and see where you can shore things up in your relationship.

———— ✦ ————

NOTES

1 Hess, J. A., and Coffelt, T. A., "Verbal Communication about Sex in Marriage: Patterns of Language Use and Its Connection with Relational Outcomes," *Journal of Sex Research* 49(6) (2012): 603-612. doi:10.1080/00224499.2011.619 282.

2 Timm, T. M., and Keiley, M. K., "The Effects of Differentiation of Self, Adult Attachment, and Sexual Communication on Sexual and Marital Satisfaction: A Path Analysis," *Journal of Sex & Marital Therapy* 37(3) (2011): 206-223. doi:10.1080/0092623X.2011.564513.

3 Headley, Jason, "It's Not About the Nail," YouTube video, 1:41. Posted May 22, 2013. https://youtu.be/-4EDhdAHrOg

4 Brotherson, Laura M., *And They Were Not Ashamed: Strengthening Marriage through Sexual Fulfillment*. Boise, ID: Inspire Book, 2004, 199.

5 Ibid.

6 MacNeil, S., and Byers, E., "Role of Sexual Self-Disclosure in the Sexual Satisfaction of Long-Term Heterosexual Couples," *Journal of Sex Research* 46(1) (2009): 3-14. doi:10.1080/00224490802398399.

7 Lankveld, J., "Self-Help Therapies for Sexual Dysfunction," *Journal of Sex Research* 46(2/3) (2009): 143-155. doi:10.1080/00224490902747776.

8 Emmons, Robert A., and Mccullough, M. E., "Counting Blessings Versus Burdens: An Experimental Investigation of Gratitude and Subjective Well-being in Daily Life," *Journal of Personality & Social Psychology* 84(2) (2003): 377-389.

9 Kogan, I., "When Words are Used to Touch," *Psychoanalytic Psychology* 20(1) (2003): 117-130. doi:10.1037/0736-9735.20.1.117.

CHAPTER VIEW

SECTION I — OUTSIDE THE BEDROOM
   The Missing Ingredient of Touch
   Touch Homework with No Strings Attached
   Therapeutic Touch
   Brainstorming Affectionate Behaviors
   Restoring the Lost Art of Kissing
   The Bliss of a Kiss
      Kissing Inhibitors
      Kissing Homework
   Re-awaken the Pleasure of Making Out
   The Kissing Closet

SECTION II — INSIDE THE BEDROOM
   No May Not Always Mean No
   Talk and Touch Her Into It
   Intimate Touching, But Not Sex Yet
   The Blissful Caress
      How To's of the Blissful Caress
      Benefits of the Blissful Caress
   Naked Cuddling
   Clitoral Stimulation — Is She Getting Enough?
Self-Evaluation - "Touch"
ACTION ITEMS — Chapter 7 - "Touch"

Chapter 7

TOUCH — TOUCH ME INTO IT

I feel like my husband is always groping me. He doesn't hold my hand when we're walking together. He doesn't put his arm around me when we watch TV. He doesn't even hug me unless I ask, but he's all hands when I'm trying to make dinner or when we're in the bedroom. Is it too much to ask for him to be just tender and sweet and affectionate sometimes just for no good reason other than to be sweet?

It's hard for me to want to be intimate with him when it feels like I'm just a sexual object to him. If we had more loving touch that didn't have sexual overtones or always lead to something, then it might be easier for me to want to have sex with him. It's kind of funny that I feel touch deprived and touch resistant all at the same time.

The primary purpose for this chapter and this "T" for "Touch" is two-fold: 1) to be sure couples are including enough non-sexual touch or affection in their relationship (outside the bedroom), and 2) to make sure couples are seeing that she gets enough (inside the bedroom) Touch—especially clitoral stimulation—as a part of lovemaking.

SECTION I — OUTSIDE THE BEDROOM

The Missing Ingredient of Touch

A missing intimate ingredient for many women is non-sexual touch or affection that doesn't always have strings attached to sex. Before marriage, there is generally plenty of affection between a man and a woman, but after marriage many women argue that once sex is an option, then the tender touch that used to occur is all but forgotten. In a rush to get to the "good stuff," many men overlook the need for loving touch outside the bedroom as a pleasure in its own right. When this happens, women begin to shut themselves off from all touch when it is only associated with and experienced as a part of sex.

There is a message that unwittingly gets sent to wives when sexual touch is the predominant touch they receive. The message is that they are only appreciated for their sexuality rather than being seen and loved as a whole person. When there is an abundance of affectionate, non-sexual touching in marriage, it reinforces the message that a woman is loved and valued by her husband in all ways—not just in the bedroom.

I like the term shared by one husband that touch is "Skin Time" with couples having a Minimum Daily Requirement almost like a necessary vitamin—Vitamin "T" for Touch. There's something magical about skin-to-skin contact, and all humans need it. We get it as babies, and then spend much of our time craving it as we grow older. Skin Time can be had by holding hands as often as possible. You might touch your honey's face, neck, arms, or even give your spouse a good hand or foot massage. That can be heavenly. Skin time is obviously easy to accomplish when making love. The invitation here is to find more ways to enjoy skin-to-skin contact without it always being sexual.

"A missing intimate ingredient for many women is non-sexual touch or affection that doesn't always have strings attached to sex."

Touch Homework with No Strings Attached

I often assign "Touch Homework" to couples. This is where they set aside some time—maybe on Sunday night after kids are in bed—where they cuddle, hold hands, practice 10-second hugs, or just lie next to each other purely for the pleasure of intimate physical contact, both knowing that sex is not on the menu for that night. What this touch homework does is helps husbands and wives begin to enjoy non-sexual touch again all by itself. It helps wives to re-train themselves and their husbands that tender touch doesn't always have to lead to something else. When the reservoir of affection is filled back up in a marriage, the wife feels more loved and wanted as a whole person—not just sexually. This helps her say yes to sex much more easily.

Therapeutic Touch

Touch has the power to heal. Human touch induces the release of the cuddling, bonding hormone oxytocin, which creates a wonderful feeling of comfort and connection.[1] Skin-on-skin contact decreases physical stress by sending a message to the adrenal glands to lighten up on the production of the stress hormone, cortisol. This results in a relaxation response.[2][3] Oxytocin released during affectionate touch or the orgasmic response has an amnesiac effect that lets you feel that all is well in the world for awhile.[4] The parts of the brain that govern fear, anxiety and stress are shut off, inhibiting the release of cortisol. The rush of oxytocin is a great reason to get in the habit of sharing 10 or even 20 second hugs.[5] There's nothing more therapeutic than loving, tender touch when one is hurt, afraid, stressed or lonely.

I've often told my family (somewhat in jest) that if I'm ever in the hospital, they just need to make sure someone is always there to hold my hand the whole time. They think that's a little over the top, but I know that's what I would want and need most during such a time. I remember being really sick during finals one semester in college. A friend of mine skipped her own classes to sit by my bed and hold my hand while I rested. It was so calming and reassuring. One wife shared that when she is feeling stressed or overwhelmed, she will often walk up to her husband and ask him to just hold her for a minute as she melts into his arms. It's as if all is well in the world again after a warm embrace.

When I wake up in the morning, I sometimes walk into the office where my husband is already working and sit on his lap just to connect with him for a few moments. It almost feels like I am plugging myself into a power source. Human touch provides a power supply that needs to be honored in its own right, not just as a part of the act of lovemaking. Don't overlook the endowment of emotional connection that comes from non-sexual affection. It can be even more powerful, at times, than the act of lovemaking.

That wonderful hormone oxytocin is released with a variety of touch—including hand holding, kissing, caressing and orgasm. It's even released simply with eye contact. This reinforces the need for eye contact (and undivided attention) during conversation, and may be especially powerful during lovemaking. Women especially appreciate the restraint that accompanies affectionate touch when it doesn't lead to sex. This act of restraint can create deep feelings of trust, love and connection, and may even fuel desire for future sexual encounters.

Brainstorming Affectionate Behaviors

I encourage couples to make a point to increase the loving touch between them. You and your spouse could sit down together and brainstorm different ways you both could be more affectionate outside the bedroom. Here are a few ideas to get started:

- Hold hands whenever you are walking together.
- Brush up against each other in the kitchen, bathroom or walk-in closet instead of avoiding each other.
- Sit close enough on the couch to touch in some way.
- Sit close enough to touch when at a movie, church or some other function.
- Seek each other out for a welcome home hug or a goodbye kiss.
- Give each other a foot, back or hand massage…with no strings attached!

Restoring the Lost Art of Kissing

As we make our way towards bedroom-kinds-of-touching, another missing ingredient for many couples is kissing and making out. Joanne hates kissing. She and her husband rarely kiss inside the bedroom or out. It's simply not on the menu. Many couples have lost that lovin' feeling when it comes to kissing. When was the last time you and your

spouse just made out for the fun of it? When couples are dating, kissing is usually a significant part of their connection and courtship. It's generally an exciting and anticipated
experience. But after marriage, many couples seem to abandon sensual, lip-to-lip (face or
neck) kissing. The pleasures of sex itself often overtake the simpler sensual pleasures of a
kiss.

Sex therapist Dagmar O'Connor suggests that kissing is actually far more intimate
than sexual intercourse. Over time, couples may avoid kissing for deeper reasons. When
couples kiss, they cannot depersonalize the experience the way they more easily can
when just "having sex." Kissing as part of lovemaking makes the experience more intimate and connected by helping to keep the relationship and each other more present.[6]

One wife confided that this was especially true for her. She shared, "If I have any
resentments toward my husband on my mind, it is hard for me to kiss him. I think kissing (or my lack of desire thereof) is usually a good indicator for me that we need to talk
some things out."

The Bliss of a Kiss

It's time to learn to love kissing again, whether it be in the course of lovemaking or
as a standalone activity. Let's discuss some of the common complaints that get in the
way of kissing. We'll then suggest some "kissing lessons" for what you could do to more
fully enjoy and engage in the bliss of kissing. How cool would that be if we all became
intentional and expert smoochers to regularly enjoy the bliss of a kiss! This discussion is
for both those who may need some encouragement for getting back into the swing of
kissing again, and for those who already enjoy kissing. Hopefully you'll get your creative
juices going to expand your kissing repertoire even more.

Kissing Inhibitors

What are some of the main inhibitors of blissful kissing? Here are six of the common
complaints I hear from wives about why they don't like to kiss:

1. *"It always leads to sex."* Many women hesitate to kiss or touch at all because
   they come to believe it will lead to something more. The touch homework above
   to re-learn the pleasure of affection, for its own sake, is critical here. Certainly the
   focus for this chapter is to also restore kissing to a standalone pleasure. It's also
   important for women to address the need to enjoy what might follow the kissing
   as well, so they can enjoy it as a lead-in to lovemaking. In this book, each chapter
   is designed to address a component of a woman's sexual wiring where she may be
   living below her potential for intimate pleasure and connection. Husbands can
   help by making sure their wives get to experience the bliss of a kiss without it
   always leading somewhere.

2. *"I can't stand kissing when either of us has bad breath."* Both husband and
   wife need to practice good oral hygiene. One husband told me how he always
   puts a new stick of gum in his mouth on his way home from work just so that

it is more enjoyable for his wife to kiss him when he gets home. It goes without saying to make it a point to brush your teeth and use mouthwash before an anticipated intimate event. You might also be sure to have mints or gum on hand for an unexpected opportunity.

3. *"We don't kiss (during lovemaking) because I'm not really in the mood anyway, and I just want to get it over with."* In Chapter 8 - "Technique," you'll see the rocket diagram with four steps providing Fuel for Female Sexual Desire. With this kissing inhibitor, it could be any of the four steps that might be impeding intimate kissing: 1) The wife does not have enough warmth in the emotional climate of the relationship to fuel her sexual desire; 2) The mental switch hasn't been flipped to decide to "go there" sexually; 3) There hasn't been enough connecting conversation to help "talk her into it" as part of her emotional foreplay; or 4) She has not received or won't let her husband provide the touch necessary to help her up the arousal scale in order for her to want to fully participate sexually. She may just be tired. But hopefully that is not her regular response.

4. *"It's hard to really kiss if we haven't talked or connected at all during the day."* Kissing (and lovemaking) requires some degree of emotional connection for women to respond most easily. Hopefully Chapter 3 - "Tenderness" made it abundantly clear how important emotional intimacy is. Husbands can help by making sure they are reaching out throughout the day in simpler ways to show their wives that they care. That may be a hug when you leave for work, a phone call or text at lunchtime, or a thoughtful act when you get home. It really does help to have some caring thoughtfulness throughout the day to warm her intimate fires.

5. *"I get grossed out because the kisses get too slobbery."* While some women tend to like their lip-locking a little less wet, her receptiveness to a kiss may be influenced by her current state of arousal. As couples learn more about what her arousal process looks like in Chapter 8 - "Technique," they can both be better able to recognize the level of passion she may be ready for at any given time. This can be a pretty easy fix for most couples if they realize, or make it known, that this is an issue. Many husbands simply don't realize that keeping their kisses a little drier can make a big difference in her responsiveness to him, especially in the earlier stages of arousal.

6. *"I get claustrophobic—like I can't breathe."* This is amazingly common for many women who hesitate to kiss. Feeling claustrophobic can again be a function of her level of arousal, but husbands sometimes just come on too strong in the beginning. And if you've had even one really bad experience of feeling suffocated or overpowered while kissing, it's enough to develop a negative association and want to avoid it. Rachel struggled with allergies, so it was already hard for her to breathe while kissing. She began using a nasal spray that helped

keep her airways open. She found that being able to breathe deeply through her nose during the face-to-face contact of kissing helped her get enough arousal, and oxygen, so that she could climax. Before using the nasal spray, she had a hard time reaching orgasm. She grinned when she said, "I think oxygen is pretty important in lovemaking!" By changing the dynamics of kissing between husband and wife, you can unlearn negative associations and replace them with new, more positive and liberating experiences.

Maybe husbands and wives need some kissing lessons. In the kissing homework that follows, I suggest that women take the lead to regain a sense of control regarding what goes on during kissing. This can help them learn to enjoy this kind of intimate connection better. But before we go there, it can be helpful to start with some understanding of your current pros and cons of kissing. Take a few minutes for both of you to jot down five of your favorite things about kissing and five of your least favorite things about kissing. If you can, share that information with each other prior to doing the Kissing Homework exercise below.

Kissing Homework

We've talked about some common complaints wives have about kissing. Now let's talk about some specific suggestions for changing the kissing dynamics in your relationship. We want to help restore kissing (and making out) to its pre-marital status as something anxiously anticipated. You might consider this going to "kissing school." One smart-alec husband asked if this kissing homework was akin to giving his wife "lip-service." Funny guy!

The following five suggestions are for you to use or adapt to your situation until you find something that works for increasing your enjoy-ability of kissing your sweetheart. Let's begin the kissing lessons:

1. ***Talk to Your Spouse.*** When wives are ready and willing to work on this aspect of touch and intimate connection, it is important for them to let their husbands know. It is much easier for husbands to participate effectively if they know their wife has deliberately decided to work on making kissing more enjoyable for both of them—especially as a standalone activity that doesn't always have to lead to sex. Learning to like kissing as a pleasure all its own helps to make it a more enjoyable and an anticipated aspect of lovemaking as well. Sometimes wives may not enjoy kissing, but also don't want to create a problem, either. They know they should talk about it, but prefer to avoid conflict even if it might eventually bring them closer. These women often suffer in silence just to keep the peace. This simply continues the pattern of unhealthy ways of interacting while limiting their potential for connection. Talking about preferences regarding kissing can help both spouses enjoy a closer connection and much more intimate and enjoyable lovemaking.

2. ***Choose a Time and Location.*** Wives might suggest a specific time and location to have "kissing class" to practice. The objective here is to set it up as a standalone activity with no associated pressure or expectation that it will lead to anything else. This is one of the common complaints associated with kiss resistance. This kissing exercise might be something you do on a date night if you decide to go park somewhere. It might even work best in the beginning if you simply set up a chair (with no arms) in your bedroom or walk-in closet, or somewhere else. Be creative. It's whatever works for you. The key here is for it to be somewhere different, if possible, yet private and not terribly easy for it to lead to sex. That helps to keep expectations out of the equation.

3. ***Preparation.*** Eliminate bad breath by brushing your teeth and using mouthwash. You can be clothed in whatever way is comfortable for you. Even though kissing is generally about connection, the primary purpose of this exercise may be to simply get reacquainted with the act of kissing as pleasurable. Certainly if you are willing and able to spend a little time connecting emotionally prior to this exercise, it can only help.

4. ***Kissing Session.*** Ultimately, the objective of this homework assignment is to help re-awaken the pleasure and sensuality of it all. For this first kissing lesson, the generally less interested spouse gets to go first as the "Kisser" and the other gets to be the "Kissee."

   KISSER: If the wife is the first Kisser, then she would sit on her husband's lap facing him lap dance style. I realize this is a position that is likely to be arousing to the husband. A secondary learning opportunity here is for both husband and wife to practice being okay when there is arousal, and not have to do anything about it. The Kisser gets to be fully in control of the kissing for the specified time, which lets them experience kissing without feeling overwhelmed by passion or saliva. You might just start with five minutes to ease into it. You might find it helpful to set a timer, so no one has to watch the clock. The Kisser is to simply, sensually and playfully, if possible, explore the spouse's face, lips, mouth, neck, ears, and/or eyelids with kissing, licking, nibbling, or touching in some way—be as creative as you can. There is no pressure that it will lead to something more. The less interested spouse will continue as the Kisser in these kissing sessions until they feel comfortable being the receiver. Through this assignment, the Kisser is to get comfortable with kissing again, and have the freedom to explore at their own pace and in their own way to identify what they like and how they like it.

   KISSEE: While the Kisser is in charge, the Kissee is to sit back, relax, focus, take it all in and enjoy every touch and sensation, doing their best to not exert any pressure. They are to just *receive*. The Kissee needs to be very much the receiver, NOT the kisser. That may mean the Kissee doesn't even kiss back, and definitely bridles their excitement—otherwise that could put pressure on the Kisser. When the Kissee can't kiss back, the Kisser gets to experience kissing without being drowned by saliva or having any other expectations involved. The key in this step is for the less interested spouse to experience being in control of and to be the initiator of the kisses.

5. ***Add Creativity.*** This kissing exercise is a sensual exploration to really pay attention to the touch and the sensations, so be creative. Be gentle, be aggressive. Switch it up and try new things. You might even try a 10-second kiss, even if it's just touching lips-to-lips with no movement for 10 seconds. It may be helpful to use a timer again. Whether these exercises are hilarious and hard to keep a straight face, or are serious business for a serious non-Kisser, it's all good. Whatever you do, try to make it fun. Both Kisser and Kissee are to relax and enjoy. Just take it slow as best you can. Allow yourself to enjoy this pleasurable delight, as if it was all new to you. Imagine you are figuring out how to kiss for the very first time. Some ideas for creativity:

   - Vary the intensity, tempo, and/or duration of the kisses.
   - Gently kiss or nibble on the Kissee's lower lip.
   - Run your tongue along the inside of the Kissee's upper lip.
   - Kiss his closed eyelid, kiss or nibble on his ear, or kiss and nibble on his neck.
   - Just barely tease his lip with the tip of your tongue.
   - Pause with your faces barely touching to simply take and breathe each other in.
   - Give butterfly kisses by fluttering your eyelashes against his skin.
   - Add some verbalization if you want, even just some Mmmm's and Ahhhh's.
   - Take in the scent of his skin as if you are breathing him in.
   - Try kissing with your eyes open as well as closed.
   - Gently tug or run your fingers through his hair.
   - Don't underestimate the power of the pause; stop and just breathe for a moment.

6. ***Watch Your Thoughts.*** As you both do this exercise, remember that whatever is going on in your mind is going to come through in your kiss, so keep it positive and lovingly focused. Kiss with conscious intention—get your mind into it, and it'll increase the pleasure for both of you. You can even engage your mind by using your imagination to fuel your fire. Think of romantic or sexy scenarios that you can play out together or just have playing through your mind. Of course, keep your thoughts on your spouse, but you can still change up the circumstances, locale or whatever else you want for variety and greater mental engagement during this sensual, oral exercise.

7. ***Share Your Experience.*** For just a few moments after the kissing exercise, each of you take a few minutes to share some of your thoughts about the experience of kissing or being kissed. It may not be a bad idea to do this kissing exercise as often as you can or at least once a week until feelings shift about kissing.

I hope you can see how identifying and addressing common complaints about kissing, along with actively engaging in kissing class, can change the experience of making out. But don't just take my word for it—try it out and see how you can make things better together.

Re-awaken the Pleasure of Making Out

I encourage couples to re-awaken the pleasure and enjoyment not only of kissing within lovemaking, but also to enjoy and engage in more kissing outside the bedroom for its own sake—you know, making out! Developing the habit of kissing affectionately and even passionately outside the bedroom every now and then will make it so much easier for that to be a welcome ingredient in lovemaking as well.

Make out on your couch, or plan to go park somewhere after date night. Before you arrive, have a conscious agreement to sensually and/or teasingly explore the other's face, lips, mouth, neck, ears, and eyelids with kissing, nibbling, touching—being as creative as possible—without any pressure or expectation that it will lead to something more. You could pause with your lips barely touching to simply take each other in. Whatever you do, be playful, tease a little, and have fun! Just remember to keep your thoughts positive. What a tantalizing adventure to make making out a fun new part of your marriage.

Some hungry husbands may not especially like the idea of kissing that doesn't lead to "something more." This is especially true when they feel that there's already not enough of the "something more" in the relationship. But learning to re-enjoy kissing for its own sake is one of the greatest ways to make it easier for lovemaking to more naturally follow a make out session. If there are specific inhibiting factors that are keeping you from engaging in this important aspect of affection and intimacy, then discuss these things with your spouse, and see if you can come up with ways to make things better for both of you.

The Kissing Closet

In addition to making time for making out, you might also create your own "kissing closet" in your kitchen pantry. It's a great way to torture your kids, and have a little fun as husband and wife as well. A kissing closet can add a bit of fun and flirtatiousness to your relationship. Our kids took issue with the fact that this kissing closet idea was technically a "kissing pantry" in the kitchen. They thought we ought to move the PDA to the closet in our bedroom. But what fun is that if we can't gross them out at the same time as having a little fun!

Part of the fun of a kissing closet (in the kitchen) is to tease your kids with appropriate public displays of affection. They may protest, but deep down it's good for them to see that their parents actually like each other. It's also a quick and easy way to steal a kiss. It could also help bring back that loving feeling with regard to kissing.

You can check out some kissing closet photos on StrengtheningMarriage.com. You'll see that there can be functional purposes of the kissing closet as well. With a husband who is a foot taller than me, it's convenient to have a nice step-stool already there for me to actually be able to reach my husband's lips without straining myself. (It looks like I still need a taller stool!)

SECTION II — INSIDE THE BEDROOM

In this chapter, we've talked about increasing non-sexual touch outside of bedroom activities. We've talked about kissing and reawakening the bliss of a kiss, and just plain old making out—both important aspects of Touch and its effect on lovemaking. Let's shift gears a little and move toward inside-the-bedroom kinds of Touch.

No May Not Always Mean No

The heading here, "No May Not Always Mean No" is likely to cause some misinterpretation or misapplication. I am trusting both husbands and wives to hear what I'm saying about the unique sexual wiring of women, and to work together to apply it appropriately to their situation as husband and wife. Given how much we've talked about the feeling of connection that must first be present, if this section is misused it will likely be apparent to both husband and wife.

I have a secret for men to know about their wives that is pretty important. I also want to apologize in advance for the fact that women can be kind of confusing sometimes, and a little hard to read if men don't fully understand how women are wired sexually. Husbands may be missing out on sexual intimacy unnecessarily because they don't understand that women tend to be a few steps away from sexual interest or desire much of the time. Men generally have a much shorter distance to get to a state of desire.

The secret is that in otherwise healthy marital relationships, "No" may not always mean "No." Of course, there are times when "No" really does mean "No." As couples develop the ability to read and tune into each other better in Chapter 9 - "Tuned In," they will know when "No" doesn't exactly mean "No." It goes without saying that in a loving, respectful relationship, one person being controlling or demanding of sexual favors is unacceptable. It runs contrary to the nature of a connected, romantic relationship. Let me share a story that may help you understand this concept—a key insight into the female psyche:

> *A client was explaining to me how she and her husband had been pretty disconnected for a couple weeks because of the busyness of their summer. One evening, her husband came and sat down by her and started rubbing her tired shoulders. She thought to herself how nice it was that her husband noticed her stress. She wondered if he also missed the closeness and wanted to reconnect.*

Then she had a horrifying thought! What if he was just trying to have sex with her, even though they had been distant for so long? Making love without feeling some emotional connection first is a pretty foreign concept to most women. They need some warm up prior to feeling connected enough for sex.

What came next confirmed her suspicion when he asked if they could have sex. She shook her head in disgust, feeling like a piece of meat. How could he even think of such a thing after giving each other the cold shoulder for a week? She explained that if her husband had just spent a few minutes talking with her first about how she was doing so that they could connect emotionally, then she could have easily been willing and able to be talked and touched into it!

Talk and Touch Her into It

The secret is that an initial cool response from a wife to a husband's advances may not really mean "No" if both understand that she may just need to be talked and touched into it first. We'll discuss this more in Chapter 8 - "Technique," but for many women, it takes four steps for her to get in the mood. It's important for women to know that a husband cannot get her in the mood if she does not first make the decision in Step 1.

Step 1: She makes a mental decision to go there.

Step 2: She needs some conversation to get her emotionally connected.

Step 3: She needs some form of touch to begin the physical arousal process.

Step 4: She can actually "feel" some desire to have sex. (Step 4 is where men generally begin.)

Now, in defense of the husband in the story, the way men are wired is that they generally connect best through sex. If things aren't going well between you and your spouse, the quickest way to close the gap for a man is to be sexually intimate. It's an amazing eraser of worries or hard feelings that a husband might be feeling. Unfortunately that's not usually the case for women. It's a funny paradox that men are wired to prefer going directly to the physical—often bypassing the talking or emotional dimension—whereas women tend to be wired to prefer to start with the emotional before they are revved up enough to move into the sexual. Couples do best to accept this reality, and then learn how to work within it effectively.

Men can come to understand and accept this wiring. They can learn to warm her up with talk and touch before diving into the sexual arena. It's a win/win for both husband and wife if he will do this. It can potentially bring about more frequent and enjoyable lovemaking opportunities. So the next time this type of scenario happens to you, I hope husbands will take this information and use it wisely to help talk and touch her into connecting sexually. You might even get lucky!

Intimate Touching, But Not Sex Yet

We can't have a discussion about Touch without highlighting the incredible value of sensual touch exercises like those suggested by many sex therapists. When there is any history of sexual difficulty, or a need to overcome past negative sexual experiences for either husband or wife, the 7-week Sensate Focus exercises like those suggested in my book, *And They Were Not Ashamed: Strengthening Marriage through Seuxl Fulfillment*,[7] not only increase the connection through touch, but also help to provide healing as well. My specialized version of Sensate Focus exercises is great for couples to learn to savor each touch or sensation and be more fully present and connected during the entire lovemaking experience. The Sensate Focus exercises encourage couples to focus on one dimension of lovemaking at a time, without strings attached to intercourse or orgasm.

These exercises are especially helpful for both husband and wife to learn to slow down, relax more fully, and savor each touch together. It may be a bit of a soul-stretching experience to embark upon these exercises and awaken dormant sensuality, but it is worth the time and effort. Husbands often teasingly suggest that we need to give out t-shirts that say, "I survived the 7-week challenge!"

The Sensate Focus exercises are a series of graduated sensual touch consisting of:

1. Nonsexual touching
2. Spooning
3. The blissful caress
4. Touching and caressing while avoiding genitals
5. Kissing
6. Touching and caressing including genitals
7. Orgasm and intercourse

It can be used as a 7-week program or as a menu. From it, you can choose to either clean the slate and start over sexually when healing is needed, or as a great way to jump-start a sexual relationship that has gone stale. Because the entire process is well laid out already in *And They Were Not Ashamed* I won't repeat it here, but let me touch on the "Blissful Caress."

The Blissful Caress

One of the uniquely exquisite forms of touch is something called the Blissful Caress. It is something you can either add to your foreplay and lovemaking repertoire, like a variation of a full-body massage, or something you can do as part of the Sensate Focus exercises to awaken and develop your sexuality as a couple. What is this Blissful Caress, you ask? It's the most exquisite, barely touching-touch that you can imagine. It sensitizes the body and electrifies it everywhere fingertips touch the skin. I like to call it the "Silent Sizzle." It's great sex therapy for you and your spouse! Here's how I describe it in my book *And They Were Not Ashamed*[8] as part of the Sensate Focus exercises:

As the giver, imagine your hand drawing sexual energy to the surface of the skin everywhere you touch. You will barely touch the body as your hand slowly glides over his/her skin from head to toe—including sexual areas. Like a soft breeze blowing across the body, the giver should caress both the back and front of the body with his/her open hand. As the giver's hand slides along the body, it will feel almost as if tiny soft kisses are being placed wherever it touches.

The intent of the Blissful Caress is to awaken sexual sensations from the depths of the soul rather than to simply arouse sexually. This caress sensitizes the body and helps awaken the sexual responses. The giver should make every caress a conscious movement, being attentive to the awakening energy in his or her spouse. As the receiver closes his/her eyes and concentrates on savoring every sensation, she/he may begin to feel sexual stirrings. The whole body should feel electrified with energy, like electricity being brought to the surface just below the touch of the hand.

How To's of the Blissful Caress

Both of you (or at least the receiver of the caress) need to be completely undressed. You may want to turn up the thermostat, or have a small heater in the room. This helps to keep the temperature sufficiently warm, since you'll be lying on your bed naked without covers. When you are in a relaxed and comfortable environment, the body is more able to instinctively let go, so that the natural bodily responses can occur. During the Blissful Caress, it may be helpful to add bedroom music and dim candle light. Decide who will be the giver and the receiver first, then switch after 5-10 minutes each. This exercise can be done where each of you has a turn giving and receiving during the same sexual encounter, or you can let just one of you have the full focus of the Blissful Caress at a time.

The Blissful Caress is an excellent standalone activity when intentionally structured to not lead to intercourse. It's a wonderful way for women to learn to feel safe sexually. It can work especially well for a reticent spouse to just lie naked on their stomach with the other only administering the Blissful Caress to the backside of the spouse's whole body. It's less vulnerable, and yet can still be a sensually exquisite experience. Depending on how you want to use this technique (as foreplay or as a way to develop sexual safety or healing in the relationship), you can lightly caress the whole body or avoid sexual areas. I'd suggest you add this Blissful Caress into your lovemaking this week, even if it's just five minutes front and back for one of you at a time.

Benefits of the Blissful Caress

There are many benefits of the Blissful Caress. For one thing, they build up positive, pleasurable associations, memories and experiences with touch and sensuality. Here are more benefits:

1. To awaken and increase sensual awareness.
2. To get to know each other's bodies better.
3. To learn to enjoy giving and receiving sensual touch without it leading to sex.
4. To learn to be more conscious, attentive or more fully present in lovemaking.
5. To help women transition into lovemaking by helping her to mentally and physically prepare.
6. To help women tune out mental distractions by focusing on and tuning into physical/sensual sensations.
7. To refresh and re-energize one's sexual relationship.
8. To awaken and excite the mind and body due to its novelty.
9. To help make sure women are getting the foreplay they need in order to fully engage in the lovemaking experience.

So many couples don't spend enough time prior to the main event to help her get sufficiently aroused. This keeps her from experiencing the full extent of the pleasure available in lovemaking. Giving yourself this "foreplay homework" by adding the Blissful Caress to your lovemaking repertoire is a great idea for any couple.

Naked Cuddling

Another fun way to enhance your touch repertoire as husband and wife, and to get in some good Skin Time, is to include some naked cuddling once in a while. One couple calls it "Huggling." It's a great tool for restoring a feeling of emotional and sexual safety between husband and wife. It can also be just a nice, novel, tactile experience—especially when it has no strings attached to sex.

> *Andrew and Tanya were struggling to connect sexually due to the negative experiences she had with her previous husband. She wanted to be intimate with her new husband, and meet his needs for sexual touch, but it evoked a lot of fear for her. She got the idea that if they could cuddle naked but not have it lead to anything, it would help her get more comfortable in feeling safe with her husband sexually.*
>
> *We discussed a time they could schedule this naked cuddling. It became an opportunity for her learn that non-sexual touch could be something they could enjoy in and of itself. They also learned that they could be sexually intimate without actually having intercourse. Both of them reported that it had become an anticipated event. It ultimately became another means of foreplay that helped them transition into lovemaking much more easily.*

Clitoral Stimulation — Is She Getting Enough?

I chuckle any time I hear the words "clitoral stimulation." When I first taught the marriage course that later became my first book, one of the husbands was pretty taken aback with how much I talked about it during one of the classes. He told me later that he had turned to his wife and said, "If she says 'clitoral stimulation' one more time, I'm going to die!'" Well, I guess he got the message about its importance at least.

One of the most common female physiological inhibitors of a full sexual response is insufficient clitoral stimulation. Only about 30 percent of women reach orgasm through intercourse alone (and some research suggests the number is even less), leaving about 70% of women who don't.[9] [10] That's vital for all couples to realize.

Vaginal stimulation alone through intercourse is often insufficient for sexual climax. The vagina has few nerve endings—with most located in the first few inches. There are significantly more nerve endings located in the clitoris, which is nearly an inch away from the vagina. When a woman is not fully enjoying sex, nor having regular orgasms, it may be that the couple has not yet figured out how to be sure there is sufficient clitoral stimulation. It must be a primary component of lovemaking.

Most women do not experience an orgasm without some form of direct clitoral stimulation. Direct stimulation does not generally occur automatically during intercourse. It is curious that women would be designed that way. Most women need to be on top, or need their husbands to manually stimulate their clitoris. This is in addition to needing other forms of sexual stimulation, such as kissing and/or caressing other erogenous zones, in order for her to reach orgasm.

While it's important to understand a woman's need for direct clitoral stimulation, it's best to take the path of indirect stimulation to bring about some arousal before focusing on her hot spots like breast and genitals. If husbands will slowly take their time to enjoy the landscape of his wife's whole body before employing direct clitoral stimulation, she will be more ready to go. You will then have a green light to go for the "good stuff" as her arousal increases.

With clitoral stimulation, some women even find that it's not so much the actual touch, but the pressure on the clitoris that makes the difference. Already being sufficiently lubricated, or adding lubrication, is necessary. Couples need to practice and have patience as they figure out the specifics of clitoral stimulation needed for their sexual style and satisfaction. Some factors may include when in the lovemaking process clitoral stimulation is most effective. Sometimes starting there without other forms of foreplay first can be irritating. The clitoris needs time to get engorged with blood, similar to the functioning of the penis.

How much clitoral stimulation is needed? How much pressure is desirable? What kind of stimulation is best and when? Other considerations include which body parts work best to provide the stimulation—the penis, thigh, hand, etc., and in what positions is it most comfortable and feasible? Especially in the beginning, women may need 15-45 minutes of clitoral stimulation to reach the peak of climax.

For some couples who have struggled for many years for her to have an orgasm, it may be an option to try using a vibrator. A vibrator provides a unique and powerful kind of touch that can help make an orgasm easier. A vibrator can also be a helpful tool in the lovemaking experience as couples get older. It can make up for the possibility of an erection not lasting long enough for her. It does have some draw backs, as I discuss more thoroughly on my website StrengtheningMarriage.com, but it could be a viable solution for some.

The action of a vibrator is certainly difficult to humanly recreate in lovemaking. If an orgasm is not already pretty well established, then using a vibrator on a regular basis could make it difficult to orgasm without it. Some who have struggled to even have an orgasm may feel that it is better to use a vibrator than for her to have no orgasm at all.

Exploring all the options of intimate touch is an important endeavor for every couple. It's necessary to find just the right kind of clitoral stimulation (i.e., direct or indirect), the right quantity (i.e., lots or little), the right quality (i.e., gentle or firm), and at the right time (after some arousal has already occurred) to create a sexual connection resulting in orgasm. Couples will need to communicate well and experiment creatively in order to identify the specific sexual ingredients that will provide the stimulation needed for mutual sexual satisfaction.

Of course, it is ideal if couples can figure this out together. But some women may need to be willing to take the lead to identify what works best for her, and share that with her husband. Women can take their husband's hand, finger or other body part and guide him to provide the kind of stimulation she enjoys most. Keeping this learning in the spirit of fun, without adding pressure to reach a certain outcome, works best for a mutually enjoyable learning process. Couples might consider it to be a fun sexual adventure to try all kinds of touch, positions and stimulation they can think of, as if doing a fun research project. You might think of it as obtaining a "master's degree" on your sexual relationship.

This discussion of clitoral stimulation and orgasm connects back to every other chapter in this book, but especially to the discussion of transcendence and surrender. If husbands play the primary role in getting the touch just right, women play a vital role in creating the mental conditions for orgasm. "Orgasm isn't just something that a man with intimate knowledge and skillful stimulating techniques provides a woman—it is something she must also be willing and able to let herself experience."[11] Adding the necessary touch to the relationship both outside and inside the bedroom is an important ingredient for intimate and fulfilling sexual experiences.

Self-Evaluation - "Touch"

To give yourself a guide as to how you are doing in this dimension, how would you currently rate yourself and your spouse overall in the area of "Touch"? Write your thoughts in your Sexual Self-Discovery Journal. — *My spouse and I have ample non-sexual touch, with no strings attached. We have a sufficient amount of sexual touch, and the right kinds (especially clitoral stimulation) for us both to be intimately and sexu-*

ally fulfilled. We enjoy kissing each other both inside and outside the bedroom. We enjoy a plentiful amount of Skin Time overall.

RATING (0 - disagree to 10 - agree):   You _____   Your Spouse _____

ACTION ITEMS — Chapter 7 - "Touch"

- To make sure you and your spouse are getting your daily quotient of Skin Time, find more ways to enjoy skin-to-skin contact without it always being sexual. Brainstorm different ways you both could be more affectionate outside the bedroom, and commit to these behaviors as often as you can. Both of you jot down five of your favorite things about kissing, and five of your least favorite things about kissing. If you can, share that information with each other prior to doing the Kissing Homework exericse.

- Your Touch Homework is to set aside some time each week after kids are in bed where you cuddle, hold hands, practice 10-second hugs or just lie next to each other purely for the pleasure of intimate physical contact knowing that sex is not on the menu for that night.

- Do the Kissing Homework exercises. Adapt it as needed to find what works for increasing your enjoyment of kissing your sweetheart.

- Re-awaken the pleasure of making out by kissing passionately on your couch or plan to go park somewhere after date night. Get in the habit of kissing affectionately and maybe even passionately outside the bedroom every now and then, with no expectation that it will lead to sex. Have fun making out with the conscious agreement to sensually and/or teasingly explore the other's face, lips, mouth, neck, ears, and eyelids with kissing, nibbling, touching—being as creative as possible—without the expectation that it will lead to something more.

- Create your own Kissing Closet in your kitchen to steal a kiss every now and then.

- Remember that wives may need to be talked and touched into lovemaking. It's part of their foreplay or warm-up before they may feel the desire to be sexually intimate.

- Utilize the 7-week program of Sensate Focus exercises as a menu to choose from to either clean the slate and start over sexually when healing is needed, or as a great way to jumpstart a sexual relationship that has gone stale.

- Use the Blissful Caress as foreplay or as a way to develop sexual safety or healing in the relationship. Add it into your lovemaking this week even if it's just five minutes for one or both of you.

- Try some naked cuddling as an excellent way to increase your touch time, or Skin Time, as a pleasure in and of itself, or as a means of foreplay.

- Be sure to figure out how much and what kind of clitoral stimulation is needed for her to regularly experience orgasm in lovemaking.

NOTES

[1] Johnson, Dr. Sue, *Love Sense: The Revolutionary New Science of Romantic Relationships.* New York: Little, Brown and Company, 2013.

[2] Field, T., Hernandez-Reif, M., Diego, M., Schanberg, S., and Kuhn C., "Cortisol Decreases and Sertonin and Dopamine Increase Following Massage Therapy," *The International Journal of Neuroscience*, 115(10) (Oct 2005):1397-1413.

[3] Wardell, D. W., and Weymouth, K. F., "Review of Studies of Healing Touch," *Journal of Nursing Scholarship* 36 (2004): 147-154. doi: 10.1111/j.1547-5069.2004.04012.x

[4] Love, Pat and Stosny, S., *How to Improve Your Marriage Without Talking About It.* New York: Broadway Books, 2007.

[5] Erickson, Kelly, "The Power of Touch: Snuggling = Better Performance?" House Call, MD, accessed June 10, 2016. http://www.myhousecallmd.com/tag/oxytocin.

[6] O'Connor, Dagmar, *How to Put The Love Back Into Making Love.* New York: Doubleday, 1989.

[7] Brotherson, Laura M., *And They Were Not Ashamed: Strengthening Marriage through Sexual Fulfillment.* Boise, ID: Inspire Book, 2004, 242-251.

[8] Ibid, 246.

[9] "Female Orgasms: Myths and Facts," The Society of Obstetricians and Gynaecologists of Canada, accessed May 31, 2016. http://sogc.org/publications/female-orgasms-myths-and-facts.

[10] Dingfelder, Sadie F., "Understanding Orgasm," American Psychological Association, accessed May 31, 2016. http://www.apa.org/monitor/2011/04/orgasm.aspx.

[11] Brotherson, Laura M., *And They Were Not Ashamed: Strengthening Marriage through Sexual Fulfillment.* Boise, ID: Inspire Book, 2004, 51.

CHAPTER VIEW

Chapter 8

TECHNIQUE — THE INTRICACIES OF *HER* SEXUAL WIRING

Your book has changed my life! I believe everything happens for a reason. Your book came into our lives at just the right time when we could truly accept it. I don't know if I would have been so open to the teachings in your book before now, but it has hit me so poignantly. I am absorbing it like a sponge. I think if I would have read this book earlier, it may have been able to change some things for us for the better. But, I will take it now and be grateful it came along when it did. It was obviously intended for me at this time.

More importantly, my husband is loving it. He can sense the change in me. I feel so free and lighthearted now about sex from the learning I have received. I always considered myself to be pretty smart, but I had no idea what I didn't know. Boy, was I missing out! It's been absolutely amazing to finally understand how sex works for me. It's been amazing for my husband and I to both know so much better now what we need to know!

Sexual Compatibility/Incompatibility

The purpose of this chapter is to provide education and techniques for both husbands and wives to better understand how women are wired sexually. Husbands and wives are naturally incompatible in this area of marriage, given their different sexual wiring. It's part of the adventure! Common challenges in incompatibility include differences in desired frequency and variety, as well as the physical and emotional priority given the intimate relationship. Personal preferences and unique arousal styles are additional factors. Most often so-called "sexual incompatibility" is due to a lack of understanding and acceptance of each other's sexual wiring.

Just as an engaged couple might begin to discuss finances, children, or household responsibilities ahead of time, they should discuss the intimate aspects of their marriage as well. By reading and discussing this chapter, couples will have a better grasp of what turns the other on and off, so that they won't have to keep stumbling around in the dark.

Sexual Compatibility is a Learned Behavior

Sexual compatibility is a learned behavior. It's something that comes with time, effort and lots of practice within the unique relationship of marriage. Orgasm, for many couples, is a learned behavior. It's not always easy or automatic—especially for women. Compatibility is definitely not something you can accurately "test" for. It's a myth to think that if people just had sex before they got married, then they wouldn't have any sexual incompatibility issues. Sex outside of marriage is a different context than the long-term, complete package that comes with the psychological commitment of marriage.

Conditions over the course of the marriage are completely different than the "honeymoon" stage of pre- and immediately post-marriage. The unique personal, psychological and physical factors inherent in marriage make sexual compatibility something that couples need to plan to work through together throughout the different stages of married life. What works in early marriage sexually may change as different seasons of life come around (i.e., childbearing, stressors, teenagers, illness, aging, etc.). Sexual incompatibility can be diminished as couples better understand each other's sexual wiring, and together build their own unique style of mutual sexual fulfillment.

Sexual Compatibility is Possible

Couples should expect a sexual learning curve in marriage, and again as life circumstances change. With effort, there is hope for couples to create a mutually fulfilling, passionate and intimately connected relationship. God seems to have designed husbands and wives with inherent sexual "incompatibility," so that couples have the opportunity to learn and work together to overcome their differences. I can't help but wonder if developing faith, patience, trust, charity and compassion are really what sexual incompatibility in marriage is designed to help us with anyway. I can't think of a better motivator for people to have to learn to develop these Christ-like characteristics than struggling with some sexual incompatibility issues.

The compassion and tenderness we develop in the process enhances intimacy. Unfortunately, that's not something you're likely to read much about in women's magazine articles on how to spice up your sex life. Nevertheless, it may be a key overlooked aspect along the journey to sexual compatibility. Our job as couples is to: 1) get educated, 2) be willing and able to discuss sexual issues and preferences, 3) acknowledge and accept our differences, and 4) be willing to make some potentially challenging personal changes. This is needed to diminish the sexual incompatibilities often found between a husband and wife.

Many couples have entered my office with serious sexual difficulties between them. If a wife, for example, decides that she's not going to accept how she is wired sexually, or won't work on her sexual inhibitions, or if the husband decides he's not going to work on being more thoughtful or trustworthy, then those needed personal changes are going to keep couples struggling sexually. By accepting the fact that some sexual incompatibility may be inevitable in marriage, we can shift our energies from fighting or wallowing in what we don't like, to proactively addressing and changing what we can. I hope couples will be encouraged to take the necessary steps to increase their sexual connection and enjoyment of this vital dimension of marriage.

Lovemaking Takes Effort

The mechanics of "having sex" are fairly simple, but really "making love" and developing a good, intimate relationship takes time and effort. The kind of sex we're talking about is where there's mutual giving and receiving—fully, naturally, and enthusiastically. Movies, pornography and other media tell us that sex is—or should be—easy, spontaneous, and always toe-curling. In our heavily sexualized culture, it's difficult to NOT be negatively affected by its erroneous messages. It's a set up for problems in real-life relationships. That's especially true given the relational trauma spouses often experience when pornography addiction has a hold on one's partner.

Pornography significantly affects the intimate relationship. Think of how many facets of women's sexual wiring (the 12 T's) are affected by a husband's pornography use (i.e. her body image issues—"Thoughts"—being exacerbated by his comparisons to fantasy women). For those who have ingested pornography, it's difficult to have a healthy and accurate perspective of the intimacies of human sexuality, not to mention having the ability to effectively engage with each other intimately.

Pornography – The Sex Mis-Educator

Pornography and most of society's portrayal of sexuality is a terrible way to learn about the tender sexual intimacies between a husband and wife. It's a dangerous sex educator presenting many misconceptions. In pornography, "sex" is one-dimensional, focusing on the physical. But true "lovemaking" encompasses all dimensions of the marriage relationship—mental, emotional, spiritual, and physical. People may believe that what they see in the sexualized media is realistic and normal. This can be especially hazardous given that good, real-life lovemaking is so much more than what pornography portrays.

Porn leads people to believe that men and women are both always and equally interested in having sex at a moment's notice. Imagine the surprise when a husband, for instance, finds that his spouse needs to feel close emotionally before she is interested in and ready for sexual expression. Porn is all about self-gratification, not mutual connection and enjoyment. Porn leaves out the interpersonal and emotional elements of lovemaking, focusing solely on the physicality of sex. This can make lovemaking frustrating for those who don't want to have to put in the extra effort to mentally and emotionally connect. This isn't optional as a vital component of healthy, human relationships.

Pornography portrays sex as easy. No relationship issues. No rejection. No foreplay needed. No hassle. There's no need to even be nice or loving toward the other throughout the day. Porn can also be very violent. This is the antithesis of tender intimacy. Porn performers are merely strangers playing out an unrealistic fantasy on the screen.

Porn is sex without intimacy. Sex without the context of intimate connection is empty and never fully satisfies. Ask any husband who is getting only "duty sex" without any emotional engagement. It's a recipe for disaster. If your blueprint of a "normal" sexual relationship comes from pornography, you might be surprised to find that your spouse has a different idea of what's acceptable sexually.

> *Katherine asked her husband to list all the characteristics he could think of that would describe healthy sexuality between a husband and a wife. She was shocked to hear his answers. She could see that he had no real understanding of what healthy intimacy was all about. He had been conditioned by porn. They began reading* And They Were Not Ashamed: Strengthening Marriage through Sexual Fulfillment *together each night. He began to understand what a healthy sexual relationship looked like.*

Porn teaches that men and women are both equally enthusiastic about engaging in any kind of sexual behavior. It suggests that people can make demands without regard for the feelings or preferences of the other. In fact, porn desensitizes men to women's genuine feelings. If couples aren't communicating sexually, their two different sexual blueprints are likely to collide.

When parents don't have open discussions about sex and intimacy with their children, then porn, other media, and friends are taking their place as sex educators. This also affects spouses who do not talk openly with each other about their sexual relationship. For many people, media is not only the *primary* source of sex education, but often the *only* education they receive.

Intimacy is Scary

Compared to the ease of virtual sex, healthy sexual intimacy is inherently anxiety producing as a pretty vulnerable endeavor. It requires self-awareness, self-disclosure, and self-acceptance. It involves sharing the good, the bad and the ugly about your inner self with another. If you don't necessarily like who you are, or are afraid you won't be accepted, it seems dangerous to openly share yourself with your spouse. It's also scary when your spouse doesn't notice or appreciate your efforts.

> *Megan felt extremely vulnerable anytime they were intimate. It only got worse when during an argument, Jason said it had been forever since they had sex. In fact, it had been less than a week. Megan remembered it clearly because it was the only night the kids were gone. She'd made a special point to wear lingerie and was more engaged than usual.*
>
> *She told me how painful it was to hear him overlook her recent efforts. She felt cheap—like a prostitute—given that her strenuous efforts were so unacknowl-*

edged and unappreciated. She felt ashamed of herself for even trying to go there so fully for him. She said, "He doesn't understand that trying to meet his sexual needs is like walking on water naked for me."

Megan felt disgusted with herself for putting herself out there so vulnerably, only to feel like her efforts were being spit upon. Jason acknowledged the severe misstep he'd made. He realized how recent it had actually been that they'd been intimate. He tried to undo the damage. He could see what he'd done to her heart. He provoked shame in her and made her vulnerability feel cheap.

Megan explained that she thought Jason finally understood the depth of her feelings after she told him, "Jason, you know how I feel loved when you do acts of service for me, and you feel loved when I'm physically intimate with you? I'm trying to love you the way you need me to, but you don't seem to realize what it means for me to have to get naked for you. So, from now on, anytime you do the dishes, you need to do them naked, so you can see what it feels like for me!"

That clicked for Jason. He made a complete turnaround. He's acknowledging and appreciating her efforts so much better now. He told me he just hadn't real-ized how scary sexual intimacy was for her, and how much of a challenge it was for her to work on that aspect of herself.

Intimacy involves being emotionally and physically accessible, responsive and vulner-able. It involves exposing ourselves—body, mind and soul. It's akin to "walking on water naked." Intimacy—whether emotional or sexual—can be especially frightening if you have been wounded by experiences in your past. Sex is easy if you can just avoid the inti-macy stuff. But it's the intimacy stuff that is what turns "sex" into "lovemaking."

When a husband is the lower-desire spouse in the marriage, one reason for that dynamic is that intimacy is too risky for them. They'd rather not. They'd rather just keep their distance—physically and emotionally. This can also make porn a seemingly perfect avenue, because they can get the physical pleasure of sex without the complicated and "scary" intimacy stuff. The antidote to fears about intimacy, or performance pressure, shame, or trauma, etc., is working together to make the relationship emotionally safe for each other and your individual insecurities. Getting professional help may also be a necessary ingredient.

Sexual Progress List

Intimacy was so scary for Miranda, due to past experiences, that we had to go very slowly in her and her husband's therapeutic efforts. It got discouraging for Miranda and Eddie at times, so we started keeping track of little pieces of their progress. This exercise could be helpful for any couple on their own journey to improving their sexual relation-ship. Keeping this "Progress List" was very encouraging to them both. It helped them see their improvement, and kept their minds focused on the positives, so neither could get too discouraged and want to give up. Some of the items they identified were:

- Eddie asks how I feel before he assumes that he knows.
- I stay with our hugs longer.
- Instead of pushing away negative feelings, I paid attention to what they were.
- We talked about, "What if we never had sex again in our marriage?" Eddie assured me he would be able to deal with it and be ok with it.
- I laid on Eddie's back while he was kneeling to pray. It surprised him and made him laugh.
- He listened to me talk about my difficult day and didn't try to offer advice about what I should do.
- We hugged without our shirts on.
- I didn't freak out when Eddie shared his feelings about being lonely and sad about our lack of intimacy.
- We learned that "silence" is our biggest block to progress.
- I'm thinking more on my own about how I might remove obstacles to intimacy.
- I playfully kissed Eddie's neck.

Your Sexual Template

In order to overcome unhealthy assumptions and expectations sexually, couples need to get educated not only about healthy sexuality, but also to identify their own mental template about sex. The media-educated mind has some sexual "unlearning" to do and new learning to acquire. It requires each of us who have had a less-than-an-ideal sexual education to face up to what we've accumulated from various questionable sources. We must work to change, even if it's simply overcoming fears about sexuality itself.

One way to help make sexual connection easier is to follow sex therapist Dr. Douglas Rosenau's advice, and provide each other with a template of what an ideal lovemaking encounter together might be. Your homework is to write out your ideal lovemaking scenario with as much detail as possible and share it with your spouse (perhaps in your Sexual Self-Discovery Journal). This not only begins the process of identifying and sharing your own sexual template, but also helps each of you learn your spouse's specific sexual desires and accelerators.[1]

Why You Should Get Educated

My husband told me that what he has learned from your book about women and the way our minds and bodies work has given him a greater appreciation, as well as a deeper understanding and love for me. I'm so glad this information has finally come from a woman's perspective. It's so much easier for me to take it in, too. Your descriptions in the book are right on in describing exactly how I feel. I feel like a light has come on for both of us! I feel like shouting out to the world that there is

HOPE for any couple struggling sexually in their marriage! There is a way, an answer, a solution if people will just learn how!

———◆◆◆———

So often people are afraid of stumbling across inappropriate material that we are hesitant to study and learn what can help our sexual relationship. I believe God expects us to get educated on these issues, though, and not act like ostriches putting our heads in the sand. I am so amazed at how much pleasure and joy my husband and I now know we were missing out on before we read your book! Thanks so much for helping me open my dungeon doors and break free of my self-imposed prison walls.

Getting educated sexually is a big deal. I rarely meet men or women who fully understand how their spouses are wired sexually. Husbands often joke with me about what in the world there could possibly be to say about sex to cover so many pages. They give me the attitude of, "what's there to know?!" Men often think there's nothing to learn, because it's all pretty easy in their mind. The reality is that there's quite a bit more to know when you factor in the intricacies of female sexuality. While sex (the physical aspects) may tend to be easier for men, in general, intimacy (the emotional aspects) is generally easier for women. Together they can influence each other for a richer, fuller, sexually intimate relationship. This young husband was especially glad that he'd been able to get better educated particularly about the intricacies of intimacy for women:

This is a must read for anybody who is about to get married, and even some who already are. I recently got engaged. My mom gave me your book to read saying, "I wish something like this would have existed when your father and I got married." All I can say is WOW! Talk about eye-opening! I had no idea. I don't think I would have even clued in after getting married. I had no idea that intimacy was such an involved and complicated thing. I have been given a new perspective going into marriage that I suspect will help to prevent many problems that might have otherwise developed. I appreciate that the book is designed to put the woman and her needs first. You encourage a very loving and selfless approach to intimacy. Women are too often forgotten and neglected in the sexual realm. I hope I can do a better job making my wife's needs the focus in our relationship.

What you don't know can certainly hurt you, or at least create a lot of unnecessary pain and negative sexual experiences in your marriage. Understanding that we're all wired differently and being okay with that is necessary to being able to work together to create a mutually enjoyable sexual relationship.

How to Get Educated

How do you get educated sexually and safely in our sexually toxic environment? You're already on your way by reading this book. Below are three important ways to get educated sexually.

1. Read and Discuss Books

Many couples have made it a point to read books together as illustrated by some of the comments shared above. For some, it's so much easier to have a written form of "sex therapy" to digest in the comfort and privacy of their own bedrooms than to see a sex therapist. Self-help sex therapy, by way of reading and discussing good books, is clinically called bibliotherapy. It can be very effective for addressing sexual issues.[2]

Many thousands of couples have been able to read good books and make improvements in their intimate relationships. That's a lot more than the number of couples that may make their way into a therapist's office. One wife recently told me that she and her husband started reading a couple pages of my book in the evening as part of their pillow talk. It helped them emotionally connect prior to lovemaking. Other couples have made it a separate learning exercise not attached to lovemaking. Reading a book allows the author to bring up touchy subjects for you without couples having to do that themselves. Couples don't always know what they need to do or talk about to make things better. See the Recommended Resources in the Appendix for ideas.

2. Learn from Each Other

Nothing compares to the specific sexual education couples must receive from each other in order to create a mutually fulfilling sexual relationship. In Chapter 9 - "Tuned In," there's a section about "Learning Each Other's Specific Sexual Preferences." There are multiple exercises to help make it easy for you and your spouse to discuss sex and learn each other's intimate intricacies.

Some of my favorite exercises for couples to learn from each other are to share their ideal lovemaking scenario, to identify each other's sexual brakes and accelerators, and to play the game "20 Questions–Your Conversation Starter about Sex" (see Chapter 9 - "Tuned In"). Specific sexual learning directly from each other is vital, but is often missing from many couples' sexual knowledge. You will have the opportunity to learn these important insights throughout this book.

3. Get Professional Help

In working with couples on their sexual relationships, there often comes a time when they realize that reading books together and trying to discuss each other's sexual desires just isn't quite enough. They need a more tailor-made approach to understanding and addressing their specific sexual and relational issues. One such couple had a pretty good marriage overall and had recently read my book, which had changed many things for the better. But they both had accumulated resentments that kept them from really opening their hearts to fully understand what the other needed. It kept them both from having sufficient desire to change things.

Sometimes couples know how they are wired and what they each want or need sexually, but they still have underlying relationship issues. Couples are often unable to identify or surmount these barriers on their own. This couple knew what they needed to know, but their previous efforts at change had simply not taken them far enough. This is where a therapist can help by seeing and hearing your interactions, identifying your rough spots, and helping you overcome those issues.

What You Need to Know

It's Not All about Technique

Often when it's the husband initially trying to improve the sexual relationship, he will tend to hone in on sexual techniques or new positions—thinking that's how to make things better. He might also think, "My wife just needs to get her hormones adjusted." It's usually much more than that. While techniques and hormones are important, specific sexual techniques are usually toward the bottom of the list of things couples need to be focusing on, especially when she's not enthusiastically interested in sex. Couples need to take a multi-dimensional view in addressing sexual issues.[3] We can get the mechanics of sex right, but it's the emotion behind it and spirit of it that we want to get right as well. We're looking for a "heart" change, not just behavior change.

When I mentioned to Mindy that I was working on the "Technique" chapter of my next book, she said, "I'll tell you what 'techniques' my husband needs to learn if he wants things to be better sexually." She then went on to list the following items to her husband as he sat there listening:

- Help me around the house that evening, so I'm not so tired by the time we head to bed.
- Be more affectionate with me during the day, so I don't just feel like a sex object.
- Let some of our sexual encounters be about me and how I like things, instead of always doing things the way you like.
- Do missionary style more often instead of talking me into trying some crazy new position.
- Don't have the television playing in the background.
- Take more time, and go slow. I need a good 45 minutes for lovemaking to be the way I like it.
- Kiss me more than you usually do.
- Stay awake after sex and cuddle me for a while.

This is a common dynamic for many couples. They need things to be different, but it's not usually all about sexual positions or technique (things that happen "inside the bedroom"). Instead, many of the factors focus on things that happen "outside the bed-room" as well.

> *Karl ended one of our counseling sessions with a request for the next time by say-ing, "I just want Janice to get better educated about sex." When they returned the next week, she spelled out how much that had offended and hurt her. Not only did that statement completely discount what to her was really lacking in their sexual relationship (trust, tenderness and thoughtfulness), but it also sent her the message that she was the problem, while he wasn't.*
>
> *As we discussed it, he realized that in his mind he did think he knew what was what, and that she didn't so much. This didn't help their emotional connec-tion. She could sense his thoughts. Like many husbands, he also thought they just needed some tips and tricks, until he learned how differently women are wired.*

Unfortunately, many women buy into this notion as well. Women's magazines and other media send women the message that if they don't act in certain ways, or enjoy sex like the women in the movies, then something's wrong with them. Sexual tips and tricks alone don't directly address the foundation of the emotional components of desire and arousal that women tend to struggle with the most. This relational foundation is addressed extensively in Chapter 3 - "Tenderness." Any of the "T's" throughout this book might be the key missing ingredient to creating your sextraordinary marriage.

> *Lynn and Kent had done a lot of work on their relationship issues. Kent had also adjusted how he interacted with Lynn during lovemaking. After a lot of trial and error on both of their parts, Lynn found a particular, playful sexual activity that allowed her to get turned on enough to finally experience orgasm. That had been their hope. It wasn't just one thing. It started with a combination of addressing their relationship issues and her own mental focus that were key to her orgasm. With those things now in place, this particular bedroom activity helped push her over the edge into orgasm.*

Especially when there's a desire for more consistent orgasms, it's not just techniques, but the following issues that couples really need to understand in order to be educated well sexually:

1. An awareness of common sexual wiring differences between men and women (addressed in this chapter).
2. Understanding the intricacies of female sexual wiring and wholeness (the primary purpose of this whole book).
3. A knowledge of specific intimate needs and sexual preferences of your spouse (personal sexual brakes and accelerators addressed in Chapter 9 - "Tuned In").
4. Having tools and techniques to help you merge your differing sexual wiring into a fun and mutually fulfilling relationship (shared throughout this book).

Sexual Wiring Differences

One of the more common questions I get from engaged couples is, "What do I need to know for our honeymoon if I don't have time to read a whole book?" Invariably I explain that they need to at least read Chapters 3-5 in the book *And They Were Not Ashamed.* Those chapters walk them through 1) the entire female sexual response, and 2) address the major differences in sexual wiring between men and women.[4]

Those two topics are key missing ingredients for many couples prior to marriage and the honeymoon. This chapter's "T" for "Technique" comes from the constant issue I see in working with couples, where those topics are critical for them to get a good sexual start for their marriage. Here I list those differences and highlight just a few additional thoughts. Many of the key points regarding female sexual wiring are already expanded upon throughout this entire book.

Please realize that there are always exceptions to the commonly encountered issues addressed in this book. I hope that those who fit more into the exceptions category will understand my intent to keep things as simple as possible by speaking to the majority situations. For those where their situation is reversed, I recommend a couple of other good books that address the not as common, but still important scenarios where the husband may have less sexual desire than the wife. These books more fully address the sexual wiring differences of these couples:

- *The Sex-Starved Wife: What to Do When He's Lost Desire* by Michele Weiner Davis
- *Why Men Stop Having Sex: Men, the Phenomenon of Sexless Relationships, and What You Can Do About It* by Bob Berkowitz & Susan Yager-Berkowitz

The following are 18 important differences between men and women to make it easier to understand and accept how and why husbands and wives interact they way they do sexually:

1. Stronger Sex Drive / Weaker Sex Drive. This difference is actually a myth, with the reality being that men's sex drive tends to be more constant and readily available, whereas a woman's sex drive is more of an emotional drive for connection and intimacy. The drives are simply different. She tends to have more of a receptive drive than a spontaneous hunger for sex itself.

2. Fast and Furious / Slow and Satisfying. While this tendency is still true for many men, as men age they tend to move more toward a woman's style of lovemaking. He becomes better able to enjoy the slower, more emotionally connected experience. Many women, as they come to fully embrace their sexuality and desire some variety themselves, find that they too like it faster and more passionate at times.

3. Ready to Go / Need Warm-up. While women do tend to need more warm-up time, this difference is again similar to the previous item where men may need a little more time, stimulation and connection to get into sex as they age. As women learn to embrace the things I teach in this book, they too can begin to have a much shortened warm-up period, and they can more actively help to get things going more quickly.

4. Desire Is Primarily Physical / Desire Is Primarily Emotional. It's amazing how many of these general differences begin to come together as couples get older. Again, in time, men's desire, while still being primarily physical, becomes more emotionally based. Women's sexuality still tends to be based primarily on the emotional connection in the relationship, but can certainly take on a more physical dimension. This is especially true as women develop and embrace their sexuality and physicality for the purpose of becoming a more complete and whole person.

Jackie wanted me to be sure the spiritual element was emphasized as much as the emotional. She said, "For my husband, it's the touch that soothes his soul, but for me it's the spiritual stuff that fuels my desire. I long for him to engage in discussing things of a spiritual nature. That's a big part of foreplay for me."

5. Body Before Person / Person Before Body. This issue is connected to the "men are more physically driven" and "women are more emotionally driven" difference mentioned previously. It illustrates the notion that men can be sexually turned on more easily by a stranger or some other sexual stimuli, whereas women tend to need the emotional or contextual component.

6. Need Sex to Feel Love / Need Love to Desire Sex. It is true that most husbands feel loved best through sexual expressions of love. When those needs aren't being met for a man, it affects their willingness to provide the more emotional components of love to their wives. The same circular pattern applies to women. When a woman's emotional needs are being met (see Chapter 3 -"Tenderness"), it is much easier for her to meet her husband's sexual needs.

7. Sex as a Reaction / Sex as a Decision. This difference is discussed in great detail in the section below, "Steps to Fuel Female Sexual Desire." It is a huge missing piece of the puzzle for understanding female sexual desire. Men can feel sexual fairly quickly with a bit of mental or visual stimulation. Women don't tend to respond quickly with sexual feelings just from a thought or something visual. Women, instead, have to consciously decide to go there, like flipping a mental switch. This begins a multi-phased process where she can begin to warm-up to the idea, and get turned on, as both emotional connection and some physical arousal occur.

8. Stimulated Visually / Stimulated Mentally and through Touch. It's important for women to understand how important it is for their husbands to be able to see them sexually. It's a big part of the turn on for them to have that visual element. That can create a perfect storm for couples, because most women have some body image issues, regardless of how they look. Tackling body image issues is addressed more thoroughly in Chapter 2 - "Thoughts."

Women do tend to be more stimulated mentally, emotionally and through touch. I would add through auditory means as well. With the proliferation of pornography and the constant visual stimuli now being ingested by girls through cell phones, iPads, etc., women seem to be beginning to shift to having a more visual orientation like men.

9. Direct Stimulation / Indirect Stimulation. Men do tend to prefer going right to the "good stuff." Because of the warm-up period needed by women, where they need some degree of arousal before they feel desire, they tend to prefer a more indirect and whole-body approach to stimulation. It's much more effective for husbands to spend some time on other body parts before diving directly into the main hot spots.

When husbands take their time, the anticipatory buildup can get their wives to the point of them practically dying for their husbands to get to the good stuff. This concept of women wanting indirect stimulation is a bit foreign to men because they prefer direct touch, especially the hot spots. Other body parts may not do much for them, and may even seem like a waste of time.

For women, touch—especially attentive touch in non-sexual areas—conveys profound and symbolic meaning. If her husband is willing to touch her neck and arms and the sides of her body, then it conveys a holistic sense of love and caring for her as a whole person, not just as sexual body parts. Again, this may seem strange to men that their wives might even prefer the non-sexual caresses because of the emotional closeness and loving romance it conveys.

10. Excited Quickly / Excited Slowly. Related to the previous item, men do tend to get aroused more quickly than women, but that changes some with age. I am constantly assigning "homework" to couples to add at least 15-20 minutes of foreplay before they can touch any of the main erogenous zones. This gives women a better chance at catching up with her husband's sexual state.

11. Pleasure as Release / Pleasure from Buildup (Anticipation). It makes sense that men would get excited more quickly, since the primary focus of their pleasure is the release of orgasm. For women, their keyword could be "Anticipation." A man can drive his wife crazy if he will exercise the restraint to touch and caress her whole body before he moves onto the lips, breasts and genitals. Taking his time before getting to the good stuff is a great approach for husbands to drive their wives wild.

Keith and Madison were watching a popular English period movie well known as a "chick flick." Keith kept shaking his head every now and then as if to say, "What is the big deal about these movies?" Thoroughly enjoying the romance of it all, it dawned on Madison that it was all about the build-up for her. The excitement was in the slow boil heightening her feelings of longing. The movie provided the perfect mental and emotional warm up to help prepare her heart and mind to be ready to let go. Women are as much about the anticipation as the main event. So men, go slow and bridle your passion in order to send hers skyrocketing.

12. *Constant Sexual Desire—Predictable Orgasm / Variable Sexual Desire— Unpredictable Orgasm.* Men have fairly consistent sexual desire and orgasms, but they do frequently run into the effects of stress and erectile difficulties as they age. With a woman's orgasm being quite a bit more complex and unpredictable than a man's, it does have an effect on her sexual desire. If a woman is rarely experiencing an orgasm, it would make sense that she wouldn't be terribly anxious to have sex again the next time.

13. *One Orgasm / Multiple Orgasms.* This one's pretty obvious for men and particularly exciting for women. Women are wired for multiple orgasms, so the pleasure doesn't have to end with one climax, if the needed stimulation continues. If women can learn to relax and surrender to the sensual pleasure, the "shock and awe" of multiple orgasms is possible. While it may be automatic for some couples, others may need to discuss this and work together to assure that the right combination of efforts are made to maximize this female potential.

14. *Penis as Sexual Center / Clitoris as Sexual Center.* Truly fulfilling sexual encounters require that a woman be willing and able to pay special attention to her husband's penis. As a common inhibitor for women, this can be a tough issue for thoroughly enjoying sex. Professional help may be needed or other therapeutic tools like the Emotional Freedom Technique (EFT tapping) to help a woman let go of this inhibition and fully enjoy all of her husband's body.

The concept of the clitoris as the sexual center is another key ingredient missing for many couples. It's keeping them from enjoying the full measure of pleasure in lovemaking. This important point is discussed in Chapter 7 - "Touch." Like the penis, without sufficient clitoral stimulation, most women will have a hard time experiencing full arousal and a climactic release. For women to have a body part—the clitoris—that has no other purpose than pleasure, attests to the fact that God wants women to find pleasure and enjoyment in their sexuality.

While there has been some discussion in the past about different types of female orgasm, i.e., vaginal versus clitoral, etc., it's important to be okay with whatever way works best for you and your spouse. The higher priority is that there be mutual sexual enjoyment instead of having a specific kind of orgasm at a specific time or way.

15. *Peak in Morning / Peak in Evening.* Testosterone does peak in the morning for men, and it tends to be later in the day for women and during the ovulation phase of their monthly cycle. As children grow and are off to school, mornings can become a favored time for lovemaking, where fatigue is less likely to rob couples of romantic opportunities for lovemaking as compared to late in the evening.

16. *Lovemaking Ends with Orgasm / Lovemaking Ends with Afterglow.* It's pretty difficult for men to stay awake after sex because of all the endorphins and other hormones that flood them, enticing them to sleep. If they will exercise restraint and stay engaged with their wives after lovemaking, that can be a rich time of connecting and bonding their hearts together even more deeply.

17. Need to Control Sexual Energy / Need to Awaken and Free Sexual Energy. Women almost have to do the exact opposite of what we teach our boys and encourage men to do. While men need to learn to bridle and control their sexual feelings, women generally need to awaken and nourish sexual thoughts and feelings, which are discussed more thoroughly in Chapter 1 - "Transformed" and Chapter 2 - "Thoughts." Sexual thoughts and feelings are already generally plentiful for men, but women almost need to nurture appropriate romantic thoughts and feelings toward their spouse throughout the day. This helps them have a head start, so they aren't trying to get all the way from 0 to 60 at a moment's notice when lovemaking opportunities occur.

18. Simple Sexual Fulfillment / Complex Sexual Fulfillment. It may be true that male sexual fulfillment seems simpler, especially in the earlier years of marriage, and women seem to be more complex due to the emotional nature of their sexual desire. But the good news is that over time, male and female sexuality tends to become more balanced and similar. Men tend to become a little more complex as their emotionality is developed and embraced. Women tend to become a little simpler sexually as they come to understand and embrace their sexuality. As the emotional dimension in the marriage is enhanced, both husband and wife come together in a more emotionally and sexually balanced way. Remember, emotionally connected sex is the best sex!

Why Women Don't Want to All the Time

When couples don't fully understand or accept the sexual differences between husband and wife, it can lead to frustration and misunderstandings. One husband said to his wife, "Do you ever hunger for me sexually?" She said, "Yes, but it's different. I don't have the testosterone you do. I hunger for you emotionally, whereas you hunger for me physically."

Another husband was frustrated that his wife didn't seem to like sex like he did. Many men think, "What's not to like?!" Jane tried to explain to James that it takes a while for her to even be interested in having sex. She explained that sometimes she feels like she's at a -5 on the "interested" scale. She hardly ever thinks about it. She agreed that she generally needs to be "talked and touched into it," once she can get to the point of even flipping the mental switch to say "yes" to sex. This was mind boggling to James. He said, "I don't get it. How could anyone not like sex?" Because men frequently ask this question, here are a few thoughts for both men and women to consider about why women may not be interested in sex all the time like men seem to be:

1. Women don't tend to be walking around with feelings of sexual desire like men.
2. As multi-taskers, women generally have many other equally important things competing for their attention, time, and energy, i.e., children, work, household responsibilities, etc. For men, with sex as their most powerful form of feeling

loved (…and feeling really good!), it's easier for them to shut out other things and make sex their highest priority.

3. Women tend to have many more sexually inhibiting thoughts and feelings than men, i.e., body image issues, fear of pregnancy, relationship issues, etc.

4. Orgasms aren't as predictable for women, so the "Wow" factor of climax is less of a sexual motivator as it is for men. Men are pretty likely to orgasm each time they have sex.

5. An orgasm actually takes a fair bit of work—mentally, emotionally, and physically. It's not generally as quick and easy as it tends to be for men. Women generally need 20 minutes, whereas men could get by with 2.

Female Sexual Wiring Phases

As an overview of the entire lovemaking process, the following diagram will help you see how the sexual response phases connect with the steps I suggest later to Fuel Female Sexual Desire. These steps reflect the female sexual wiring initially discussed in *And They Were Not Ashamed*,[5] while including the findings of Dr. Rosemary Basson's important research on female sexual desire.[6] It's so important that both husbands and wives understand that women have quite a few steps before they get to the place where men more naturally reside—at the Desire phase. Women tend to start from a sexually neutral state. Thus, the need for a Warm-up/Preparation Phase for women to be able to catch up to where their husbands are already at in the arousal process.

Overall Phases of Female Sexual Response	Specific Steps to Fuel Female Desire
Phase 1 — Warm-up/Preparation Phase	*(Where women's sexual response begins…)* Step 0 — Relationship Climate Step 1 — Deciding to "Go There" Step 2 — Emotional Connection (Talk)
Phase 2 — Some Arousal	Step 2 — Emotional Connection (Talk) Step 3 — Physical Foreplay (Touch)
Phase 3 — Desire *(Where men's sexual response begins…)*	Step 4 — Desire shows up
Phase 4 — Continuing Arousal	
Phase 5 — Orgasm/Release	
Phase 6 — Afterglow	

Because "Desire" tends to garner the most difficulty for women, the following section "Secrets of Female Sexual Wiring" will specifically address Phase 1 — Warm-up/ Preparation, Phase 2 — Some Arousal, and Phase 3 — Desire. Part of the intricacy of female sexuality is that it doesn't go in a straight line from point A to point B. It includes many multi-faceted factors for desire, arousal and release as indicated by the 12 "T's" discussed throughout this book.

Secrets of Female Sexual Wiring

My husband and I have been married for five years. We have struggled with intimacy problems since a few months after we got married. I was just never in the mood, and I didn't know how to get there. I wanted to have that closeness with my husband, but just didn't know how to get my body to want it. It got to the point where I would dread getting into bed at night with my husband, because I knew he was going to try to initiate sex, and that I would say no, then he would be hurt, and want to stay up all night talking about it and ask me questions I didn't have the answers for. We have had countless arguments over intimacy. We would always go around and around in circles, having the same argument every time. We were so frustrated. We wanted to fix the problem but didn't know how.

The clinical models of the sexual response cycle generally put "Desire" as Step 1. While that tends to be more true for men, "Desire" needs to be thought of as the 4th step for women. Many women see themselves as being "never in the mood." What women don't understand is that the elusive "mood" takes some conscious effort. Desire for women doesn't usually show up until after they: 1) mentally decide to "go there," and 2) begin to have some degree of emotional arousal, and 3) some degree of physical arousal as well. Of course, there are always exceptions of women experiencing desire followed by arousal similar to how men are wired.

It is very common for husbands and wives to misunderstand what it takes for women to "feel" some desire to have sex. Women are generally not walking around with the feeling of sexual interest. Female desire is more responsive to or "induced" by other factors than it is spontaneous in its own right. Female desire tends to be rooted in a need for emotional intimacy and closeness (e.g., respect, trust, affection, communication). It's about them wanting to express love to their husbands, to feel close, or because of their desire for oneness with their spouse based on their own sexual wholeness. Female desire is generally cultivated or manufactured, rather than it coming solely from a physical drive or sexual appetite. This gives women the status of basically starting from a sexually neutral position.

Even though women are sexually wired differently than men, it's okay. As couples figure out, accept, and discuss their differing wiring, they can actually make sense of ways to work things out pretty well. Chapter 5 - "Transition" discusses additional specific actions couples can take that become "Bridges to Desire" in the "Warm-up/Preparation" phase of lovemaking. These bridges can help women get from a state of "haven't even thought about sex" to "yeah, let's do it!"

I Want to Want to

Angie came to see me frustrated because she wanted to figure out how to want to want sex. She said her husband often asks her if she wants to have sex, and when she is honest with herself she would generally say, "No." He'd then ask her when she thought she might want to have sex, and she'd usually say, "I don't know," but what she really wanted to say was, "Probably never."

For many women the feeling of "wanting to" is multiple steps away from where they usually are. I designed a "Fuel for Female Sexual Desire" diagram shown here in this chapter to help couples understand that they are pretty normal. Wives and their husbands just need to understand what those steps are and how to get to a feeling of "wanting to." As Angie and I discussed this handout, she realized how normal she actually was. She was so relieved. She had been feeling "broken" sexually, as many women do when they feel like they are never in the mood for sex. She began to see how she might actually be able to want to.

Thinking from a man's perspective, it makes sense that his wife may seem broken somehow. As was discussed above, why in the world would anyone NOT want to have sex given how great it feels? Women do wonder if they are broken somehow, and men are only happy to agree. That's the only thing that makes sense. In my book *And They Were Not Ashamed,*[7] I list over 30 different physiological, psychological and relational factors that contribute to "not wanting to" or low sexual desire, which is the most common sexual complaint. For now I'd like to focus on low sexual desire from the perspective of the more universal cause that men and women simply need to better understand her sexual wiring.

Accompanying Causes of Low Sexual Desire

Most of the causes of low sexual desire require some help from a counselor or preferably a sex therapist. If the guidance I share here isn't quite enough to get you where you want to go, that will be a sign that you may need additional professional help. When medical or physiological issues are affecting sex, it's important to be sure those are addressed first, otherwise psychological or relational approaches won't be as effective. Let me share just a few of the common accompanying causes of low sexual desire to give you an idea of what other factors may be at play for women who aren't that interested in sex:

Physiological Causes—Medications, hormones, painful intercourse, illness, fatigue, lack of orgasm/fulfillment, etc.

Psychological Factors—Body image issues, childhood abuse/neglect, previous negative sexual experiences, cognitive inhibitions, stress, fear, etc.

Relationship Issues—Resentment, anger, insufficient affection, lack of sexual understanding, lack of emotional connection or safety, addictions, etc.

HOW WOMEN GET IN THE MOOD

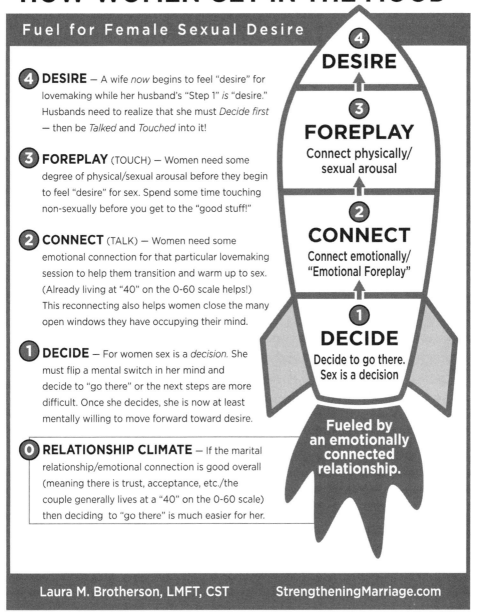

Fuel for Female Sexual Desire

4 DESIRE — A wife *now* begins to feel "desire" for lovemaking while her husband's "Step 1" *is* "desire." Husbands need to realize that she must *Decide first* — then be *Talked* and *Touched* into it!

3 FOREPLAY (TOUCH) — Women need some degree of physical/sexual arousal before they begin to feel "desire" for sex. Spend some time touching non-sexually before you get to the "good stuff!"

2 CONNECT (TALK) — Women need some emotional connection for that particular lovemaking session to help them transition and warm up to sex. (Already living at "40" on the 0-60 scale helps!) This reconnecting also helps women close the many open windows they have occupying their mind.

1 DECIDE — For women sex is a *decision.* She must flip a mental switch in her mind and decide to "go there" or the next steps are more difficult. Once she decides, she is now at least mentally willing to move forward toward desire.

0 RELATIONSHIP CLIMATE — If the marital relationship/emotional connection is good overall (meaning there is trust, acceptance, etc./the couple generally lives at a "40" on the 0-60 scale) then deciding to "go there" is much easier for her.

4 DESIRE

3 FOREPLAY
Connect physically/
sexual arousal

2 CONNECT
Connect emotionally/
"Emotional Foreplay"

1 DECIDE
Decide to go there.
Sex is a decision

Fueled by an emotionally connected relationship.

Laura M. Brotherson, LMFT, CST   StrengtheningMarriage.com

Steps to Fuel Female Sexual Desire

Jackie was happy that I discussed how women are wired sexually. She explained, "After our first visit where you explained the steps that fuel female sexual desire, I felt so validated. It was what I had been trying to explain to my husband, and he was finally able to hear it from you. I felt so understood and liberated. We connected intimately those next few weeks better than we had in a long time. When we got kind of stuck one night, my husband pulled out the diagram and started to ask where I was in the four step process. He wanted to know how he could help. It was such a turn on for me that I literally threw it aside and we made love."

Let's talk more now about each of the steps that are needed for women to fuel their sexual desire and get from 0 to 60 sexually.

Step #0 - Relationship Climate (CONNECTED)

This "step" is so important and so all-encompassing that the entire Chapter 3 - "Tenderness" is dedicated to how to create this secure connection in your relationship. I term it as "Step #0" because it isn't so much of a step as it is a contextual factor. It's a necessary pre-requisite for a woman to take Step #1 of making a decision to move forward sexually. Female sexual desire is primarily fueled by a warm and emotionally connected relationship. Step #0 is all about providing an environment where she'd want to say "Yes" to sex. Kari had to continually remind her husband that for her to "want" to make love required that they first feel like friends, since they often didn't. His pouting about the lack of sex just made things worse.

The relationship between husband and wife, including her perception of how she feels she is generally treated by her husband, is her primary source of intimate fuel—even though she may not necessarily be aware of it. For women, sex begins in the heart and mind, with the body that follows. If the marital relationship or emotional connection is good overall (there is trust, safety, acceptance, friendship, etc.—Chapter 3 issues), and the couple generally live at a "40" on the 0-60 scale, then deciding to "go there" is much easier for her. One wife explained that it's taken 10 years for her husband to learn how to be "thoughtful." That was the fuel she'd been missing. Hopefully husbands won't take 10 years to learn this lesson.

People often ask me how I've been able to turn things around sexually in my own marriage. I have personally worked at most of the things I teach my clients and that I share in this book. But a big part of our success goes to my husband for creating an environment that allows us to live in the upper range of the 0-60 scale. Cindy had a huge "Ah-ha" moment when she came to a similar realization of how much of a role her husband played in her sexual availability:

I know I'm a pretty judgmental person. So, I tend to do that to my husband as well. In reading your book I was feeling pretty proud of myself for my non-typical ability (as a woman) to always be willing and ready for sex. I have hardly ever turned my husband down in our 14 years of marriage. Lately I've noticed myself being really critical of my husband though about his weight and eating habits. He never says anything back to me in reaction. I actually don't remember him ever saying a negative word to me at all. I knew I needed to change how I was acting, so I talked with some friends about it (who themselves have had a hard time with weight and their eating habits, too). They set me straight and helped me change my perspective—that I don't have to understand him or fix him. I just have to trust him to do what he can. I just need to let go and let him be him.

As I have been reading about this 0-60 concept, it finally it hit me. My husband already does 99% of everything you teach in your book to help us feel connected. It's no wonder I live at a 60 all the time! I had been crediting myself for always being ready for sex, when it was really the environment my husband had created FOR ME that has helped me be that way. This has been a huge revelation! What a major mental shift.

Another way to think of the connection between emotional intimacy and sex in a marriage is: "Sex is to a marriage what oil is to an automobile engine. Intimacy is the fuel, and sex is the lubricant."[8] Intimacy for women is not just physical, but emotional, and spiritual. Having the "fuel" of emotional connection is what makes it possible for women to decide to start their sexual engines.

Being sexual can be a scary and vulnerable endeavor for a woman. She has to wade through a few extra steps before she is feeling arousal and desire. It's this very arousal and desire that helps her overcome her fears, frustrations, or mental distractions that otherwise threaten to derail her pleasure train. Wives need to be able to trust that their husbands will take the necessary time for intimacy—not just sex, but also the intimacy.

As men begin to understand the unique sexual wiring of women, they may become more aware of how to approach their wives effectively. There is a definite difference between "male foreplay" and "female foreplay." Due to the emotion-based and all-encompassing nature of female foreplay, this Step #0 addressing the emotional climate attests to the reality that every interaction as a couple either fuels desire or diminishes it. Leanne struggled with her husband's advances. He'd often reach over and put his hand up her shirt. When she'd cringe he'd say, "We're married. We can do this now."

Just because you *can* do something doesn't mean you *should*. With female foreplay, the elements in Chapter 3—tenderness, thoughtfulness, respect, etc.—are paramount. Leanne felt like a sex object, not a beloved wife. She related, "His actions don't feel like expressions of love or connection. I feel like a piece of meat. I don't think he even cares about me and my needs outside of what I can do for him sexually. Female foreplay for me is him talking with me and listening to me. It's being respectful. It's being interested in all of me—not just my body."

If the climate of the relationship isn't so good, or if there are any of the additional causes of low sexual desire mentioned above, then imagine how challenging it would be for a woman to say "Yes" to sex. She has to do so without any actual feelings of desire in hand, and in Leanne's case, may even have relationship obstacles to overcome. Jan too lamented, "It would be much easier for me to go there, if I knew he had my back and loved me unconditionally. I just don't feel like he does, so why should I go there sexually?" The following steps provide the blueprint to help couples understand and work through the unique elements of female foreplay.

Step #1 - Make a Conscious Choice (DECIDE)

For women, sex is a decision. It's an act of faith to move forward while you have no actual feelings of sexual desire in hand...yet! Women have to consciously choose to flip a mental switch and decide to "go there"—like unlocking the deadbolt on a door, and cracking it open a bit as well.

Michele Weiner-Davis, in her book *The Sex-Starved Marriage,*[9] suggests the Nike approach of encouraging women to "Just Do It!" trusting that the feelings will follow. She highlights the idea that women don't have to be a victim of their current emotions, since those feelings can change as you move into arousal. With the right mindset and relationship climate, you can more easily count on the amorous feelings to show up if you willingly step into the process and allow yourself to get started.

Husbands often feel like the stars must align for wives to say "Yes" to sex. This may seem especially true if any of the following are true: couples don't have an understanding of the wife's sexual wiring; she hasn't fully embraced her sexuality nor developed her sexual wholeness; she struggles with body image issues; her husband was kind of a jerk that day; she's still recovering from some kind of betrayal or relationship trauma; or if she doesn't usually have a climax anyway (all fairly common conditions). Saying "Yes" to sex might feel like she's saying yes to walking on water naked.

Struggling through the many challenges of a husband with a pornography addiction, Sandra shared how she considers it a real accomplishment for her to even get on the fence about saying yes to the possibility of sex. She has a lot of pain, distrust, and feelings of betrayal that she must wade through to get her mind to even unlock the door to sex. This is particularly true for any wife dealing with issues that have weakened her trust in her husband. (See the list of Recommended Resources in the Appendix for additional help.)

If she is either pressured into sex or says "Yes" without really mentally deciding to open the door (which actually happens quite a lot), then "duty sex" or "dead-fish sex" is the result. But, if she makes the decision to unlock the door to her heart, body and soul, she is now at least mentally willing to move forward toward the actual feeling of desire.

For some women, it can be helpful to actually choose to "schedule" lovemaking. It makes Step #1 easier because it's already done. Scheduling sex also helps make it easier for women to get themselves mentally prepared for making love on a given day. They know it's coming. If they willingly choose to schedule it, and if they learn about and accept how they are wired, then it's a helpful reminder for them to put some focus on preparing to "go there" later that day. This concept of scheduling sex works well for some couples and not so well for others. Scheduling lovemaking is really not much different than scheduling date night. It's something husband and wife need to discuss to see if this idea would help or hinder them in their relationship.

Sex starts in the mind, and a woman does have some power over her thoughts. She can learn to focus on things that help her "warm-up" mentally and emotionally get her in the mood for lovemaking. Women are not helpless victims of their husbands' actions or lack thereof. It's just a lot harder if a woman feels like her husband has been a jerk.

Step #2 - Connect Emotionally/Emotional Foreplay (TALK)

Steps #2 and #3 are the phase where the husband gets to take the lead to "Talk" and "Touch" his wife into wanting sex—remembering that she may not be "feeling it" quite yet. After learning about these steps to get to a state of sexual desire, Cindy started telling her husband, "I can flip the switch to a yes, but you're going to have to talk and touch me into it!"

Women need some degree of emotional connection for each sexual occasion to help them transition from mommy mode, or work mode, or where-ever-her-brain-has-been mode, to start warming up to sex. I call these two steps (2 and 3) the "Warm-up" or "Preparation Phase" of lovemaking.

One husband asked me what the difference was between Step #0 (the emotional climate) and this Step #2 (talking to connect emotionally). While similar, Step #0 is the connecting that happens outside the bedroom on a day-to-day basis. The emotional connecting in Step #2 is specific to getting re-connected emotionally for a particular lovemaking experience. I call this "Emotional Foreplay" to emphasize the emotional component of the intimate experience. Others call this "Love Play" over the standard idea of "Foreplay."[10]

Keep in mind that if there isn't enough emotional connecting at the Step #0 level, then the efforts at Step #2 will tend to feel disingenuous to the wife. She may feel that the connecting is all about the sex (the physical act), rather than about connecting with each other on a broader basis.

There are two main purposes for these warm-up steps: 1) to re-connect emotionally as husband and wife, and 2) to help her shut down the many windows or "computer screens" she has open in her mind. Talking together about your day or other thoughts and feelings begins to help her focus on you—and the beginnings of lovemaking. For husbands, the Bridges to Desire items identified in Chapter 5 - "Transition" are likely to be the best ways to talk and touch her into a feeling of sexual desire.

Husbands can also help by removing expectations of sex as *the* purpose for connecting. It feels more genuine to a woman and is less likely to induce resistance or frustration. Creating a space of emotional connection and safety is key. The wife does need to ultimately be responsible for getting her needs met during Step #2 and #3 of the desire-building process, but it's obviously a lot easier for the man to take the lead in "Talking" and "Touching" given that she may not be really feeling it yet.

As major multi-tasking, World-Wide-Web-type thinkers, women do have a particular struggle with stopping all the plates that are usually spinning in their minds. Developing the mental discipline to shut things down and focus on the lovemaking experience is such a big challenge for women that it is the primary focus of Chapter 2 — "Thoughts."

Connecting conversation helps women close the many open windows they have occupying their minds. When I began to explain this Step #2 to Angie, she said she noticed that she needed more than just "How was your day?" kinds of conversations. She said the way she explains it to her husband is to say, "Tell me some nice things." I often suggest couples use some of the pillow talk and "Positive Flooding" techniques discussed in *And They Were Not Ashamed*[11] and highlighted below as well.

So, what are some helpful hints for connecting emotionally and providing some of that vital emotional foreplay? The following are some ideas to get you going:

Sharing your day. While some of the initial "How was your day?" talk may occur before the couple is in the bedroom, it can also occur once in the bedroom where you are both more able to focus on each other. You might share some of your highs and your lows from the day to reconnect.

Sharing your experiences with particular emotions. Husbands could take it to the next level and ask their wives to share and/or themselves share an experience they've had that day (or any experience that comes to mind) with any or all of the following "9 Core Emotions": 1) anger, 2) fear, 3) guilt/shame, 4) joy, 5) loneliness, 6) love, 7) sadness, 8) pain, 9) passion/enthusiasm. You could begin by taking turns sharing an experience you've each had with "anger." The other listens without responding, then you both move onto the next emotion. This provides a unique forum for couples to share parts of themselves and their lives that don't always get shared. This is connecting material. With the negative emotions, you might want to choose an experience that isn't about your spouse when you use this exercise for foreplay.

Couples Questions. Another favorite exercise for connecting emotionally is to ask each other a few of the Couple Questions listed in the Appendix and on my website, StrengtheningMarriage.com. These questions help you get to know each other a little better. They steer the conversation away from the common topics of daily logistics, work, kids, finances and household stuff to more personal and intimately revealing information. Here are a few to get you thinking:

1. What is something you are looking forward to today, this week or this month?
2. What are three of your favorite things about me?

3. If you could go back in time to your teenage self, what would you say?
4. What would you do if you could do anything you wanted for a day/week/ month/year?
5. "If I could change one thing about myself, I would change _____."
6. What would you do if money weren't an issue?
7. How could I make your day/life easier/better right now?
8. How do I tend to express anger or handle conflict? (Each partner asks themselves and answers to the other.)
9. What are some of your fears?
10. What are some of your favorite memories?

Reading and discussing sexual materials. Ken and Janet found it helpful to read or listen to part of my book as a way to learn, connect and begin the warm-up phase leading to lovemaking. Some couples prefer that this activity be disconnected from the act of lovemaking, while others find it to be a helpful part of the foreplay process.

Share your Stress List or Happy List. If a wife is particularly stressed, her husband could ask her to tell him 10 things that she is feeling stressed or frustrated about. This can be a great way to let her take all the concerns spinning in her mind and release them. This helps her to let go so she can focus on her pleasurable senses, instead of the distracting thoughts. But a word of caution to husbands—don't try to fix any of the items on her Stress List or provide feedback. Just listen! This is a venting session only, not a search-for-solutions session. It could also be fun and helpful to invite her to list 10 happy things about her day. This helps her focus on the positives, and makes it easier for both to feel connected.

Words of appreciation. Husbands could tell their wives "nice things" by listing things they like and/or appreciate about their spouse, like: "I sure love what a great mom you are," or "Thanks for taking care of such and such today," or "I liked the sexy text you sent me this afternoon!"

Acknowledging attractive physical qualities. A husband might progressively move on to things he likes about his wife's body, being careful to read how she's responding to what is being said. He might say something like: "I love your pretty smile," or "You have beautiful eyes," or "I think you have the softest hands ever."

Remember, connection and arousal is beginning to develop for the woman somewhere along this path, so a focus on her physical/sensual traits is actually helpful at some point. Many women who struggle with their sexuality often tend to struggle with their physicality as well, so this particular exercise assists with both connection and arousal, while also helping a woman be more comfortable and accepting of her physicality.

More sensual communication. Husbands can move even further into more sensual communication like that found at Level 2 of the "Auditory Arousal" in Chapter 6 - "Talk." This communication might sound something like: "Your body is so beautiful!" or "I love it when you touch me like that!" or "I love how you kiss my neck like that!"

or "I love you so much!" All of the "talk" in this Step #2 not only serves to emotionally connect, but also can easily lead into serving as sexual arousal as well.

Adding a spiritual dimension. As an added component, many women wish the connection here was not just emotional or physical, but spiritual as well. Jane explained how she wished she and her husband could maybe pray together before lovemaking, or read some kind of religious materials during this warm-up phase to connect more on a spiritual level, not just a sexual one. This kind of spiritual connecting could also be Step #0 type fuel for sexual desire if it were occurring more regularly as an outside-of-the-bedroom activity. An action item here for wives might be to share with your husband if this is a missing element of satisfying lovemaking. Brainstorm ways to add in more of a spiritual element.

Step #3 - Connect Physically/Physical Foreplay (TOUCH)

In addition to emotional arousal, women also need some degree of physical or sexual arousal before they generally begin to feel the feeling of "desire" or "wanting to." This might include snuggling, spooning, a back, foot or hand massage, caressing, kissing, etc. Female foreplay tends to be slower, softer, and more gentle—especially in the beginning. They are looking for a slow boil. Men tend to prefer more overtly sexual foreplay that's fast and furious, so remember to stick to her speed.

Gail had given Jack the go-ahead, letting him know sex was a possibility. But instead of a soft and slow approach, he dove in with "male foreplay." "Instead of grabbing for my sexual spots, I wanted him to pull me close and caress my arm while nibbling on my neck. He rarely kisses me. But, I wish he would."

Understanding the specific foreplay needs of one's wife necessitates some communication and intimate direction, preferably during outside the bedroom activities. Kissing is one of those things that especially kick-starts the release of the bonding hormone oxytocin. It helps reduce stress and boosts mood, not to mention all the pleasure-producing nerve endings packed into the lips. You'll generally have a better sexual experience if you include kissing as part of the pre-intercourse activities.

This "Touch" step may (but not always) be occurring in conjunction with the previous step of emotionally connecting. It all depends on where the wife is at on the arousal scale. It's critical that husbands read their wives well. This is the sole focus of Chapter 9 - "Tuned In." Husbands must get good at reading their wives during sex, without having to distract them with questions about how she's doing. Rylie's experience may help illustrate the dilemma men have in reading their wives well:

My husband has a hard time reading where I'm at on the arousal scale. He wishes I would be more vocal about it. But I am naturally more quiet. I am trying to say more about what I am enjoying or how I'm feeling. But it takes a lot of effort. And if he asks me where I am arousal-wise, it really distracts me from the good feelings

I'm trying to focus on. It easily pulls me back into my head, where the multi-tasking thoughts start spinning.

Instead, I really need to stay focused on relaxing and getting in touch with my sensual instincts. I don't want to feel like a temperature gauge or a gas tank reading. I guess this is why I need to get better at talking about my feelings outside the bedroom, so that he can read me better inside the bedroom.

On some occasions, a wife may need the focus to be solely on verbally connecting first before she can even move into affection and connecting physically. Other times she may be able to engage in both at the same time. Again, husbands need to remember that at this stage, they are still working to "touch" her into a state of "desire" where husbands already are…and probably have been for a while at this point. This step is NOT to touch her into an orgasm quite yet.

What that means is that husbands need to spend at least some time affectionately touching non-sexual areas before they dive into the other more erogenous zones. Maybe it would be helpful for men to think of this Step #3 as "pre-foreplay touch"—the affectionate touch before the sexual touch. Hopefully men can learn to enjoy this indirect foreplay as much as the overtly sexual foreplay.

The biggest challenge for most men at this point is to keep their own desire and arousal in check, so that they don't get too far ahead of their wives on the arousal scale. It's like a couple getting ready to board an airplane together to go off to an exotic or "erotic" destination. If he doesn't stay tuned in to her and doesn't keep his own arousal in check, it's like him hopping on the plane without her, leaving her standing there on the tarmac all alone as he flies off into the wild blue yonder of arousal and climax.

Step #4 - Sexual Desire Shows Up (DESIRE)

In this step, a wife now begins to feel desire for lovemaking. Having now made it through Phase 1 — Warm-up/Preparation, and Phase 2 — Some Arousal, she reaches the feeling of "wanting to" (Step #4 - "Desire") and is likely to already be up the arousal scale at least 3 to 5 points. I laughed when one husband, after discussing the "Fuel for Female Sexual Desire" rocket diagram, shook his head and said with a grin, "It seems like it would take less to launch a nuclear strike!" So, you're not alone if it seems pretty intricate. While his comment may seem like it's true in the beginning of trying to figure things out, it's worth breaking down each step to be sure you understand the process. In time, if couples will apply the information throughout this book, the whole desire and arousal process can actually become fairly easy to flow through. This is especially true as couples work together as a team to bring about a mutually enjoyable sexual relationship.

Continuing Arousal

Following the Warm-up, Arousal and Desire phases of female sexuality, continuing arousal is still needed to bring a woman to the climactic release of orgasm. Since arousal is unique to each woman, it is particularly important to help couples identify specific turn-ons and *when* they are best played out in the course of lovemaking. Sufficient arousal and lubrication is very important at this stage. Some couples may find it helpful to have additional lubrication on hand to add to the equation. This helps assure that clitoral stimulation and intercourse go smoothly.

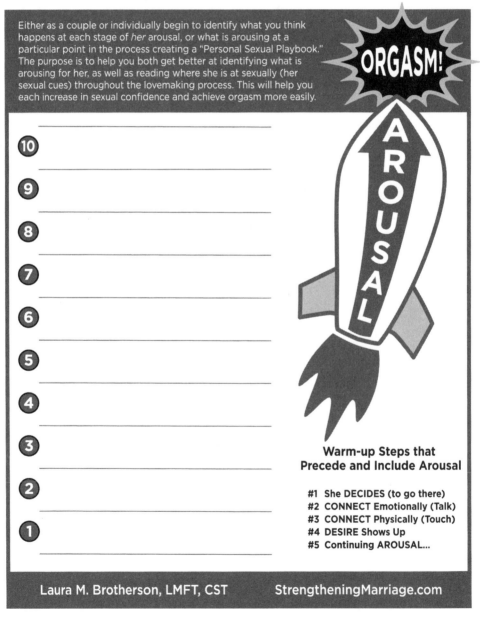

YOUR PERSONAL AROUSAL SCALE

Either as a couple or individually begin to identify what you think happens at each stage of *her* arousal, or what is arousing at a particular point in the process creating a "Personal Sexual Playbook." The purpose is to help you both get better at identifying what is arousing for her, as well as reading where she is at sexually (her sexual cues) throughout the lovemaking process. This will help you each increase in sexual confidence and achieve orgasm more easily.

ORGASM!

AROUSAL

10
9
8
7
6
5
4
3
2
1

Warm-up Steps that Precede and Include Arousal

#1 She DECIDES (to go there)
#2 CONNECT Emotionally (Talk)
#3 CONNECT Physically (Touch)
#4 DESIRE Shows Up
#5 Continuing AROUSAL...

Laura M. Brotherson, LMFT, CST   StrengtheningMarriage.com

One of the additional tools I've developed for my clients is the "Your Personal Arousal Scale" exercise where couples (or even just the wife) can identify what actions, techniques or approaches are particularly arousing to her and at what stages in the arousal process. This is helpful to not only identify arousing sexual activities or behaviors, but also to identify where in the arousal process they work best.

Candace noted that if her husband went straight for her clitoris when she was maybe at a 3 or 4 on the arousal scale, it was not sexually helpful, but actually quite irritating to her. If he instead kissed her neck, or tickled down the sides of her body, paying special attention to her breasts, she moved up to a 6 or 7 on the arousal scale. She was then more ready for clitoral stimulation either by hand or through intercourse. Completing your own sexual arousal template will be so helpful to the many good husbands out there who want to meet their wives' sexual needs, but don't always know exactly how to go about it effectively.

When I shared this exercise with Brandie, she was eager to be able to put things in writing (in her Sexual Self-Discovery Journal), so that her husband would know that when she did initiate sex, she was probably already at a 7 on the arousal scale. This meant she didn't want him to be messing around or be silly with her. She wanted him to be serious and get down to business. She wanted to be taken! I asked what it meant to her to be "taken" sexually. I wanted her to be able to share what that might look like so that she could communicate it clearly to her husband. She identified what she was looking for in the following descriptions:

- If we're in the living room when I give you "that look," turn toward me, and come at me, gently pushing me back on the couch.
- Just start undressing me without saying anything.
- Pick me up and carry me to the bedroom.
- Start kissing me on the neck.
- Don't touch the hot spots until you've spent some time elsewhere first.

When I asked her what about if *he* initiates sex, she stopped and thought for a moment, then laughed as she said, "Actually, I'd like him to do what I just spelled out whether I initiate or he does the initiating. He just needs to be sure he gets a look from me first that says I'm open to it." She was able to recognize that regardless of who initiates, she doesn't like him teasing her or being silly because it makes her feel like she's having sex with a kid. She doesn't like him asking questions, but confidently taking charge. She wants a man's man to make love to her, not an unsure guy who's being silly.

It's clear that husbands and wives really need to spell out their personal preferences and desires. If not, husbands may be doing things that aren't helping to fuel her fire. Wives need to make it a priority to figure these things out by writing in their Sexual Self-Discovery Journal. That way they can identify and share their personalized sexy information with their spouse.

193

Sexual Arousal Template

Your homework is to create a sexual arousal template. This is to identify for your husband what you think you may be feeling, experiencing, or wanting at each step of arousal. You might include what specific actions you enjoy best at each stage of the arousal process. You can also indicate what order you prefer things to go to help you achieve orgasm. What's arousing to you will likely include that which connects you both—mentally, emotionally, physically and spiritually.

This exercise works well in conjunction with the list you'll be making of your sexual Accelerators (turn-ons) and sexual Brakes (turn-offs) in Chapter 9 - "Tuned In." The ideal lovemaking scenario you wrote out from above will also help in putting together "Your Personal Arousal Scale."

Extraordinary Sex

This entire book has been created with the primary purpose of exploring the essential ingredients for "extraordinary sex," founded upon what I call a "sextraordinary marriage." Connected sex is the best sex. It's what defines a sextraordinary marriage. It's the bliss of connection. The 12 areas (12 T's) that couples need to address for female sexual fulfillment include: 1) Transformed Sexual Identity, 2) Thoughts, 3) Tenderness, 4) Time, 5) Transition, 6) Talk, 7) Touch, 8) Technique, 9) Tuned In, 10) Teasing, 11) Treats, 12) Transcendence.

Keep in mind that "the Big O" is not just orgasm, but a more encompassing "Oneness." Extraordinary sex includes that multi-dimensional oneness that we crave even more than just the physicality of an orgasm. I like this description by Dr. Sue Johnson, founder of Emotionally Focused Couples Therapy, of the kind of sex we're shooting for as husband and wife. She calls it Synchrony Sex:

> *Synchrony Sex is when emotional openness and responsiveness, tender touch and erotic exploration all come together. This is the sex that fulfills, satisfies and connects. The key prerequisite here is not wild sexual techniques but a safe emotional bond. The safer we feel emotionally, the more we can communicate, express our needs, play and explore our responses and relax into sexual feelings. We can literally tune into each other and co-ordinate our sexual dance, sensing each other's inner state and responding to how arousal shifts and peaks.*[12]

Other Key Ingredients of the Big "O"

This book is not only to better understand female sexual wholeness, but also to more passionately and regularly achieve pleasurable orgasmic sexual experiences for both husband and wife. Although the 12 T's above are the main ingredients for orgasm to occur, the following highlights a few additional points to consider. These emphasize other specific things to remember about the, at times, elusive nature of female orgasm:

1. *A learned response.* Female orgasm is a learned response for many couples requiring time, effort and lots of practice to master.

2. *Relax and let go.* Being relaxed and focused on enjoying your husband and the sensuality of the experience regardless of the outcome is key. Don't put pressure on yourself or your spouse for a certain outcome. It increases psychological pressure and the potential for spectatoring (mentally watching yourself go through the motions rather than being fully present and engaged). Just relax into it and let the passion and arousal build. Growing anticipation is a big part of the turn on for women. Be okay with whatever happens, knowing it will be enjoyable and good enough! Letting go is necessary for orgasm to show up.

3. *Orgasm is a by-product.* Because orgasm is an involuntary response, you need to focus on the fun and pleasure. Make your orgasmic efforts a playful adventure. Let an orgasm just happen as you barely pay attention to it directly. Bask in the emotional and tactile experience as you play around together. It's tough to not focus on the desired outcome when you may be frustrated about not experiencing an orgasm. Orgasm isn't something you can go after directly. It happens as a result of the 12 T's listed above and throughout this book. It occurs best in a relaxed environment, as a side-effect of genuinely connecting.

4. *Take the lead.* Women need to take some responsibility for their orgasms. Men can't do all the work for them. A woman may need to take the lead in directing things sometimes in order to figure out what kinds of touch are most arousing to her. She may need to teach these things to her husband.

5. *Know your body.* Women need to have some understanding of their bodies and how they work. If women don't know where their clitoris is, for example, they may need to get a mirror and figure it out. It's located just above the urethra under a bit of a retractable hood. It's very sensitive to the touch until it gets aroused and engorged with blood, similar to the functioning of the penis.

6. *Know what you're shooting for.* It's helpful for women to have a pretty good idea of what an orgasm feels like. If you haven't yet experienced one, it may be helpful to read the three descriptions of an orgasm I share in *And They Were Not Ashamed*.[13] You can also simulate the involuntary vaginal contractions that occur during orgasm by voluntarily contracting your pubococcygeus muscle (P.C. muscle), or pelvic floor muscle. This can help you learn a little bit about what an orgasm feels like.

7. *Develop your pelvic floor muscles.* You may have heard of the pelvic floor muscles in reference to Kegel exercises (contracting your "P.C. muscles"). Doing the Kegel exercises regularly (and during lovemaking) can help with achieving climax. It can strengthen the orgasm as well. Doing Kegels during sex can help you focus on the sexual sensations, and increase your pleasure as well. Using pelvic weighted exercise balls is a great way to help strengthen the pelvic floor muscles. You might look up Lelo Balls or Luna Beads for more information.

8. ***Don't let discouragement get you.*** Past failures at achieving orgasm can create discouragement and feelings of failure. It makes it hard to keep working toward orgasm. Don't let the self-defeating cycle of doubt, fear and frustration happen to you. It's paradoxical, but you must maintain faith and keep believing it will happen, while not putting too much focus on it. A state of mind of hopeful surrender works best.

9. ***Try other positions.*** I mention a few sexual positions in the "Treats" - Chapter 11, but trying new positions can also be important from a "Technique" angle as well. Try searching for "Christian" and "sexual positions" as search terms to hopefully avoid pornographic images. This is obviously a delicate issue especially if pornography has been a problem, but it may be helpful to consider to get the stimulation she needs.

10. ***Get some help.*** If you feel like you've tried everything, and haven't been able to figure it out yet, then it may be time to get some help. Utilize the assistance of a marriage counselor or sex therapist to help you dig into the specific areas of your relationship that may need some extra help.

Self-Evaluation - "Technique"

To give yourself a guide as to how you are doing in this dimension, how would you currently rate yourself and your spouse overall in the area of "Technique"? Write your thoughts in your Sexual Self-Discovery Journal. — *I understand the importance of getting educated sexually both from reliable resources and from my spouse. I understand and accept the sexual wiring differences between men and women addressed here. I willingly work within those realities to find what works for us intimately and sexually. I understand that there are some extra steps for me to feel sexual desire. We are working together to help address those needs. I can see which of the 12 T's I most need to work on in order to make our sexual relationship all it can be.*

RATING (0 - disagree to 10 - agree):   You _____ Your Spouse _____

ACTION ITEMS — Chapter 8 - "Technique"

- Make a "Progress List" by keeping track of the progress along your journey to improving your sexual relationship.
- Write out your ideal lovemaking scenario with as much detail as possible, and share it with your spouse. This not only begins the process of identifying and sharing your own sexual blueprint, but also helps each of you learn your spouse's specific sexual accelerators.
- Add at least 15-20 minutes of foreplay to your lovemaking before either of you can touch any of the main erogenous zones.

- Create a sexual arousal template for your husband by identifying what you think you may be feeling, experiencing or wanting with each step of arousal. You might include what specific activities you enjoy best at each stage of the arousal process, and what order you prefer things to go, to help you achieve orgasm.

- Start brainstorming a list of at least 20 specific sexual activities that you enjoy. Rate each item from 0 - 10 (totally turns me on) to indicate how much of a turn-on each one is. Pinpoint the potential order in which these activities might be preferred.

- Start brainstorming a list of at least 10 specific sexual activities that turn you off. Rate each item from 0 - 10 (totally turns me off) to indicate how much of a sexual brake each one is to you.

- Share your lists of sexual brakes and accelerators with your spouse, if you can. It can be fun to both do this exercise of identifying your brakes and accelerators, exchange lists, and then discuss anything that surprises you and/or note anything you already knew pretty well. You might also ask each other what it was like to do this exercise as an added insight into each other's sexual psyche.

NOTES

1 Rosenau, Dr. Douglas, *A Celebration of Sex: A Guide to Enjoying God's Gift of Sexual Intimacy*. Nashville: Thomas Nelson, 2002.

2 Lankveld, J., "Self-Help Therapies for Sexual Dysfunction," *Journal of Sex Research* 46(2/3) (2009): 143-155. doi:10.1080/00224490902747776.

3 Hertlein, Katherine M., and Weeks, Gerald R., "Toward a New Paradigm in Sex Therapy," *Journal of Family Psychotherapy* 20(2-3) (2009): 112-128. doi:10.1080/08975350902967234.

4 Brotherson, Laura M., *And They Were Not Ashamed: Strengthening Marriage through Sexual Fulfillment*. Boise, ID: Inspire Book, 2004.

5 Ibid, 47.

6 Basson, Rosemary, "Female Sexual Response." Clinical Fact Sheets. Association of Reproductive Health Professionals (March 2008), accessed June 29, 2015. http://www.arhp.org/publications-and-resources/clinical-fact-sheets/female-sexual-response.

7 Brotherson, Laura M., *And They Were Not Ashamed: Strengthening Marriage through Sexual Fulfillment*. Boise, ID: Inspire Book, 2004.

8 Penner, Clifford L., and Penner, Joyce J., *Restoring the Pleasure: Complete Step-by-Step Programs to Help Couples Overcome the Most Common Sexual Barriers*. Nashville: Thomas Nelson, 1993.

9 Weiner-Davis, Michele, *The Sex-Starved Marriage: Boosting Your Marriage Libido: A Couple's Guide*. New York: Simon & Schuster, 2004.

10 Granvold, D. K., "Promoting Long Term Sexual Passion," *Constructivism in the Human Sciences* 6(1) (2001): 73-83.

11. Brotherson, Laura M., *And They Were Not Ashamed: Strengthening Marriage through Sexual Fulfillment*. Boise, ID: Inspire Book, 2004, 53-54.

12. Johnson, Sue, "The Three Kinds of Sex," *Creating Connections* (2013), accessed June 29, 2015. http://www.drsuejohnson.com/attachment-sex/three-kinds-sex.

13 Brotherson, Laura M., *And They Were Not Ashamed: Strengthening Marriage through Sexual Fulfillment*. Boise, ID: Inspire Book, 2004, 72-73.

CHAPTER VIEW

The Need for Tuning In
Knowing Your Communication Styles
Tuning Into Self
Tips for Tuning Into Self
    Process Writing
    Attend to Your Emotions
    5 Minute Meditation
Tuning Into Your Spouse
Tips for Tuning Into Your Spouse
    Talk and Listen
    Pay Extra Attention to Nonverbal Communication
    Learn to Think Like Your Spouse
    Check Out Assumptions
    Ask Questions
    Eye Contact
    Tuning In/Observation Exercise
    Go With Me Emotionally
Tuning Into Your Own Sexuality
    Keep a Sexual Self-Discovery Journal
    Identify Your Sexual Accelerators
    Identify Your Sexual Brakes
Tuning Into Your Spouse Sexually
    Reading Her Winces
    She Doesn't Want to Direct the Traffic
    20 Questions–Your Conversation Starter about Sex
Tips for Tuning Into Your Spouse Sexually
    Talk to Each Other about Your Lovemaking
    Eyes Open Sex
    Find Your Spouse's Hot Spots
    Do the Sensate Focus Exercises
    Tune In to Her Arousal
    Turn it Off
Self-Evaluation - "Tuned In"
ACTION ITEMS — Chapter 9 - "Tuned In"

Chapter 9

TUNED IN — GETTING IN SYNC
EMOTIONALLY AND SEXUALLY

Jared and Allison had been struggling with their sexual relationship. She had some issues from her past that made sexually connecting scary for her. Through counseling, they were both coming to better understand the impact of her past experiences. Jared became better at empathizing with her feelings and fears. One night, Jared was giving Allison a foot massage as a way to help her relax after a long day. He had been doing this more often lately, which helped his wife internalize that she was safe with him and could relax and let go a little more. She could enjoy the pleasure of the foot massage without worrying about it leading to something else.

Allison was so thoroughly relaxing and enjoying the massage that Jared thought this might be a possible green light for him to go further. Slowly he began to work his way up her legs, massaging them gently. He felt her begin to tense and emotionally shut down. Reading her cues, he quickly adjusted his approach and returned to casually massaging her feet.

Because we had previously talked about how women are wired sexually (meaning that sometimes we just need to be "talked and touched into it"), Jared explained that this had been his take on her in that moment. While it had been more wishful thinking on his part, I acknowledged how wonderful it was that he understood her reaction so well, and that he was able to adjust to where she was at emotionally. Allison shared how reassuring it had been to see that Jared was able to read her and was willing to kindly adjust to her state of being rather than be upset. She ultimately felt so relaxed and close to him that she ended up allowing the interaction to go further, ending in a very positive sexual experience for both.

The Need for Tuning In

As I work with couples, I realize that the ability to "know" and "read" each other well is missing for many. Couples aren't always good at reading between the lines. They aren't especially adept at suspending their own perspective and empathically seeing things from the other's point of view. We may talk about being able to read each other's minds and finish each other's sentences, but that may not be true enough for some couples. It's a skill to be able to sense each other's inner state and respond accordingly. Especially in the bedroom, much of the sexual communication is conveyed nonverbally.[1] It is important for couples to be skilled at sending and receiving effective verbal and nonverbal cues in order to tune in well.[2]

Couples spend a lot of time being mis-attuned to each other. The goal is simply to keep working to tune in even better next time. Being tuned in to each other is a reward that comes only after a lot of time and effort has been expended. Couple attunement is "in-to-me-see" intimacy on a whole new level. Connection at this psychological level has an upward self-perpetuating cycle because of the oxytocin that is released when couples tune in to each other effectively through touch, eye contact, and other emotionally supportive behaviors. Mirror neurons additionally help us read each other better and develop empathy, which continually improves the connection.[3]

Without being attuned to each other well outside of the bedroom, it is very difficult to "know" each other well within the sexual dimension of the marriage. This chapter highlights the need to truly *know* your spouse, especially so that lovemaking can be a flow of reading and responding effectively to each other's vibes. It's not terribly romantic to say (or hear) in the heat of the moment, "Should I do this or that?" Instead, a tuned-in couple will read each other's nonverbal cues and communicate well when they are outside the bedroom; this helps husband and wife more confidently move forward inside the bedroom.

One couple was reminiscing about a recent intimate exchange they had. The husband commented that he hadn't been planning on kissing her at that moment. She asked, "So, why did you?" He responded, "Well, I read your body language and knew it was a go!" It was a great example of him being tuned in to her nonverbal cues. That's a real turn on for women to know their spouse will read them and confidently respond. It's a powerful skill for couples to have.

In order to truly know each other, husband and wife must both feel safe and be willing and able to expose their true selves to each other. Both need to know and accept the other's idiosyncrasies as part of a package deal that comes with one's spouse, and take those things into account within their intimate interactions. Couples need to open up to each other, check assumptions, and get good at reading each other well. It is only from a place of emotional safety, openness, honesty and transparency over time that couples can come to truly know each other and be able to read each other well.

Tuning in is about reading each other's verbal and nonverbal cues. You might compare it to listening to a song. The music is the nonverbal message, while the words are the verbal message. Tuning into and responding accurately to both messages takes a lot of practice and communication to become skilled.

With repeated experiences of sharing your true selves, you both come to know each other well. That is when it becomes second nature to sense what your spouse is thinking or feeling at any given time. In Chapter 3 - "Tenderness," I suggested spouses start asking each other, "How can I make your day better today?" In this chapter, we're working towards couples getting to where they already know the answer because they have learned to read their spouses well, and have developed the habit of regularly doing things that make their life better every day. This is the kind of relationship dreams are made of.

Founder of Emotionally Focused Therapy, and researcher of adult attachment and bonding, Dr. Sue Johnson asserts that the key ingredients—the make-it-or-break-it elements in strong relationships—are the ability to be emotionally open, accessible, and responsive to your spouse. This means being able to tune in to the psychological channel (thoughts and emotions) of your sweetheart by reading and understanding their emotional cues.

The ability to be seen, understood and "known" so deeply at an empathic level builds a bond profoundly safe and secure, because you know that they are always there for you. You know that they get you, and that they fully know you, and love you anyway. You can see it in their eyes. It takes courage, and a willingness to be vulnerable, to be able to tune in and respond emotionally and empathically with your spouse.[4][5] In order to create this secure bond in marriage, partners need to be "Accessible" and "Responsive," as well as physically and emotionally "Engaged."[6] You can remember these key components with the easy acronym A-R-E. Not only are these factors necessary for knowing and tuning in to your spouse, they are also the foundation for the emotional foreplay discussed in Chapter 3 - "Tenderness."

When couples don't realize that such emotional attunement is possible and necessary, it can create misunderstandings and emotional distance that can be detrimental in marriage. For example, if the husband in the scenario above didn't believe that his wife ever made it a priority to positively respond and engage emotionally, he may have either been emotionally wounded from her shutting down response, or he might have ignored her cues and continued his sexual advance. Both of these scenarios would lead to a deeper entrenchment of the negative sexual pattern they are trying to change.

"Without being attuned to each other well outside of the bedroom, it is very difficult to 'know' each other well within the bedroom."

Knowing Your Communication Styles

Tuning in requires that each spouse understand each other's personality—their strengths and weaknesses that may get in the way of how openly, honestly and kindly they communicate. Another couple in my office struggled with the common relationship dynamic of the husband being very expressive and open with his thoughts and feelings, while she tended to keep her thoughts and feelings more to herself. This couple's past experiences and innate personalities had lead her—the more reserved spouse—to withhold profound opinions and feelings. When she was finally able to share them in counseling, it caused her husband a lot of insecurity and a major loss of confidence in the relationship. It was one of the few times she felt safe enough to share her true feelings. After so many years of marriage, he was completely shocked and unprepared to take in how unhappy she had been. Everything about their relationship that he thought was real became a big, painful question mark in his mind.

As is common with most couples, the circular nature of their communication contributed to his painful new realization about their relationship. She withheld critical information, while he unwittingly contributed to her withholding by often responding with anger or frustration. Neither realized how difficult it was for her to openly and honestly share her opinions. They weren't aware of how his dominant personality was unintentionally sending the vibe that it was unwise for her to speak up. Both of them contributed to the lack of open and honest communication, one by not willingly saying things that may have been difficult, and the other by not recognizing the emotionally unsafe environment he was inadvertently creating that kept her quiet. Their marriage reflected the common codependent relationship dynamics that often develop into significant dysfunction in a marriage over time. Situations like this often require counseling to help mediate an emotionally safe environment for true feelings to flow.

Another approach for couples to communicate more openly is to share their thoughts and feelings in writing. This often levels the playing field. The hesitant one can speak more freely and safely on paper, while the more expressive one has to restrain their responses because the other isn't usually present when they first read the spouse's writings. This written form of communication provides a layer of protection, especially for the spouse who tends to struggle with being more open and honest.

By tuning in to each other, both husband and wife can recognize each other's strengths and weaknesses with regard to communication. Couples can make room for both to satisfactorily feel heard and understood. This type of understanding ultimately leads couples to be able to know, read, and tune in effectively to each other not only mentally and emotionally, but also sexually. Husbands can help by willingly working on their ability to read their wives well, so that they can respond and engage more effectively. I've encountered many men who aren't terribly interested in this endeavor.

> *I had been working with Dave to help him understand his wife's concerns. I would often say, "What do you think your wife would say or feel about that?"*
> *In the beginning, he would often be a bit exasperated, as if I had asked him the dumbest question. He'd say, "I have no idea."*
> *Other times he would ask me to just tell him so he didn't have to figure it out. I'd then explain that the key here was for him to develop the ability to watch,*

listen, and learn so well that he would sense what she was thinking simply from the verbal and nonverbal cues she gave him. This also helped him step outside of himself and begin to see things through her eyes, so that he could respond more sensitively to her needs.

Tuning Into Self

Before we explore tuning in sexually, we must first be sure husband and wife are able to know, read and tune in to themselves and each other outside the bedroom. Once tuned in to self, they can then use those skills to tune in to each other in the midst of lovemaking. What does it mean and what does it take to be able to tune in to one's self? Tuning into oneself is to be self-aware—to know your strengths, weaknesses, opinions, preferences, vulnerabilities, etc. It takes some time and effort to really get what makes you "You."

It requires time and effort to really understand your and your partner's core self. Once you truly know who you and your spouse are, then you can better see how "You" inter-acts with your spouse and what to do about it. For example, as my husband and I would interact over time, and be honest with each other—sometimes even painfully—I came to realize that I have a pretty quick response to almost anything. Also, I generally have an opinion about almost everything, but my husband didn't as much. That realization about myself and my husband helped me to ensure I didn't always impose my opinions on him just because they tended to be stronger and more quickly expressed. It helped me make time and room for my husband to think, feel and respond differently than me.

Tips for Tuning Into Self

Some of the best ways for individuals to build a foundation for tuning into them-selves are as follows:

Process Writing. Regularly engage yourself in "process writing" (i.e., your Sexual Self-Discovery Journal) to become more familiar with your thoughts and feelings. I invite my clients to have ongoing written conversations with God or themselves or even me about whatever is going on in their minds—especially when they are struggling.

One upset client contacted me about some things that were happening in her rela-tionship. We had an appointment in the next few days, so I suggested she try doing some process writing. She later told me that writing had been very therapeutic. Writing a conversation as if talking with me was beneficial because she could easily hear what I would say or ask her.

Another client uses this writing therapy to tune in to her own thoughts and feelings and to help clear out the trauma of dealing with her husband's porn addiction. She told me that when she writes, it feels like she purges the feelings. She lets go so much that when she rereads the writings later, it often looks foreign to her—as if someone else had written it because the issue had dissolved. It's a great tool to get your thoughts/frustrations/anger down on paper, so that your brain can stop stewing on it.

Process writing is simply putting on paper what is going on in your mind to allow you to "process" or make sense of your internal experience. This helps you not only become more familiar with yourself, but it also helps you process and dissolve painful, accumulated thoughts and emotions that often get in the way of interacting in healthier ways in our relationships.

It's important to really know your weaknesses as well. Make a list of everything you can think of that you don't like about yourself. As you review each one, decide if you are willing to forgive yourself for being imperfect. If so, you can let go and turn it over to God. Things we've said or done that we are ashamed of create a heavy weight that we carry around until we acknowledge our foibles and let them go.

The same process can be done with our strengths, so that we can each reinforce our value and worth as a person. List every positive thing you can think of about yourself. Add to it as often as you can. This becomes a list that you can review to remind yourself of all the positives about you. Having a clear understanding of your strengths and weaknesses makes you more in tune with who you really are as you tune into and interact with your spouse.

Attend to Your Emotions. Pay attention to any negative emotions. This helps you to figure out what you are feeling and why. Negativity is not a natural state, but a psychological alarm that something is off. For example, you might overreact to something trivial, like spilled milk. By noticing or attending to the negative emotion, and taking a few minutes to do some process writing, you may discover that you are actually upset about something else. Understanding your trigger and why you are taking it out on someone else is valuable information. It can also be helpful to make a Stress List or Anger List or Frustration List of everything you are currently feeling upset about. It's another way to be more aware of the context of your negative emotions and tune in to them so they can dissipate.

5 Minute Meditation. I highly recommend clients do a simple 5-minute meditation each day (see Chapter 2 - "Thoughts"). This provides an opportunity to be more present, slow your thoughts, and tune in to your deeper/divine self. This creates a solid foundation for knowing and being with yourself. Since women tend to always be doing, and have their minds going a million miles a minute, this opportunity to just sit and *be* can be profoundly transformative.

Tuning Into Your Spouse

Like tuning into yourself, the gist of tuning into your spouse is for you to know them emotionally—their strengths, weaknesses, opinions, preferences, vulnerabilities, sensitivities, tendencies, and style of interacting, etc. Being already tuned in to yourself, you can see better how "You" are distinct from your spouse. You can see what unique characteristics you bring to the table and the particular ways you interact with them.

Chad and Kathy had been married for more than 30 years, but when I asked them to tell me what the other most liked to do on date night, they were stumped. I was surprised how little they knew about each other's likes and dislikes in a variety of areas. We set up homework opportunities for them to start asking each other a variety of questions to get to know each other at a deeper level. They decided to get the book 365 Questions for Couples *to ask each other on a regular basis.*

A little later we were talking about an issue that came up regarding a sexual behavior he wanted to try. I could see Kathy was resistant to the activity and hesitant to share her thoughts. I asked Chad what he thought Kathy's opinions were on the subject. Without even glancing her way, he replied that she just "wanted to talk about it later." He thought that meant she was probably fine with it.

I offered them both an observation that Kathy tended to not say what she really thought a lot of the time, so as to not hurt, offend or upset Chad. I offered that she tended to give general responses, or offer distractions, delays or other means of avoiding conversations where there may be a difference of opinion. I suggested Chad look into her eyes for a moment to see if he could tell what she was really thinking about it. As he did so, she began to tear up. He could see that she was not okay with it.

Chad defended himself by saying that she had seemed fine with it. He added that he told her she could say no if she wanted to. I asked him what he thought about how easy that would be for her, considering that he had already begun to move forward in that direction and was pretty intent on it. His eyes registered the beginnings of awareness. He curtly said, "So, what am I supposed to do then?" I shared with him that he and I shared some similar characteristics. Most couples are made up of someone who tends to not say so much and is more tuned in to the other's feelings (like Kathy), and the other who generally has a lot to say about everything and is generally less tuned in to the other's feelings (like he and myself).

I explained that for people like him, it's easy to say what he thinks and to not get too concerned about how others may feel. We also tend to assume other people think like we do, so he might make an implicit assumption that if people have an opinion or feel strongly about something, they will speak up. But for those like Kathy, they may instead keep quiet so as to not cause any problems. They also tend to wonder how people can be so thoughtless and inconsiderate. While speaking up may be easy for him, it's probably not so easy for his wife.

The job of the more dominant or verbally expressive spouse is to: 1) be more sensitive and inquisitive about their spouse's thoughts and feelings; 2) to keep their thoughts and desires more neutral, so as to send a message that it is okay if they have a different opinion; and 3) to read and listen to her nonverbal communication, because it would always be more accurate than what she might say verbally.

I noticed Kathy moving toward Chad on the couch, putting her hand on his leg, as if to protect him from the painful realizations he was having. I asked Kathy what she thought her job was in all this. She rightly suggested that she needed to try to speak up more and to say what she really thought. I added that she might even need to be willing to do so even if it might unsettle Chad or upset him. Attending to the circular nature of their interactions, her job was to learn to be less sensitive to Chad, while Chad's job was to be more sensitive to her. They both chuckled at the paradoxical nature of their relationship and their homework.

Communication and emotional responsiveness are the primary means of becoming attuned to each other. The more you communicate and really get to know each other at a deeper level on an ongoing basis, the more attuned you will become.

Even after 30 years of marriage, Randall and Shannon still misread each other's sexual cues and had many mismatched expectations. Shannon figured Randall would want to have sex that evening, since she'd been out of town for a few days. But when he didn't wear his silky boxers that night like he usually did, Shannon assumed he was too tired for sex. The next morning she was awakened to his intimate caresses. It was their usual time for lovemaking. She longed to catch up on the sleep that had been desperately lacking while she was away. Frustrated that he didn't realize the depth of her sleep deprivation, she hesitantly succumbed to his advances, then fell immediately back to sleep.

With both of them misreading each other's cues, and neither making the extra step to check their assumptions, additional negative experiences were added to their pile of missed opportunities for emotional responsiveness and mutually enjoyable intimate connection.

Tuning in obviously goes both ways. Husbands and wives both want the other to pick up on their vibes. As Jane talked to me about wanting to help her husband tune in to her better, he said, "You know, I wish you would read me better, too. Can't you tell when I'm stressed and need a stress reliever like sex?" She admitted it almost startled her to remember that it's not all about her needs, but his, too.

We all tend to project our own thoughts, feelings, and opinions, etc., onto others, because we tend to think that others must think the same way we do. This can hinder us from tuning into others, especially if we don't realize this human tendency. When you know what your thoughts, feelings, strengths, weaknesses, opinions, preferences, vulnerabilities, and tendencies, etc., are, it's easier to clearly distinguish what are yours and what are someone else's.

Being tuned in means you are able to "share" experiences instead of having two different experiences simultaneously. You can stay tuned in with your spouse mentally and emotionally by asking questions and continually getting to know them better. This helps you stay current as they continue to evolve and become. Your spouse's interests and opinions can change over time. As you stay tuned in to your spouse, you can gain a greater appreciation for their interests and goals and be better able to support them.

Maybe your husband has always wanted to scuba dive. Maybe your wife used to go rock climbing. Maybe your spouse has always wanted to feed the homeless. Such discoveries could not only spark ideas for more meaningful activities, but also help you to understand and work toward fulfilling both your dreams and your spouse's dreams as well. "Shared" or "tuned-in" experiences are like intimacy superglue that can make your relationship stronger and the sexual connection even better. As you and your spouse feel more known and appreciated by one another, that closer connection will be evident in the bedroom. Make it a priority to continue to ask your spouse deeper questions about who they are, how they think, what they like, and who they want to be.

As evidenced by the story of Chad and Kathy, couples need to make sure they know which side of the complimentary/codependent cycle they tend toward in their relationship. This will help them understand whether they need to work on speaking up more, or speaking up less to really tune in to each other well.

Tips for Tuning Into Your Spouse

The following are some ways to practice better knowing and tuning into your spouse in non-sexual ways:

Talk and Listen. This one may seem pretty self-evident, but make sure you have enough time to talk together and continually get to know each other. After a day of working with clients, I sometimes feel like my husband has no idea who I am now, because I have learned and evolved so much even just in the course of a day. Staying connected through pillow talk or taking advantage of other opportunities to share thoughts and feelings even in little pieces helps you both keep up with who your spouse is becoming each new day.

Pay Extra Attention to Nonverbal Communication. As you can see in the story of Chad and Kathy, nonverbal communication is huge. I use the 80/20 analogy that when you say something, only 20% of it is through words. The other 80% is nonverbal, which comes from your tone, body language, facial expressions, gestures, eye contact (or lack thereof), and even posture. What is lesser known about one's "tone" or nonverbal communication is that it comes from the thoughts, feelings, and beliefs or the internal self-talk we are having inside our minds. The reality is that our thoughts get communicated to our spouse as nonverbal messages whether we want them to or not. Husbands and wives need to be more attentive to their thoughts and beliefs, so that their words and their thoughts match when they are communicating. Otherwise, in such mixed messages, our spouse will tend to focus on and believe what they felt (the nonverbal vibe) rather than what they heard.

To tune in well with your spouse, it's not enough to just keep your mouth shut if you can't say something nice. You have to also change the way you are thinking and seeing your spouse. This is so they will not be hurt, offended, or constantly on the defensive by the "attitude" they feel from you. Whatever you are thinking comes through louder than what you are saying.

Learn to Think Like Your Spouse. Many couples have little understanding of how their spouse thinks or feels about things. After discussing a thought or concept in counseling, one of my most common questions to couples is, "What do you think your spouse thinks about that?" I do this even while their spouse is sitting right beside them and could easily answer the question themselves. The spouse is often stumped. They're curious why I don't just ask the spouse. I push a little to give them an opportunity to think from their spouse's perspective. It's a way to practice empathy and to learn to think like their spouse. It's key to tuning into each other.

> *Hoping to help Andrew understand his wife better, I asked him what he thought it felt like for his wife to hear him say, "I'm trying to work on our marriage, but she's not!" Turning to his wife, I asked, "What do you think causes him to say that?" This gave her a chance to step into his shoes, and for him to hear how he was coming across to her. She shared some thoughts.*
>
> *I asked Andrew if what she was saying made sense to him. He quickly responded no, but I continued. "If you think from her perspective, does it make sense?" He reluctantly agreed. Throughout the session I asked them both various questions like, "What do you think it's like for her to be your wife?" or "How is it for Andrew being married to you?" As we neared the end of the session, I asked them both what their takeaways were. It surprised me to hear him say he needed to work on seeing things from her perspective more. I was thrilled. He understood the need to think like his spouse. That's exactly what being "tuned in" is all about.*

Determine to ask yourself often what your spouse would think, say or do in a given situation. Don't let yourself off the hook too easily by saying you don't know or have no idea. Try to step into your spouse's shoes and think about how your spouse might feel, and how your spouse might answer a particular question. When clients try to get out of it, I often ask, "But if you had to guess, what would you say?" Even if your answer isn't spot on, the effort to understand them better will create emotional connection and give them a chance to clarify. Create opportunities to check in with your spouse and see how well you "know" them.

John's experience provides another example of how to tune in to your spouse better. Out of frustration, he had written a list of all the ways he was disappointed with his wife and their intimate relationship. I asked if he could do the same thing from her perspective, as if he was his wife. Knowing her pretty well after 30 years of marriage, he did a good job of identifying what his wife's truths were about their relationship from her perspective. Given Leanne's overwhelmed and discouraged state at the time, we decided it wouldn't be helpful for him to share his list with her.

Instead, he was able to see her through different eyes, as he reminded himself of her difficult realities when he was tempted to focus on his own. This process helped him have greater patience and compassion for her. It significantly improved the way he interacted with her. You too might write out a list of thoughts and feelings (in your Sexual Self-Discovery Journal) you think your spouse has about your marriage and intimate relationship. If it is doable, you might share your writings with your spouse to see how accurate your perceptions are of their perspective. You might even consider asking them to do the same to see how well they understand what your relationship is like for them.

Check Out Assumptions. While it's good to learn more about what the other is thinking, it's not good to assume you know until you ask. Candace had been panicked about some random thoughts she had been having about a former boyfriend. She felt terrible and didn't know why it was happening. Shane knew about her thoughts and was beginning to be concerned, given the way she was acting. She felt anxious every time Shane asked her about it. Her weighty responses flared his own insecurities and made him think there was really something more to the feelings she was having.

When she finally explained what exactly she'd been thinking, Shane was relieved. He almost chuckled as he tried to explain that her concerns were nothing compared to what he thought they might be. They both learned how important it was to be more open and honest with each other and to check with the other about any assumptions they were making. It was an opportunity for both of them to also get better at factoring in their personalities and sensitivities and be better attuned to each other. It's never a great idea to assume anything about your spouse or how they are thinking, as you'll likely be wrong. One husband said, "Our new philosophy is, 'When in doubt, clarify.'"

If you do make assumptions, go with the concept of "assuming good intent" as your default.[7] Most of us are trying to do the best we can. By assuming good intent about our spouses, we change the way we feel about them and what they may be saying or doing. That changes and improves the way we think. As you begin to practice thinking like your spouse, it may also be important that you get in the habit of double checking your assumptions with each other. You might do this as a part of pillow talk as you go to sleep at night or as part of your conversations during date night.

To practice, think of one assumption you had about the other in the past week. Describe it and ask your spouse if your assumption was correct, i.e. "Last night when you didn't say 'good night' before going to bed, I thought you were upset with me about.... Was that correct?" They then get a chance to confirm your assumption or correct it. This helps you not only understand their thoughts and feelings better, but also helps you get better at reading their future verbal and nonverbal communications. This will come in handy in the bedroom.

Ask Questions. I'm a big fan of books, articles, websites, etc., that provide questions for couples to ask each other. This allows their conversations to extend beyond the regular day-to-day kinds of subjects. I often assign homework to couples to keep some questions handy so that they can ask each other even just one question a day, or more if it's Date Night. Some of my favorite resources for Couples Questions to get to know and tune in to each other better are:

- *365 Questions for Couples* by Michael J. Beck
- *101 Conversation Starters for Couples* by Gary Chapman
- *101 More Conversation Starters for Couples* by Gary Chapman
- *Love Talk Starters: 275 Questions to Get Your Conversations Going* by Les Parrott
- *Important Questions to Ask Before and After Marriage* by Claude Strayhorn
- "Table Topics for Couples," Tabletopics.com

Eye Contact. Make a point to look your spouse in the eyes as often as you can. This provides a snapshot into their soul if you will take the time to look. It's great practice for paying attention to what's behind their facial expressions—reading between the lines. Eye contact shows that you care enough to give your spouse your undivided attention. Eye contact is also one of the tuning in behaviors that can induce a release of the bonding hormone oxytocin. Eye contact leads to greater understanding and empathy between husband and wife. In the section on Tuning Into Your Spouse Sexually, we'll talk more about how eye contact can also be utilized during lovemaking for greater sexual attunement.

Tuning In/Observation Exercise. On the TV show *The Mentalist*, the main character works with law enforcement not as a psychic, but as an amazingly perceptive consultant. Working a fresh homicide case, he is often able to determine many otherwise unknown things about a victim simply by his exquisite observation skills, using all his senses—sight, smell, sound, taste and touch. He is also able to quickly read many things about a potential suspect simply from their nonverbal (and verbal) cues. Although this is just a TV show, we can all learn to improve our ability to watch, listen, observe, and notice our spouse. In time we can come to learn (or at least have a really good idea) what our spouse is thinking and feeling.

Developing this ability to observe and tune in allows husband and wife to come to truly "know" and "be known" by each other. This is one of the deep longings of the soul. To practice your tuning in abilities, consider doing the following exercise occasionally. This exercise is a fun way to really see and know each other:

> *Sit facing each other knee to knee either on chairs or sitting cross-legged on a bed or floor. Simply observe each other with a pleasant face and maintain eye contact for two minutes. Then take turns telling each other 10-15 things you noticed or think you know or understand about the other. Some examples might be: "You*

looked a little uncomfortable doing this exercise," or "This made me think about the time we…," or "I think you have a great smile."

I asked a couple to do this exercise and got a humorous response. The wife reported, "My husband *did not* want to do this. He was surprised (and disappointed) that you didn't make us to do this naked." (It's not a bad idea, actually!) "We kept laughing a lot through the exercise, but it was fun. We had a good talk afterwards. We both actually enjoyed doing it, despite his prior grumblings. We were able to share both observations and general affirmations of each other and found it to be a good experience."

Go With Me Emotionally. One way to truly connect with your spouse is to go with them emotionally. That is to read and match their emotion—like sitting in sadness with them. Helen and John had been struggling with feeling connected and being there for each other emotionally. Helen was especially feeling the lack. John had been working on it, but didn't really understand until a "gift of crisis" occurred in their marriage. A "gift of crisis" is what I call something that happens in a relationship that is so bad, or so painful, that it demands change. It paves the way for that change to occur that may not have happened without the "gift of crisis." John explained his awakening during one of our individual counseling sessions:

I got the wake-up call of a lifetime. My wife was struggling, and I could see that what I was doing wasn't helping her or our marriage. Things happened between Helen and her family that demanded I finally and fully step up to the plate to be there for her. In counseling when we first discussed what Helen needed from me emotionally, it was like being enrolled in the class where I was learning new concepts. When she was abandoned by her family, it became the "lab" where I had to put into action being there for her emotionally. I now get what she has been asking of me—"to go with her emotionally." I've had to read her, and see where she's at, and then go with her into the pain, if necessary.

I vividly recall when she shared some painful emotions she was having about feeling abandoned by a friend. In that moment, it was as if I was walking up to a gate on a path I usually didn't take with her. I started to do my old thing of looking for the positive intention in them, almost as if I was defending them. But this time I thankfully noticed that she began shutting down like she normally did when I wouldn't go with her emotionally. I immediately switched course, even though that wasn't easy or natural for me. She helps me be there for her now. She's learned that she can speak up and let me know I'm abandoning her emotionally instead of just shutting down like she used to.

I know now that I need to really hear her feelings, so she can open up to me emotionally. She needs to know I'll be there for her. She needs unconditional, strong, quiet support, and my emotional presence. She needs me to be available to her emotionally and not interrupt with my problems. I need to listen with sensitivity and softness. I need to get better at feeling what she feels and to vali-date what she feels, instead of minimizing or discounting her feelings. I've finally learned how to be there for her. She made it clear for me when she said, "Where ever I go emotionally, go with me." I know that despite the hell we are going through, we'll be able to come out stronger. We are creating something so much better than we could have ever had before I was awakened to her pain and the emotional void in which I was letting her live all alone.

Tuning Into Your Own Sexuality

As you get to know yourself more thoroughly in an effort to connect better with your spouse, you might also tune in to your sexuality by learning more about your specific sexual wiring.

Keep a Sexual Self-Discovery Journal

I've been married for 20 years and I've never had an orgasm. In your book you ask: Do you know what turns you on? Do you know what works best for stimu-lating your clitoris? Have you determined what kind of touch or stimulation is needed? Do you know when in the lovemaking process the stimulation works best, and what quantity, intensity, or speed is most arousing? My answer is, "I genu-inely don't know. I don't know even after all these years, and I'm not really sure how to even figure it out!"

For many wives, especially those who have not made sex a high priority, or made it an area of personal expertise, it can be valuable to begin keeping a simple and private Sexual Self-Discovery Journal of things you notice about your lovemaking experiences. Get in the habit of noting two or three things you liked most and liked least about that session of lovemaking. Be specific. Vanessa started writing in her Sexual Self-Discovery note-book regularly. She'd write a few things after each time they had sex, and leave it where her husband could read it. She said, "It's so much easier if he just reads what I write instead of me having to tell him to his face. It's worked really well for us."

Taking a few minutes to jot down a few things can be very helpful. It will help you remember what you experienced and what you liked or didn't like. This helps women to be more sexually self-aware and to identify their intimate brakes and accelerators. Your Sexual Self-Discovery Journal is a key part of processing the exercises throughout this book, and increasing your intimate understanding. This process writing helps you put concerted effort into figuring out the specific ingredients for you to experience the ecstasy of sexual intimacy.

Identify Your Sexual Accelerators

Your "Sexual Accelerators" are those things that lead to greater interest and arousal. Sexual accelerators are your sexual "likes" or "turn-ons"—that which fuels your fire. These can be things *you* do, *your spouse* does or that you *both* do to light the intimate fires.

> *Kari loved it when her husband would lightly kiss her lips, as she passively "received" his intimate affection. At first she would just bask in his kisses without even kissing him back. It was a way that she could warm up and get into the action. She liked to just lay there taking it all in, as she enjoyed the sensual touch on her lips. To her this was a way for her to be "kissed into sex" during that "touch-me-into-it" phase of lovemaking.*
>
> *At first her husband was a little put-off when she didn't kiss him back, thinking she wasn't into it. He misunderstood the acceleration effect of this activity for her, until he learned how much she loved to just be kissed and adored without having to actively participate. It was a perfect part of her warm-up process. It made her feel as if she was being gently seduced.*

Getting to know each other's sexual accelerators (and brakes) is a necessary part of being able to tune in to each other sexually without always having to speak words. Carl struggled to understand his wife's body language and nonverbal messages. He fumbled around, keeping them both somewhat distracted during the sensual experience. Not knowing what his wife wanted sexually affected their ability to really connect and enjoy each other intimately.

> *Howard didn't know when to be soft and slow and when to get serious about things sexually. It often frustrated Julie that he didn't get it until she was able to explain it to him. She let him know that if she had sweats on when he came to bed that she definitely need a fair bit of warm up. She'd have to be "talked and touched into it."*
>
> *Sometimes she was already in bed wearing lingerie, but felt like he'd fiddle around with her instead of going for it like she was wanting. She told him that if she was already wearing lingerie, then that was one of those times when she was feeling a little more frisky and wanted to be "taken" instead of getting a soft and slow approach. She chuckled when adding, "And if I'm going to wear lingerie, it would be nice if he would at least admire the wrappings before he rips them off!"*

With a little extra communication, Howard came to understand her nonverbal body language differences and was able to adjust his sexual approach accordingly. This scenario provides a good example of how husbands need to understand what the wife's sexual code means. Wives need to be sure they articulate their sexual language. The following "Sexual Accelerators" exercise will help you both understand each other better.

One of the challenges many women face is that they themselves often have no idea what they like or what accelerates their arousal. My oft-given homework to women is to brainstorm a list of at least 10 specific sexual activities, ("favorites") that they enjoy. I then have them rate each item from 0 (not much of a turn on) - 10 (totally turns me on) to indicate how much of an accelerator each one is.

A few helpful hints to start your thought process for this sexual accelerators exercise might be to fill in the following sentence stems:

- "I love it when you…"
- "It feels really good when we…"
- "It really helps me when you…"
- "It really puts me over the edge when you…"

Here are some common accelerators to get you started in identifying your own. They might be things you do or things your spouse does in the lovemaking process that turn you on:

- Talking together.
- Making sure teeth are brushed and mouthwash is used.
- Having romantic music or candlelight.
- A nice backrub without touching sexual zones too early in the process.
- Hearing loving words and expressions of your pleasure.
- Verbally expressing my own pleasure during foreplay with "Mmmms" and "Ahhhhs."
- Tickling my tummy or other body parts without touching the hot spots at first.
- Nibbling on my neck and sides of my breasts.
- Actively caressing your body and enjoying the firmness of your arms, muscles and shoulders.
- Breathing you in and basking in the sensual pleasure of it all.

An additional piece of the puzzle in figuring out the intricacies of female intimacy is to pinpoint the timing or order in which these activities might be preferred. Most women won't necessarily know until they stop to think about it. An example might be where you enjoy your husband kissing your breasts, but not if he hasn't first kissed and caressed other parts of your body (like your neck, shoulders, and lips). It is a good rule of thumb for men to spend at least some time on the less obviously erotic body parts before going for the breasts and genitals. It's an important part of the warm-up process that many women need, to help them get fully engaged sexually. It also sends an important message that her whole body and whole self is desired, not just her sexual parts.

Identify Your Sexual Brakes

Sometimes it's easier to start with identifying your sexual brakes if you can't figure out what your accelerators are. The turn-offs are usually more obvious to women. Sexual brakes are those things that hinder your arousal or enjoyment of sex. These are the activities you dislike that dampen your fire and turn the arousal process off.

> *Sandy felt like her husband was like a little kid in a candy story when they had sex. It was a real turn-off for her to see him so excited. It made her feel self-conscious, especially when she wasn't feeling the same giddy excitement. She enjoyed kissing, but felt like he was so over-anxious and into it that it put the brakes on her growing arousal. He needed to be cool and take on a more casual and confident manner.*
>
> *She was able to identify this sexual brake and even had an idea for a solution. She explained how much better it would be if her husband would almost play hard to get during foreplay. She explained how that really turned her on and made her anticipation skyrocket. She wanted to be able to kiss him and have him almost brush her away playfully. She said, "When he is playful and even a little teasing like that, it just makes me want him even more!"*

Identify your sexual brakes by creating a list of at least 10 specific sexual actions that you don't like about the lovemaking process. To identify your turn-offs, for this exercise you might fill in the following sentence stems:

- "I get distracted when you…"
- "I get annoyed when you…"
- "I get stuck in my thinking when you…"
- "When you _____ my arousal seems to slowdown or come to a standstill."

Sexual brakes and accelerators can be: physiological, psychological, relational, mental, emotional, physical/sexual, spiritual, environmental—sights, sounds, smells, activities, words (said or not said), location, time, place, pace, etc. So, let your mind roam free to identify both your sexual accelerators and sexual brakes, then share that information with your spouse. Some common sexual brakes for women are:

- Bad breath.
- Letting negative thoughts get the better of them.
- Inhibitions due to body image issues, negative sexual conditioning, feeling unsafe emotionally.
- The husband getting aroused too fast when she's still warming up.
- Having the bedroom too warm or too cold.
- Accidentally leaning on or pulling her hair.
- French kisses too soon and too wet.
- Focusing too much on breasts and not enough on other body parts.
- Getting frustrated or being impatient when arousal isn't happening quickly.
- Being tired/stressed.
- Being too passive or disengaged.

Depending on who struggles the most with sex, it may be helpful to let that person do this exercise of identifying and sharing their brakes and accelerators without the added pressure of the feedback from the person who already gets into sex easily. You may want to think about how to do this exercise to fit your circumstances. If you aren't sure, I'd suggest the wife do both of these exercises (accelerators and brakes) even if it's just for her own awareness.

Sharing this with your spouse would be the next important step. This is where a counselor can be helpful if this is a difficult subject. The hope for this exercise is to unlock some of your sexual secrets together as a couple in the spirit of helpfulness. It is not to offend each other with what they may be "doing wrong." It can be fun to both do this exercise, then exchange lists and discuss anything that surprises you and/or note anything you already knew pretty well. You might also ask each other what it was like to do this exercise as an added insight into each other's sexual psyche.

Tuning Into Your Spouse Sexually

Tuning into each other sexually means different things for a wife versus a husband. In lovemaking, the wife generally needs to focus on tuning into her own pleasurable sensations—at least at first—in order to shut down all the open windows occupying her mind that distract her from her sexual self. Because of how women are wired sexually, tuning into herself first allows her to focus and more easily get into the state of arousal. Then she is better equipped to tune in to her husband sexually. This allows her to be more active sexually, as well as more emotionally and sexually present.

In lovemaking, the husband needs to be especially attuned to his wife first (rather than himself) because arousal is generally easier for him. This way he can then focus on reading her subtle cues within the lovemaking experience, especially as she works her way into a higher state of arousal. Reading her breathing, her facial expressions, her movements, her sounds, and her body all become vital components of great lovemaking.

Reading Her Winces

Mitch and Elizabeth's experience illustrates how vital it is to know your spouse and be able to tune in and read her well.

Elizabeth was working through some difficult experiences from her teen years. During one of their intimate homework exercises, things went a little further than planned. Mitch said he noticed that she seemed to tense up a bit and almost wince, but decided to push forward anyway, thinking she'd relax into it. I asked Mitch if he thought his wife was more likely to speak up when something was off, or to not say anything. He said she probably wouldn't say much.

I wondered out loud if he realized that Elizabeth also tended to say what she thinks he wants to hear rather than what she really feels to not upset him or hurt

*his feelings. He hesitantly agreed that was probably true. I explained that some-
times people who are more reserved will unwittingly "lie," or at least withhold
information, so as to not seem rude or cause problems. I suggested that he may
need to get better at reading her, so that he doesn't push forward with things she's
not quite ready for—especially intimately. If he did, it would just reinforce the
negative beliefs she already has about men and sex.*

Certainly in an ideal world, each spouse clearly communicates their true thoughts
and feelings. But the reality is that it isn't always the case. It's usually more true for one
spouse over the other. Both Elizabeth and Mitch recognized that she does tend to withhold her true feelings, and he tends to take her at her word.

> *Elizabeth acknowledged needing to work on expressing her thoughts and needs
> more forthrightly. While both of them could work on their communication, it
> seemed more appropriate at the moment for Mitch to work on reading Elizabeth
> better until she was able to speak up more freely.*
>
> *At their next counseling session, Mitch decidedly stated, "I want to get better
> at noticing her cues—even her 'winces'—especially as I approach her sexually. I
> don't want her to feel like she needs to keep lying to me just to save my feelings. I
> see this as an opportunity to really figure her out and understand what she's trying
> to communicate even when she doesn't use her words. I've been assuming I could
> rely on what she tells me. I know now that I need to pay better attention to her
> subtle cues. I'm hoping that will eventually help her feel safe enough to be more
> honest with me."*

During lovemaking, husbands should pay more attention to their spouse's body language. They might ask themselves, "Does she tense up and pull away or relax into me
and draw towards me?" Men will greatly benefit if they will get good at reading her.

She Doesn't Want to Direct the Traffic

In Chapter 6 - "Talk," we discussed the value of women sharing their feelings during
lovemaking (particularly the positive ones). It certainly helps her husband learn how to
tune in to her better. But it's a bit of a buzz kill for her if she has to spell it all out for
him *during* sex. This is where having a husband who has learned how to tune in to his
wife, and read her cues outside the bedroom, will pay off big time inside the bedroom!

One wife said it this way: "It's just not that sexy for him to ask me how I liked something in the middle of lovemaking. I especially don't like it if I'm wanting to be 'taken.'
It's a turn off to have to say, 'Um, that's not working for me. Can you do something different?' I need him to pay more attention to what has happened before, or what I have
said in past conversations outside the bedroom, so he can use that information on the fly
within the bedroom. I definitely don't want to have to direct traffic for him while trying
to focus on getting turned on."

This is especially important for men to understand because one lovemaking session her cues might say, "Take me!" and another session might induce a "soft and slow" or, "Can we have a quickie?" response. The same approach may lead to a variety of different outcomes. It's part of what makes sex new and exciting, even after many years of marriage.

20 Questions—Your Conversation Starter about Sex

Both husbands and wives, but especially wives, need to identify what turns them on and what turns them off. Then they need to communicate that vital information to each other. This intimate information becomes the erotic intelligence husbands and wives need in order to truly "tune in" to each other. To help make it easier for you and your spouse to learn from each other and discuss the specifics of your sexual relationship, I suggest an exercise called "20 Questions–Your Conversation Starter about Sex."

This exercise is another great way to help you identify your sexual brakes and accelerators. Discussing the questions below can make a fun date night activity or something to discuss as you go for a walk together. This could be part of your pillow talk, with no expectation that it will lead to anything. You may want to take turns with who answers each question first.

1. What do you think are three of my favorite parts of lovemaking?
2. What are three of your favorite things about lovemaking?
3. What are three things you think I like *least* about sex?
4. How often do you think most couples have sex? How often do you wish we had sex?
5. What do you remember about our first kiss?
6. On a scale of 0-10 (0 = not at all, 10 = a lot), how much do you enjoy kissing in general? What could make it better?
7. What misconceptions did you have about sex before we got married?
8. What is one of your favorite memories of us being intimate?
9. What are three things that happen "outside the bedroom" that make you *most* interested in being intimate?
10. What are three things that happen "outside the bedroom" that make you *least* interested in being intimate?
11. On a scale of 0-10 (0 = not at all, 10 = a lot) how important is non-sexual touch and affection to you in our relationship?
12. When we engage in non-sexual touch or affection (i.e., holding hands, hugging, sitting close, etc.) what does that communicate to you or mean to you?
13. What are some of your favorite places on your body to be touched, kissed, or caressed during lovemaking?
14. What kinds of things do you most like me to say to you during lovemaking?
15. What does sex mean to you?

16. What is something you've thought might be fun to try sometime?

17. What do you wish we would have done differently on our honeymoon?

18. How much do you think our honeymoon experiences affect the sexual relationship we have today?

19. What would your ideal lovemaking experience be like? Share as many details as you can.

20. What are some of the biggest obstacles or biggest challenges when it comes to sex?

If it is particularly difficult for either of you to answer these questions, you may want to consider writing out your answers, and then give them to your spouse to read on their own before discussing them. Carl and Stephanie were going through this list of questions while on an anniversary getaway. They decided to create a list of their favorite sexual experiences from throughout their marriage. It was a highlight for them both to reminisce about their enjoyable intimate memories. This is another fun idea for couples to tune in to each other intimately by creating such a list of favorite sexual experiences.

Tips for Tuning Into Your Spouse Sexually

The following are some specific ways to practice tuning in and reading your spouse's sexual cues:

Talk to Each Other about Your Lovemaking. It is important for husband and wife to have some discussion about their lovemaking, including their likes and dislikes. This can help them both learn each other's sexual specifics, even if it seems uncomfortable at first. This is not a great conversation to have during lovemaking or even immediately after. Maybe the next day would work for some mutual sharing about the experience. It's also best to keep any verbalizations within lovemaking positive whether it is "Mmmmms," or "Ahhhhs," or simply moving a spouse's hand or lips to a different location. In a mutual coaching conversation later on, you can discuss things more fully. Like the 20 Questions above, it will help husband and wife get to know each other better sexually.

Eyes Open Sex. In lovemaking, specify occasions when you both will try to keep your eyes open during sex, even during orgasm. This takes lovemaking from simply sexual, to simply amazing with the added intimate connection. As Dr. David Schnarch states in his book *Passionate Marriage,*[8] many couples do not really connect emotionally while they are connecting physically. It's almost as if couples tune each other out rather than tune each other in. This eyes open exercise may be uncomfortable for couples at first, since it requires a strong sense of self and a willingness to be vulnerable—body and soul. *Eyes open sex* has the added benefit of seeing how your lovemaking is affecting her. You can see in her eyes what exactly turns her on.

Find Your Spouse's Hot Spots. To tune in to each other better during sex, make a conscious effort to touch new erogenous zones on your honey, and see what kind of response you get. If you rarely touch his backside during lovemaking, try it. If you rarely kiss her on the ear lobes, try it. If you rarely give him a hickey somewhere, try it!

Do the Sensate Focus Exercises. Another intelligent way to identify each other's sexual accelerators and sexual brakes is to do the 7-week program of Sensate Focus exercises mentioned in Chapter 7 - "Touch," and more completely spelled out in my first book *And They Were Not Ashamed: Strengthening Marriage through Sexual Fulfillment.*[9] This 7-week program of gradually increasing sexual touch gives you both a unique opportunity to see what lights your fire and what doesn't.

The Sensate Focus exercises are sexually therapeutic.[10] They allow for a fun, sensual exploration to help you both get to know each other better sexually. These exercises require you to experience your sexuality more slowly and in smaller compartments, which helps you see your sensuality and sexuality with new eyes. It can help provide intimate insights for identifying your sexual accelerators and sexual brakes. Sensate Focus exercises are a great way to learn new techniques for your lovemaking repertoire that you may have never considered before.

Tune In to Her Arousal. Husbands might want to get in the habit of noting where on the arousal scale of 0-10 they think their wife is at any given moment in the lovemaking process. By tuning into her arousal level, husbands can learn to be more aware of their own arousal, master their own sexual feelings, and help to be more in tune with her arousal process. Additional help will come from their wives completing the "Sexual Arousal Template" exercise in Chapter 8 - "Technique," and sharing those insights with their husbands.

The objective is for husbands to get good at noting things like, "She's still at a 3, so I need to keep things slow and stay away from her breasts." "I think she's around a 6 now, so this is when she seems to like me to touch her breasts more." "She's probably around an 8 now, because she is a lot more active and kisses me more. I know she likes me to be more aggressive and put more pressure on her clitoris as she gets closer to her climax." As husbands are able to mentally identify where she is at arousal-wise during lovemaking, it can significantly help him to know what to do, and when, to make sex a blissfully exquisite experience.

Turn it Off. It should go without saying that cell phones, iPods, iPads, laptops, the television, etc., should be nowhere near the action when you're getting it on. Mental distractions occur easily enough during lovemaking—especially for women—so make it as easy as possible to "turn on" and "tune in" to each other by turning distractions off!

Tuning into yourself, your spouse and each other sexually is another key ingredient of a sextraordinary marriage. Like tuning into a radio station, when the sender and receiver are "tuned in" to each other, the messages of love and ecstasy can be relayed simultaneously without interference. To be truly tuned in to each other both inside the bedroom and out results in being more fully present mentally, emotionally and physically. This allows husband and wife to be securely attached, as well as more actively engaged participants in more passionate and mutually fulfilling lovemaking. Being tuned in to each other requires emotional strength and vulnerability, but it's worth it!

Self-Evaluation - "Tuned In"

To give yourself a guide as to how you are doing in this dimension, how would you currently rate yourself and your spouse overall in the area of being "Tuned In"? Write your thoughts in your Sexual Self-Discovery Journal. — *I am tuned in to myself and my spouse sexually both "outside the bedroom" and "inside the bedroom." I can read my spouse's body language and nonverbal cues and respond effectively in both the emotional and sexual dimensions of our relationship.*

RATING (0 - disagree to 10 - agree):   You _____ Your Spouse _____

ACTION ITEMS — Chapter 9 - "Tuned In"

- Be sure that both husband and wife feel safe enough and are able to be open and honest with each other. This will tend to be easier for one spouse over the other.

- An approach for couples to communicate more openly is to share their thoughts and feelings in writing.

- Regularly engage in process writing, written conversations with yourself or God, and notice and attend to your emotions.

- Make a list of everything you don't like about yourself. As you review each one, decide if you are willing to forgive yourself for being imperfect. If so, you can let go and turn it over to God.

- Make a list of every positive thing you can think of about yourself. Add to it often. This becomes a list that you can review to remind yourself of all the good things about you.

- Ask yourself often what your spouse would think, say or do in a given situation. Don't let yourself off the hook too easily by saying you don't know or have no idea. Try to step into your spouse's shoes and think about how your spouse might feel, and how your spouse might answer a particular question. Create opportunities to check in with your spouse and see how well you "know" them.

- Write a list of thoughts and feelings you think your spouse has about your marriage and intimate relationship. You might share your writings with your spouse to see how accurate your perceptions are of their perspective. You might even consider asking them to do the same to see how well they understand what your relationship is like for them.

- Double check your assumptions with each other. You might each think of one assumption you had about the other in the past week. Describe it and ask your spouse if your assumption was correct, i.e., "Last night when you didn't say 'good night' before going to bed, I thought you were upset with me about…. Was that correct?" They then get a chance to confirm your assumption or correct it.

- Get one of the books of questions for couples. Use it regularly to get to know each other better.
- Do the Tuning In/Observation Exercise.
- Regularly write in your Sexual Self-Discovery Journal to tune in to yourself mentally, emotionally and sexually and to identify your sexual brakes and accelerators.
- Create a list of your sexual accelerators by brainstorming at least 10 specific sexual actions "favorites" that you enjoy. Rate each item from 0 (not much of a turn on) - 10 (totally turns me on) to indicate how much of an accelerator each one is.
- Create a list of your sexual brakes by brainstorming at least 10 specific sexual actions that you *don't* like about the lovemaking process. Share your sexual accelerators and sexual brakes with your spouse.
- Play the game "20 Questions–Your Conversation Starter about Sex" to make it easier for you both to learn from each other and discuss the specifics of your sexual relationship. This exercise is another great way to help you identify your sexual brakes and accelerators and better tune in to each other sexually.
- Together create a list of your favorite sexual experiences or memories.
- Consider doing the 7-week Sensate Focus exercises to get better tuned in to each other sexually.
- Husbands might want to get in the habit of noting where on the arousal scale of 0-10 they think their wife is during various stages of the lovemaking process.

NOTES

1. Hess, J. A., and Coffelt, T. A., "Verbal Communication about Sex in Marriage: Patterns of Language Use and Its Connection with Relational Outcomes," *Journal of Sex Research* 49(6) (2012): 603-612. doi:10.1080/00224499.2011.619282.

2. Granvold, D. K., "Promoting Long-term Sexual Passion," *Constructivism in the Human Sciences* 6(1), (2001): 73-83.

3. Johnson, Dr. Sue, *Love Sense: The Revolutionary New Science of Romantic Relationships.* New York: Little, Brown and Company, 2013.

4. Johnson, Dr. Sue, "The #1 Way to Build a Stronger Connection with Your Partner," Mind Body Green, December 29, 2014, accessed April 28, 2016. http://www.mindbodygreen.com/0-16781/the-1-way-to-build-a-stronger-connection-with-your-partner.html.

5. Johnson, Dr. Sue, *Hold Me Tight: Seven Conversations for a Lifetime of Love.* New York: Little, Brown and Company, 2008.

6. Johnson, Dr. Sue, *Love Sense: The Revolutionary New Science of Romantic Relationships.* New York: Little, Brown and Company, 2013.

7. Harker, Emil, *You Can Turn Conflict into Closeness: 7 Communication Skills of Successful Marriages.* Brigham Distributing, 2015.

8 Schnarch, David, *Passionate Marriage: Keeping Love and Intimacy Alive in Committed Relationships.* Holt Paperbacks, 1998.

9 Brotherson, Laura M., *And They Were Not Ashamed: Strengthening Marriage through Sexual Fulfillment.* Boise, ID: Inspire Book, 2004, 242-251.

10 van Lankveld, J., "Self-Help Therapies for Sexual Dysfunction," *Journal of Sex Research* 46(2/3) (2009): 143-155. doi:10.1080/00224490902747776.

CHAPTER VIEW

Touch and Respect
Understanding Her State of Readiness for Playfulness
Challenges of Being Playful
Benefits of Fun and Flirty Playfulness—Inside the Bedroom and Out
  Helps you feel more relaxed
  Takes away discomfort or embarrassment about sex
  Adds a lighthearted, playful tone to the marriage
  *Allows you to take yourself and others less seriously and to approach life more
    enjoyably*
  Adds fun and spice to the relationship
  Reduces focus on a particular outcome; less goal orientation to sex
  *Helps re-kindle the initial attraction of the relationship where fun
    and flirty was the norm*
  Helps develop the friendship in the relationship
  Increases playful anticipation
  Helps increase spontaneity
  Helps get you out of the loop of negative thinking and distraction
How To Be More Playful in Your Marriage—Inside the Bedroom and Out
Self-Evaluation - "Teasing"
ACTION ITEMS – Chapter 10 - "Teasing"

Chapter 10

TEASING — PUTTING THE FUN
AND FLIRTY INTO SEX

Flirting with my honey can be so much fun! It's been really helpful to me in culti-
vating my own sexual feelings towards him. I used to hate it when he'd try to flirt
with me or be sexual toward me in any way outside the bedroom. But all that has
thankfully changed. It has become a frequent joke for me to say, "Hey babe, you
wanna get lucky?!" I especially love to say this to him when there is no chance of
follow through…just to torment him…like on the way to church or right after
we've already been intimate.

At first my husband would look at me with this surprised—almost unbeliev-
ing—look that said, "Are you kidding me? Are you really serious? Now don't kid
me!" In time his response developed into a simple, "Yeah. Sure, I wanna get lucky."
He got even wiser when he began to say, "I already am!" This playfulness has
made our relationship so much fun. It helps me keep my intimate fires flickering
throughout the day.

This story is one of my favorites from a client who had discovered the fun in being
flirty with her husband. A missing ingredient in many couples' lovemaking repertoire is a
dash of fun and flirty playfulness. It's almost a mindset you're wanting to develop in your
marriage—to naturally think in fun and flirty ways. When sex (or the relationship) gets
too serious, it loses a lot of the joy and passion it can otherwise have. When there isn't
much playfulness or humor either outside or inside the bedroom, it can negatively affect
the whole marriage…including the sex.

Some couples have nearly forgotten how to flirt. By definition, flirting or teasing is
playfully tempting your spouse or communicating interest and attraction, but without a
direct intention to follow through. From a wife it might sound something like, "Do you
wanna mess around!?" with no intention to do so, or a suggestive, "How did I get such
a hot honey?!" Writing flirty notes on his mirror with lipstick or giving him any kind of
suggestive look or touch can add a bit of fuel to the intimate fires.

Sometimes it easier to remember how to flirt and be playful when we imagine our
husband as our boyfriend. Women may want to think back to the days of being his girlfriend and rekindle some of those thoughts and feelings. Thinking like a girlfriend is
a great way to keep the fun and flirty in your relationship. I can hear many husbands

saying, "I am sexually playful with my wife outside the bedroom and she hates it." The key words are "sexually playful." It's easy for men to tease and be playful with their wives sexually, but they tend to struggle with being playful with no strings attached. Women find it difficult to receive playfulness that seems like it always has an ulterior—sexual—motive. What women really need, especially in the beginning, is overall playfulness in the relationship.

Touch and Respect

Mark just thought his wife wasn't comfortable with PDA (public displays of affection) until we dug a little deeper. Jackie explained that most of the time, his PDA was in front of their children or their teenage sons' friends. She was concerned about how others might feel during such interactions. She felt like he sometimes took things a little too far, so she went on guard to protect those around her.

We discussed that what is going on in his mind at the time is the vibe he is sending out—which can ultimately be for anyone in the room to pick up on. He had thought it was a good thing that their kids saw him "loving" his wife. But, when I asked what he thought his young daughters might be thinking or feeling, he paused. He realized they might be a little confused.

I asked what messages they might take in seeing their mother not enjoying the interactions, but him continuing them anyway. Would he want them to let boys treat them that way? He hadn't ever thought of it from their perspective and realized it all might be a little too much for their young minds to understand. I also asked, "What about your older sons?" Was there any negative messages they might get from seeing their dad "playfully" touch and tease their mom? Would he want his sons to treat young women that way? As he thought about it, he considered that it might come across as objectifying if he was after something without respecting her feelings about it. Certainly it is a wonderful thing for kids to see their parents be fun and playful with each other. There's a big difference between behaviors that have a sexual overtone and those that are "just playful." It takes a lot of self-insight to be aware of the difference.

The key issue is that of showing respect. If Jackie was genuinely uncomfortable with the teasing, it might be good for him to find out what she was feeling. Jackie admitted that until this discussion, she hadn't been able to put her finger on what she was feeling, but that this was right on. She had been thinking with her "mom brain" and trying to protect those around her from being uncomfortable. She genuinely wanted Mark to know she liked to be playful with him, but that it needed to be more appropriate or in private. He acknowledged that his behavior probably had been a little unseemly now that he was thinking differently about it.

I wondered out loud if he had inadvertently trained his wife to not be flirty and affectionate with him because she felt unsafe in these moments.

I mentioned my "Seesaw Principle" where one spouse is up in the air on one side of an issue (Mark being overly touchy in public), with the other spouse down on the ground on the opposite side of the issue (Jackie being pretty resistant to any touch in public). If either of them would consciously move themselves toward the middle, it would naturally bring the other more toward the middle as well. What I love about resolving couple conflicts is that even if only one spouse will change, it can still help and often change them both. Now that this topic had been brought into the light with more understanding added, I challenged Jackie to shoot for a bit of a "shock and awe" approach to being more flirty and sexually playful with Mark when it felt appropriate to do so. She was happy to take that on. Mark didn't need any prodding to change how he was being "flirty" with his wife.

Understanding Her State of Readiness for Playfulness

Many women have complained to me about their husbands groping them or kissing them too passionately in the kitchen. It often feels inappropriate to them. That may be especially true if it's happening in front of children, who may not be old enough to understand or appropriately process experiences of a sexual nature. It can be an unintended form of sexual abuse for children to be exposed to sexual behaviors before they can properly process it.

To wives, any unwelcome sexual teasing or suggestiveness tends to feel similar to affection that always leads to sex. This one-directional playfulness tends to have a negative effect on women because it reinforces the idea that everything is about sex to a husband, or that that's all their husbands really love about them. A wife wants to be loved and wanted for her whole self, not just her sexuality. It can also send a message that the husband doesn't really understand her or care that she is wired differently—more emotion-based than sexually.

When there are strings attached to even playful touch in the marriage, and wives have not yet developed or embraced their sexuality (or their playfulness), they tend to be turned off by *any* kind of teasing touch, like Jackie in the story above, instead of being warmed up by it. Men and women are wired differently in and out of the bedroom. Since men tend to have easier access to feelings of sexual desire, it's more natural for them to be playful sexually. Women, however, are still a few steps away from feelings of desire, so it feels out of place—and can even feel violating at times—instead of playful.

Men, if you aren't getting a positive response to your playfulness, here are some suggestions. Be more attentive to your wife's response to your teasing and playfulness. If you aren't getting a warm response, then tone it way down. Maybe just stick to non-sexual playfulness, until you can build her trust in you and the relationship that everything you do isn't about leading her to sex.

For men, non-sexual teasing and playfulness requires that their thoughts also be non-sexual. That means there is no thought or expectation that it will lead to anything sexual. You need to think through how you come across to your wife. Neutral thoughts about your loving playfulness must be in place long before you even speak. If you are thinking, "I sure hope we finally get to have sex tonight," while tickling her or playfully telling her not to rip your clothes off that night because you're too tired, then the playfulness will likely bomb. Instead, if you were to tease her in ways where you couldn't follow through anyway, you are more likely to get teasing points. For example, you might kiddingly tell her that it's too bad she's not going to be able to "get lucky" because you're heading out of town, or because you are sick with the flu. If you genuinely are headed out of town or actually have the flu, then it will work much better.

Keep in mind that it's all about what you are genuinely thinking and feeling when you are interacting with her. Your thoughts and feelings behind your words and actions are felt more keenly than the words or actions themselves. Your teasing needs to be expectation-free in order for it to be most successful. Another option is to discuss the idea of adding playfulness to your relationship, but let her take the lead in doing so until she feels ready or safe to make it mutual. Letting her take the lead will help you refrain from putting unproductive pressure on her.

Challenges of Being Playful

Keep in mind that being more playful in your marriage has some challenges. Playfulness doesn't come naturally for many women, although some personalities have an easier time being playful and spontaneous. Self-esteem and self-acceptance also play into the ability to be playful and spontaneous. It's a learned behavior for many women. When couples are dealing with a painful past, or have a lot of accumulated anger and resentment, it may not be the best idea to start working in the area of teasing and playfulness. Professional help may be needed, and other ingredients from this book may be better suited to begin your marital enhancement journey. It's generally best if the less-inclined spouse decides to develop her playfulness and spontaneity, rather than be encouraged by her husband. Trying to change someone else generally has the effect of frustrating the initiator and creating defensiveness on the part of the recipient because of the pressure they feel.

A word to husbands…this whole concept of adding teasing, playfulness, and spontaneity requires that the initiating spouse (often the husband) be carefully tuned in to the wife. If a husband's efforts to encourage more playfulness in his wife are falling flat, it may be good to re-read Chapter 9 – "Tuned In" to help you focus on tuning into your spouse first. This can help you be conscientious in your approach to increasing playfulness in your marriage. There's a chance your spouse may not yet be ready to focus on adding this ingredient, so it's best if you can be okay with that until they come into it themselves.

> *"Teasing and being flirty and playful with each other is probably one of the best indicators that things are going really well within a marriage."*

❧

Benefits of Fun and Flirty Playfulness—Inside the Bedroom and Out

Assuming we're good to go in adding some fun and flirty playfulness to your relationship, let's talk about some of the benefits inside and outside the bedroom. Consider all the different ways that adding in the ingredients of teasing and playfulness into your marriage can help, in both the emotional and sexual relationships.

Helps you feel more relaxed. Being able to relax is vital for women to be able to step into the sexually intimate experience. When there is playfulness in the marriage, the mental switch to take things into the bedroom is much easier.

Takes away discomfort or embarrassment about sex. Sex can be a pretty taboo topic fraught with anxieties. But when there's an element of playfulness to the relationship, and even more so in the lovemaking experience, it naturally reduces feelings of discomfort or embarrassment.

Adds a lighthearted, playful tone to the marriage. Life can be pretty serious sometimes. It's easy for marriage to not only get a bit stale, but also to develop a serious—even stifling—tone. It's no fun to live in a fuddy-duddy mode of relating. The practice of playfulness lets life be a little more fun and enjoyable. One wife told me how much her husband loved it when she was able to respond in a more lighthearted way. Rather than get upset by his sexually oriented teasing, she was able to say to him with a smile, "When the kids are asleep you can 'handle me' all you want!" Finding ways to laugh and keep things light is great foreplay for fun and playfulness in the bedroom as well.

Teasing and being flirty and playful with each other is probably one of the best indicators that things are going really well within a marriage. I can often see how a couple's marriage is doing just by how a husband and wife interact with each other. A client said she could always tell when their relationship was flourishing. They would laugh a lot more and be playful with each other. She felt that was also the first thing to go when things weren't going well.

Being appropriately flirty and playful in front of your kids sets a good example for them of how to have a healthy and fun relationship in their marriages. As kids see that their parents like each other and have a desire to be with each other, it reinforces feelings of love and security in the home and family. Reawakening a playful vibe in your interactions with each other not only feeds the emotional relationship and the family stability, but enhances the more intimate, sexual interactions as well.

Allows you to take yourself and others less seriously and to approach life more enjoyably. Teasing and playfulness are an invitation to focus a little more on the lighter side of life. Not taking ourselves too seriously can pay dividends in multiple dimensions of life and marriage. A client shared how she'd been struggling with intimacy a lot in her marriage. She felt that her husband made sex so serious and intently focused that it inhibited her sexual response and reinforced her feelings of sex as a chore. He was uptight, and he didn't smile much or act playful. He had many expectations sexually.

She always felt like he was getting right down to business instead of connecting with her and helping her warm up to him first. His seriousness made her feel self-conscious and fearful that she wouldn't be able to meet his expectations. After her husband adjusted his approach and stopped being so serious about it, things significantly changed for the better. His newfound playfulness and learning to relax into it freed them both to enjoy lovemaking so much more and to make it a more pleasurable experience.

Adds fun and spice to the relationship. In Chapter 11 - "Treats," we'll talk more about specific ways to add spice and novelty into the intimate relationship, but suffice it to say that playful teasing is a great way to spice things up inside the bedroom and out.

Reduces focus on a particular outcome; less goal orientation to sex. When couples are being playful with each other, there's almost an unspoken message that says, "It doesn't really matter what happens here, 'cuz it's all gonna be fun!" Goal-orientated sex is a real downer. It increases performance pressure on both husband and wife and decreases the chances of a mutually fulfilling experience. Focusing on the fun and playfulness of sex helps couples let go of the need for any particular outcome. Playfulness in the bedroom can create a bridge between what you wanted to have happen during sex, and what actually did happen—making both outcomes equally positive and fulfilling.

Helps re-kindle the initial attraction of the relationship where fun and flirty was the norm. In the beginning of a relationship, there is continuous flirting and fun. Sometimes as the realities of life happen, husband and wife lose that aspect of marriage. When couples re-kindle that kind of fun and flirty relationship, many of the initial feelings of attraction are then more present in the whole relationship. Those feelings of attraction stir the sexual pot for more passion in lovemaking as well. Another benefit of flirtatiousness in the marriage is that there is less pull of flirtations outside the marriage. Never stop flirting with your spouse!

Helps develop the friendship in the relationship. The degree of friendship in the marriage is part of the emotional foreplay for lovemaking. Being playful and kidding around like good friends sets the stage for relaxed playfulness and greater sexual connection inside the bedroom because of the friendly and connected relationship outside the bedroom. Some wives may think it should be the husband's responsibility to develop this area of friendship, since he is the one generally wanting more sex. As we discussed in Chapter 3 – "Tenderness," it certainly behooves men to put their best effort into the emotional connection between husband and wife. It's probably the area they have the most control over to help improve things sexually.

Women, too, have a vested interest in developing the friendship and flirtatiousness of the marriage. It helps to make the relationship that much more sweet and satisfying for her as well. It helps develop her wholeness and completeness as a human being. Rather than being a passive recipient, wives can be proactive participants in creating a playful, fun and flirty marriage relationship.

Increases playful anticipation. Anticipation is powerful fuel for female sexual desire and arousal. Playful teasing outside the bedroom has the effect of putting women a couple steps ahead mentally. This helps them make the transition to lovemaking so much easier. When there is an element of playful, even prolonged teasing between husband and wife—especially in the bedroom activities—it can shoot anticipation and arousal through the roof.

One couple shared how the wife was finally able to have an orgasm after many years of marriage because her husband discovered a way to playfully tease her sexually in the course of lovemaking. He found that if he would tease her as he undressed her, it would take her arousal to the next level and over the edge! It took a lot of practice for them to get to this point, but by adding in the elements of teasing and playfulness, both of them felt more relaxed, less concerned about the outcome, and more willing to go whereever the experience took them.

Helps increase spontaneity. Another benefit of flirty playfulness is that it helps with spontaneity in the relationship. I like to say, "I'm very spontaneous…if it's planned!" Letting go of things at a moment's notice is tough for me and tough for a lot of women. Living such a busy, fast-paced lifestyle, people tend to live a pretty planned out and structured existence. Having things planned out and sticking to the plan can create a sense of safety and control. This is especially true in the context of marriage and the bedroom. Being flexible, going with the flow, or allowing for impromptu activities—whether inside the bedroom or out—is often something wives need to practice in order to develop. It definitely didn't come naturally for me. The very act of being playful or teasing your spouse in some way is a great way to practice spontaneity.

Spontaneity is an ability that many husbands would love for their wives to develop, especially given that spontaneous sex is high on a husband's list of fun things to do!

That may yet be a distant goal for some women, but having that objective in mind is a great way to work toward developing one's spontaneity skills. Expressions of spontaneity are especially enhancing sexually, given that it's a conscious act of self-will or choice. Husbands want to be wanted, rather than simply being serviced on demand. Wives who work at being more playful and spontaneous, or even initiating sex once in a while, really amp up the excitement and connection in the relationship.

Joan was working diligently at trying to initiate sex with her husband more often. She felt a bit deflated, though, when he commented that he appreciated her efforts to initiate, but sometimes felt like sex was mostly on her terms and her timetable. He was right. She had worked hard to be able to initiate sex, but wanted to take on this additional challenge as well. He had been so patient with her throughout their efforts to overcome their sexual issues. She began to work at being more consciously prepared for *his* advances, even though it was much harder for her to do. Here are some ideas that may be helpful in getting your gears grinding to initiate or be more sexually spontaneous:

- Initiating lovemaking could include a simple text that says, "Hey, wanna get lucky tonight?!" Or you could leave some lacy panties in his car, lunch, or briefcase, etc., with a note that says, "For a good time call, xxx-xxxx!" Initiating sex can also be as simple as getting into bed naked or rolling over to snuggle him if that's not your norm.
- Practice preparing yourself mentally to be able to say, "Yes" to sex when he initiates. It might help to start out with saying, "Yes" to outside-the-bedroom invitations (i.e., to go for a walk, or to meet him for lunch, etc.). Going with his preferred time and way sexually is often tough for women, but is so heartily welcome to husbands. Being spontaneous sexually means that you have developed the ability to work through some of those first steps of fueling female desire discussed in Chapter 8 - "Technique." These are, namely, 1) deciding you can and will go there, 2) taking responsibility for your emotional foreplay by initiating more connecting contact that day, and 3) getting yourself in a relaxed, ready-to-receive-sexual-stimulation state, so that he can take it from there.

Helps get you out of the loop of negative thinking and distraction. Especially in the context of lovemaking, being playful and teasing each other is a great way to distract your mind from negative thoughts and other intimacy distractions.

How to Be More Playful in Your Marriage—Inside the Bedroom and Out

With a better understanding of some of the challenges and many of the benefits of being more playful, here are some specific ways to include more fun and flirty playfulness in your marriage—inside the bedroom and out:

- Send fun and flirty texts to each other throughout the day. Be sure to let your spouse know if you specifically want them to not read something sexual into it. Some spouses may need to overtly understand that flirty playfulness in their wife isn't necessarily a direct invitation to something more. The more a wife can experience giving and receiving teasing and playfulness without it leading to anything sexual, the easier it will be for her to continue to develop her playful side organically. Develop a repertoire of pet names or code words for sex or sexual things just between you to add that element of playfulness. It can also reduce discomfort and embarrassment about sexual things. Like the wife in the opening scenario, she referred to sex as "getting lucky." It could also be called "nooky" or "getting it on." Personal pet names like "baby doll," "honey bun," or "hot mama" give couples a chance to have a private language that includes sexual connotations that in time decrease the taboo nature of the subject itself.

- Share funny video clips or other humorous anecdotes to bring more lightheartedness and laughter into the relationship. Taking turns sharing the latest joke can be another fun way to laugh together.

- Even consciously smiling more at each other can help you both take life a little less seriously. My husband and I have often noticed a stressed or worried look on the other's face. We will gently touch the other's furrowed brow to remind each other to relax and help them immediately release the tension they are feeling. It's a fun little tool for lightening the load of life.

- Winking is another amusing habit to get into as husband and wife. It's kind of fun to steal a wink across the room or to give a big, obvious wink just to be silly! One husband froze when he caught the eye of a woman winking at him suggestively. He didn't know what to do, until he turned and noticed the woman's husband behind him. He breathed a sigh of relief, then thought what a lucky guy that man was.

- Any kind of unexpected action has the potential for creating a playful moment. Whether it's a wife who unexpectedly goes up and kisses her husband's neck, or a husband who unexpectedly tells her wife how cute she is—these moments can add a bit of spice and put a smile on everyone's face.

- A great way to decrease focus on a particular outcome is to playfully plan on a completely different outcome than orgasm. This could be a session of naked cuddling with no intercourse allowed. It could be to do the kissing homework suggested in Chapter 7 - "Touch" or on my "Bliss of a Kiss" Marital Intimacy Show podcast, episodes #026-#028. It could be to plan to go park and make out somewhere, where intercourse is not even an option, to re-kindle the fun and enjoyment of just plain old making out!

- It might be fun to just be a little playful and silly about changing the whole sexual scenario. You might let your hair down during a sexual escapade like naked tickling matches, dancing naked, or just some intimate snuggling…unless you simply can't contain yourself!

- After many years of marriage, it can be difficult to remember the fun and flirty times you had together in the beginning of your relationship. Why not role play a first date together? You could also role play as if you are in the beginning stages of courtship as you go about your daily lives. Perhaps there are some playful texts, emails, phone calls, random flowers you could send and receive. If this wasn't your forte back in your earlier days, now is a great opportunity to develop that playful side of yourself.

- Playing a little hard to get is another great way to increase teasing and playfulness in your marriage. Talk about fun and flirty! One wife told me about her efforts to kiss or hug her husband when he got home from work. At first it was a bit of a drudgery to her, but then we suggested he play a little hard to get sometimes. When he started doing that, everything changed. It started to drive her crazy, in a good way. She went from it feeling like a duty to finding it a fun challenge to "get him" when he came home.

- In the bedroom, there are all kinds of fun and flirty ways to tease and be playful with each other. You could undress each other playfully, teasing all along the way. You could play some peek-a-boo. You could do a striptease. You could play some of the fun bedroom games available out there. It's all about brainstorming ideas and identifying those that both of you are willing to try.

- Playfulness in the bedroom has the added benefit of helping women close down the many mental windows open in their minds. Playing out a sexual scenario, for example, allows wives to more fully engage themselves in the lovemaking experience. Teasing them with tickling or non-sexual caressing helps them to be more present and more actively participate in the process of lovemaking.

- Orchestrating surprises for each other increases spontaneity and playfulness. Oftentimes, one spouse has a greater preference for surprises and may even be better at pulling them off. There's something about setting up and receiving surprises that provide some fun stretching for the soul. It's can help us break free of needing to be in control or of having to follow a plan in order to be okay. Setting up a surprise getaway or just surprising your spouse with a night off to go and do whatever she wants are a couple of suggestions. It may be more difficult to willingly go with the surprise or spontaneous opportunity presented. It's something some may need to keep practicing.

- One of my favorite fun ideas for couples is to create a "kissing closet" out of the kitchen pantry. It's a great way to be fun and flirty and to freak your kids out a bit as well. And who doesn't love doing that—especially if you have teenagers! If you search "kissing closet" on StrengtheningMarriage.com, you'll see some fun photos and more about how you, too, can create your own kissing closet. It might be fun to send pictures of you and your spouse utilizing your own kissing closet to share on our website.

- You might consider stealing a kiss in public every now and then. It will catch your sweetheart off guard at first and create some of that unexpected spice in your marriage. This is especially good homework for the spouse who tends to be more reserved. One wife decided she would kiss her husband in the movie theater at the end of every movie they saw. At first it was a little unnerving for her, but with a positive response from her husband, they've kept at. They've even gotten better at being playfully surreptitious about it. It is good for kids to see their parents loving each other, so a random appropriate kiss or hug in front of them is another fun and flirty idea to consider.

- When either husband or wife has to travel, it provides a perfect opportunity to tease and be playful with each other. Another favorite idea for travelling is to take your "Flat Spouse" with you. It's a full body cutout picture of your spouse, maybe even pasted onto cardboard that you take with you when you travel. You then take pictures of you and your Flat Spouse at various locations during your travels to send by phone or email back to your spouse at home. (Search "Flat Spouse" on my website, StrengtheningMarriage.com, and you'll see some fun photos and how to do this for yourself.)

- If you forget to take your Flat Spouse, you could even just take some selfies with your cell phone and send them back home with a flirty text message. My husband is not a big fan of selfies. It just makes it mean even more to me when he does, as a way to stay in touch when we are apart.

These fun and flirty ideas for you and your spouse could be incorporated into your marriage, especially if teasing and playfulness are some of the missing ingredients in making your marriage and intimate relationship all it can be. All of this teasing and play-fulness is ultimately designed to help improve the friendship and emotional connection between husband and wife. This, in turn, helps make it easier for women to "decide" to go there sexually. If teasing, playfulness and fun have not been a focus of your marriage, I encourage you to make it a priority and a personal area of expertise.

Using the "Progress List" exercise in Chapter 9 - "Tuned In," you could start jotting down in your Sexual Self-Discovery Journal any times you are consciously fun, flirty, playful or spontaneous, whether inside the bedroom or out. What you keep track of you are more likely to pay attention to and ultimately increase. You might also keep track of times your husband is flirty and playful and what your response is to him. If it isn't a great response, see if you can identify ways to change things in order to respond to him more positively.

The teasing and playfulness discussed in this chapter is a mindset you're striving to develop. In the next chapter, Chapter 11 - "Treats," we'll delve further into taking this teasing and playfulness into the bedroom to add fuel to the fire with variety, novelty, and adventure.

Self-Evaluation - "Teasing"

To give yourself a guide as to how you are doing in this dimension, how would you currently rate yourself and your spouse overall in the area of "Teasing"? Write your thoughts in your Sexual Self-Discovery Journal. — *Being fun and playful with my spouse is an important way to keep the spark alive in our relationship. I often tease, flirt and be spontaneous with my spouse, and enjoy it. I have developed (or am developing) a playful mindset that is making our marriage more fun than ever before.*

RATING (0 - disagree to 10 - agree):   You _____ Your Spouse _____

ACTION ITEMS — Chapter 10 - "Teasing"

- Discuss the idea of adding playfulness into your relationship. Consider letting her take the lead if she is hesitant to make it mutual.

- On a scale of 0 (none) - 10 (a lot), where would you currently rate yourself in the area of teasing and playfulness in your marriage and then in your sexual relationship?

- Review the suggestions for teasing and playfulness in this chapter and brainstorm some ideas of your own.

- Together, or individually, choose at least a few ways you could integrate more playfulness in your marriage.

- Start a "Progress List" of playfulness by jotting down (in your Sexual Self-Discovery Journal) any time you are consciously fun, flirty, playful or spontaneous, whether inside the bedroom or out. You might also keep track of times your husband is flirty and playful and what your response is to him. Identify ways to be able to respond to him more positively.

CHAPTER VIEW

Chapter 11

TREATS — KEEPING THE SPARK ALIVE

"Guess what, Laura?! I have a sex 'bucket list'!"

"You do?" I replied enthusiastically.

"Well, my husband and I were just thinking we ought to have a bucket list of sexual things we'd like to try or do someday."

"That's awesome!" Intrigued, I said, "Tell me more."

"Well, so far we've been able to pull off the 'under-the-moon-in-the-backyard' bucket list item, and we're working on adding more things to our list!"

"I love it!" I said.

You can bet that I was impressed with the progress and proactivity of such an idea for this client! She had been working on being more playful and spontaneous sexually, so this was a perfect next step for her. Her story provides a great transition from our previous chapter about teasing and sexual playfulness to this chapter about sexual "Treats!"

I mentioned in Chapter 10 - "Teasing" that the primary purpose of the "teasing and playfulness" concept was particularly to encourage a more playful state of mind in the overall relationship and within the bedroom. In this chapter, the concept of "Treats" takes the teasing and playfulness more from a mindset to action. The idea behind the Treats "T" is to encourage novelty, creativity and adventure in marriage and in the intimate relationship as well. The goal is long-term, mutually fulfilling marriages. It's a pretty safe bet that the single best treat a woman can give her husband is some good, passionate lovemaking.

A fun, flirty intimate relationship provides a protective layer for marriage that must be constantly nourished. God made sex the ultimate treat with no other natural substance or experience coming close to the pleasure and connection it can provide. With boredom as its own brand of stress in marriage, the ideas in this chapter can help you ensure that a humdrum bedroom routine won't become an Achilles Heel in your marriage.

Novelty, Familiarity and Connection

In the beginning of marriage, sex tends to be automatically novel and varied. But as time goes on, we get used to and adapt to things. Thus familiarity often overruns novelty and newness.

Before we dig in to encourage more novelty, a few words about the power of familiarity and connection as a means of novelty. A good, solid, emotionally intimate relationship, in and of itself, can be a vital source of enduring excitement. Building on earlier chapters that address emotional connection, feeling safe and secure is what allows women especially to explore and be sexually adventurous. If she can trust that her partner is there for her, then she can relax and let go. Physical, mental, and emotional safety foster a willingness to experiment, because of the protective emotional bond.[1]

The strength of the attachment a couple has affects their sexual behavior. Well connected couples, where the bonding hormone oxytocin flows freely, are less likely to experience habituation or boredom. Instead, their interactions remain vital and rewarding, because of the depth of the intimate bond.[2] If the focus of a couples' sexual relationship is primarily physical instead of emotional, then novelty and variety will be much more needed. When couples are tuned in emotionally, sexual encounters are naturally unique and interesting. Emotionally "tuned-in" sex reduces the need for novelty and variety because of the oxytocin that is readily present in each spouse. This comes from the abundant emotional and physical affection in the relationship.[3]

A strong, bonded marital relationship has additional benefits, such as decreasing stress, easing depression, speeding healing, and helping to ward off addiction.[4] The marital foundation of emotional connection is vital. Novelty simply adds some spice—making marriage even better! Adding the seasoning of novelty into what's familiar requires us to stretch outside our comfort zone. In moderation, doing something new and different awakens your senses and changes your brain chemistry in good ways.

Brains Need Novelty

Within human relationships, there are competing needs for connection and stability, as well as newness and novelty. Newness and novelty stimulate the neurotransmitter dopamine in the brain, creating a feeling of excitement, optimism and elation. It's the pleasure chemical.[5] Dopamine is not to be confused with oxytocin, which brings about bonding and connection, over excitement and passion.[6] The importance of this chapter on "Treats" is that those who stay married well for the long haul are those who are not only securely connected, but are also willing and able to keep the excitement of new love alive. This means continually nourishing their relationship with some newness and novelty. Couples can maintain and/or regenerate passion throughout their marital journey by infusing it with novelty, excitement and surprise.

While brain studies do propose the need for novelty, it's a careful balance. Too much novelty and stimulation can actually decrease one's ability to connect well emotionally. The novelty and overstimulation of things like pornography, infidelity, addictive substances, etc., can create an overdose of dopamine. This can rewire the brain's reward circuitry, making every day love, commitment and sex seem humdrum.[7] If you or your spouse have gotten caught up in the overdose of addictive substances or behaviors like pornography, you will likely need professional help to unwire and re-wire your brain properly. The sooner you get serious about working on that, the sooner your marriage can be all that it was designed to be. (See the Recommended Resources in the Appendix for understanding pornography and addiction recovery.)

It's important to note that the vital ingredients of a sextraordinary marriage are not primarily novelty and breathtaking passion. What's foundational is loving and secure companionship, fun and flirty behavior, sex that's not necessarily perfect, but "good-enough," and lots of affectionate touch.[8] Novelty is the seasoning, not the main course in a sextraordinary marriage. With that said, there is still some credence to the neurological need for novelty both in marriage and the bedroom. Boredom can increase the likelihood of couples taking each other for granted, decreasing marital and sexual satisfaction, and increasing one's vulnerability to outside temptations.[9]

This chapter is chock full of boredom-busting ideas to keep things fresh, new and interesting, especially within the bedroom. Get ready to knock your spouse's socks off… and a few other articles of clothing as well! Taking action of any kind breeds motivation to continue to pursue your goals for variety, fun and more creativity in the bedroom.

Being Interesting Outside the Bedroom First

Before we get into bedroom activities specifically, there are a few overall concepts that can help couples naturally infuse novelty, variety and adventure into their own lives and marriages. This can then flow over into the bedroom relationship. These two elements are: 1) keeping yourself interesting, challenged and mentally stimulated, and 2) leaving a little room between you and your spouse for some mystery and intrigue. This facilitates the ongoing excitement of two ever-changing, multi-faceted individuals.

Mentally Stimulated. One of the primary ways to keep your bedroom and your relationship interesting is to keep yourself new and interesting. Having endeavors that fuel your own passion for life adds fuel to your marriage and intimate relationship as well. Continuing to develop and challenge yourself in ways that "complete" you will keep you growing and help you become more alive. When you are interesting to yourself, you will be more interesting to your spouse as well. And you will also be accomplishing one of the divine purposes of marriage—for individuals to become whole and "One" as husband and wife. It reminds me of the concept of marriage, illustrated by the diagram below, "Two Halves-Become Two Wholes" where ultimately it isn't two half individuals that make marriage whole. It's two individuals who work to become whole so that they can more easily become one.

When I am learning new things, I have new insights to share and new information to think and talk about. For example, the passion I feel in my work of strengthening marriages spills over into my marriage and my family. I often come home from work enthused about a new concept a client and I have fleshed out together in the thick of their raw, marital challenges. Cultivating a hunger for knowledge keeps your thoughts

TWO HALVES - BECOME TWO WHOLES

Before Marriage

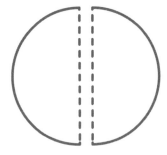

1/2 + 1/2 = 1

Before marriage two imperfect 1/2's are attracted to each other to create what feels like a complete whole. ("He/she completes me!")

Within Marriage

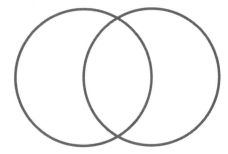

1 + 1 = 1

In marriage God's design for two imperfect individuals is to be stretched and polished to become two whole/ complete individuals.

StrengtheningMarriage.com

fresh with new worlds to explore and new insights to share. To stay interesting—keep learning. Take a class on something you are passionate about. It may be an art class, a karate class or tennis lessons. Even just reading a new book, such as this one, expands the mind and provides all sorts of new information to bring home to the marriage and the bedroom.

Pursuing new and/or challenging activities either individually or as a couple keeps you mentally stimulated and enhances your emotional connection as well. Doing that might also remind you that you matter—that you are worthy of investing some time and effort into yourself. Learning together as husband and wife by taking classes, reading new books and articles or attending seminars not only helps keep each of you interesting individually, but also infuses the relationship with creativity and novelty. Do new things together to catch your mind off guard and keep things fresh, new and exciting.

Having a shared hobby as husband and wife can help to reignite passion and connection. You could hike, work out, visit museums, or attend art shows or high school plays. You might learn a new skill like cooking, dancing, skiing or playing racquetball—whatever puts a spring in your step and takes you off your beaten path. Rita shared her experience with learning something new, and how it blessed her life and her family, too:

When our children were still pre-school aged, I was feeling overwhelmed with the responsibilities of raising young children. Being home to raise them full-time was what I had always wanted, but I felt a need for a creative outlet and some time away from home and kids for grown-up conversation. I enrolled in a weekly cake decorating class—something I'd always wanted to do. My husband took care of the children while I attended the classes. I appreciated his willingness to help me attend to my needs, too.

Each week when I came home I felt energized. I was learning something new! I came to realize how much I needed this break and a little "me time." It made me feel better about myself, and more positive toward home and family. My family especially loved helping me eat the beautiful cakes I was making! I felt even more loved by my husband as he helped facilitate this opportunity for me. I think he liked seeing me learn and grow in new ways. It almost seemed to make me more interesting in his eyes. I know he especially liked seeing me excited and happy about my new skills—not to mention the noticeable change in my stress levels after an evening out.

The Need for Mystery and Distance. This concept of allowing for some distance and mystery in your marriage may seem a little paradoxical after talking so much about closeness and connection. It may be better understood as akin to the concept of "absence makes the heart grow fonder." The ability to have a passionate, fulfilling relationship requires that a couple balance our two primary drives—intimacy (connection) and independence (distance). It's almost a spiritual concept that may be best understood from a metaphoric standpoint. This may allow you to more accurately and appropriately internalize and apply the concept. Deanne shared an experience she and her husband had that wonderfully illustrates this concept of distance and intrigue in marriage.

Last night, we went out to dinner with a large group of people. My husband came late and was not able to sit next to me. When we got home, he told me that as he watched me across the table he found himself even more attracted to me from a distance. He said it was almost like being in high school again watching the popular girl from across the room and lacking the courage to ask her out, but wanting to. Then he said he smiled to himself and thought, "Whatever, that's my wife! I get to take her home!"

Life's inevitable occurrences of distance between husbands and wives provide an opportunity for mystery and longing. I find wisdom in this inspired poem by Kahlil Gibran about the need for some separateness as a strengthening agent in marriage.

On Marriage
You were born together, and together you shall be forevermore.
You shall be together when the white wings of death scatter your days.
Ay, you shall be together even in the silent memory of God.
But let there be spaces in your togetherness,
And let the winds of the heavens dance between you.

Love one another, but make not a bond of love:
Let it rather be a moving sea between the shores of your souls.
Fill each other's cup but drink not from one cup.
Give one another of your bread but eat not from the same loaf.
Sing and dance together and be joyous, but let each one of you be alone,
Even as the strings of the lute are alone though they quiver with the same music.
Give your hearts, but not into each other's keeping.
For only the hand of Life can contain your hearts.
And stand together yet not too near together:
For the pillars of the temple stand apart,
And the oak tree and the cypress grow not in each other's shadow.

I hope the rich metaphors in this poem can more elegantly help you to see the deeper meaning behind the need for mystery and distance in marriage. This poem suggests forever togetherness as the end goal of marriage, but letting your togetherness have room to breathe and freely flow is needed. It's like a profound gift requiring trust in oneself and each other, knowing that hearts will always return home.

It reminds me of the wife who shared how interesting it was to experience her husband at a distance as she watched him up on the stand conducting church services each week. It somehow made her hungry for him in a way she hadn't experienced in a long time. It seemed that because of the distance they now experienced in their marriage, she almost felt butterflies in her stomach when she again came into his presence. It was as if the distance had created some mystery and magic between them.

Continuing with the poem, the foundation of connection should allow for drinking not from one cup, but of having a variety of interests and sources of nourishment. This allowance brings an added depth and richness to the relationship, as well as a wholeness to the individuals who then come together in marriage as ONE. Husband and wife grow not in each other's shadows where there is no light or fresh air. Instead, they have the trust and freedom to grow wherever they may be—yet connected by unbreakable heart strings, like the wife who watched her husband serve and lead from afar. The distance and mystery is a means of bringing newness, experience and growth back home where it can enrich the marriage and family relationships.

When the foundation of a marriage is firmly rooted in God, then there need be no fear about some separateness or distance in the marriage. Instead, it's about allowing each other the space to fully be, allowing each full access to their own agency. For when you are "chosen" by your spouse—knowing your spouse has the freedom to choose elsewhere (i.e., how to spend their time, energy or affection)—then how much sweeter it is when it is you he freely chooses.

Rachel shared her concerns with me about her husband going back to school. She was worried about how he would be spending so much time away from home, meeting new people, and being in study groups with other women. She worried that he might not like coming back home to her after all of his new and exciting experiences with other people. As we discussed her concerns, she realized that it had actually been good for them to have some distance. She was able to see it as him having agency, and yet he was still choosing her. He still came back home to her and wanted her help with his studies and to discuss all the cool things he was learning. She came to feel that her faith in him had actually been strengthened, as she was able to push past her fears.

Intimacy vs. Desire

While intimacy tends to improve with closeness, "desire" may be heightened by some degree of separateness. Balancing distance and closeness is the challenge of intimate relationships. How do we maintain our individual identities while also being so intimately intertwined? This question embodies the challenge of "differentiation" in intimate relationships. It's the ability to maintain the elements of togetherness and connection with that of autonomy and separateness. This is used as fuel for desire in the bedroom environment. In marriage, we need both the intimacy fueled by connection and the desire fueled by separateness.

We may have taken a round-about road to get to talking about "Treats" for the bedroom, but these overarching concepts of staying individually interesting while allowing for some mystery and distance provide a foundation and prepare the way for more specific and intimate "Treats" for the bedroom.

"It doesn't take much to add novelty and creativity to your lovemaking. Whatever you are currently doing, just doing something different can spice things up."

Ideas for Novelty and Creativity in the Bedroom

Let's talk about a bunch of fun, intimate ingredients to add novelty, newness and adventure to your bedroom experience. If you're looking to add a little "shock and awe" to your intimate relationship, or more mystery and intrigue, you'll note these ideas double as great ways to infuse a spark of fun and variety into lovemaking. They are also quite useful in helping women get and stay emotionally present and mentally focused during sex. You'll not only have a quick and easy list of new things to try, but will hopefully be inspired to create many grand new ideas of your own. A guiding concept as we discuss a variety of novel ideas is to be creative when it comes to your sexual relationship. You don't have to get all crazy, but by thinking outside the box, you can even just do something a little different that awakens some sizzle in the mind and enlivens all the senses.

It doesn't take much to add novelty and creativity to your lovemaking. Whatever you are currently doing, just doing something different can spice it up. It can be a fun novelty to "ban" a particular activity from your lovemaking for a time. Going without something you normally do creates a novel buzz in the brain as well. I am often amazed at how something as small as a different touch in a different way at a different time can awaken the sexual senses and create a novel response in the mind and body.

I love companies like The Dating Divas that provide hundreds of creative dating ideas and even some creative lovemaking ideas to help us keep the spark alive in our relationships, so be sure to check them out at TheDatingDivas.com.

A Word of Caution

Just a word of caution—these extra treats for a sextraordinary marriage may not even be feasible for wives if they have not yet done the work in previous chapters, especially Chapter 1 - "Transformed" that addresses one's self-concept as a sexual being, or Chapter 2 - "Thoughts" that addresses one's inhibiting thoughts and beliefs about sex. These foundational issues lay the groundwork for a woman to not only embrace her sexuality to the fullest extent, but also provide the impetus for her to be willing and able to take lovemaking to a whole new level of novelty, adventure and connection.

Categories of Creativity

Below are some of the different categories of ideas with which you could begin to experiment. They will help you break free of boredom and routine, enhance the ambience, and add a little variety and excitement to your sexual encounters:

Locations. Try having sex in different locations, like your walk-in closet, the bathroom counter, the shower, a hot tub or bath, your swimming pool, a tent in your backyard, your car (in the garage or at a remote location), a hotel, or you could even try skinny dipping if you can find a good secluded spot. You may also be fulfilling a fantasy for your husband with some of these ideas. Indulge your senses with a romantic getaway to a place with themed suites like The Anniversary Inn—one of my favorite places! You can escape to the beaches of Hawaii or live in a romantic fairy tale for the night. Every couple needs at least a few nights away without kids to keep the romance rolling along.

Durations. Time spent making love can be a few minutes to a few hours. Go for a quickie when time is short, or take time and plan an hour or more for some luxurious lovemaking. Whatever you do most often, vary it by utilizing different durations. If quickies are not your regular sexual fare, they are a nice gift to your spouse when time or energy is limited or for trying out new locations. To learn more about the benefits of quickies, listen to my Marital Intimacy Show podcast episode #029, "A Quickie about Quickies," available at TheMaritalIntimacyShow.com.

Time. Testosterone peaks between 6 and 8 a.m. and often creates erections, so morning sex is a favorite time for a lot of men, though often an inconvenient time for their wives. It's nature's way of saying, "Gentlemen, start your engines." Morning sex can balance hormone surges because vaginal intercourse provides a "hormone exchange"—men absorb estrogen and women absorb testosterone.[10] Whatever your regular fare, adding in some early morning sex, a "nooner," or waking him up in the middle of the night could add some welcome variety to your lovemaking schedule. One husband told his wife he was more than happy to have her wake him up anytime, even in the middle of the night. She shook her head, rolled her eyes and said, "Okay, but if you ever do that to me you're in big trouble!"

For another angle on the "Time" concept, think back to your early days together. What did you do then that you don't do much of anymore? Did you make out more then, and don't much now? Did you have a wider variety of fun date nights than you do now? Role playing earlier times or scenarios is a great way to intensify erotic emotions and command your attention to the lovemaking experience as well.

If we add an "s" to the word "Time," we might consider how many "times" we have sex in a given period. As a fun idea for your 7th anniversary, for instance, have sex seven times in a day, week or during an anniversary weekend getaway. If you've been married for 24 years, rather than trying to have sex 24 times you could utilize a little creativity and have sex 2 + 4 times in a day or week to celebrate your 24th anniversary. Ten days of sex might be a fun 10th anniversary gift for your sweetheart. The ideas are limitless.

Speed. Making love either fast and furiously or leisurely slow and soothing are two more ways to change it up. You might even include some of both by starting slow and speeding things up as arousal grows. Most husbands would do well to default to starting with slow and gentle, unless you are getting erotic indications to the contrary as illustrated by the story of Kristi below.

Intensity. Women tend to like things slow and gentle in the beginning to help them get into a deeper state of relaxation and arousal. But there are times when the extra intensity of rough and rugged may be a fun change of pace not only for husbands, but also for their wives. Kristi explained that if she came to bed with her sweatshirt and yoga pants on, then it was a sign for her husband to start slow to help get her in the mood. If she was already barely clothed then she wanted to be "taken." Husbands can help a lot by mastering their wives' communication styles and signals…especially in the bedroom.

Positions. There may be hundreds of different sexual positions to try. Certainly some positions may work better than others. It all depends on the objective of the experience—to help her orgasm, or just for some added novelty and pleasure. Men are always anxious to try a new sexual position. Some positions may work best for mutual comfort and effectiveness, but it may not be a bad idea to try a few just for fun and variety, or to fulfill a fantasy! Listed below are just a few of the many positions you could try. You might carefully search the internet for "Christian sex positions" for more options to choose from. Christian sites tend to be more conscientious about presenting things like sexual positions without being pornographic.

- *Woman on Top.* The woman on top position is an easy change of pace for those who tend toward the man-on-top missionary position. It's a fun way for wives to have more control and to get the angle just right for good clitoral stimulation. There are many variations to this one, so make it an adventure for you both to find just the right position that pleases.

- *Forward Missionary Position (or The CAT).* The man is on top like in the missionary position, but he is higher up on her body. She lies beneath him with her hips arched over a small pillow keeping her legs straight and close together. This helps his pubic bone and base of the penis come into more direct contact with her clitoris during intercourse. Rather than thrusting, you're both engaging in a slow, sensual rocking motion to grind the pubic bone and clitoris together. This position is also called the coital alignment technique (CAT).

- *Elevated Doggy Style.* Have her kneel forward leaning up against a wall or the bed's headboard, and have him enter her from behind. With her supporting the position against the wall, his hands are free for other things! This position is a bit more comfortable for women than classic doggy style where her hands are at the same level as her knees. This position is often considered a favorite for men.

- *Lap Dance.* She can try a lap dance where she straddles him on an armless chair—with her feet touching the floor, wall or bed for support. He could also sit on the bed up against pillows against the headboard or a wall while she straddles him kneeling with each leg on one side of his legs.

- *Man Standing.* With her laying on her back at the edge of the bed, the husband would hold up her legs, as he stands next to the bed over her. This position makes for great eye contact.

- *Spooning.* Both husband and wife lie in bed on their sides. He spoons her from behind, entering her slowly, with his hands available for other enjoyable sex play.

Scenarios. Mentally and verbally role playing various scenarios like a redo of your honeymoon, or a passionate encounter on a sandy beach of a deserted island, can be an easy way to try something a little adventurous within the safety of your own home. The mind is a powerful tool for adding a little adventure within the bounds that are appropriate for you and your spouse. Brainstorm together as husband and wife a few ideas of scenarios that might be fun to try out. Romantic scenarios are part of Level 3 Auditory Arousal discussed in Chapter 6 - "Talk."

Foreplay. The possibilities are endless for adding variety, adventure and sizzle to foreplay. Foreplay is often minimal or neglected outright by many couples. Without good foreplay, you can pretty much guarantee that the experience will not be as satisfying for the lower-desire spouse, who likely needs the extra warm-up foreplay provides.

If foreplay usually starts with kissing, start with a foot or back massage instead. If you usually start in bed, begin with dancing to a fun upbeat song or slow romantic music. You could even do that half naked or in some sexy lingerie. Begin by dancing clothed, then undress as you go. Dancing naked in your bedroom can be a great form of foreplay! It's a fun way to warm up and connect both emotionally and physically. If foreplay usually starts just a few minutes before the main event, try encouraging some outside-the-bedroom emotional foreplay in the form of texts, emails or flirty conversation throughout the day. You or he could send kissy face selfies with a little love note text to start the sizzle.

Another fun way for foreplay to start earlier in the day is to flash him a "sneak peek" that morning just to tease him. You could also teasingly play hard to get, letting him know all the things he "can't" do to you as he's on his way out the door to work. You would surely get his attention by seductively sliding your hand into his pocket to reach for his keys…or something.

During lovemaking, if your husband usually goes right to the "good stuff," let him know he can't touch any of the hot spots for at least 15 minutes. It's a fun form of torture, but good for your husband to develop self restraint. Let him know he will have to figure out something else to do to warm you up. It might be just snuggling while talking, or dancing with you to a slow song, or he could just hold you or give you a 10-second hug, or do a hand massage.

Foreplay is a great time to discover new erogenous zones for both of you. Wives often tell me that they don't know what they like until they experience it, so foreplay may be the perfect time for playful trial and error to find her hot spots. Exploring new forms of foreplay is likely to bring up issues of personal preference, and what is or isn't okay. Be sure to review that section in Chapter 2 - "Thoughts" if any conflicts occur over what new sexual activities to try.

Ambience—Lights/Candles. Are you usually a lights off or lights on kind of gal? Try changing it up a bit by adding candles for lighting or getting colored light bulbs to put in a small bedroom lamp. If you rarely make love in the light where your husband can more fully enjoy the visual delights, then give him a treat of lighted lovemaking.

I'm a big fan of using candles, especially those candle warmers where nothing actually burns. They not only give off a romantic colored glow, but also make the room smell delicious. The purpose of candles is to create an ambience that not only helps women transition from mommy mode to wife and lover mode, but it also adds to the novelty and sensuality of the experience. Candles easily change up the environment based on the color and/or scent of the candle.

Bedroom Music. It's amazing how you can be immersed in your day-to-day thinking, and then a romantic song comes on the radio and causes a pause. It can immediately shift your focus to amorous thoughts and feelings. Music is one of the quickest ways to shift one's mood. Music has the power to help women get and stay in a state of arousal more easily during lovemaking. I often encourage couples to create their own bedroom music or "mood music," not only to arouse romantic feelings, but to help women keep their minds on the sexual experience instead of being distracted by something on their mental to-do list.

There's a wide variety of music to choose from to utilize the power of music in your lovemaking. It's a great idea to create a playlist that encourages intimate feelings. Try out some Caribbean music and escape to the Bahamas in your bedroom. Classical, jazz, country, instrumental, soft rock, nature sounds, or maybe even music from your teen years can bring back a flood of memories and new emotions. It can completely change the sexual experience without ever having to leave your bedroom. You might also choose music that makes you want to dance and move your body, so as to get more in tune with your physicality and ultimately your sensuality. White noise may also be helpful, not so much for the novelty, but for the "protection" it provides if there are logistical concerns about being heard.

Props/Toys/Games. Mirrors in the bedroom can add an erotic element and potentially fulfill a fantasy for your husband as well. It may not be feasible to cover your ceiling with mirrors, but even bringing out a few full-length mirrors for the occasion can be kind of fun and create some new sexual sizzle. Consider testing out a new sex toy like a small vibrator. Vibrators can add some novelty and fun to the experience. They can even help a woman experience an orgasm if she hasn't yet been able to do so. Vibrators do have some downsides, though, as we've mentioned before in Chapter 7 - "Touch." Some couples have found though that having an orgasm with a vibrator is better than no orgasm at all, so the addition of a vibrator in lovemaking may need to be a topic of discussion if it's for anything other than some variety and fun.

Another helpful prop could be sexual positioning foam pillows like the Liberator ramps and wedges. These fun additions can increase the pleasure of lovemaking and help with sexual positions that may be more mutually satisfying. Other potential additions might include intimate card games, board games or games you make up using the roll of the dice. You might add in feathers, a silk scarf, massage oils or fun edible items like whipping cream in a can or chocolate syrup.

You might break up the routine and predictability of sex by using a blindfold during lovemaking. What a way to awaken your sexual senses by having the sense of sight impaired. Foreplay without eyesight can heighten the sense of touch, taste, smell and sound, while decreasing inhibitions. It just may add some mystery and intrigue given the erotic vulnerability it engenders.

Attire/Lingerie. If you usually start foreplay already naked, try starting fully clothed and slowly undress each other as part of the process. If you normally have intercourse fully naked, try leaving on as many clothes as you can. If you normally wear your sweats or big t-shirt to bed, try something a little more seductive. And if you go for role playing a scenario, you could get out your Halloween costumes for some added fun!

Many women have found that wearing nice lingerie adds to the newness and novelty of the experience, and it also helps them make that mental, emotional and physical shift into lovemaking mode. Just putting on lingerie helps them with that first step of deciding to "go there" and getting in the mood, even if they aren't yet feeling desire. Lingerie can also help women stay more present and focused on the intimate experience and feel sexier about themselves. Lingerie may be as much for the woman's benefit as it is for her husband's visual delights. Have a variety of lingerie options on hand and add something new to the mix every so often.

Senses. How many of the senses (sight, sound, smell, touch and taste) do you usually use in lovemaking? The varieties are endless for visual, auditory and tactile delights in addition to utilizing your taste buds and sense of smell. If sight and touch are the only senses you tend to use, then add some auditory sensuality with music, romantic sounds, or by the words expressed during lovemaking. Don't forget some olfactory sensuality with scented candles, perfume, cologne or essential oils. Allow yourself to be soothed by the natural scent of your loved one by pausing for a moment to inhale and take in their unique scent. Add the sensation of taste with yummy lip gloss, or fun edible items such as canned whipped cream, chocolate syrup, caramel syrup, or creamy peanut butter.

To enhance tactile sensations, try cashmere or silk instead of flannel, or give each other a luxurious massage with scented massage lotion or oils. You can enhance the visual senses with lingerie—for you and for him—or with more or less clothing than usual. A unique approach to visual variety is to consider "eyes-open sex" if you normally keep them closed during lovemaking. This is a powerful way to connect emotionally and even spiritually during sex as well.

As mentioned earlier, try having sex blindfolded for added intrigue while heightening the other senses. The varieties are endless for visual, auditory and tactile delights in addition to utilizing your taste buds and sense of smell. Paying special attention to the senses during lovemaking is a form of mindfulness that can help you feel more relaxed and present, providing for greater enjoyment in the sexual experience.

How about your spiritual senses? You might consider including some of the spiritually connecting activities of Tantra. A tantric sensual approach can make the sexual experience closer to that of its originally intended divine experience. Tantra, a mindful, meditative approach to sex, focuses more on connecting in the moment and even being one with God[11] rather than just climaxing. It encourages calming the mind, body and soul with spiritually meditative practices in order to be more fully present and tuned in to the sacred and sensual delights of lovemaking.

A few basic exercises in Tantric lovemaking are included in the Sensate Focus exercises found in Chapter 12 of my book, *And They Were Not Ashamed: Strengthening Marriage through Sexual Fulfillment*, such as spooning and the blissful caress. Even just focusing on your own breathing during lovemaking, then synchronizing it with the breath of your spouse, can amazingly heighten the senses and spiritual connection.[12]

Who Initiates? In your marriage, who tends to initiate lovemaking? Who tends to be more passive, and who is more assertive? Change it up by taking turns initiating sex. In my work with couples, it's usually the husband who initiates most. It makes sense, given that women don't tend to be walking around with sexual desire on their minds. For women, sex is a decision. I encourage wives to take the challenge to initiate sex more often. It's a great way to boost the intimate fires and get a very enthusiastic response from your husband as well. He may even say, "Who are you? And what have you done with my wife?!" with a big smile on his face.

The first time I was challenged at a marriage workshop to initiate sex with my husband, it was a little scary and overwhelming. I couldn't remember ever having done so up to that point in our marriage. It created a real shift in my brain just from the thought of me proactively taking the lead to initiate sexual encounters once in a while.

Other variations of the "who initiates?" variety might include the way you initiate. You could try initiating sex without using any audible words, or only with written words, or only with seductive nonverbal communication. You could take turns being completely in charge of the lovemaking experience, doling out directions for any of the novel variations listed in this chapter. It could be that you take turns taking the lead in what gets touched when and how. It might be fun to brainstorm all the different ways you each could initiate lovemaking. Spicing up your sexual relationship need not be difficult or overwhelming, considering the many simple ways to do something a little fun and different in (or out of) the bedroom.

Other Ideas to Add a Spark

Below are some other ideas of things to consider to add a little spice to your sexuality:

Making Out. Many couples never make out anymore. It seems that once sex becomes an option, then kissing and making out fall by the wayside, leaving many women, especially, to miss the subtler forms of lovemaking. Scheduling a make-out only session could be fun in and of itself, or good fuel for future desire…especially when you have both pre-determined that it won't lead to anything else. Just knowing that the no-sex limitation is in place often allows women to be able to let go and go for a great make out session. This fun endeavor often sparks pre-marriage memories that can transport you to an earlier, exciting time. Find a fun place to park and make out in your car sometime.

Surprises. Anytime we are surprised, it is more memorable and fires off more pleasurable chemicals in the brain. Even just something out of the ordinary in the course of lovemaking can create an unexpected boost of excitement and pleasure. Sexual surprises that take extra effort and planning are often seen as an even greater gift given the fore-thought it required. Surprises can be tricky, though, especially if one of you isn't a fan of the unexpected. You'll need to read and know your spouse well, and then plan carefully to pull off a good surprise.

Seduction. Mastering the art of seduction in your marriage can be as simple as under-standing your honey's hot spots, coupled with an awareness of your spouse's unique ways of feeling loved and cherished. I often encourage couples to develop the habit of looking at their spouse with loving, wanting eyes. This is best done when the thoughts behind the looks are genuinely loving and desirous as well.

A longing I often hear—especially from husbands—is the desire to feel truly wanted (especially sexually) by their spouse…not just loved. A wanting, seductive look that you are willing to follow up on is a great way to send the message, "I want you!" Because women are wired differently than men, husbands can help best by looking at their wives with "love" instead of wanting. Women often complain that all their husbands ever want is sex, so make sure your thoughts and gazes toward your wife send the message that they are loved for their whole self, not just as a sexual partner.

Sensate Focus Exercises. An excellent way to add newness, novelty, adventure and wonder to your sexual relationship is to take on the challenge of my version of Sensate Focus exercises in my first book *And They Were Not Ashamed*, explained in detail on pages 244-251. The Sensate Focus exercises are a 7-week or 7-step graduated sexually connecting process. They can bring many new benefits to any couple's intimate relation-ship. Here are just some of the bounteous benefits of participating:

- To develop and build up positive, pleasurable associations, memories and experiences with touch and sexuality.
- To awaken and increase sensuality and awareness of new positive and pleasurable sensations in the body.
- To get to "know" or acclimate husband and wife to each other's bodies, sexual preferences and desires.
- To learn from each other where, how and what touch is most pleasurable and stimulating.
- To learn to enjoy giving and receiving the tactile pleasure of sexual intimacy (stroking and being stroked) for its own sake without the psychological pressure and expectation to proceed to climax.
- To help couples learn to be more conscious, attentive, and fully present in their lovemaking.
- To help individuals develop greater control over their sexual energy and greater discipline over their thoughts.
- To provide an opportunity for couples to "clear the slate" and start over sexually.

Sharing Fantasies. Sharing fantasies with each other is a great way to increase emotional connection. But it takes a lot of vulnerability and trust. Fantasies can enhance lovemaking and put some real sizzle in your sexual life. Eliciting the power and excitement of the imagination can keep the intimate relationship fresh and thriving. It need not be too intimidating if both husband and wife are attentive to the other's needs and sensitivities. One husband sent me the following email illustrating the desire husbands often have to add some novelty and fun into the bedroom activities:

> *I'd like to share my fantasies with my wife, but I feel reluctant because I don't want to come off as selfish or make her feel bad in any way. My fantasies aren't weird. I think they are healthy, fun, and playful…like making out with our clothes on until we can't stand it. Or taking turns wearing a blind fold to accentuate touch, or playing around in the shower, or trying a new lovemaking position, or making love in the morning instead of always at night, etc. Ultimately what I'd really like is to feel "wanted" on occasion, or to feel that my wife wanted to be sexually playful with me. I don't want her to be intimate with me out of duty, guilt, or even kindness. I want it to be a mutually enjoyable and fun experience.*

Many people immediately think of fantasies as something bad or lustful. Another way to think of it in a more positive light is that of utilizing creativity in lovemaking and the power of the mind and its "mental imagery." Our mind is our most erotic body part. What's going on in the mind during lovemaking is a very important part of being fully engaged and more active sexually.

Some keys to appropriately using fantasy or mental imagery as an intimate enhancement are to keep the focus of the fantasy on your spouse, and to be respectful of the other's desires and boundaries regarding what feels acceptable and doable with no pressure applied. This needs to be a mutually enjoyable erotic endeavor, but both spouses may need to stretch a little in order to be able to meet each other's sexual needs and healthy desires. Sharing such fantasies gives you both greater access to the mysteries of the other's mind.

Many of the ideas shared in this chapter for adding novelty simply play out as sexual preferences of one spouse or the other. If something is not your particular preference, then doing it anyway to add adventure and variety can turn it into a gift for your spouse, especially if your attitude is positive. Sharing and potentially playing out some of your fantasies (preferences or creative ideas for lovemaking) can be especially excitement inducing for long-term marriages.

One wife shared how scary it was when she found out that her husband would love to have sex in the car out in the middle of nowhere. She worried whether they'd get caught, and a host of other concerns. She also felt, if she kept her fears in check, this was probably something she could feasibly do to fulfill this fantasy for her husband. She felt some anticipatory excitement of the planned event. Later she told me that she actually enjoyed it as much or more than her husband and even seemed to do a little better than him at keeping worries in check.

One how-to for sharing fantasies is to create a shared "sex bucket list" of fun things to try. Another idea is to exchange erotic letters or emails with each other, detailing your ideal lovemaking scenarios or a dream scenario of seduction. There's nothing like imagination and creativity to counter the boredom of a bedroom routine. Just keep in mind the other's sexual state of mind so as to not get too far ahead of each other.

In discussing fantasies, assure each other that there's no pressure to act out any or all of the proposed ideas. Rather, it's just a means to gather and share some fun new possibilities. Sharing such vulnerable things in writing (utilizing your Sexual Self-Discovery Journal) for your spouse to read on their own before discussing it together later, helps minimize the potential negative impact. It provides a little time to mentally process the information. Sexual scenarios can be used for role playing purposes or as simply a means to learn about each other's erotic wishes and desires.

A softer approach to fantasies might be for husband and wife to each create a list of all the things they individually like or love about lovemaking, providing erotic insights for each other. Because of the power of the mind, remember that even just role playing a fantasy during sex can have as powerful a sexual effect as carrying out the fantasy in real life, which may not always be feasible or desired. To learn more about sharing fantasies, listen to episode #031 "Sharing Fantasies—Q&A" of my Marital Intimacy Show podcasts available at TheMaritalIntimacyShow.com.

So Many Options

When Stan and Carrie wanted to know what new things they could do to make their intimate relationship better and change things up a bit, we discussed some of the novelties suggested in this chapter. I reminded them of the other exercises throughout this book that can have the same powerful effect, and maybe even at a deeper level.

In addition to things like changing the ambience, location or trying a new position, keep in mind things like the following activities from throughout this book that can also be a treat and put a spark in your sexual relationship:

1. Find ways to include more Auditory Arousal in your lovemaking as addressed in Chapter 6 - "Talk."
2. Write out your ideal lovemaking scenarios as discussed in Chapter 8 - "Technique."
3. Do the Accelerators and Brakes exercise in Chapter 9 - "Tuned In" to identify your turn-ons and turn-offs.
4. Discuss the "20 Questions–Your Conversation Starter about Sex" listed in Chapter 9 - "Tuned In" either verbally or in writing to learn many new things about each others' likes and dislikes.

Much more could be suggested as additional ways to add novelty, variety and adventure into your marriage and bedroom relationship. Hopefully this chapter has at least started you brainstorming ways you can incorporate more creativity and newness into your sexual relationship.

Self-Evaluation - "Treats"

To give yourself a guide as to how you are doing in this dimension, how would you currently rate yourself and your spouse overall in the area of "Treats"? Write your thoughts in your Sexual Self-Discovery Journal. — *I strive to keep myself learning and developing to stay challenged and interesting to myself and my spouse. I am excited about adding more novelty, creativity and adventure into our lovemaking. I know it's a great way to keep our relationship fresh and new for the long haul.*

RATING (0 - disagree to 10 - agree):   You _____   Your Spouse _____

ACTION ITEMS — Chapter 11 - "Treats"

- Figure out something you could do or a class you might take to keep learning and growing so as to be even more interesting to yourself and your spouse.
- Think through the categories of "Treats" addressed in this chapter: locations, durations, time, speed, intensity, positions, scenarios, foreplay, ambience, bedroom music, props/toys/games, attire/lingerie, senses, and who initiates. Choose just a couple new things to add to your lovemaking repertoire.
- Consider the additional ways to add a spark to your sexual relationship and choose at least one to commit to do: making out, unexpected surprises, seduction, Sensate Focus exercises, sharing fantasies.
- Consider sharing your fantasies with each other, by either creating a shared "sex bucket list," or by writing out your ideal sexual scenario, or by listing all the things you currently like or would like to do sexually. You decide if it would be best to share such information in writing first or to simply discuss it verbally.

NOTES

[1] Johnson, Dr. Sue, *Love Sense: The Revolutionary New Science of Romantic Relationships.* New York: Little, Brown and Company, 2013.
[2] Ibid.
[3] Ibid.
[4] Robinson, Marina, and Wilson, Gary, "Pair Bonding 101: Beware Novelty-As-Aphrodisiac," accessed April 26, 2016. http://www.reuniting.info/pair_bonding_101_beware_novelty_aphrodisiac.
[5] Ibid.

6   Health & Sex, "How the 'Love Hormone' Works Its Magic," accessed April 26, 2016. http://www.webmd.com/sex-relationships/news/20131125/how-the-love-hormone-works-its-magic.

7   Robinson, Marina, and Wilson, Gary, "Pair Bonding 101: Beware Novelty-As-Aphrodisiac," accessed April 26, 2016. http://www.reuniting.info/pair_bonding_101_beware_novelty_aphrodisiac.

8   Metz, Michael E., and McCarthy, Barry W., "The 'Good-Enough Sex' Model for Couple Sexual Satisfaction," *Sexual and Relationship Therapy* 22(3) (2007): 351 - 362.

9   Granvold, D. K., "Promoting Long Term Sexual Passion," *Constructivism in the Human Sciences* 6(1), (2001): 73-83.

10 Dr. Gregory Olson of The Nevada Clinic, personal communications with author, April 7, 2016.

11 Bullis, Ronald K., "Biblical Tantra: Lessons in Sacred Sexuality," *Theology and Sexuality: The Journal of the Institute for the Study of Christianity and Sexuality* 9(1998): 101.

12 Muir, Charles and Muir, Caroline, *Tantra: The Art of Conscious Loving.* San Francisco, CA: Mercury House, Inc., 1989.

CHAPTER VIEW

What is Transcendence?
Challenges of Letting Go
Husbands' Challenges of Letting Go
The Spirituality of Sex
    Connecting Sex with Godliness
    Lovemaking as an Expression of Wholeness and Oneness with Spouse and God
    Sex as a Rejuvenation of the Soul
The How To's of Sexual Surrender
    Relaxing into the experience
    Letting go of control
    Trusting ourselves, our spouse, and God that all will be okay
    Letting go and trusting in God
    Connecting sex with spirituality
    Being and feeling emotionally safe; letting go of fears
    Being emotionally and physically vulnerable
    Surrendering to the present, to the unknown, to sexual sensations
    Transcending minor disturbances in your life
    Detaching from expectations and allowing the experience to take over
    Willingly moving into a sexually aroused state
    Letting go of unnecessary inhibitions
    Exercising mental discipline from mental distractions
    Keeping a Sexual Self-Discovery Journal
The Splendor of Sexual Surrender
Self-Evaluation - "Transcendence"
ACTION ITEMS — Chapter 12 - "Transcendence"

Chapter 12

TRANSCENDENCE — LETTING GO AND TRUSTING GOD

For the first several years of our marriage, sex was "nice," but it was not like what you hear or see on TV or in the movies. My world was not "rocked," my toes did not curl. I finally started to realize it was "ok" to want sex, to enjoy it, and to be actively involved. I started telling my husband what I liked, and guiding him to what felt good in the moment. I finally had a real orgasm. NOW I REALLY WANTED SEX! I went from only having sex because my husband wanted it, to wanting it myself. We finally started to figure it all out. I think one of the biggest factors was realizing that I, as a woman, have to let go. I have to relax and not try to control everything.

Our lovemaking has really evolved as we have learned more about each other. I have had several different orgasms. I am not sure why they are different or what causes the differences, but in the last few years I have had ones that are so intense that I personally do not have control over my body. I have convulsions, for a lack of a better word, when my body jerks and jolts every which way. I strongly believe all these different orgasms are now possible because I have learned to completely let go and give myself to my husband.

What is Transcendence?

Transcendence in lovemaking is the ability to relax into the experience. It is letting go of control with a "take me" attitude. It's the ability to be vulnerable and surrender to the present moment, trusting that all will be okay. Sexual surrender includes detaching from expectations and allowing the experience to take over and go where it will. It's the ability to let go and let God. "Letting God" is trusting in God, His plan, His timing and His purposes, even in the sexual dimension of life. Transcendence is the power to move beyond one's non-aroused self, and its attending inhibitions, into the consummate state of sexual arousal and orgasm. Orgasm isn't something you can will yourself to do, but something you surrender into. It's a physical and psychological surrender.

Women must be able to let go and surrender to the sensual pleasure and passion of the sensations they are experiencing in lovemaking. They need to transcend any mental or physical distractions. It may also mean transcending minor disturbances in the relationship or in one's day in order to let go and connect with one's spouse sexually.

Understanding and practicing transcendence and surrender in a sexual context is a vital ingredient for a sextraordinary marriage. For a woman to fully experience the ecstasy of sexual intimacy, as it was intended, she needs to be able to regularly experience orgasmic release—the ultimate transcendent experience of letting go into sexual surrender. The endgame of sexual surrender and transcendence is to share the sublime, sensual satisfaction of making love and becoming *one* with one's spouse.

Challenges of Letting Go

The element of transcendence and surrender to the sexual experience highlights many of the challenges women inevitably face in lovemaking. Relaxing can be a challenge. Letting go of control can be a challenge. Trusting in our spouse, or God even, can be a challenge. Surrender requires a level of self-mastery and self-development that demands intentional effort. Sex therapist Dr. David Schnarch states, "Letting go requires a strong grip on yourself."[1] "Doing" and "being done" require that you are able to hold onto yourself, but also fully let go—knowing you'll find your way back. Schnarch reminds us that because sexual intimacy includes disclosing ourselves through sex, then those who let themselves be fully "known" have greater potential for profound sexual experiences.

Additionally, feeling safe enough in the relationship and the sexual encounter itself—emotionally and physically—can be a challenge. Trusting in the unknown of an involuntary sexual response, such as orgasm, can be intimidating. How will I look? How will I act? What will happen? What will my husband think about what I do? All of these can be obstacles to letting go and surrendering to the unknown, altered, yet exquisite state of sexual arousal and orgasm. Such obstacles inhibit the sexual response. The most pleasurable part of sex is the involuntary orgasm, where you are momentarily "out of control." If you struggle with "letting go," then you are likely to struggle with having an orgasm, and will be limiting the experience of oneness.

Sheralyn was terrified to lose control during sex. She was afraid of being unladylike. She was afraid of losing control of her faculties. She didn't want to act in a carnal manner, because she wasn't that kind of person. These fears inhibited her sexual response. While writing this chapter and thinking of what many women go through to "get" the concepts of "Transcendence" or surrender, I was taken by the enormity of what is required. The ability to "do" sexual surrender is a lot like jumping from a secure place into the darkness, believing that a strong and loving husband/God will catch you. Here are the necessary components for sexual surrender discussed in this chapter:

- Relaxing into the experience.
- Letting go of control.
- Trusting ourselves, our spouse, and God that all will be okay.
- Letting go and trusting in God.

- Connecting sex with spirituality.
- Being and feeling emotionally safe; letting go of fears.
- Being emotionally and physically vulnerable.
- Surrendering to the present, to the unknown, to sexual sensations.
- Transcending minor disturbances in your life.
- Detaching from expectations and allowing the experience to take over.
- Willingly moving into a sexually aroused state.
- Letting go of unnecessary inhibitions.
- Exercising mental discipline from mental distractions.
- Keeping a Sexual Self-Discovery Journal.

Husbands' Challenges of Letting Go

For a husband, the biggest challenge of surrender is letting go of trying to "fix" his wife sexually. It's also removing the inadvertent pressure of wanting sex so desperately that she can never freely give it to him because his intense desire usurps her ability to freely choose him. This sets her up to have sex out of guilt or duty. Duty sex is not mutually fulfilling or enjoyable. When sex, or any discussion of it, has become practically off-limits in the marriage, husbands need to partner with God to let go, if they want their wives to have a chance to choose. They will also need to be patient as they both work on the many areas affecting the sexual relationship.

The paradoxical reality is that people change best when no one needs them to. It's counterproductive when a husband tries to control something he doesn't really have control over anyway. He needs to transcend his desires and let go of attachment to a certain outcome in the sexual relationship. It may be a necessary step to grieve the loss of his sexual hopes and dreams, trusting God (and his wife) that all will work itself out (*see* Romans 8:28). Surrendering on a spiritual level invites husbands to choose to totally believe that all their righteous desires will come true, while also being totally okay if they don't. To do this requires accessing God's enabling power to carry them through the challenges. It's the only way to really be okay when you're not okay. God has powerful divine purposes for the sexual relationship in marriage, if men will turn the matter over to God and trust in His purposes and His timing.

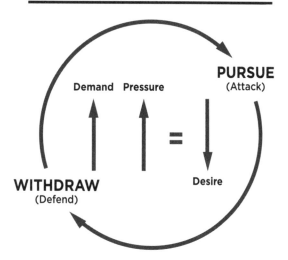

The Pursue/Withdraw Cycle

PURSUE
(Attack)

Demand   Pressure

=

Desire

WITHDRAW
(Defend)

While reviewing the list of 12 T's of female sexual wiring, Troy said, "I feel like I'm doing all these things already." I asked if he was doing them out of genuine love for Lindsay or if he had strings attached, hoping to get sex. When you have strings attached it creates psychological pressure, which inhibits female sexual desire. Lindsay turned to me and said, "I actually think my love language is him doing this surrender thing, so that I don't feel the pressure and his sexual expectations all the time—even when he may not say anything."

This illustrates the "Pursue/Withdraw"[2] dynamic husbands create when they are so needy for sex that it pushes the wife even further away. I call this the "Hungry-Dog Syndrome" (see The Marital Intimacy Show podcast, episodes #058 – 059). This pressure and neediness is not attractive. It's counterproductive to what the husband is wanting to achieve. Another helpful approach for husbands is to use Michele Weiner Davis' Divorce Busting "Last Resort Techniques" where husbands redirect more of their focus and energy elsewhere.[3][4] They "stop the chase" and "get a life." Even though it may seem counterintuitive, this approach, coupled with the spiritual surrender strategies addressed above, can work wonders on changing the pursue/withdraw cycle and genuinely increase the chances of a positive intimate outcome.

The Spirituality of Sex

The ability to surrender ultimately requires faith. Faith provides the fuel for trusting in and surrendering to something unknown. Sex, in essence, could be considered a spiritual and physical expression of faith, trust and surrender. When women let go sexually, it's symbolic of surrendering to God. With God as the creator of sex itself, one cannot undertake to truly surrender without understanding the spiritual nature of sex.

In the grand design, it is in the context of divinity that transcendence and true surrender are even possible. Many couples have experienced a transcendent sexual connection during sex. It is one of God's great gifts to husband and wife. Lovemaking might be considered a type of worship, similar to worshipping and communing with God. Sexuality in its most sacred context is that of oneness with God.[5] Sexual communion could be considered a spiritually altered state. The act of sex itself is a spiritual process to know, experience and unite in oneness with your spouse and with God. Sex ought to be seen as sacred, where husband and wife honor each other and open their minds and souls to the presence of a Higher Power.

One of God's first commands was for husband and wife to cleave (or join) unto each other and become one flesh...not just one heart, but one flesh (*see* Genesis 2:24). It seems that God intended physical and sexual communion as a vital part of His plan for marital oneness. Rather than seeking sex solely for its physical qualities, putting sex in its spiritual context can help us truly transcend society's view of sex to its higher and holier state. Because of God's influence in our lives, sex can be a spiritual experience for a husband and wife. If we see sex as solely a physical or carnal act, we miss out on its grander meaning and godly purposes.

When we ignore or avoid developing and mastering this sacred part of our being, we are incomplete. We will ultimately sense the absence of joining ourselves in oneness with our spouse and with God. It is our spirit within, longing for wholeness, that directs us toward the path of perfection and completion. It is our spirit that ultimately guides us to seek the spirituality of our God-given sexuality.

Sexual development within the context of marriage and spirituality is a refining process for the soul. It is intended to awaken in us higher faculties and nobler traits of human nature, moving us closer to reaching our divine potential. Sexual surrender is almost symbolic of what God asks of us—that we give to Him our lives, our heart…our everything—holding nothing back. Surrender to our spouse is an opportunity, if you will, to practice the surrender God asks of us. It takes faith. It takes trust. It's an opportunity to truly transcend.

Connecting Sex with Godliness

To reconnect sex with the spirituality of sex, we must adjust our beliefs to allow spirituality and sex to coexist. If that is just too much of a mental stretch, then it will be difficult to find the spiritual connection inherent in God's designs for sex. Reprogramming our minds with positive and productive beliefs (as discussed in Chapter 2 - "Thoughts") can uninstall the negative conditioning we may have accumulated, and allow us to better experience the spirituality of sexuality. One woman shared her struggle to connect the concept of sex and God, which was inhibiting her intimate relationship with her husband. She wrote:

> *I was especially happy and relieved to read your simple statement that opened the doors for me—GOD APPROVES OF SEX and (here is the crucial point) WANTS YOU TO ENJOY IT! Logic has always told me that God approves of sex. It's how we make babies. It's what draws men and women together. Adam and Eve had sex or no one would be here to worry about it! But for most of my adult life, I reasoned that it is "OK" to "let" your husband have intercourse with you, but actually wanting to be kissed and touched, or becoming aroused myself was something I was ashamed to express. During the times I got turned on and found enjoyment in sex, it was barely over when I would begin to wonder if God was disappointed in my behavior. I can't overemphasize how much that simple statement, WANTS YOU TO ENJOY IT, has freed me and made all the difference.*

Recognizing the sanctity of sex and sexuality naturally imbues it with reverence and respect. It is a gift from God. While sex does not need to be a solemn, spiritual experience every time, it certainly can be. Being aware of the divinity of sexuality can turn ordinary into sextraordinary. It can remind you that you are not only becoming one with your spouse, but you are also becoming one with God.

Lovemaking as an Expression of Wholeness and Oneness with Spouse and God

For spiritual and sexual union, husband and wife must connect more profoundly on an emotional and spiritual level, rather than merely going through the motions physically. Couples need a multi-dimensional approach to sex by developing and investing themselves spiritually as well as emotionally and physically. If couples experience sex from a state of neediness or emptiness, instead of from a place of wholeness and genuine sharing, the spirituality of sex will remain limited. This places a responsibility on both husband and wife to develop themselves into whole persons as much as possible. This includes developing whatever dimensions are lacking. This work can be done within the context of their daily interactions or by intentionally doing personal growth work.

Couples must be striving to overcome, or at least make peace with their individual challenges and weaknesses, to the point of obtaining a strong, accepting sense of self. Each must strive to bring to the marital bedroom a self grounded in a divine sense of well-being, continually seeking to become more whole. Lovemaking housed in the context of wholeness and oneness requires a healthy mental, emotional, spiritual and physical sense of self. There exists a shared trust and confidence between husband, wife and God flowing over into one's personal well-being, resulting in peace and acceptance with self and spouse.

A spiritually based, sexual desire stems from feeling good about oneself, one's standing with God, and wanting to share it with your spouse, rather than coming from feelings of inadequacy or dependency. A client once asked how to have confidence and this sense of wholeness and well-being. I responded that when you feel at peace, and securely connected to God, then little else can negatively affect you.

The divine power of the sexual union requires and pushes a couple toward greater wholeness. This is especially true given the differences and intricacies of a husband's and a wife's sexual wiring. As evidenced by the many dimensions (12 T's) discussed throughout this book, mastering these aspects makes sex a divine experience and expression of one's wholeness and oneness with spouse and God. It positively flows into every aspect of one's life. This is a significant motivator in my strivings to help strengthen marriages sexually.

Sex as a Rejuvenation of the Soul

With one's heart in the right place, sex can literally rejuvenate the soul, as husband and wife join their bodies and spirits in an act of soulful communion with God. This divinely designed expression of love can provide mutual joy and pleasure, and heal wounds in the relationship and the soul. It can cleanse, refresh and develop the mind, body and spirit, refueling both husband and wife with God's exquisitely energizing intimate nourishment. There are few things that can bring greater joy and richness to a husband/wife relationship than spiritually connected sex. This might simply mean having God in mind as a part of the sacred sexual union.

Sharing a sacred sexual union moves a husband and wife closer to each other and to God, protecting them from divisive influences. It enhances and strengthens the relationship at its core, which boosts the power and effectiveness the couple has in all areas of life. Sex connected with spirituality makes you want to be a better spouse and a better person. Harold shared the spiritual empowerment he felt as he and his wife began to experience the spirituality of sexuality. He wrote:

> *Joy and I keep working on the things you've suggested, and we keep progressing in our intimate relationship. Lately I have just felt so full of love for everyone I meet or talk to—at work, at church, socially, and everywhere. I am more in love with my wife than ever! My whole countenance seems lifted to a higher plane.*

When the intimate relationship in marriage is right, everything just feels right, and the world seems brighter. Does sex as a spiritual experience mean that it must be somber and solemn? No. Spiritual sex can be soft and slow, or passionate and powerful! It's the intent of the heart and the depth of emotional and spiritual intimacy that makes the difference. As a consummation of emotional, physical and spiritual connection, sex can truly be a sublimely spiritual experience.

The How To's of Sexual Surrender

Let's discuss some suggestions for actively incorporating the points of sexual surrender mentioned above:

Relaxing into the experience. The key point in relaxing into the experience, and the climax, is that women may need to develop a repertoire of relaxation techniques such as the Arousal Helpers in Chapter 5 - "Transition." These are used to slow down the mind and body to prepare for surrendering to the sexual experience.

One mother shared a wonderful conversation she had with her daughter that planted a seed of the need to relax regarding sexual things. She was talking with her daughter about tampons and how to use them for the first time. She explained the importance of training her body to relax, so that the tampon would be easier to use. She went further to explain that learning to relax would also make her experience with lovemaking much smoother as well. These kinds of conversations with the next generation help them develop healthier sexual beliefs and experiences that pave the way for a healthier and more fulfilling sexual relationship in marriage.

Some additional examples of relaxation techniques for women may include taking a warm bath or going "off duty" from some of the evening responsibilities. This could also include going for a walk, reading a book, listening to music or relaxation audios, lying still on your bed, or meditating in silence. Relaxing into the experience can be developed into a special, built-in part of foreplay during lovemaking. During the act of sex itself, women can learn to focus on their breathing and the sensual touch given and received during lovemaking (as discussed in Chapter 2 - "Thoughts"). This can help her keep her mind focused on making love to her spouse, instead of being distracted from thoughts and feelings that might otherwise get in the way.

Letting go of control. Letting go of control is a difficult thing to learn. It's challenging for women outside of the bedroom, so it's even more difficult within. Surrender is the ability to let go of the need to control and direct things. This is counter to the way many women are wired. Surrender is recognizing your powerlessness over some things. To work on this area of letting go, try practicing imperfection. This might mean letting the cleanliness of your home be "good enough," or letting your day be acceptable, even if it didn't go quite as planned. I'm not an expert at "letting go of control." But, I am consciously practicing letting my husband and children be in control of things that I might have wanted to go differently. Life gives us opportunities to practice letting go of control. When you have a problem that doesn't seem fixable, or is under the charge of someone else's agency, we get to practice letting go. It's an opportunity to yield to others, which is an act of trust itself.

Trusting ourselves, our spouse, and God that all will be okay. On a higher level, sexual surrender is the manifestation of trust not only in one's spouse, but also in one's self. Sexual surrender is an act of faith in yourself, your spouse and God. Trust leads to transcendence. It's the embodiment of vulnerability emotionally and spiritually, so intricately intertwined in the intimate relationship of marriage. Sometimes women question their own judgment because they have not had their own voice, or haven't been able to develop confidence in themselves due to experiences from their past. Trusting themselves is vital to truly surrendering to someone else.

When there is trust and emotional safety in the marriage relationship, and a generally high level of emotional connection and responsiveness, the sexual experience exceeds expectations. Once inside the bedroom, it is much easier to let down one's guard, close one's mental windows, set one's daily cares aside, relax, and immerse one's self in the sensual experience. Within this heightened spiritual and sexual state, you transcend your regular station, being lifted into a higher plane of existence, even if only for a short period of time.

Trusting one's spouse gets even trickier in today's society with the prevalence of pornography and other betrayals that weaken trust in a marriage. Trust is the foundation of a strong and sexually connected marriage; so when women feel they can't trust their spouse, it's a huge barrier to overcome in the bedroom. When women have felt pressured to do things they don't feel comfortable with intimately (often from the influence of pornography), then it's difficult for them to let go sexually. Husbands can help by being transparent with their thoughts, feelings and struggles, so that they can work as a team to overcome what may be chipping away at the trust in the relationship. In lovemaking, sexual surrender is an act of trusting your husband with your very body and soul.

Letting go and trusting in God. Underlying letting go and trusting your husband sexually is the ability to let go and trust God. Sometimes feelings of anger, resentment and distrust for various life experiences get turned toward God. Maybe things haven't turned out as you wanted and you blame God. Maybe you feel God has promised you certain things that haven't happened. These kinds of feelings can get in the way of a divinely and deeply rooted spiritual and sexual surrender.

I encourage clients to process those kinds of thoughts and feelings in writing (like in your Sexual Self-Discovery Journal), as if having a conversation with God. Tell Him everything you want Him to know—your hurt, your resentment, your anger. List it all. This can often help to remove the thorn in your soul. Working through such issues can also be something a counselor can help with.

> *Kendra was struggling with the "letting go" part of lovemaking. She'd get to the peak, then be unable to go any further. Her husband was doing so much better, but there were still some residual issues from his pornography problem. I reminded her that although her husband was imperfect, she did have a perfect God that she could trust. She had already learned how to surrender his addiction recovery to God, so I suggested she practice doing it again within lovemaking.*

People may disappoint you or fail you, but God won't. When you trust in God, you can better trust in others who may not be so perfectly trustworthy, because you know God's got your back. It's within that mindset that you can thoroughly let go within the sexual experience. An orgasm is an involuntary response, so if you can't let go into the sensuality of it all, it will be difficult for an orgasm to happen. Sex provides a wonderfully symbolic opportunity for learning to let go and trust in God.

As a child when you are securely attached to your parents, you feel safe to roam, explore, and grow because of your secure base. As an adult, if you will securely attach yourself to God, then surrender (and "differentiation"—having a solid inner base, and being separate but connected in a healthy way)[6] is much more doable. At the ultimate level, sexual surrender may have more to do with your relationship with God than even your spouse.

Like having a secure attachment to your spouse, when you are securely attached to God, you know you can trust Him. You know God will bring about the best possible circumstances and outcomes, even if they are different than what you thought they should be. That secure base of trusting and being connected with God provides the foundation for you to be strong, secure and stable in your own right. It is because a perfect God is providing your sustenance and validation rather than imperfect human beings.

Connecting sex with spirituality. Making a connection between sex, God, goodness and spirituality can go a long way toward assisting in the process of sexual surrender. In my first book, *And They Were Not Ashamed: Strengthening Marriage through Sexual Fulfillment,* Chapter 2 was devoted to helping bridge that gap between society's view of sex and God's designs for it. I have often assigned that chapter as homework to read or listen to over and over for clients who struggle with the spirituality of sex. It gives them an abundance of positive, affirming statements about sex to feed their minds in an effort to overwrite the negative belief systems so many women have about sex. Men's sexual addiction groups have used this book to connect sex with spirituality, or to simply see what healthy sex might look like. It has helped many men obtain a whole new understanding of the sacredness of sexuality, and the delicate nature of the intimate relationship between husband, wife and God.

Some couples have made it a priority to pray together as husband and wife before being sexually intimate. Others make the spiritual connection a stronger dimension of their marriage by reading and/or discussing scriptures or other spiritual literature. This adds a spiritual base to the emotional foundation many women long for in their lovemaking.

Being and feeling emotionally safe; letting go of fears. Much of the feeling of safety comes from the quality of the marital relationship. If there are issues with feeling emotionally safe with your husband, then you may want to work with a therapist to help sort those out. Part of this is about you and your ability to transcend your fears, and to maintain a state of faith despite whatever obstacles are in your way.

When a wife feels emotionally safe with her husband, there is honesty and transparency with each other. This lets her know that even though he really knows her, warts and all, he still loves her. I've seen many clients where their spouse does love them that way, but their own fears and insecurities get in the way. One way husbands can help is to be open and honest, yet attentive and sensitive to their wives. They can love, affirm and appreciate them, rather than criticize or condemn. The way husbands and wives listen and communicate with each other does a lot to help or hinder the emotional safety of the marriage.

A woman needs to develop that strong sense of self, so that her husband is able to be honest with her and share his truths, even if it may be unintentionally hurtful to her at times. Whether intentional or not, wives need to have the strength to be able to hear and handle uncomfortable information that their husbands may have to share—especially about sex. This goes back to her needing to shore up her connection with herself and God, so she is less negatively affected by negative thoughts and feelings of others.

Sometimes your only true source of strength has to come from God and your relationship with yourself. That strength becomes the source of combating fears. People have often asked me what it's like to take on this work of strengthening marriages and helping couples sexually—given the challenges and criticism that may come my way. I always respond that as long I know I am good with God, then most everything else is irrelevant. If God is for me, what can it matter who is against me (*see* Romans 8:31).

Discussing my fears and insecurities with my Heavenly Father and keeping myself aligned with Him gives me the strength to move onward and upward, despite challenges. This includes embracing my imperfections along the way. This divine connection allows me to have my voice, and to confidently stand up for myself no matter the situation. It allows me to also have more compassion for others' weaknesses and vulnerabilities.

A personal partnership with God is exactly the inner strength we all need. It allows you to be truly open and vulnerable, and yet willing to tackle difficult things all at the same time. A strong relationship with God is how you and your marriage relationship can be sealed with a powerful protective layer. God helps make you and your marriage more than it could be without Him and all it is meant to be. Rita shared some of her struggles with connecting with God and her husband, too:

> *There was a time when I was feeling criticized by my husband, so I turned to God and found my value there. It was powerful to be able to rely on Him. I may have taken it a little too far though by not remaining open and vulnerable with my husband. I had the attitude of, "I don't need my husband to feel good about myself. I depend on my God." While this worked for a time, as a short-term survival tactic, it didn't work in the long run.*
>
> *I want to care more about connecting emotionally with my husband and relying on him. The "I can't depend on you" attitude is not faithful, hopeful, or charitable. It is accusatory and unforgiving. It seems protective even when there is no longer a threat coming my way. I like how you talk about having a partnership with God as being the best way to be open and vulnerable with our spouse. I think I was relying on God, but in Satan's way because it wasn't strengthening my marriage.*

Being emotionally and physically vulnerable. Being emotionally and physically vulnerable sexually is certainly related to being able to feel emotionally safe in the relationship. If a wife doesn't feel that it's safe to share her innermost thoughts and feelings, you can bet she won't be terribly excited to share her naked body and soul. This is a team process of both a husband helping in every way he can to make his wife feel safe emotionally, physically and sexually, while the wife must also be willing to be vulnerable in ways that sexual surrender requires.

Surrendering to the present, to the unknown, to sexual sensations. Sexual surrender requires multiple forms of surrender. Surrendering to the present means that a woman must stay focused on the experience of that moment, instead of letting her mind wander into the future or the past. This requires mental discipline that women often have to develop. Surrendering to the unknown means stepping into the darkness, believing it will all be okay. This is even more difficult when past experiences have taught her that she'd be a fool to trust anyone ever again. She may be able to experience some of the pleasures of sexual connection, but may not quite be able to let herself go far enough to slip into that uninhibited wonderland, where full arousal and sexual climax is possible.

Letting go into the state of sexual arousal and orgasmic expression may seem scary and unknown, but it is necessary. Being okay with how you might look or what you might do or say when you are not in control is critical to surrendering. An orgasm is not just something that a skillful husband is able to provide his wife. It is also something she must be willing and able to let herself experience. Fearing or resisting sexual touch and other sensations is counterproductive to a full sexual response.

Surrendering to sensual pleasure and the passion of sexual sensations is another difficult thing for many women. But, if women do the work in Chapter 1 - "Transformed," embracing one's sexual nature and surrendering to sexual sensations will be easier. If it's too difficult to let go, then professional help may be necessary. Therapists can help to resolve current and/or past hurts that have become continuing fears. Trusting yourself, your spouse and the sexual experience is a conscious act of faith because we all continue to make mistakes and mistreat each other at times. Leaning into fears and embracing unknown, yet positive possibilities, can allow us to ride the wave of sensual surrender into the divinely ordained wonderland of erotic bliss.

Transcending minor disturbances in your life. I often hear from husbands that it feels like the stars must align for their wives to be willing to be intimate with them sexually. I get that female sexuality is generally more complex than what a man may personally understand. There is also a need for wives to be able to let go and transcend minor disturbances in their lives, especially in the relationship with their husbands.

This is no small feat for many women, since our arousal tends to be easily thwarted. A client recently shared how their date night had been quite nice and romantic, so he had real hopes of making love that night. When they got home, something happened with one of the kids that threw everything off. Because of that, his wife couldn't get herself back on track intimately. Staying on track sexually is so much easier for men to do for two reasons: 1) they are better able to compartmentalize different aspects of their lives, and 2) they can more quickly and easily get into a pretty enduring state of arousal.

In contrast, their wives are like the World Wide Web, with everything ever-present on the stage of her mind. She also has a harder time getting far enough into the state of arousal to even remotely guarantee that it will continue forward, despite interruptions. Women must consciously practice letting go of disturbances, in order to be transported to sexual pleasure-land and not be derailed. The more practice, the easier it becomes.

One way women can work on this is through process writing (in a Sexual Self-Discovery Journal). It's very helpful for women to write down "disturbances" as if listing them, or conversing with someone directly, or as if talking to God about it. It allows women to feel "heard" and validated, allowing the issue to more easily dissolve into the ethers of the universe…at least long enough to take a little trip with their spouse into sexual pleasure-land. It's empowering for women to develop the ability to not let minor disturbances have so much influence over them. If there are serious, ongoing issues in the relationship, it may be wise to seek professional help to work those out, so that they don't get in the way of connecting sexually.

Detaching from expectations and allowing the experience to take over. One of the challenges inherent in many sexual dysfunctions is having a goal orientation to sex. Many couples go into lovemaking with expectations, such as needing her to have an orgasm or him being able to not ejaculate too quickly. When there is an emotional attachment to a certain outcome in lovemaking, it creates psychological pressure. Instead of relaxed enjoyment of whatever pleasure lovemaking affords, expectations are counter-productive to surrendering to the sexual experience and letting it take you where it will.

It's such a tricky balance between having absolute faith or belief that a particular love-making session will be great for both of you, while not getting unduly attached to a specific outcome like mutual or simultaneous orgasms. This is where playfulness in love-making (discussed in Chapter 10 - "Teasing") becomes an important factor. Playfulness can create the bridge between what you may want to have happen during sex and what actually does happen—making both outcomes equally positive.

Willingly moving into a sexually aroused state. In sexual surrender, a woman must literally transcend her regular state of being and open the door to this wonderland of sexual pleasure. Because the process of arousal is so much slower in general for women, there is a lot more conscious thought that goes into a wife's journey into arousal. This is why I often talk of the first step toward sex for women as a "conscious choice" to go there even when sexual desire does not yet appear to be on the horizon.

A woman must willingly and consciously surrender her safe and more familiar state of being in order to go into a sexually aroused state. I think men strain their brains when they try to imagine there being such a dilemma, because they often have no frame of reference for not easily and willingly going there with no reservations. Thus, husbands can help out by patiently and perceptively walking their wives through foreplay into the wonderland of sexual arousal and surrender.

Letting go of unnecessary inhibitions. Part of the surrender in a sexual context is let-ting go of inhibiting thoughts and behaviors, at least to some degree, due to the unique, altered state of arousal. What may seem completely out of place to you in the kitchen, for instance, could be a welcomed and even warranted change in attitude and activity in the bedroom. Something you may not do or say in the day-to-day moments of your life may be completely appropriate within the context of sexual expression with your spouse. This is why getting the concept earlier in the book (Chapter 1 - "Transformed") of transforming your identity into that of a sexual being puts the whole package of sexually relating to your spouse into a protected and sacred sphere.

It reminds me of the scene from the movie *My Big Fat Greek Wedding,* where the mother is telling the soon-to-be-married daughter on her wedding night that she is to be a "lamb in the kitchen, but a tiger in the bedroom." This is a great metaphor for letting go of unnecessary inhibitions within the context of lovemaking. This counsel from the mother suggests embracing and whole-heartedly participating in sexual relations, even if that may not be your familiar personality outside the bedroom. While not fully understanding the mind of the Lord with regard to the state of arousal, I encourage you to embrace the uniqueness of arousal knowing that God created that heighten state of sexuality for the purpose of marital bliss.

Exercising mental discipline from mental distractions. One of women's biggest challenges with lovemaking, in general, is to quiet their thoughts enough to let the senses overtake thinking. It's like turning off or transcending the mind in order to turn on the body and soul. It means not thinking too much about anything, but just feeling. This is a necessary prerequisite for the sexual surrender crucial to the sexual climax of orgasm. This difficult aspect of sexual surrender requires that you set aside any negative or unproductive thoughts that may get in the way of focusing on the pleasure at hand. It is literally a mental discipline for women to be able to stay focused on the present moment and the pleasurable sensations they are experiencing in lovemaking. Developing these abilities are discussed more fully in Chapter 2 - "Thoughts."

Keep a Sexual Self-Discovery Journal. To surrender sexually, it helps to spend even just a few minutes free writing in a simple notebook about any thoughts, beliefs, fears, feelings, etc., that you may have associated with sex, and the letting go it requires. Such writing gives you a chance to process things that otherwise rarely have a forum in your life for exploration and resolution. After identifying and writing about any issues you find regarding sex, letting go, or losing control within lovemaking, etc., I recommend husband and wife discuss these issues to work together to alleviate fears, build trust, and increase emotional connection.

The Splendor of Sexual Surrender

In closing, let me share a wonderful success story one of my clients shared with me about the power of sexual surrender, despite the difficult healing journey that's often involved:

> *It's been a challenging quest to learn to surrender myself to my husband and the sexual experience. I now understand why you are so passionate about helping couples with sexual intimacy in marriage. I never knew what I was missing. Now, I won't ever have to miss out again...Just a few short years ago the term "sexual surrender" would have sent me into a tailspin. Both of those words are loaded*

with negativity, hurt and pain. Putting the two words together in a positive form would have been unthinkable. It wasn't until I learned how to change my feelings about sex and sexual enjoyment from an unnecessary evil, and negative part of life, to something I now yearn for with my spouse.

Sexuality, for me, had been a trigger. Coming from a sexually abusive background, I used to associate anything having to do with sex as bad, wrong, hurtful, violating and ugly. Surrender used to mean giving in, giving up, and being overcome with darkness. When I was young, I had to walk a fine line between surrendering just enough that I wouldn't get hurt any worse than I already was, and giving in completely to that darkness.

Sexually surrendering to any man was just not an option for me until recently. I have had so many preconceived notions of what sex meant, or was supposed to be. I never once imagined that it could ever be anything beautiful, joyful, and exquisite, nor something I longed for more of in my life. It has taken me many years to overcome my past, in order to be fully present with my husband when making love. He has been so patient with me as I have learned to bury my past and embrace a bright and beautiful future. Sexually surrendering to my husband is now a sacred and beautiful experience. This is definitely something that required much effort and practice. It was a learned behavior.

First, I had to overcome my sexual abuse, and all of the atrocities that happened to me. It has not been easy. Next, I had to learn that I was still beautiful and someone worth loving. I still have to work on being fully present, at times, during lovemaking. I can always tell when those walls are up. Sometimes all it takes is doing a quick mental check in to fully let go of whatever is holding me back. I remind myself that I am safe, loved, wanted, and cared for.

Being able to give this gift of sexual surrender to my husband and myself has made all the difference in the world to me. It gives me a sense of honor and dignity. I feel so much closer to God. Today I look at my sexuality as a beautiful, glorious gift that was given to me by God. Surrendering to it is now empowering, rather than something to be feared. The intimate times when I am able to fully engage and completely surrender to my husband are some of the most sacred and beautiful experiences I have ever had. It is a glorious gift that we all can have with time, patience, love, and supporting one another throughout the sometimes difficult process.

As we come to the end of this book, I encourage you to re-take the Sexual Self-Evaluation assessment in the Appendix to see how much your sexual wholeness and the various aspects of your intimate relationship have improved. Now is a good time to remember the phrase, "The best evidence that I learned is that I changed." God bless you in your continued journey to *happily ever after* with your honey!

Self-Evaluation - "Transcendence"

To give yourself a guide as to how you are doing in this dimension, how would you currently rate yourself and your spouse overall in the area of "Transcendence"? Write your thoughts in your Sexual Self-Discovery Journal. — *I am able to relax and let go within the sexual experience. I embrace the spiritual and sacred nature of sex. I realize sexual satisfaction isn't just something my husband can* do *for me, but something I must be willing and able to let myself experience.*

RATING (0 - disagree to 10 - agree):   You _____   Your Spouse _____

ACTION ITEMS — Chapter 12 - "Transcendence"

- Relax into the experience of lovemaking. Develop a repertoire of relaxation techniques to slow down the mind and body to prepare to surrender to the sexual experience.
- Let go of control. Practice imperfection. Practice "good enough." Practice letting others be in control of things that you might want to do differently.
- Trust yourself, your spouse, and God that all will be okay.
- Let go and trust in God.
- Process your thoughts, feelings, hurts, resentments, etc., about sex in writing (like in your Sexual Self-Discovery Journal), as if having a conversation with God.
- Connect sex with spirituality.
- Develop emotional safety as husband and wife. Let go of fears.
- Be emotionally and physically vulnerable.
- Surrender to the present, to the unknown, to sexual sensations.
- Practice letting go of minor disturbances in your life.
- Detach from expectations during lovemaking, allowing the experience to take over.
- Willingly move into a sexually aroused state. Make a decision to let yourself go there.
- Let go of unnecessary inhibitions.
- Exercise mental discipline from mental distractions.

NOTES

1   Schnarch, David, *Passionate Marriage: Keeping Love and Intimacy Alive in Committed Relationships.* Holt Paperbacks, 1998, 287.

2   Penner, Dr. Clifford and Joyce, "Counseling for Sexual Disorders,"Richmont Graduate University, Atlanta, GA. November 6-8, 2009. Advance Sex Therapy Training.

3   Weiner-Davis, Michele, *Divorce Busting: A Step-by-Step Approach to Making Your Marriage Loving Again.* New York: A Fireside Book, 1993.

4   Weiner-Davis, Michele, "How To Prevent a Divorce—The Last Resort Technique," Divorce Busting, accessed July 9, 2016. http://www.divorcebusting.com/blog/how-to-prevent-a-divorce-the-last-resort-technique

5   Bullis, Ronald K., "Biblical Tantra: Lessons in Sacred Sexuality," *Theology and Sexuality: The Journal of the Institute for the Study of Christianity and Sexuality* 9(1998): 101.

6   "Differentiation of Self," The Bowen Center for the Study of the Family, accessed June 13, 2016. http://www.the-bowencenter.org/theory/eight-concepts/differentiation-of-self.

Appendix I

Knowing HER Intimately—12 Keys for Creating a Sextraordinary Marriage

As you begin your journey to the intimate relationship of your dreams, you may want to start by taking this "Sexual Self-Evaluation" to see where you currently are in the 12 dimensions of sexual wholeness. It would be great for your spouse to take it as well. This will be a guide for you to know where to put your focus to best improve your intimate relationship. As you take it again after reading and applying the concepts in this book, you will be able to see your progress.

Chapter 1 — "Transformed Sexual Identity"

To give yourself a guide as to how you are doing in this dimension, how would you currently rate yourself and your spouse overall in the area of a "Transformed Sexual Identity"?

— I embrace the idea that I am a sexual being. It is a good and important part not only of my marriage, but also of my wholeness and aliveness. I commit to awakening and nurturing my sexuality, and take responsibility for my sexual desire and fulfillment.

RATING (0 - disagree to 10 - agree):   You _____ Your Spouse _____

Chapter 2 — "Thoughts"

To give yourself a guide as to how you are doing in this dimension, how would you currently rate yourself and your spouse overall in the area of "Thoughts/Beliefs"?

— I have positive and affirming thoughts and core beliefs, not only about sex, my sexuality, and my body, but also about my husband, his body, and our marital/ sexual relationship. I have the mental discipline needed to be able to focus my thoughts and keep out inhibiting mental distractions during sex.

RATING (0 - disagree to 10 - agree):   You _____ Your Spouse _____

Chapter 3 — "Tenderness"

To give yourself a guide as to how you are doing in this dimension, how would you currently rate yourself and your spouse in the area of "Tenderness"? This ingredient is the primary foundation of emotional connection upon which a sextraordinary relationship is built.

— I am doing well with the 20 characteristics of emotional connection. I make couple time and date night a priority. I know and speak my spouse's love language well.

RATING (0 - disagree to 10 - agree):   You _____ Your Spouse _____

Chapter 4 — "Time"

To give yourself a guide as to how you are doing in this dimension, how would you currently rate yourself and your spouse overall in the area of "Time"?

— I make my sexuality and my intimate relationship with my spouse a high priority. I make time to be together with my spouse. I find ways to cut back on other less important things in order to make time for developing my sexual self, strengthening my marriage relationship, learning sexually, and having enough time for fulfilling sexual intimacy.

RATING (0 - disagree to 10 - agree):   You _____ Your Spouse _____

Chapter 5 — "Transition"

To give yourself a guide as to how you are doing in this dimension, how would you currently rate yourself and your spouse overall in the area of "Transition"?

— I understand the need for a transition process to warm up into lovemaking. I have some "bridges" that help me transition into desire and arousal. I am developing the mental discipline to help me stay focused.

RATING (0 - disagree to 10 - agree):   You _____ Your Spouse _____

Chapter 6 — "Talk"

To give yourself a guide as to how you are doing in this dimension, how would you currently rate yourself and your spouse overall in the area of "Talk"?

— I talk with my spouse in ways that help us connect. I can share my inner self. I am comfortable talking with my spouse about sex to better understand each other intimately. I utilize sensual communication as an arousing part of lovemaking.

RATING (0 - disagree to 10 - agree):   You _____ Your Spouse _____

Chapter 7 — "Touch"

To give yourself a guide as to how you are doing in this dimension, how would you currently rate yourself and your spouse overall in the area of "Touch"?

— My spouse and I have ample non-sexual touch, with no strings attached. We have a sufficient amount of sexual touch, and the right kinds (especially clitoral stimulation) for us both to be intimately and sexually fulfilled. We enjoy kissing each other both inside and outside the bedroom. We enjoy a plentiful amount of Skin Time overall.

RATING (0 - disagree to 10 - agree):   You _____   Your Spouse _____

Chapter 8 — "Technique/Education"

To give yourself a guide as to how you are doing in this dimension, how would you currently rate yourself and your spouse overall in the area of "Technique/Education"?

— I understand the importance of getting educated sexually both from reliable resources and from my spouse. I understand and accept the sexual wiring differences between men and women addressed here. I willingly work within those realities to find what works for us intimately and sexually. I understand that there are some extra steps for me to feel sexual desire. We are working together to help address those needs. I can see which of the 12 T's I most need to work on in order to make our sexual relationship all it can be.

RATING (0 - disagree to 10 - agree):   You _____   Your Spouse _____

Chapter 9 — "Tuned In"

To give yourself a guide as to how you are doing in this dimension, how would you currently rate yourself and your spouse overall in the area of being "Tuned In"?

— I am tuned in to myself and my spouse sexually both "outside the bedroom" and "inside the bedroom." I can read my spouse's body language and nonverbal cues and respond effectively in both the emotional and sexual dimensions of our relationship.

RATING (0 - disagree to 10 - agree):   You _____   Your Spouse _____

Chapter 10 — "Teasing/Playfulness"

To give yourself a guide as to how you are doing in this dimension, how would you currently rate yourself and your spouse overall in the area of "Teasing/Playfulness"?

— Being fun and playful with my spouse is an important way to keep the spark alive in our relationship. I often tease, flirt and be spontaneous with my spouse, and enjoy it. I have developed (or am developing) a playful mindset that is making our marriage more fun than ever before.

RATING (0 - disagree to 10 - agree):   You _____ Your Spouse _____

Chapter 11 — "Treats"

To give yourself a guide as to how you are doing in this dimension, how would you currently rate yourself and your spouse overall in the area of "Treats"?

— I strive to keep myself learning and developing to stay challenged and interesting to myself and my spouse. I am excited about adding more novelty, creativity and adventure into our lovemaking. I know it's a great way to keep our relationship fresh and new for the long haul.

RATING (0 - disagree to 10 - agree):   You _____ Your Spouse _____

Chapter 12 — "Transcendence/Surrender"

To give yourself a guide as to how you are doing in this dimension, how would you currently rate yourself and your spouse overall in the area of "Transcendence/Surrender"?

— I am able to relax and let go within the sexual experience. I embrace the spiritual and sacred nature of sex. I realize sexual satisfaction isn't just something my husband can do for me, but something I must be willing and able to let myself experience.

RATING (0 - disagree to 10 - agree):   You _____ Your Spouse _____

Appendix II

RECOMMENDED RESOURCES

Throughout this book, I have recommended various books and have directed you to this "Recommended Resources" list for additional learning to strengthen your marriage intimately. Additional resources will also be available on my website:

*Visit **StrengtheningMarriage.com/KHIbook/** where you will enter your email address to receive special access to worksheets and other helpful resources.*

Disclaimer: *Be aware that some of the books listed here may have pictures or language that some may be uncomfortable with given the subject matter. Please read at your own discretion.*

Favorite Resources for Intimacy and Sexuality

- *And They Were Not Ashamed: Strengthening Marriage through Sexual Fulfillment* by Laura M. Brotherson — Great book to help women embrace and develop their sexual identity, reprogram negative sexual conditioning, and better understand inhibitors and intricacies of a woman's sexuality.
- *The Good Girl's Guide to Great Sex (And You Thought Bad Girls Have All the Fun)* by Shelia Wray Gregoire — Great book to help women embrace and develop their sexual identity and reprogram negative sexual conditioning.
- *The Sexually Confident Wife: Connecting with Your Husband Mind Body Heart Spirit* by Shannon Ethridge — Great book to help women embrace and develop their sexual identity and reprogram negative sexual conditioning.
- *Sheet Music: Uncovering the Secrets of Sexual Intimacy in Marriage* by Kevin Leman — Good book for general sexual relationship improvement.
- *When Two Become One: Enhancing Sexual Intimacy in Marriage* by Christopher and Rachel McCluskey — Good book for general sexual relationship improvement.
- *Passionate Marriage: Sex, Love and Intimacy in Emotionally Committed Relationships* by David Schnarch — Great book for helping couples confront the internal challenges inherent in developing one's sexual relationship.
- *Intimacy and Desire: Awaken the Passion in Your Relationship* by David Schnarch

- *Tantra: The Art of Conscious Loving* by Charles and Caroline Muir — Great book to add a more spiritual element to lovemaking, and be more conscious about connecting intimately.
- *A Celebration of Sex: A Guide to Enjoying God's Gift of Sexual Intimacy* by Douglas Rosenau
- The *Sex-Starved Marriage: Boosting Your Marriage Libido: A Couple's Guide* by Michele Weiner-Davis
- *Hot Monogamy: Essential Steps to More Passionate, Intimate Lovemaking* by Patricia Love
- *The Gift of Sex: A Guide to Sexual Fulfillment* by Dr. Clifford and Joyce Penner
- *52 Ways to Have Fun, Fantastic Sex: A Guidebook For Married Couples* by Dr. Clifford and Joyce Penner — Great book for helping to add fun and variety to your sexual relationship.
- *The Way to Love Your Wife: Creating Greater Love and Passion in the Bedroom* by Dr. Clifford and Joyce Penner

Favorite Resources for Marriage in General

- *The 5 Love Languages: The Secret to Love that Lasts* by Gary D. Chapman — Excellent book for learning what makes each other feel loved.
- *Love Sense: The Revolutionary New Science of Romantic Relationships* by Dr. Sue Johnson — Excellent book about the power of emotional connection as the foundation of relationships.
- *Hold Me Tight: Seven Conversations for a Lifetime of Love* by Dr. Sue Johnson — Help for couples to learn how to communicate with each other more effectively by addressing underlying attachment needs for connection.
- *The Marriage Clinic: A Scientifically Based Marital Therapy* by John M. Gottman
- *The Seven Principles for Making Marriage Work* by John M. Gottman and Nan Silver
- *His Needs, Her Needs: Building an Affair-Proof Marriage* by Willard F. Harley, Jr.
- *Getting the Love You Want: A Guide for Couples* by Harville Hendrix
- *Laugh Your Way to a Better Marriage: Unlocking the Secrets to Life, Love, and Marriage* by Mark Gungor — Hilarious book for understanding key differences between men and women.
- *You Can Turn Conflict into Closeness: 7 Communication Skills of Successful Marriages* by Emil Harker
- *The Love Dare* by Alex Kendrick and Stephen Kendrick
- *Becoming One: Emotionally, Physically, Spiritually* by Joe Beam
- *The Proper Care and Feeding of Marriage* by Dr. Laura Schlessinger
- The Dating Divas, thedatingdivas.com — Great for fun dating ideas and such!
- *Happy Wives Club: One Woman's Worldwide Search for Secrets for a Great Marriage* by Fawn Weaver

Favorite Resources for Self-Development

- *Boundaries: When to Say Yes, How to Say No to Take Control of Your Life* by Henry Cloud and John Townsend — Great book to read or listen to in order to help with having healthy emotional boundaries.
- *I Thought It Was Just Me (But It Isn't): Telling the Truth About Perfectionism, Inadequacy and Power* by Brené Brown — Empowering book for helping to overcome shame, codependency and perfectionism.
- *Daring Greatly: How the Courage to Be Vulnerable Transforms the Way We Live, Love, Parent, and Lead* by Brené Brown
- *A Return to Love: Reflections on the Principles of "A Course in Miracles"* by Marianne Williamson — Great book for helping to make peace with yourself and developing spiritual surrender.
- *Loving What Is: Four Questions That Can Change Your Life* by Byron Katie and Stephen Mitchell — Great book for helping to make peace with yourself and developing spiritual surrender.
- *Healing Trauma Through Self-Parenting: The Codependency Connection* by Patricia O'Gorman and Philip Diaz — Great book that uses the 12 steps to help readers overcome unhealthy behaviors.

Favorite Resources for Specific Sexual Dysfunctions

- *Restoring the Pleasure: Complete Step-by-Step Programs to Help Couples Overcome the Most Common Sexual Barriers* by Dr. Clifford L. Penner and Joyce J. Penner
- *A Celebration of Sex: A Guide to Enjoying God's Gift of Sexual Intimacy* by Douglas E. Rosenau
- *When Sex Hurts: A Woman's Guide to Banishing Sexual Pain* by Andrea Goldstein, Caroline Pukall, and Irwin Goldstein
- *The Problem of Pain* by C.S. Lewis
- *Coping with Premature Ejaculation: How to Overcome PE, Please Your Partner & Have Great Sex* by Barry W. McCarthy and Michael E. Metz
- *Coping with Erectile Dysfunction: How to Regain Confidence and Enjoy Great Sex* by Barry W. McCarthy and Michael E. Metz

Favorite Resources for Pornography and Sexual Addiction Recovery

- *Out of the Shadows: Understanding Sexual Addiction* by Patrick J. Carnes
- *Healing the Wounds of Sexual Addiction: Sexual Integrity in a Fallen World* by Mark Laaser
- *Shattered Vows: Hope and Healing for Women Who Have Been Sexually Betrayed* by Debra Laaser — Especially for those dealing with a spouse with a porn addiction.

- *What Can I Do About Me?* by Rhyll Croshaw — Especially for those dealing with a spouse with a porn addiction.
- *The Porn Trap: The Essential Guide to Overcoming Problems Caused by Pornography* by Wendy Maltz and Larry Maltz
- *No Stones: Women Redeemed from Sexual Addiction* by Marnie C. Ferree — Especially for women dealing with love/sex/pornography addiction.

Favorite Resources for Sexual Abuse and Trauma

- *The Sexual Healing Journey* by Wendy Maltz — Especially helpful when there are issues with past sexually abusive experiences.
- *Mending the Soul: Understanding and Healing Sexual Abuse* by Steven R. Tracy
- *Sex and the Soul of a Woman: How God Restores the Beauty of Relationship from the Pain of Regret* by Paula Rinehart — Great book for understanding the sacredness of sex, especially from the perspective of women, and the power and protection that comes from having healthy sexual boundaries.

Favorite Resources for Couples Questions

- *365 Questions for Couples* by Michael J. Beck
- *101 Conversation Starters for Couples* by Gary Chapman
- *101 More Conversation Starters for Couples* by Gary Chapman
- *Love Talk Starters: 275 Questions to Get Your Conversations Going* by Les Parrott
- *Important Questions to Ask Before and After Marriage* by Claude Strayhorn
- "Table Topics for Couples," Tabletopics.com

Additional Resources

- PODCAST — The Marital Intimacy Show by Laura M. Brotherson. Listen and discuss with your spouse the brief audio podcasts available on iTunes and at TheMaritalIntimacyShow.com. See Appendix III for a list of episodes.
- ARTICLES — Read and discuss with your spouse any of the many articles available on StrengtheningMarriage.com.
- YOUTUBE — Watch and discuss the "Marriage Messages" videos available on our Strengthening Marriage YouTube channel.

RECEIVE ADDITIONAL RESOURCES

Visit *StrengtheningMarriage.com/KHIbook/*
where you will enter your email address to receive special
access to worksheets and other helpful resources.

Appendix III

THE MARITAL INTIMACY SHOW PODCAST

Episode List

- Learn the secrets of sexual satisfaction
- Find solutions to the intimacy issues that plague so many marriages
- Create a mutually fulfilling, intimately connected, and passionate relationship…emotionally, spiritually and sexually!

TheMaritalIntimacyShow.com

Listening to these Marital Intimacy Show podcast episodes can be helpful both for learning purposes and to help change negative sexual conditioning to be more positive. Episodes are available at TheMaritalIntimacyShow.com, or on iTunes, so they are easy to listen to as you go about your day.

Episode	Title	Length
#001	Six Tips to Strengthen Your Marriage Sexually — Part 1	(18:44)
#002	Six Tips to Strengthen Your Marriage Sexually — Part 2	(21:20)
#003	Jumpstarting Your Marriage — Part 1	(14:07)
#004	Jumpstarting Your Marriage — Part 2	(19:01)
#005	Affair Proofing Your Marriage, Part 1 — What's Not Enough	(18:35)
#006	Affair Proofing Your Marriage, Part 2 — Specific Steps	(15:35)
#007	Affair Proofing Your Marriage, Part 3 — Dealing with Your Issues	(15:58)
#008	Affair Proofing Your Marriage, Part 4 — Vulnerability and Opportunity	(15:31)
#009	Secrets of Sexually Satisfied Wives — Part 1	(17:17)

#010	Secrets of Sexually Satisfied Wives — Part 2	(17:43)
#011	Tiger Woods, Marriage and Infidelity	(17:18)
#012	Three Keys to Help You Thrive in Your Marriage	(15:57)
#013	Awakening Sensuality	(12:41)
#014	Auditory Arousal	(11:29)
#015	Making Passion a Priority	(12:40)
#016	What Sex Means to a Man	(14:28)
#017	Desire is a Decision	(13:28)
#018	Stories of Hope — Finding Fulfillment	(15:23)
#019	Overcoming Obstacles of the Big "O" — Part 1	(17:05)
#020	Overcoming Obstacles of the Big "O" — Part 2	(13:28)
#021	Overcoming Obstacles of the Big "O" — Part 3	(15:12)
#022	Where Do I Start in Strengthening My Marriage Intimately? — Q&A	(13:57)
#023	Mood Music — Q&A	(08:19)
#024	The Blissful Caress	(09:53)
#025	What You Need to Know about Loving Your Spouse	(13:10)
#026	The Bliss of a Kiss–Restoring the Lost Art of Kissing, Part 1	(07:54)
#027	The Bliss of a Kiss–Restoring the Lost Art of Kissing, Part 2	(08:54)
#028	The Bliss of a Kiss–Restoring the Lost Art of Kissing, Part 3	(09:41)
#029	A Quickie about Quickies	(07:24)
#030	I Am a Sexual Being, and It's Good–Developing a Sexual Identity	(10:45)
#031	Sharing Fantasies — Q&A	(09:25)
#032	Husbands, Housework, Divorce and Sex	(14:10)
#033	Body Image and Lovemaking — Part 1	(09:01)
#034	Body Image and Lovemaking — Part 2	(08:33)
#035	Beating the Body Image Blues: Part 1 — What is Real	(09:54)
#036	Beating the Body Image Blues: Part 2 — Emotional Eating	(10:58)
#037	Beating the Body Image Blues: Part 3 — Making Peace with Your Body	(11:05)
#038	The Good Girl Syndrome	(08:47)
#039	Overcoming The Good Girl Syndrome	(12:54)
#040	Lovemaking: When Couples Have Teens at Home — Q&A	(12:04)
#041	Five Key Times to Talk to Your Kids about Sex — Part 1	(10:45)
#042	Five Key Times to Talk to Your Kids about Sex — Part 2	(09:58)

#043	Let's Play 20 Questions	(08:42)
#044	No, May Not Always Mean No	(06:44)
#045	Raising the Bar on Date Night	(09:36)
#046	Why I Wrote the Book *And They Were Not Ashamed: Strengthening Marriage through Sexual Fulfillment*	(07:32)
#047	Good Girls Do! Countering the Good Girl Syndrome in Marriage	(09:14)
#048	The Importance, Inhibitors and Intricacies of Intimacy	(08:08)
#049	What's Up with the Bait and Switch in Marriage? — Q&A, Pt 1	(07:51)
#050	What's Up with the Bait and Switch in Marriage? — Q&A, Pt 2	(07:42)
#051	The Agony and the Ecstasy of ONEness in Marriage	(09:05)
#052	50 Reasons to Make Love	(11:59)
#053	What He Really Wants for Christmas	(07:38)
#054	Healthy Sex	(07:31)
#055	Sexual Surrender	(08:10)
#056	Differences in Sexual Wiring – Bridling vs. Awakening Sexual Energy	(09:03)
#057	Self-Help Sex Therapy	(10:05)
#058	Hungry Dog Syndrome, Part 1	(09:15)
#059	Hungry Dog Syndrome, Part 2	(09:30)

Available at TheMaritalIntimacyShow.com
and iTunes

Appendix IV

Increasing Emotional Connection

Ask each other some of the following questions as a fun way to stay better connected. These are great questions for date night, pillow talk, or as part of the emotional foreplay/warm-up phase of lovemaking.

1. What are some of your favorite memories from any time in your life?
2. What are your favorite holidays and why?
3. If you had to select three possessions to represent your personality what would they be?
4. What is something you are looking forward to today, this week and this month?
5. If you could go back in time to your teenage self, what would you say?
6. What would you do if you could do anything you wanted for a day/week/ month/year?
7. "If I could change one thing about myself I would change _____."
8. If I spent a typical day in your shoes, describe what I would experience?
9. What are three of your favorite things about me?
10. What's something I could do to be a better spouse?
11. What would you do if money weren't an issue?
12. How was your day today?
13. How could I make your day/life easier/better right now?
14. How do I tend to express anger or handle conflict? (Each partner asks themselves and answers in front of the other.)
15. What are some of your fears?
16. What has surprised you about life?
17. What are three things you like about yourself?
18. How would you describe your family?
19. What are your least favorite household chores?

20. What are your favorite foods?

21. What are your favorite treats?

22. What's something I may not know about you?

23. What do you think are our most difficult topics to discuss?

24. How would you describe yourself?

25. Who have been some of the most influential people in your life?

26. What is your least favorite color?

27. What's your least favorite type of food?

28. If you were asked to give yourself a nickname, what would it be?

29. If you had to chose a new first name what would you choose?

30. When was the last time you thought about me in a positive way?

31. What are three of your favorite things about my body?

32. What's your favorite non-sex activity that we do together?

33. Are there times when you ever feel like you aren't my priority? When?

34. What are some things you learned about marriage from your parents?

35. Tell me about what you were like as a child? As a teenager?

36. What is one negative memory you have as a child?

37. Which of your personality traits do you wish you could change?

38. What are three things you hope to do/accomplish before you die?

39. How am I different than others you dated?

40. Do you ever wish I could read your mind? When?

41. What are your favorite things to spend money on?

42. Make it a fun game to take turns sharing something you like/love/appreciate about the other person until you have shared at least five things each.

References:

- http://psychcentral.com/blog/archives/2014/02/22/17-questions-to-ask-your-partner-to-deepen-your-connection/
- http://www.relationshipquestionsonline.com/relationship/questions/fun/
- http://www.lifehack.org/articles/communication/list-100-questions-ask-your-partner-date-nights.html
- *365 Questions for Couples*, Michael J. Beck

INDEX

❧

Laura M. Brotherson, LMFT, CST, CFLE

Licensed Marriage and Family Therapist and Certified Sex Therapist, Laura M. Brotherson, is the author of the best-selling book, *And They Were Not Ashamed: Strengthening Marriage through Sexual Fulfillment*, and host of "The Marital Intimacy Show." Laura works in private practice serving couples, individuals and families. Also a Certified Family Life Educator, Laura is actively engaged in providing marriage education through Couples Cruises, articles, radio and television broadcasts, and presenting at conferences and workshops.

Laura is passionate about helping couples navigate the intricacies of intimacy to help build stronger marriages and families. Laura and her husband, Kevin, of 25 years have three children and are the founders of StrengtheningMarriage.com —*your trusted resource for education, products and services to strengthen marriages ... intimately!*

To learn more, visit StrengtheningMarriage.com.